ID Nos
9

TRIUMPH & BEYOND

THE EAST COAST MAIN LINE, 1939 - 1959

PART ONE

CHALLENGER PUBLICATIONS

THE EAST COAST
MAIN LINE
& certain
connecting railways
1939

EDINBURGH
Berwick
NEWCASTLE
DARLINGTON
Stockton
Northallerton
Scarborough
Harrogate
YORK
Leeds
Hull
DONCASTER
Cleethorpes
Sheffield
Newark
GRANTHAM
Nottingham
King's Lynn
March
PETERBOROUGH
Cambridge
Hitchin
Hatfield
LONDON

N

"This work is dedicated to the management and staff of the LNER,
whose professionalism and devotion to duty enabled the ECML to
play its triumphal part in the Second World War, and especially to
those railway personnel who were killed or injured in the conflict"

Printed and bound by Printflow Colour Ltd. Bolton

First published in the United Kingdom by
Challenger Publications
15 Lovers Lane, Grasscroft, Oldham, OL4 4DP

TRIUMPH & BEYOND

THE EAST COAST MAIN LINE, 1939 - 1959

PART ONE

by

B.W.L.BROOKSBANK

ACKNOWLEDGEMENTS

Triumph and Beyond has had a protracted and complex development, and certainly would not have reached fulfilment without the encouragement and active help given by numerous people, from Chris Hawkins and George Reeve - who started me off on writing about the ECML, to John Hooper who has actually brought the project to fruition. Three other publishers of railway books, David St John Thomas, Stephen Mourton, and Greg Fox, have given me sound counsel and extensive aid on the way, as has Bill Rear - who has been outstanding in proffering advice and furthering 'contacts' for me. I am very grateful to all these gentlemen and to very many others to whom I have turned, being neither a professional railwayman nor a significant railway author. Although a lifelong railway enthusiast, I began this project as an almost complete outsider in the world of 'Railway Buffs', and had never worked on the railway except for three weeks as a teenager in the war - memorable and formative as those 21 days were.

However, in the process of writing this book I have come into contact with many very helpful people, most of whom were steeped in the profession and/or the hobby of railways, and several of whom have become good friends. I cannot really grade them according to the degree of benefit I have gained from them, but foremost among those who have taken very great trouble to help me I must include Walter Dendy: Walter was professionally involved in the operation and planning of ECML services for many years - albeit largely in the period after that covered in this account, and his contributions of fact and constructive criticism based on his experience and wide interest in railways have been invaluable to me. I owe him very special thanks, but I also feel abundant gratitude for the help of Geoff Hughes, John Aylard, and Geoff Goslin who are among the most knowledgeable and respected doyens remaining of the band of LNER enthusiasts and lineside observers. These good friends have not only taken a great deal of trouble to read constructively what I have written and provided me with splendid photographs but have also introduced me to many others who have been almost equally helpful. Other men who have carefully read my drafts and made wise and invaluable criticisms, and also given me priceless photographs and plans, include Ken Appleby, John Bennett, Malcolm Crawley, Willie Hennigan, the late Harold James, John McCrickard, Brian MacDermott, Roger Newman, Cecil Sanderson, Richard Strange, John Talbot, Ray Townsin, Ken Wightman, and - just before he died - the late Willie Yeadon. I warmly thank my friend Colin Stone - a well-read *non-specialist* - for his important contribution in helping to redraft the key background Chapter III. Finally, I am grateful to Christopher Garnett for 'topping up' the work with his invigorating Forward. To all I extend my warmest appreciation for their abundant and painstaking help.

I have also reaped the benefit of having been a lifelong member of the Railway Correspondence & Travel Society, in being able to rely heavily on the information published by them in the *Railway Observer* and above all in their *Locomotives of the LNER,* edited by Eric Fry, to whom as well as to Reg Wood (RCTS Publications Manager) I am indebted for their permission to 'lift' so many facts from these sources. The library of the RCTS has also been a valuable source of relevant literature, as has that of the Stephenson Locomotive Society, and I am indebted to their respective Librarians, Tony Silcock and Dick Roberts. By being also a member of the Gresley Society, the Great Northern Society, the Steam Railway Research Society, the World War Two Railway Study Group and the Railway & Canal Historical Society, I have made other friends and received further valuable help and information. I am also much obliged to members of the North Eastern Railway Association, the North British Railway Study Group, the Signalling Record Society and the LNER Study Group for their assistance in providing me with photographs, track plans and information - and further contacts. In the Gresley Society, I am especially grateful to Geoff Hughes firstly for kindly allowing me to study - and learn a great deal from - his excellent London University Thesis on the LNER, and then for publishing in the *Gresley Observer* an excerpt about the air war from this book.

Of absolutely critical importance to the research I have undertaken before writing this book have been the records concerning the British Railways made available at the Public Record Office, Kew, in their AN, RAIL and MT classes, and for the war story to an extent in their WO and AIR classes. I owe my thanks to the staff at the PRO who have willingly and efficiently helped me - almost entirely anonymously. In addition, I very much appreciate the help given to me by Philip Atkins and his staff in the Reference Library of the National Railway Museum, by the staff of the Archives Departments at the Imperial War Museum, at the RAF Museum, Hendon, and to Charles Rudd at the Brunel University Library (Clinker Collection). My thanks go to the Darlington Railway Centre & Museum, especially to Mrs Ann Wilson, Curator of the Ken Hoole Collection, for all the trouble she has taken on my behalf. Likewise, I have enjoyed the assistance of the staff at the Darlington Local Studies Library, the Doncaster Metropolitan Borough Library, and at the Nottinghamshire County Council Newark Library, as well as to the staff at several other County Libraries and public archives where I was made welcome but may not in the end have come away with material. To all I offer my warmest thanks.

Much of the information recorded in these pages was derived from Working Timetables and related documents; many were my own, but a number were in the SLS Library - also I have to thank Mike Lynch for very kindly lending me some from his collection. The elucidation of the details of the track and signalling along the ECML - which are described in Part II of this book - would have been very incomplete and perhaps most inaccurate if John Talbot had not had the kindness to lend me the relevant sections of his massive collection of signalling records, and if I had not also had the good fortune to be given copies of a wide range of track and signalling plans and related information by John Aylard, John Bennett, Malcolm Crawley, Willie Hennigan, and Ed Nicoll, while Mike Christensen and John McCrickard have been very helpful with regard to wartime new works. I am also indebted to the Cambridge University Library and to Mr Rawlings in particular for his willing help in providing copies of a large number of 25in. Ordnance Survey maps. I offer my warmest thanks to all of these fellows.

I have been fortunate in obtaining photographs from numerous people, many of whom have been kind enough to give me prints or to let me have them on indefinite loan - for what has turned out to be very nearly just that. The original photographer may have long ago passed on, and anyway is stated in the caption where known, but I would like to single out here in particular for my special thanks those who have provided photographs that they themselves took: John Aylard, Reg Batten, David Beeken, Ian Carr, Peter Cookson, Derek Dant, Jim Davenport, Walter Dendy, John Dewing, Geoff Goslin, Brian Green, Peter Hay, Frank Hornby, the late Harold James, Ed Johnson, Michael Joyce, the late Graham Lloyd, Michael Mensing, Brian Morrison, Bruce Nathan, Ken Oldham, Bill Rear, Dick Riley, Cecil Sanderson, Ernest Sanderson, John Sedgwick, Norman Skinner, James Stevenson, and Ray Townsin.

I am much indebted also to those who have supplied me with photographs from their own collections - and usually willing to make a personal selection for me to add to my own collection or to use in this book: Michael Bentley, R.K. Blencowe, Paul Bolger ('Stations UK'), Richard Casserley, Warwick Burton, Mike Christensen, Brian Cloxton, Hugh Davies, Chris Duffell (on behalf of the GN Society), Bruce Ellis, Ken Groundwater, Geoff Hughes, Robert Humm, Andrew Ingram, John McCrickard, John Smith ('Lens of Sutton'), Neville Stead, Graham Stacey and Brian Stephenson (Photomatic, RAS and other collections), John Talbot, Peter Waszak, Ron White (Colour-Rail), Henry Wilson, and Peter Wilson. Geoff Goslin has provided me with a number of photographs from the Gresley Society collection, K.R. Greenwood several from the SLS collection, and Ken Groundwater and Alan Thompson several from the Armstrong Trust collection.

Besides photographs, Walter Dendy kindly lent me a wealth of ECML material in the form of reports, brochures, leaflets and notices - mainly from the pre-war LNER, and I am also grateful to John Aylard, Tony Foster and Bryan Longbone for facsimiles of various important letters, notices and so forth. Not least, I am much obliged to Murray Hughes, the Editor of *Railway Gazette International*, for agreeing to my reproduction of a number of posters, notices, cartoons etc. published in the *Railway Gazette* in the 1940s, and I am especially grateful to Reg Carter for allowing me to borrow his set of wartime Railway Gazettes. Apart from those I have mentioned, many other people I have been in touch with over the years in connection with this work have been friendly and helpful in various ways, even if they were not able themselves to provide photographs or other material.

I offer my loving gratitude to my daughter, Clare, for using her skills to reproduce - just from photocopies of photographs - the ink-and-wash renderings featured in this book of the various ECML-related subjects, and to my son, Edmund and his wife Jan, for their encouragement and for choosing the title. Lastly, everything - but everything - has depended on the continuing support and forbearance of my wife, Rosemary.

Ben Brooksbank, Morden, Surrey 1997.

FOREWORD

There is a British tendency to look on the past with nostalgia. This particularly applies to railways, where services, standards, and ridership are popularly seen to be in terminal decline. I disagree with this premise. Today's service on the East Coast Main Line has 40% more train-miles in the timetable than it had 10 years ago with equivalent growth in passenger numbers and revenue. We are also beginning to see a remarkable turn-round in passenger sentiment for long-distance rail travel.

While BR was operationally and commercially much more successful than given credit for, it failed to maintain the reputation of the railways in Britain and lost the public regard that its predecessors had had. In a few decades, a show-case industry had become the butt of every second-rate comedian. Today of course the wheel has turned full circle, and East Coast Main Line express services are being operated by a private train company for the first time in nearly fifty years. There are differences from the LNER and its predecessors in that we do not own or operate the track since the creation of Railtrack. Great North Eastern Railway Limited only operates the main line express service and we must interface with other operators to serve those seaside resorts so wonderfully portrayed in the 'Big Four's' advertising posters.

GNER is moving forward very, very quickly with the things that require short to medium-term investment or can be improved by management action. We have taken on the mantle of a famous railway service with an illustrious history whose reputation held up despite state ownership. We advertise as 'Britain's fastest railway.' Our aim today is to be the standard-bearer for the passenger rail industry and the pre-eminent long distance travel experience in the UK. This will be achieved not through recreating the romance, the excitement, the 'myth' of the pre-war golden era of railway travel, but with modem standards of speed, passenger service, and reliability.

What of the medium to long-term future? The newly franchised train companies will only survive, never mind prosper, if they can shift up a gear commercially and achieve year-on-year growth in passenger numbers and revenue and which is well above the average levels seen under both private and state ownership since the First World War. There are pertinent questions about how this can be achieved by companies granted relatively short franchises - seven years in GNER's case - when we need to plan and invest for the long term. The author of this history writes how the double-track sections imposed severe operational - and hence commercial - constraints on the LNER. These constraints are probably more severe on some sections of the East Coast Main Line now, despite the absence of the freight trains of past decades. The sheer number of GNER long-distance and of other companies' suburban passenger trains now overwhelm the double-track section from Welwyn to Knebworth, making major investment in multiple tracking, or hard decisions on capacity allocation, inevitable as new private railway companies seek to run more trains and refuse to accept the parameters that BR had to operate within - of always living with the infrastructure that Queen Victoria bequeathed to us.

Technology is a mixed blessing too. We run a 125 mph service and aspire to go faster in the future. Mixing high-speed expresses with much slower suburban or 'regional' trains inevitably causes capacity problems and timetabling conflict. Going back to our Welwyn bottleneck, each suburban train stopping at Welwyn North station requires the track capacity of three to four non-stop GNER trains. The LNER, and later BR, faced similar conflicts of interest despite controlling their networks and all services. In theory, they could have set their priorities on purely commercial grounds, but they tended to adopt both operational and commercial compromises. If we did this now, I am sure it would create enormous difficulties for GNER as it would mean accepting artificial constraints on our prospects.

The task which we, and others in the industry, must now address is how to make the new industry arrangements overcome these and other structural problems which two previous forms of ownership and organisation ultimately failed to solve. We cannot accept stagnation or modest growth. We must deliver long-term investments and strategic vision to break out of this trap. The Victorian railway entrepreneurs understood the need for real growth. Their successors either did not, or they failed to find the vision and carry it through to reality. We will not do it alone, because governments and many other agencies have their fingers in the railway pie as they have done since the First World War. However, if GNER and other private companies get things moving in the right direction - and quickly, we have the best opportunity for many decades to set the scene for a major change in the status, role, and prospects of railways in the UK.

CHRISTOPHER GARNETT

CHIEF EXECUTIVE
GREAT NORTH EASTERN RAILWAY

CONTENTS

APPENDICES

    Damage on the ECML due to Enemy Action
      Introduction
      London area
      York
      Newcastle
      Miscellaneous
      Attacks on moving trains
    Aircraft Crashes and related Incidents

    Serious Accidents
    Less Serious Accidents - Wartime Only

    Snow on the Line
    The Deluge in the Borders in August 1948, and its Aftermath

A typical London Inner Suburban train of the 1930s (to 1950s): this one is made up of an ex-GNR 'quad-art' (eight bodies on nine bogies) and is ex-works in varnished teak with white roof and large shaded class numbers (1, 2 and 3) on the lower door panels. It is passing some splendid somersault signals as it approaches Harringay from Finsbury Park on its way to New Barnet, behind N2 No.4725 (BR 69504) Note the destination board, a GN innovation which was to disappear with the threat of invasion in 1940 and which often did not re-appear postwar. *Lens*

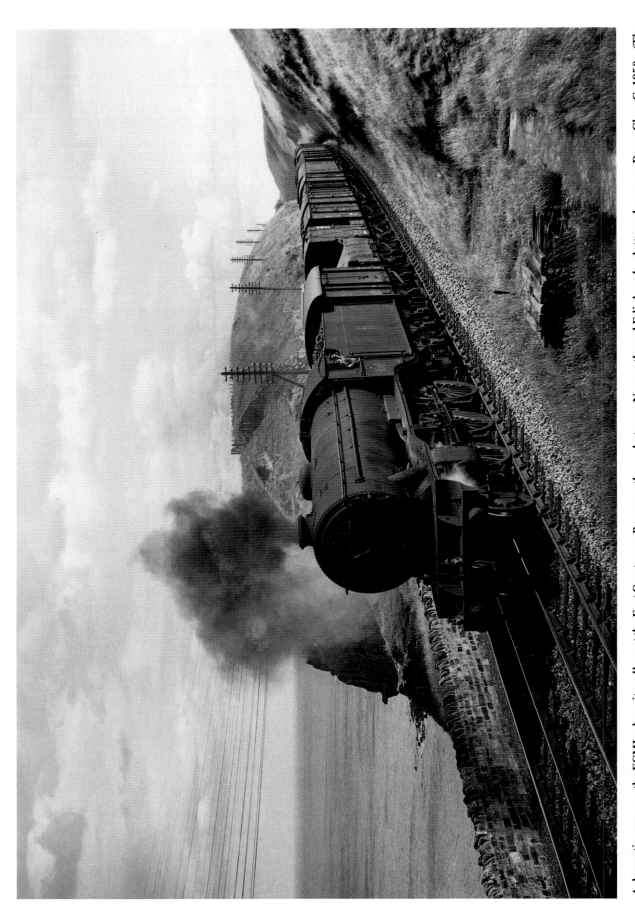

A dramatic scene on the ECML where it really met the East Coast, near Burnmouth: No.61968 (LNER No.2472), one of the K3s which were constantly working freights between Newcastle and Edinburgh, clatters along on a Down Class C, 1950s. (The crew knew to look out for the photographer, John Robertson). *J. Robertson.*

Chapter I. INTRODUCTION

A natural consequence of middle-age is the stark realization that the world around has changed, often out of all recognition. Of course you yourself have not, but everyone else has and so have the appurtenances of civilization. Technological progress and the industries of man have developed to the extent of radically altering our surroundings. Nowhere more is this the case than in the transport industry. In Britain in the space of two generations the part once played by the railways, at least for the movement of merchandise and of many raw materials, and to a large extent of people, has been shifted to the roads, and the railway system threatens to become moribund.

In the late 1930s just before the Second World War, although road transport had shown a phenomenal growth during the inter-war period of 21 years, in terms of ton-miles some 41% of the freight traffic was still being carried by rail, 17% by coasting vessels, 4% by canal, but 42% by road, the railways carrying 16,266m. ton-miles in 1938 of which half was coal class traffic. In 1993 10,500m. ton-miles of freight were being carried by rail, but this was a mere 6.5% of a much larger national total. In 1939 95% of the 230m. tons of coal mined was conveyed from the collieries by rail in 740,000 wagons - most of them privately owned, and these constituted 57% of the fleet of 1.3m. running on the railways. The four main line Railway Groups owned 19,700 locomotives, and the total route mileage of the Railways was 20,000. In 1939 there were about 2.03m. motor-cars and 0.42m. goods vehicles on Britain's roads; in 1993 there were 20m. and 2.3m. respectively. Today, while 7.5% of net mass movement[1] (passengers and freight) by UK surface transport is by rail, trains consume a mere 2.4% of the total energy expenditure. Total freight in ton-miles moved by all modes in the UK (137.2m ton-miles in 1994) is now 42% above what it was in 1952, but that carried by rail (8.1m ton-miles) is only 36.1% of the 1952 level.

In little more than one generation, a network of motorways has been constructed in Britain, at outrageous cost in public money. The new roads duplicate and often displace the railways that serve the same basic purpose of providing a track for rapid movement of people and goods. Yet, the building of roads consistently fails to keep pace with the increase in the number of private motor vehicles and seems merely to generate more traffic and more congestion. Meanwhile - unlike in many European countries, in Britain the railways have been grossly underfunded for many decades, but fares and charges have been driven up to double what they ought to be in relation to other living costs, in a despairing and self-defeating effort to recoup losses on a public service that in many respects has become progressively worse in quality. Further - again unlike on the Continent, the passenger services provided out of working hours and on Sundays and Holidays have been - perhaps until recently - so bad that ever more people are driven to depend on their cars. A transport revolution has occurred, but it is turning sour.

Belatedly, there is currently some revival of investment in the railways: at £2.96m in 1992/93 it was 'only' about 1¹/12th the total annual (public and private) investment in road transport, compared to 1¹/26th seven years ago, yet the Government of the day has still to respond effectively to two recent major Reports (Houghton, 1994; Wood, 1994)[2], written after long deliberation by men and women of international academic renown and standing. The Houghton Commission Report provides the facts and figures that describe the present position and the alarming future prospects. It emphasizes how the advantages and convenience of the car and lorry for transport have been allowed to outweigh their far higher primary energy consumption (per ton moved). The building of motorways and the great improvements in the performance of road motor vehicles in recent decades has endowed an economic advantage to road over rail on progressively greater distances. Yet there is an inexorably mounting debt to the environment, the indefinite expansion of road transport cannot be sustained and, as the SACTRA Report clearly demonstrates, the construction of ever more and wider motorways is futile because it generates ever more new traffic.

More recently, in 1995-96 we have seen not only an increasingly vociferous environmentalist anti-roads movement, but also while British railway operations and infrastructure are being hurriedly put back into the private sector by a Conservative Government bent on divesting itself of the responsibility to provide a satisfactory public service railway - and to make a short-term profit (but perhaps long-term uncertainties) for the taxpayer as it does so, the New Labour Party are responding to the ground swell of environmentalism by promising - if and when they get into power - to invest much more in rail, to shift more freight back to rail, to switch public subsidies from the Train Operating Companies onto Railtrack, and to enhance the powers of the Rail Regulator over the TOCs[3]. Thus there is hope in the air, and perhaps the privatized railway will prosper.

It would seem that the underlying factors that weigh so drastically against the railways are psychological. People love their motor vehicles that they *drive themselves* and which bring them so many basic benefits and satisfaction *vis-á-vis* public transport. They are not only obviously far more convenient and private than a bus or a train, but they nurture a sense of potency in driving a powerful vehicle and an image of social superiority (see also Wright, 1994[4]) - revealed for example by the rush to buy new cars when a new registration letter comes in. Conditioned over decades of grossly underfunded and relatively poor railway facilities, compounded by their harsh experiences of the War and subsequently by concerted advertising by the all-pervasive Road Lobby, the public in general pour odium on the Railways. The Media maintain a consistently negative attitude to them, and in advertisements the motor car is adulated. There is a popular indifference to road accidents along with a 'paranoid' concern about safety on the railways, and with lack of concern about the impossibility of reliable scheduling of a journey by road but an obsessional insistence on the absolute punctuality of the trains, and not - be it said - of the airlines. Again, the attachment of the average person to his private motor vehicle is so powerful that laws to regulate it - and insurance to protect users from its obvious perils, are resented and so widely abused as to place the Law in contempt. Now at last people are recognizing the phenomenon of 'Road-Rage': a recent MORI poll[5] of British drivers, of whom there are 26.2m, in the previous 12 months 12% of the sample *admitted* to committing serious road-rage (*i.e.* worse than just gesturing or verbal abuse) and

38% had been victims of it; there were an estimated 1.8m. instances of people being forced to pull over or off the road, 0.8m. being physically threatened and 1.0m. being attacked by other drivers or having their cars being driven into or damaged. This is damning evidence of the extent to which motor vehicles bring out some of the worst in people, and it may be that, apart from the more serious 'enhancement of self-image' induced by driving a vehicle, effects on the brain of petrol and diesel fumes (and perhaps carbon monoxide) lead to the abnormal behaviour now called Road-Rage. Most revealing of all is the fact, well-documented in several surveys, that the average person either has no idea of or does not care about the *true* costs to him of his beloved private transport, assessing it solely on running costs. Moreover, the 'company car', the provision of a minimally taxed 'perk' given by employers in lieu of higher salaries to employees who more often than not have only the vaguest idea of the car's necessity - if any - for their work and which they universally abuse for leisure, has become much more deeply enshrined as an institution in Britain than in any other European country.

People seem therefore to welcome enthusiastically the disruption of the environment by the noise, perils and pollution generated by the proliferation of the motor vehicle and the airliner, yet the construction of the essential new railway links with the Channel Tunnel[6] led to such a vehement storm of NIMBY[7] protest that it has been inordinately delayed - very nearly fatally, and this was not so in France. Indeed, the poor public image (and the excessively high fares) of British Railways are largely absent on the railways of the European Continent, where public investment in the railway 'infrastructure' has been vastly greater (in relative terms) than in Britain. The contrast on the Continent, in the clean efficiency of the system and the positive attitude of both staff and customers, is now in stark contrast with that of much of the railway system of this country.

The protagonists of road transport were already in the ascendant in the 1930s. Between the wars the number of private cars on Britain's roads had risen from 110,000 in 1919 to 2,034,000 in 1939, motor-cycles from 115,000 to 488,000, buses, coaches and taxis from 44,000 to 90,000, and goods vehicles from 62,000 to 418,000. Already in 1939 people were spending on private road transport about £135m. a year (£3,375m. - £61 per man, woman and child - in today's money); in 1990 they were spending an incredible £722 per person per year on this addiction.

There was an enforced withdrawal from the roads during the war, but soon after it pre-war trends returned more strongly than ever once the nation's wealth revived. By the end of the 1950s the share of the railways of the sum total passenger-miles[8] by all modes (including the private car) had fallen to 15.6%. In 1938, at 20,000m. their share had been 28%, and by 1993 it was down to under 6%. In 1938, passenger-miles in Britain by private car were about 25,000m. or 35% of the mileage by all modes. Fifty and more years on, the revolution in car ownership has progressed to the extent that passenger-miles by car were more than *15 times* greater still (367,000m.) in 1990 and constituted 85% of all mileage. A different lifestyle has evolved based on the motor vehicle, with dispersal of both homes and work out of towns and cities and a tendency for community life to disintegrate. Whereas in 1951 only 14.5% of British households had regular use of a private car and only 1.2% had more than one car, in 1990 two-thirds had a car and one-fifth had more than one car. In 1990, average expenditure on motoring was 13.7% of total personal income, - at the cost of 6.46 persons

being killed *in their cars* (therefore *not* including other road users) per 1,000m. passenger-miles, 12 times the corresponding statistic for rail passengers[9]. (For freight the relative safety record of rail vs. road is even more favourable). Nevertheless, in spite of the fact that in the past forty years fares have risen a great deal more than motoring costs, the railways (including London Transport and other Metro systems) are still carrying 23,000m. passenger-miles, and buses 26,000m., which all goes to show that people have become generally more mobile - or restless?

After the war there had been an opportunity for the State to integrate freight transport by confining road vehicles to the distribution from railheads of merchandise carried by rail over the longer distances, and under the 1947 Act for the nationalization of transport the long-distance hauliers had been gradually taken over by the new Road Haulage Executive. However, their lorries were decontrolled under the Conservative 1953 Act and there was positive encouragement of traders to use their own private transport unrestrainedly. 'C' licence vehicles, that had anyway not been brought under State control, then proliferated enormously, and came to do more harm than anything else to rail freight revenue. The whole concept of a unified transport policy was thrown to the winds, and the BTC was left in the impossible position of still having to balance its books while the railways were left at the mercy of unfettered road competition and starved of adequate funds to modernize. Furthermore, the construction of the motorway network and the acceptance of ever larger and faster lorries has been accompanied by the drastic elimination of not only rail freight depots but also of rail access to factories - and the erection of most new factories and distribution depots beside motorways and well away from railways. A vicious circle in the freight transport industry was started which has left British Railways in the 1990s scarcely transporting any merchandise at all.

Instead, the employment of separate small units for transport, albeit essential for strictly local journeys, has been allowed to become the predominant mode for longer distance journeys and even to a large degree for bulk overland movements. This may be though an interim aberration, for - even in Britain - the extent is beginning to be recognized to which the individual motor vehicle is grossly wasteful in the long run, and furthermore that the continued indiscriminate use of the internal combustion engine will rapidly and progressively exhaust non-renewable energy resources. It can now be seen that the environment in which we live will be irreversibly damaged, directly by the toxic pollutants derived during the combustion of fossil fuels - today predominantly petroleum, and even gas for electricity generation, and indirectly by the irreversible and disastrous change in climate due to the 'Greenhouse Effect' of the carbon dioxide formed. Consequently, in order to prevent the waste of fuel inevitably attending the operation of independent vehicles and to cut down the rate of carbon dioxide accumulation, the next generation will be forced to revert to the use of trains of vehicles for transportation. The desirable aim of integrating transport - rail and road, private and public - so far paid scant attention by politicians, is perhaps becoming a serious issue. We are still however not seeing any popular recognition of the preposterous waste of national resources - not to mention private suffering, brought about by road accidents, and, at a less obvious level, the hardship and unhappiness caused to all who are too old or infirm living in the country and unable to drive a car. Such are the 'Wheels of Progress' in the transport industry.

The reader will rightly conclude that this account is written from the viewpoint of an enthusiast for railways, and is directed primarily to like-minded individuals. The present generation is largely ignorant of the degree of comfort and convenience offered by the - privatized - Railways before the Second World War, and their fathers remember only the relative privations of rail travel after the war. Here an attempt is made to sketch these pre-war circumstances, before going on to describe how they were in wartime and afterwards - and before 'Beeching', using the East Coast Main Line (ECML) of the London & North Eastern Railway (LNER) as a example. In so doing it is inevitable that many facets of the operation of lines connecting with the ECML are encompassed, and that the fortunes of the LNER as a whole and of British Railways are relevant to the story. Indeed it is a record, representative of all British railways of the Triumph (in helping to win the war) and of the aftermath - 'Beyond'.

The Big Four Railway Groups were joint-stock companies of tremendous resources, some of the greatest privately financed corporations in the world. Yet they were struggling hard long before the war to remain profitable. The LNER had not been able to pay a dividend on the Ordinary shares since 1926, and in 1938 could not even pay any on the First Preference stock. The LNER was the second largest of the Big Four, and actually the least profitable. In 1938 it had a total route mileage of 6,258, some 1,962 stations, a staff of about 177,000, and possessed 6,518 locomotives (almost all steam), 19,600 coaching-stock vehicles (12,300 of which were passenger coaches, with seating for 683,000 people) and 258,000 wagons. Total freight carried was 130m. tons (5,600m. net ton-miles) per year, and passenger traffic amounted to 4,700m. passenger-miles per year. The spine of the LNER system was the ECML: London - Doncaster - York - Newcastle - Edinburgh. The ECML was, and still is, one of the prime trunk routes, and much of the LNER system depended on the operation of this spine. It carried a substantial proportion of the LNER's traffic, and when we study the ECML we are in many ways studying the LNER - and its successor Regions of British Railways. The trains and the installations of the ECML were both Big Business and an institution.

In the 1930s, a mystique associated with the ECML had grown up, not only in the railway enthusiast fraternity but also amongst the railway staff and the public at large. This was principally as a result of the development by the LNER of the great expresses from King's Cross to Yorkshire, the North-East and Scotland, of unsurpassed speed and comfort, hauled by some of the largest and fastest steam locomotives ever seen in Britain. Moreover - and perhaps surprisingly, the supremacy of the ECML expresses has been maintained to the present day, culminating in the provision of a totally electrified and modernized railway on which trains capable of 140 m.p.h. are scheduled to run the 393 miles from King's Cross to Edinburgh at an average speed of nearly 100 m.p.h. including several stops. And now, in April 1996, these modern and superior services are back in private hands, the new Great North Eastern Railway Company Ltd., a subsidiary of Sea Containers Ltd.

The romance of the ECML expresses has ensured the publication of numerous books and countless articles about them, illustrated with brilliant and inspiring photographs of Sir Nigel Gresley's great steam locomotives that made the line so famous. Relatively little, however, has been recorded about the more mundane operations and the layout of the ECML as a working railway and of how the rest of the railway system interconnected with it. The present account aims to fill the gap,

providing a detailed description of the line, of its traffic and its feeder services, as they were in the critical period of the 1940s and 1950s, lively in the memory of those of us with grey hairs.

A facsimile of a 1939 leaflet issued by the LNER shortly before the outbreak of war. The luxury travel offered on the *FLYING SCOTSMAN* was second only to either the *CORONATION* or *QUEEN OF SCOTS*. The 1930s did not offer much to the shareholders of the LNER but privileged passengers on the ECML certainly had a choice of luxury trains. Times were about to change drastically. *LNER*

The pastime of watching trains, arising originally out of the boyish hobby of collecting numbers, provides enjoyment for hosts of boys in Britain. A proportion of these 'afflicted' boys do not grow out of it, but develop a lasting and absorbing interest in railway matters which is often highly specialized and well-informed. Those who are *not* interested in reading this book may well ask why this is. It is a subject worthy of serious study by psychologists and sociologists, because, for example, why is it evidently more prevalent in Britain than in many other countries, and why is it almost exclusively a male pursuit? However, those who *do* read this have little need to ask; they are hooked. Men of the older generations (more than about 40 years old) who, so to speak, 'contracted the disease in its more unremitting form', remember the 'Good Old Days' when Steam Locomotives ran as a matter of course on British railways. If they are more than about 50 years old, they will remember when steam locomotives were indeed the mainstay. These men are afflicted with a profound nostalgia for those bygone days of Steam, and seem to have an insatiable need for descriptive, photographic and auditory recollection of that past Age, as well as of course helping to support the prodigious Railway Preservation Movement in this country. They will - like the author - have known the era still of the Steam Railway, not perhaps in its hey-day - which was in Edwardian times, nor yet in the dying days of the steam locomotive, but in its 'Finest Hour' in the Second World War and in the post-war 1950s when the Steam Railway had a temporary resurrection. Still, the railways are run by professionals as a business, for the benefit of the public - not for rail lovers, and this book should interest those true railwaymen also. Moreover, the account should inform the younger generations, as well as please the older men, with an element of unashamed nostalgia pervading it.

Considered in the wider context of those memorable years of the 1940s and 1950s and examined in depth, the delineation of the ECML, its centres and their operations, is a big subject, and has had to be presented in two parts. In Part I, firstly an outline is offered of the ECML and its principal centres, as perhaps seen through the eyes of the ordinary traveller. There follows a survey of the background history of the Railways of Britain during the twenty years and three months between the outbreak of the Second World War and the end of 1959, with a section about how the LNER and the ECML were affected. After that the particulars are tackled, and in Part I are described the train services and ancillary facilities provided on the ECML for passengers, and the yards and services for freight. Special attention is paid in Part I to the Second World War, with accounts of passenger and freight operations during the conflict, also Appendices on war damage and on accidents, lists of military establishments and private sidings. Much of Part II is concerned with a detailed description of the ECML itself, with its stations, junctions, yards, and the trains to be seen, also a Chapter on alterations to the Way and Structures during the war and the early years of Nationalization. The mainstream 'Railway Buff' is accomodated as well in Part II, with accounts of the Locomotive Scene and its changes during those twenty years - although without reproducing the enormous literature on the exploits of the express locomotives of the day. Lastly, there is a record of the management and staff who ran the railway in those times. Part II also contains the bulk of the reference detail of this work,

with maps and plans, and copious lists of train workings and so on. The index and bibliography will be in Part II.

No attempt is made to record the history of the ECML either before 1939 or after 1959, subjects that have been amply covered by other authors. Rather, the concern here is with what happened in the War - in so far as is possible from the surviving records, in its aftermath and in the early years of Nationalization, to one of Britain's most celebrated railway routes.

The photographs in this book are meant to support the descriptions in the text, and therefore in general their captions are intended[10] for identification more than explanation. Photographs are very largely selected from the 1939-1959 period, but with a little elasticity in some instances where the precise date was usually irrelevant and is anyway indicated in the captions.

Notes:

1. The sum of the *weight* of passengers (assuming an average weight of 50 kg) and of freight, multiplied by distance moved, and not including the empty weight of the vehicles.
2 a). Report of the Royal Commission on Environmental Pollution (Chairman, Sir John Houghton, CBE, FRS). 18th Report, October 1994. Transport and the Environment. London: HMSO. b). Standing Advisory Committee on Trunk Road Assessment, 1994.
3. Rail Freight Group Conference, June 1996.
4. Wright, C. (1994). Conflicts, accidents, catastrophes and chaos: road transport in the twenty-first century. *J. Royal Soc. Med.* 87, 403-407.
5. 1997 Lex Report on Motoring, *Driving for Safety*/MORI.
6. In any case, a Channel *Bridge* was nearly built instead, - and that would have made the Road Lobby happy.
7. 'Not In My Back Yard'
8. Passenger-miles are the product of passengers carried and the distance of their journeys; as these statistics are normally based on tickets issued, they are underestimated to the extent that fare-dodging is prevalent. Net ton-miles is the product of revenue-earning load and miles conveyed; thus the Railways' internal goods, *e.g.* permanent way material, is not included, nor are empty wagons.
9. Since 1990 the figures for road usage have increased slightly but deaths have declined from a total for all road users of 5,217 in 1990 to 3,621 in 1995.
10. Apart from publishing some of the author's *own* choice pictures?

Freight as seen on the ECML many thousands of times a year: O2/2 No. 63945 (LNER No.3500) heads an Up class H south of Retford, 7th August 1956. The railways had just helped to win one war but by this date they had a major battle themselves - against road transport - which was being lost at an alarming rate. Perhaps commonsense will one day prevail. *B.K.B.Green.*

Chapter II. THE EAST COAST MAIN LINE (ECML) IN THE LATE 1930s: AN OUTLINE

The ECML was, and remains, in many ways a coherent and integral operating system, but it cannot be studied in isolation. When looking later at the traffic, and trains, and operations on the line the wider context of the national network will have to be recognized and account taken of the services that fed into the ECML[1]. Often under examination will be the facts and fortunes of the LNER as a whole - sometimes of its three distinct Areas, and in the post-Nationalization era the Eastern, North Eastern and Scottish Regions of British Railways (ER, NER and ScR of BR). In presenting and discussing traffic statistics for example, the more global figures will be noted and taken as the basis for the assessment of trends, while estimating that about two-thirds of the LNER's traffic involved the ECML in whole or in part. After Nationalization, this trunk route, still operated as a unity, was divided commercially and administratively between the ER, NER and ScR, and this will have to be borne in mind in assessing the relevance of facts and figures to the situation on the ECML itself. The former LNER Scottish Area - of which the ECML was a relatively small part - was absorbed into a much larger ScR that also comprised the former LMS lines in Scotland, while - from February 1949 - the ER included the London, Tilbury & Southend section of the former LMSR. In April 1950 a few more former LNER lines passed into the London Midland Region (LMR), and the NER gained considerable stretches of the former LMSR in Yorkshire - albeit not until 1957 its operating functions. In February 1958 more profound changes of Regional organization were instituted, with the abolition of 'penetrating lines'. These administrative changes may complicate the interpretation of statistics to some extent, but it had little effect on the unitary framework of the ECML around which this account revolves. In any case, our theme is really the history of the railways of Britain in the Second World War and its aftermath, as *exemplified* in the scene on the ECML, in that the ECML was a major trunk railway and the core of the LNER and its successor Regions.

In 1938 the London & North Eastern Railway (LNER) Group had been in existence for a mere 15 years, formed in 1923 by the agglomeration of six great Companies: the Great Northern (GN), Great Eastern (GE), Great Central (GC), North Eastern (NE), North British (NB), and Great North of Scotland (GNS) Railways. The LNER was still divided administratively and in spirit into three relatively autonomous Areas - Southern, North Eastern, and Scottish. However, traffic agreements had long since established a close cooperation between the GNR, NER and NBR, to provide an integrated London - Edinburgh express passenger and freight service. The three Railway Companies had together built coaching-stock, the East Coast Joint Stock, specially for these services. The GNR itself had 'ended in a field' near Shaftholme Junction, four miles north of Doncaster, where an end-on union was made with the NER, but it had running powers into York - and reciprocally the NER had running powers into Doncaster.[2] Over the Border, the NER had running powers over the NBR from Berwick-upon-Tweed to Edinburgh (Waverley). Thus ECML expresses came to be worked by GN locomotives to York, where the NE engines took over (occasionally at Doncaster instead) and worked the trains through to Edinburgh.

Freight traffic, on the other hand, on the ECML in the 1930s remained relatively regionalized. A few through freight - also parcels, and particularly fish - trains ran right through between London and Scotland, far more only from York and Newcastle to Edinburgh *etc.* - again arising from the running powers of the NER over the NBR, but the great bulk of ECML freight and mineral traffic was staged: basically, London - Peterborough - Doncaster - York - Newcastle - Edinburgh. In addition, much of this traffic fed onto and off the ECML and used it only in part. Thus on the freight side the ECML was far less a unity than it was on the passenger side, and in a sense this made the traffic that much more interesting, while the nature - and often the motive power, of the freight trains differed radically at the major centres down the ECML.

The ECML was certainly not one of the easiest trunk lines to operate. There were a number of stretches of double track even at its southern end, the first coming just 10 miles from King's Cross, and indeed only 122 miles (138 from 1942 and 140½ from 1959) out of the 393 route miles from King's Cross to Waverley were provided with four tracks. Some operating convenience was gained on the southern section of the route as a result of the former GNR's rather unusual segregation on four-track sections of tracks 'by direction' instead of the more usual segregation 'by use' (*i.e.* Down Slow, Down Fast, Up Fast, Up Slow), and by the provision of a few flying junctions (at Holloway, Finsbury Park, Wood Green, and Langley), and also separate signal boxes for Down and Up directions which interacted little with each other. However, segregation by direction caused added difficulties for empty stock and light engine movements. Nevertheless, with such a preponderance of double track, if there had not been roughly parallel alternative routes over which freight traffic could be directed, it would have been impossible to run trains of a wide range of speeds from high-speed expresses to lumbering coal trains. As it was, the two-track stretches acted as severe bottlenecks that forced the scheduling of expresses in batches, with long intervals to allow the coal trains to be worked through. These were: New Barnet (Greenwood Box) to Potters Bar, and Welwyn (Digswell) to Woolmer Green Box (each 2½ miles)[3], through Arlesey and Sandy stations, and Huntingdon North to Yaxley (13½ miles - but mitigated with Up or Down goods lines part of the way). In addition, the layouts at King's Cross, Peterborough North, and Grantham and to a large extent those at Doncaster, Darlington and Newcastle, not being segregated by direction were very awkward for operating staff. Moreover, due to junctions and curvature there were very severe speed restrictions at Peterborough North, Selby, York, Durham, Newcastle and Morpeth, with less severe limits at most of the other major junctions and over several important bridges on the route. Officially, the overall speed-limit was 90 mph, but for various reasons such a speed was prohibited over much of the ECML; thus the limit was somewhat less between Retford and Selby and from Darlington to north of Newcastle, owing to the threat of mining subsidence, and in the London suburban area.

It was therefore no mean feat to run not only the *FLYING SCOTSMAN* non-stop (in summer) from King's Cross to Edinburgh (with corridor tenders to allow changeover of crews), *(above)* **Speed on the ECML: A4 No.60012 (LNER 4491) COMMONWEALTH OF AUSTRALIA, descending Stoke Bank, near Corby Glen 5th August 1957.** *M.Mensing.*

(left) **Raskelf: a 1939 view of the Vale of York 'racing ground', with one of the stations rebuilt in 1933 at the time of the addition of a new Down Slow and the full electrification of the signalling. The view is southwards towards York, and the box on the left was by then used only for working the point switches when traffic needed to be detached.** *Stations UK.*

(left) **Alne, as it was in 1939 after the 1933 widening by provision of a new Down Slow line and rebuilding of the station on that side (and - it seems - a new waiting shelter on the Up platform), also modernization of the signalling between Skelton and Northallerton. A B16 is thundering through on a Down Class B Goods.** *Stations UK.*

THE CORONATION **was not always worked by an A4 Streamliner: on 21st June 1938 non-streamlined A3 No.2744 (BR No.60090)** **GRAND PARADE had the honour. Here the Down train is seen at Newcastle Central - only two minutes late, No.2744 having worked** **it from Grantham and going on to Edinburgh. Moreover, on that day the A4 (No.4467) had failed at Hitchin and a** *K3* **(No.2428) had** **worked the train from there to Grantham.** *N.E. Stead coll.*

but also - as was done in the late 1930s - to run (on Mondays to Fridays) three high-speed trains which for their time were among the fastest in the country. These latter were: the *SILVER JUBILEE* (King's Cross - Newcastle in just 4hr, 67.1 m.p.h. with a stop at Darlington); the *CORONATION* (King's Cross - Edinburgh in just 6hr, 65.5 m.p.h. with stops at York and Newcastle); and the *WEST RIDING LIMITED* (King's Cross - Leeds in 2hr 43min, 68.4 m.p.h. non-stop, then Bradford in 3hr 5min). Thanks to the powerful class A4 streamlined Pacifics, these trains could be scheduled at those relatively high speeds in spite of the restraints of the route referred to, for the ECML had no stiff or long banks comparable to those on most other trunk routes; the steepest of any length was the $4\frac{1}{2}$ miles at 1-in-96 of Cockburnspath Bank facing Up trains.

The three Streamliners - called by the Railway the 'High-Speed Trains' - were made up of special streamlined stock of striking appearance. The *SILVER JUBILEE* was painted silver-grey and at first was a seven-coach set consisting of two articulated pairs of twin coaches and an articulated restaurant-triplet, but success led to the enlargement of the third-class twin set to a triplet. For the other two expresses, the *CORONATION* and the *WEST RIDING*, there were each four pairs of twin articulated coaches (including two kitchen cars) painted blue; the two sets for the *CORONATION* each had a 'beaver-tail' observation saloon at the rear - during the summer. The third-class coaches had two-and-one fixed but luxurious seating, while in first-class

instead of the normal type of seat there were movable armchairs. The seven coaches of the *SILVER JUBILEE* for example had seating for only 233 passengers - and certainly *no* standing. However, there was naturally an extra charge for the pleasure of using these trains: in the *SILVER JUBILEE* it was 25p[4] in first-class and 15p third-class - not a lot compared with the single fares in 1939 from London to Newcastle of £3.93 first-class and £2.59 third-class; on the *CORONATION* the supplement to Edinburgh was 20p third-class - 25p in the observation saloon.

In 1939 there was of course the *FLYING SCOTSMAN*, which in summer ran non-stop from King's Cross to Waverley in 7hr - a mere 56.1 m.p.h., but the normal consist was 12 coaches (14 in winter), heavier than that of the Streamliners because (except for the restaurant/kitchen cars) the stock was not articulated. Equally prestigious and popular for travellers were the two Pullman expresses run on the ECML: the *QUEEN OF SCOTS PULLMAN* (King's Cross - Leeds - Harrogate - Newcastle - Edinburgh - Glasgow), and the *YORKSHIRE PULLMAN* (King's Cross - Leeds, Bradford, Halifax, Harrogate, and Hull) - and on Sundays the *HARROGATE SUNDAY PULLMAN*. These comprised trains of heavy Pullman cars, both first and third-class. Staffed by a smart conductor and attendants employed by the Pullman Car Company, these luxurious expresses were in effect all-restaurant-car trains - as were the *CORONATION* and *WEST RIDING LIMITED* - with full and ample meals of good food and wine being served at all seats - and you had to pay a supplementary fare similar to that on the Streamliners. A typical dinner cost 37¹/2p, and the supplementary charge for travelling by Pullman was 60p to Edinburgh. Nowadays, you have to pay £130 for a trip to Folkestone and back on the resurrected Pullman cars of the 'Venice Simplon-Orient Express', although with a three-course meal thrown in. Such an excursion is considered a great luxury for a special occasion, while in the 1930s travel by Pullman was a normal routine. You did not have to put on special smart clothes - they were normal attire anyway, and it was worth that extra 'few bob' to travel across the country effectively in an opulent restaurant.

fares were normally calculated as the single fare plus one-third. A large variety of reduced rate fares were offered, notably Cheap Day Returns (after 09.30hr) and Early Morning Workmen's Returns (before 07.30hr), Night travel (by specified trains) or Sunday travel, all at single fare, and Season tickets (Monthly at 75% of the cost of six Ordinary Returns per week). In addition there were various Excursion Day Returns at less than single fare - down to as little as 0.10p/mile, for individuals, members of various clubs, or for organized groups - which if large enough would hire a coach or even a whole train. Reservations could be made for a small charge for not only seats but also even for a private saloon - even an Invalid Saloon with bed. Rail travel was thus good value for money, and as long as fares were not raised in line with or more than wages - which they were not until at least the 1960s, it remained so. In 1938 an average wage-earner could buy 24.5 miles of rail travel (at ordinary fares) for an hour's work, this was unchanged ten years later and by 1958 he could get 42 miles.

L·N·E·R STREAMLINE TRAINS

MONDAYS TO FRIDAYS
(will not run 23rd to 27th December and 6th to 10th April inclusive)

"THE CORONATION"
Average throughout speed 65.5 m.p.h.
Accommodation limited to 210 passengers (48 First Class, 162 Third Class.)

			p.m.			p.m.
King's Cross	...	...dep.	4. 0	Edinburgh (Waverley) ...dep.		4.30
York	...	... ,,	6.40	Newcastle ... ... ,,		6.33
Newcastle ...		... ,,	8. 0			
Edinburgh ...	...	...arr.	10. 0	King's Cross ... ...arr.		10.30

Connecting trains at Edinburgh, Newcastle and York.

"THE SILVER JUBILEE"
Average throughout speed 67.08 m.p.h.
Accommodation limited to 183 passengers (58 First Class, 125 Third Class.)

			a.m.			p.m.
Newcastle	...	...dep.	10. 0	King's Cross ... ...dep.		5.30
Darlington	...	... ,,	10.42	Darlington ... ...arr.		8.48
			p.m.			
King's Cross	...	...arr.	2. 0	Newcastle ... ... ,,		9.30

Connecting trains serve Tyneside and Tees-side.

"WEST RIDING LIMITED"
Average throughout speed between Leeds and London 67.9 m.p.h.
Accommodation limited to 210 passengers (48 First Class, 162 Third Class.)

			a.m.			p.m.
Bradford	...	...dep.	11.10	King's Cross ... ...dep.		7.10
Leeds	...	... ,,	11.31	Leeds ... ...arr.		9.53
			p.m.			
King's Cross	...	...arr.	2.15	Bradford ... ... ,,		10.15

Connecting trains at Leeds and Bradford.

SUPPLEMENTARY FARES (for each single journey.)

	1st Class		3rd Class	
	s.	d.	s.	d.
London and Bradford	4	0	2	6
London and Darlington	5	0	3	0
London and Edinburgh	6	0	4	0
London and Leeds	4	0	2	6
London and Newcastle	5	0	3	0
London to York	4	0	2	6
Newcastle and Edinburgh	3	0	2	0
York to Newcastle	3	0	2	0
York to Edinburgh	4	0	2	6

Seats can be reserved in advance through any of the Company's Passenger Agencies or Stations.

A concise summary of the schedules of the three LNER Streamline Trains in 1939. Note the substantial supplementary fares.

On ordinary trains of the time, first-class and third-class[5] passengers already had plenty of comfort, the main difference between the classes of accommodation being in the extra space - and the exclusivity - enjoyed by first-class: three-a-side seating *vs.* four-a-side in third-class. Ordinary fares in 1939 were 1.00p/mile for first-class and 0.66p/mile for third-class; Monthly Return

RESTAURANT TARIFF

AFTERNOON TEA

Tea or Coffee, Toast or Tea Cake, Bread and Butter, Cake or Pastry . .	1/-
Tea or Coffee, Bread and Butter, or Cake or Toast	9d
Pot of Tea	6d

DINNER

Table d'Hôte First Class . . .	5/-
Table d'Hôte Third Class. . .	4/6

À LA CARTE MEALS ALSO AVAILABLE

For children travelling with half-fare tickets, half-price only is charged for dinner or à la carte meals, with a minimum charge of 1/9.

TRAIN ATTENDANTS

travel with the train and will be happy to render to the passengers any service which will be helpful in ensuring the fullest possible comfort on the journey. They will undertake the posting of letters or dispatch of telegrams.

POSTCARD PHOTOGRAPHS

of the train and streamlined locomotives can be obtained (price twopence each) from the Attendant.

All served at your seat - First-class dinner at £6.25 in today's money, not bad? - and the Attendant will post your letters.

Down the ECML in August 1939 there were many fast expresses. Including the Streamliners and Pullmans, Edinburgh had four, Newcastle eight, Leeds and Bradford six, and Hull five weekday daytime services from King's Cross, and on Fridays and Saturdays these were greatly augmented. Daytime services ran through to Scarborough, Bridlington, Filey and Whitby, to Cleethorpes and Skegness *via* Boston, and there were through coaches to Kings Lynn and to Cromer. Indeed, a feature of the

ECML express services was the large number of different destinations served by through portions or coaches on the expresses from King's Cross. There were a number of overnight expresses, most with sleeping-cars, especially to Scotland, and these included through coaches to Perth, Inverness and to Lossiemouth as well as to Aberdeen and to Fort William.

At holiday times many relief trains were run, and in summer there were a number of regular Saturdays Only services - although not quite so many as were provided in the 1950s when paid holidays had become universal. In peacetime the ECML north of York also saw several night expresses from London Marylebone to Newcastle, not advertised in public timetables but most running quite regularly. In addition, numerous Cheap Day Excursions were advertised - many organized by Agencies - and were very popular. A number of these, especially on Sundays, were often regularly scheduled, while naturally events such as football matches and horse races led to the running of very large numbers of excursion trains, as did major events like the Coronation. (The Special Traffic Notice for a holiday week could run to 150 pages, listing hundreds of special and relief trains).

Needless to say, there were many trains other than expresses run at passenger train speeds on the ECML. There was one Motor-Car Train - *even in 1939* - which ran to Edinburgh, the road vehicles being conveyed in covered vans. Four regular trains were scheduled daily from King's Cross for parcels, newspapers, or mails. There was an evening Travelling Post Office (TPO) - the 'North Eastern Down' - to Newcastle and Edinburgh, and the *NIGHT SCOTSMAN* also had a TPO van, both exchanging mail bags at speed, and there were one regular and two conditional empty coaching stock trains for Doncaster or York daily (each way).

Local services were extensive in the London area, *i.e.* down the ECML as far as Hitchin, many of them continuing on to Royston and Cambridge, and many local services ran in and out of Grantham, Doncaster, Selby, York, Darlington, Durham, Newcastle, and Edinburgh. In addition, cross-country services impinged on the ECML at Peterborough North, Retford, Doncaster, Selby, York, Northallerton, Newcastle and Edinburgh, and country branch trains came onto the ECML at various other places. These will all be described in Part II.

Although diluted to a certain extent by stock of pre-Grouping origin, the normal coaching stock for the regular expresses and most of the relief trains comprised Gresley's dignified designs with bodywork of varnished teak, elliptical roofs with sloping ends, and buck-eye couplers. The majority of coaches were of compartment stock, more cosy than open saloons - if your companions were unobtrusive, or absent, but less preferred by railway enthusiasts because the view out was one-sided and the windows in the doors were often drop-lights with those heavy leather straps, rather than the picture windows of the end-vestibule stock. Open saloons were however now being employed by the LNER, including those with uncomfortable 'bucket' seats and green-and-cream exteriors. Saloon coaches were also employed of course for restaurant cars, and for the Buffet Cars - largely pioneered by the LNER. Most of the ECML expresses had restaurant cars, but buffet cars were a feature of the shorter regular services, such as on the King's Cross, Garden Cities and Cambridge 'beer' trains, and on cross-country services that impinged on the ECML, as well as on summer seasonal and excursion trains.

As on the other main lines, restaurant cars - in fact first introduced in Britain by the Great Northern Railway in 1879[6] -

were the norm. Meals were generally very appetizing, and it was the norm to have a slap-up breakfast (20p), a lunch of three to four courses (22½-25p), afternoon tea (5p) worthy of the best Tea Shoppe, and dinner of five courses (25p) with a choice of good wines[7]. The catering staff worked long hours, as often it was a return trip from say Leeds to King's Cross, going out meanwhile to Bounds Green for a break and to restock. Pay, at £3 a week for a waiter, was hardly lavish - but there were the tips.

On account of the lengthy journeys to Scotland and elsewhere, numerous sleeping-car services ran down the ECML in the late 1930s. These ran on five trains from King's Cross to Scotland, and one other to Newcastle. One train (the *NIGHT SCOTSMAN*), composed almost entirely of sleeping-cars, conveyed passengers from London only to destinations beyond Edinburgh. For those travelling first-class the sleeping-cars had luxurious single-berth compartments, a shower compartment, and electric pressure-ventilation and heating; third-class cars had four-berth compartments - and no shower section. The ride in a sleeping-car was smooth and (comparatively) quiet, and a good sleep was easy - unless you were a railway enthusiast. (If you were, you tended always to be wondering where the train had got to, and the carryings-on in the dead of night at such places as York and Newcastle, where the trains stopped if only for operating purposes, would force you to peep out in your pyjamas from behind the window-blind). It cost 37½p to cross the Border in a third-class sleeper, and a massive £1.05 for a first-class one - quite beyond the reach of any but the wealthy, or those on business expenses. The sleeping-car attendants (one per car or pair of cars) were always warm, jovial and dependable, but on £3 a week or less they had a hard life, sleeping by day and travelling every night between say London and Edinburgh; as with waiters, tipping was expected, however. (By comparison, a Top Link driver working on the *FLYING SCOTSMAN* would get £4.60 a week (plus a good mileage allowance) in 1939. Like sleeping-car attendants, and guards on the Non-Stop, he and his fireman would be away from home many nights of the week - and perhaps some men liked it that way).

THE PASSENGER'S JOURNEY

Let us recollect a journey from London to Edinburgh by the *FLYING SCOTSMAN* in the summer of 1939. We will not go first-class, nor on the *CORONATION*. We will go third-class, and take a quick look at the whole ECML as it really worked - albeit on a train of well above average comfort and speed, trying to visualize the scene from the viewpoint of the average traveller. This third-class traveller would however necessarily still be a person of adequate means, most likely middle-aged. He would not be a business man - today's 'executive', for he would otherwise imagine himself to be in too much of a hurry to travel from London to Edinburgh *by day*, and would go by sleeper overnight, and if reasonably wealthy would go first-class. We might imagine on the other hand that our traveller is a foreigner: in 1939, as today, many of those making the whole seven-hour non-stop journey third-class by day would be foreign tourists (mainly American), and it is always intriguing to try to view British institutions, like the ECML and its *FLYING SCOTSMAN*, through a foreigner's eyes.

It is a weekday, and the morning rush-hour is not quite over when we arrive at King's Cross, in good time for the 10.00 departure, and the Underground was hot and crowded - is it ever not so? - or the taxi from our hotel had crawled maddeningly

The London aspect of the ECML: the noble frontage of King's Cross station in the early 1930s, partly obscured by an assortment of 'temporary' erections - known as the 'Native Village' - that proliferated further before they were eventually swept away in the 1960s. The date of this photograph is revealed by vintage models of the road vehicles - and their sparsity, but also by the LNER lettering used being pre-Gill Sans. *H.G.E.Wilson collection.*

(left) The interior of the main section of King's Cross, as seen from near the buffer-stops of No.1 platform. The scene is way back in June 1933, as witnessed by the ancient GN coaches at platform No.7 and the siding between the platforms. *Photomatic.*

(opposite) King's Cross in the 1930s: the Suburban station (platforms 11-17), with N2s Nos.4755 (BR No.69534) and 2681 (BR No.69587) waiting to depart, for New Barnet and for Cuffley respectively. *Lens*

in streets almost as choked with traffic - but far less regulated - as they are today. From the Underground, we would have come up into the spacious circulating area (then quite new), from which a narrow passage and stairway led - if you could find it - up into the back end of the main LNER terminal. If you came by taxi, you would be dropped at an unprepossessing side entrance half way along No.10 platform and near the Suburban station; you would however land by the booking-office, which from the Underground entrance was a long struggle to reach. (Of course you might well have bought your ticket already, at one of the many agencies, a large department-store, or one of the various town offices of the LNER). If you had come by bus or on foot there seemed no real entrance. This was virtually blocked by the jumble of discordant and seemingly temporary buildings - known as the 'Native Kraal' - that disfigured the originally fine frontage of the station, and you had to go in by a grubby opening at the side on York Way, marked 'Exit', to a totally inadequate circulating area. If arriving by taxi you would be sure to be offered and accept the cheerful services of a *porter*, who for no more than 2¹/₂p would carry all your bags and find your seat - no doubt reserved in advance (for 5p), - unless you were a train-spotter, who would need to choose his Window-Seat Facing Engine (*picture*-window on *right*-hand side) and *not* be constrained by having had to reserve a seat not to his liking. Train-spotters and other energetic young people might well have brought their bicycles with them, for which a mere 0.2p/mile was charged; wealthy passengers could bring along their motor-car (for 1¹/₂p/mile); others might be accompanied by up to three dogs, for the same price as a bicycle. In those days, when you travelled with far more possessions - especially bulky apparel - than is now fashionable, luggage was a problem, but you could send it in advance for 10p per package - collected and delivered, door-to-door.

Whichever way you entered King's Cross main-line station you would move suddenly from the ozonized aroma of the Tube, or from the motor-exhaust aroma of the taxi and the street, into that of the engine smoke plus Jeyes Fluid aroma characteristic of a big station, and then the comfortable upholstery aroma of

the carriage. That was all in the normal course of things, but each Railway - each pre-Grouping Railway - had its own aromas, and the GNR/LNER was no exception, with LNER smoke and LNER carriages quite unique and recognizable if impossible to describe.

At all big stations there were crowds of people of all types, sizes and descriptions. The stations were normally full of the noises of steam engines, of the impersonal and often pompous train announcers broadcasting by Tannoy but little understood, of inspectors' and guards' whistles, of shouts of the impatient, of the wail of children, and of the slamming of doors. King's Cross was quite typical in these respects, but to the railway enthusiast it was unique. To him Gresley's great gleaming green Pacifics or his starkly bright silver or blue A4 Streamliners, and the End of No.10, saw to that. Platform 10 was a world in itself - yet with no barrier from the outside world, alike to the ordinary passenger and to the railway staff. Almost all the main station appointments were ranged along its side, and above them were the Railway Offices, both those of the Stationmaster and his assistants and also the offices of many of the LNER Headquarters Departments, including that of the famed Chief Mechanical Engineer - Sir Nigel Gresley. Along No.10 were: the Buffets (one full of men and the smell of beer and cigarette smoke; another full of harassed women and their fractious children, and the smell of fish-and-chips); the Restaurant, smelling of good food, and the 'Georgian' Tea-Room, smelling of tea and toast; the Waiting Rooms and the Ladies' (except First-class, which had a plush new lounge) and - down a dingy stairway - the Gentlemen's Lavatories, smelling of ....?, but where a bath could be had for 5p. Then there were the Booking and Enquiry Offices, still permeated by the musty, dusty smell of the Victorian days, and there was the all-important Lost Property Office. Like everything else do-it-yourself, self-service luggage-lockers came only after the War, but in 1939 the one at King's Cross - a target of the IRA as recently as that July - employed 17 men and collected about 37,000 articles a year from all over the LNER Southern Area, of which *only 20%* were claimed back. Attaché cases were abandoned at the rate of 250-300! a month, and outstanding

Welwyn Viaduct from the west, with an Up express headed by an A1, early 1950s. *Batten.*

recoveries included: a performing dog on its hind legs, a monkey, a Japanese beheading-sword, a tin of live fish, artificial limbs, a belt of American dollar bills, and ten gold dollar pieces.

The first half of No.10 had all these delights, and crowds of people hurrying in all directions. Further along, the enthusiast's determined rush to see what was 'up front' was now frustrated by piles of parcels and mailbags and the need to avoid being run down by a man on a little tractor trailing a string of ancient platform trollies; the smells were of mailbags, fish, of more Jeyes Fluid, and then of *steam locomotives*.

Our interested - but not 'railway-mad' - passenger, comfortably seated now in the *FLYING SCOTSMAN*, would be in one of the spanking new carriages that Gresley had recently had built for this prestige train, rivalling in opulence the sets used for the Streamlined Trains. Quite apart from the natural expectation that the train would leave for Edinburgh promptly at 10.0 a.m. and get there at 5.0 p.m., the prospect of seven hours 'cooped up' in a train with no possibility of escape was for the 1939 traveller by no means as daunting as it is for an airline traveller today, when at any time he faces an intercontinental or even a short-haul journey. On the train he would have not only a luxurious seat with more than ample leg-room - even room to stretch right out if he were going first-class or at a slack time - and a good view out, but he would also be able to get up and stretch and walk the corridors, even to take a draught of fresh air, as well as to smoke unless he had been unlucky enough to find himself in one of the (minority of) No Smoking compartments. He could only be more free and comfortable if he went on a sea voyage. As on today's airlines, he would be importuned by the catering staff to take not only the four main meals (according to the time of day), but also infinite light refreshments and the opportunity to plaster himself throughout the journey with booze; on the Streamliners[8] and the Pullmans this would all be brought to him at his seat. Moreover, a lady passenger on the *SCOTSMAN* could retire to a lounge, and a retiring-room with dressing-tables and a maid in attendance. The prestige trains had double-glazing and pressure-ventilation. None of this was provided on the long-distance road coaches

that competed even then for the people who could not really afford to go to Scotland by train. Like modern airline passengers, they were clamped for hours in their tiny seats, and lucky if they could get up to relieve themselves during the endless tedious hours.

However, the sense of satisfaction and security engendered in our happy passenger by being cosily settled in his seat in the train could be much upset if he happened to read the *Company's Bye-Laws and Regulations*. Then he could be severely shaken by

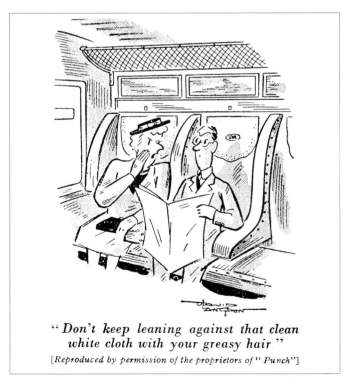

" Don't keep leaning against that clean white cloth with your greasy hair "

[*Reproduced by permission of the proprietors of " Punch"*]

The LNER had antimacassars too - and as for putting your feet on the seat opposite...!

the fear of doing something wrong in a variety of different ways, not least for example if he were a consumptive and had not obtained "permission in writing of a stationmaster or other officer of the Company, duly authorized in that behalf", for "no person suffering from any contagious or infectious disease or disorder shall enter or remain ... in or upon the Railway or in any carriage, or to travel on the Railway." If he (or "any person having the custody, charge or care" of him), had failed to do this, he was liable not only to be thrown out but was also "liable to the Company for the cost of disinfecting the Company's premises and any carriage in which such person shall have been...", etc. Or for fear of men, - as was the author so often warned about Card-Sharpers, who (unlawfully) "played for money or moneysworth at any game or pretended game of chance or skill in or upon the Railway or any carriage or vehicle thereon". On the other hand, if he had read these Bye-Laws and Regulations, our passenger might be angry that the Company was under no obligation to provide him with a seat, to run a train to time, or even to run it at all. His only recourse was to abandon his journey plans precipitately and go to the the booking-office for his money back.

Our passenger in the *FLYING SCOTSMAN* was carried away from King's Cross at 10.0 a.m. on the dot, in luxury. If a foreigner, he would then wonder when he would ever see the Beautiful British Countryside, as his train for the first half-hour fought its way out through a succession of no less than nine tunnels to escape from the Great Maw; our normal traveller would not be concerned, as was our train-watcher, with the innumerable junctions and yards and their fussing steam engines. Once out of London, the discerning tourist was rewarded briefly by a good sample of England's 'great garden', as the train cut through the pleasing Home County of Hertfordshire - a modicum of real charm in the passing scene. After that there followed endless miles of prosperous English farming country - fifty years ago a lot less expansive than nowadays, for then there were far more real hedgerows and the elm trees were still flourishing. This scene dominated the journey for 200 to 300 miles of the ECML. Our foreign traveller especially perhaps, would thrill at the sight of many of the beautiful English village churches, and briefly at the glimpses of Peterborough Cathedral, Selby Abbey, York Minster, and most of all the dramatic appearance of Durham's Cathedral and Castle as the train slowed over the viaduct before passing through Durham station. Apart from perhaps complaining about

the not very exciting English scenery he was seeing for much of the journey, from Darlington to well beyond Newcastle he would no doubt not like the many unsightly colliery waste-tips and the mean housing of the industrial North East.

He may have wondered why the route was called 'East Coast', for it was not - until he was little over an hour and a half from Edinburgh, when he *at last* saw the North Sea. After a glimpse of it at Alnmouth, for a short while the vista over the sea near Beal was however quite romantic, as on Holy Island one of the most historic sites of English Christianity was visible. Then after passing through the famed Border town of Berwick-upon-Tweed the train finally ran on the cliffs above the waves near Burnmouth. The best countryside of the journey would then be seen - the edge of the Scottish Border country, in the last 50 miles or so before Edinburgh as the train wound through the Lammermuir Hills, and came just in sight of the coast once more at Dunbar.

Our tourist on the non-stop *FLYING SCOTSMAN* would have noticed passing through during the journey some of Britain's finer towns and cities - and railway centres, such as Peterborough, Doncaster, Selby, York, Darlington, and Newcastle. The majority of daytime ECML passengers did not go through from London to Edinburgh, but were bound to and from these intermediate places and those reached from them by connecting routes. All these centres made their distinctive contributions, in terms of traffic and of ambience, to the ECML environment. Let us then imagine our 1939 traveller going, not right through to Edinburgh, but stopping off at one of the important intermediate places on the ECML. What did they impart to the scene?

Peterborough (North station) was where you got off if you were bound for many places in Lincolnshire: Spalding, Boston, Skegness, Grimsby - even perhaps that famed resort, Cleethorpes, or for places in the Fens served by the former Midland & Great Northern Joint line: Wisbech, King's Lynn, even Cromer on the Norfolk coast. At Peterborough, many passengers joined ECML trains to go north from almost anywhere in East Anglia: Cambridgeshire/Isle of Ely, Suffolk and Norfolk. In the 1930s,

In the 1930s, an Engineer's train, with one of Hitchin's old J3 0-6-0s (No.4137, later BR No.4145 - it never got its '6'), trundles down at Ganwick between Hadley North and Potters Bar Tunnels. Lens.

13

Peterborough North - in 1931, somewhat before our period but little changed before the war: the view north from Crescent Bridge. On the left, the LMS lines, their Crescent Box, Crescent Sidings, and Spital Bridge engine shed beyond; to the right of the LMS through lines, signal rodding separates an LMS siding from the LNER Down Goods line, the Up Goods, and then the Down 'Excursion' platform. The all-over roof spans the Down and Up Main lines, and on the far right is the Great Northern Hotel. *LCGB.*

Peterborough North as seen from Crescent Bridge - just after our period, 6th June 1960. A bedraggled A4, No.60031 (LNER No.4497) GOLDEN PLOVER is running through with the 09.30 Glasgow Queen St. to King's Cross, while a Derby light-weight two-car DMU stands in the Up bay; beyond is the Great Northern Hotel. *M.Mensing.*

Grim Grantham: a pre-war view looking south from the Up Main platform 2, with the bay platform 4 on the right. One of Gresley's A4's is approaching on a Down Streamliner, and behind the old GN stock, on the right, can be seen the recently built coaling plant at the locomotive shed. Note the 'Co-Op' milk churn on the Up platform - another glimpse of the past. *D.Thompson.*

few passengers so travelling could avoid having to change trains at Peterborough North, and it was not a very pleasant experience. The station was straight out of the mid-19th century - small, devoid of modern amenities and draughty. For the staff it was worse, an operating nightmare on a key position of interchange for both passenger and freight traffic. It must have been a hard task for Control to operate and for the stationmaster.

Grantham station too was an antiquated, uncomfortable station almost unaltered in nearly a hundred years. It was there that passengers for Nottingham, Derby and west thereof, and for Sleaford, Lincoln and other Lincolnshire destinations, had to get out of their comfortable ECML express and bundle into the old ex-GN carriages (some still even six-wheelers) that often formed their slow connecting trains - and there were almost no through coaches from London.

Newark was a quite important stop - but mainly just for Newark, a market town with a range of industrial establishments. At *Retford*, some ECML passengers might change for stations to Lincoln and Grimsby or to Sheffield (Victoria) on the cross-country ex-GC Manchester - Sheffield - Lincolnshire line. Sheffield was reached more conveniently from St Pancras or from Marylebone, although in pre-Grouping days the GNR had run through expresses to Sheffield Victoria *via* Retford, and these were revived by BR in the Diesel era.

Passenger interchange was essentially nil at nearby Dukeries Junction. There the residuum of the over-ambitious Lancashire, Derbyshire & East Coast Railway crossed the ECML, but there were few trains on that line and hardly any trains stopped at the ECML Low Level station. There were no goods facilities at Dukeries Junction, and the stationmaster must have had a grand time - a suitable rest-cure from the tribulations of Peterborough North, perhaps?

In terms of railway operation - and from the railway enthusiast's point of view, *Doncaster* was a key junction on the ECML. There diverged the main line on to Leeds, Bradford, and other towns in the West Riding of Yorkshire, and that to Hull, taking the through trains or coaches from King's Cross and elsewhere off the ECML; it was not normally necessary for passengers to change at Doncaster for these important destinations. Also at Doncaster the ECML intersected with the west - east artery of the former Great Central system, the line from Sheffield to Scunthorpe, Grimsby, and - again - Cleethorpes, but interchange with GC line trains at Doncaster would be

principally for local services. In addition, at Doncaster the 'Joint Line' (ex-GN&GE Joint) came in from Lincoln, Sleaford, March and hence from East Anglia generally, but through trains were few in number on that line except on Summer Saturdays; otherwise it was more convenient to change at Peterborough, Grantham or Retford. Therefore the majority of ECML expresses for York and beyond did not stop at Doncaster and from the point of view of the ECML passenger Doncaster station was for the people of Doncaster and of the surrounding district. The station was however being quite extensively modernized in 1939 - even if incompletely until after the War - and was not as forbidding as many other comparable stations.

With its pivotal position in the great South Yorkshire coalfield as the junction of various interconnecting lines, Doncaster was of paramount importance in terms of coal and heavy freight traffic. There the LNER had major Locomotive, Carriage and Wagon Works, employing over 3,000 people. So, while our ordinary passenger disdainfully ignored the busy freight yards and general railway activity, to the professional railwayman - and to the railway enthusiast - Doncaster meant everything. Although not actually created by the railway, for it was also an important market town on the Great North Road, Doncaster indeed vied with Crewe and Swindon as a Railway Town.

Few ECML expresses deigned to call at *Selby*, the next town of importance down the line, because unless destined locally or for Yorkshire Coast resorts like Bridlington and Filey ECML passengers would not need to alight there. Selby, like Retford a station of two main platforms and still with its Victorian facilities (including dining- and refreshment-rooms), was more an incidental point of intersection of the ECML with a busy west - east line, in this case the ex-North Eastern route from Leeds to Hull and to Bridlington. It was a freight junction of moderate importance, and from the viewpoint of the railway connoisseur from the South it was where he first became aware of the great North Eastern Railway system, with its own characteristics - such as powerful robust locomotives with spacious cabs, high-capacity coal wagons, and on local trains clerestory coaches with Westinghouse brakes.

(left) **Barkston: a very functional ex-GN wayside station. The view is northwards in the 1930s, showing an Up express of teak stock approaching with an A3, and the two Down platforms - one on the main line, the other on the branch to Lincoln and Sleaford.** *D.Thompson.*

(middle) **Ranskill: another of the rather mean wayside stations on the GNR section of the ECML. In this 1930s scene looking south, an Ivatt Small Atlantic (LNER Class C2) with No.2 Express Goods headcode is approaching on a strangely composed 'mixed' train. The train may have been the 07.00 'Q' Wood Green (Waterworks Sidings) to Doncaster HC empty stock and vans train. 'HC' stood for 'Horse & Carriage' (Horse & Cart' in the vernacular), the 'Carriages' having been in the olden days those normally hauled by horses and owned by the gentry but loaded onto railway wagons.** *D.Thompson.*

(below) **Track and signalling at Chaloners Whin Junction: a view southward, 20th September 1937. The ECML curves away to the left towards Selby, while the four tracks straight ahead are the Sheffield and Leeds lines towards Church Fenton.** *K.Appleby coll.*

A pre-war scene (20th September 1937) from the York Racecourse platform, showing a typical large NER signal gantry spanning the six tracks southwards from York, bearing - as well as the host of arms for Down trains - three Up distants. The box on the left housed only the ground-frame for the exit of Holgate Down Reception Sidings (behind and to the left). An LMS engine (MR 2P 4-4-0 No.498) approaches on the right and, beyond the massive road bridge, the end of a Down freight can be seen curving round towards York Yard South. *K.Appleby coll.*

York station: the main entrance, on the Up side across from the City Walls, with Thomas Prosser's rather grand porte-cochére; part of the Royal Station Hotel is seen on the right. The date of the view is 1961, but Cheap Day returns are evidently still available to Leeds and Harrogate. *H.G.Wilson coll.*

Soon after Selby came *York*, considered by many the capital of the North of England and historically England's second city. York had been the Headquarters of the NER and in the 1930s was that of the relatively autonomous NE Area of the LNER. After Nationalization it naturally became the Headquarters of the North Eastern Region of BR, and finally of the combined ER and NER. The Headquarters offices were housed in a large and imposing block, built in 1906 and symbolizing the prosperity of the proud North Eastern Railway, and with the station and the Royal Station Hotel nearby befitting the importance of the NER to the City of York. Our foreign tourist travelling down the ECML would certainly have wanted to visit York, and many of our ordinary English travellers would have been going there. In winter months when there were no through services from the London direction to Scarborough, Whitby or other Yorkshire Coast resorts, many passengers would be changing at York for these and also for other places in the North and East Ridings. (Before the War, about 2m. passengers a year came to the seaside resorts of the NE Area, mainly on Day Excursions). On the other hand, York was where passengers coming from many parts of the country and bound for the North East and Scotland joined the ECML.

York was the junction for the main lines from Leeds and from Normanton and thence from Manchester, Liverpool and the Central and Western Divisions of the London Midland & Scottish Railway generally, also for the main line from Sheffield and through there from the Midlands, South Wales, the West Country and central Southern England. Another line came in to York from Hull. Although a number of trains from these major areas of Britain, from Manchester and Liverpool, from Birmingham, Bristol, and Cardiff, and from Southampton, ran through York on to Newcastle and even Edinburgh, many - being LMS trains - terminated at York. Therefore very many passengers changed there. There was also a corresponding vast flow of freight traffic, and all this made York the greatest intermediate junction and railway centre on the whole ECML. Together with the very substantial freight traffic down the ECML *via* Doncaster, through York's great freight yards passed traffic to and from most parts of the country. Lastly, at York was one of the principal Works for the building of coaching stock, employing nearly 1,500 workers.

Commensurate with its importance, York had a station of magnificent proportions, which had been enlarged as recently as 1938. With 16 platforms on a sweeping curve, most of them under three majestic arches, the station and its sounds had a grandeur, typified by the sonorous public address announcements - it being the first British station equipped with 'Tannoy': "York. This is York station. York. Change here for ..." Almost all ECML expresses stopped at York, and even if they did not they were slowed to 15 mph to pass through its centre roads; the most blasé ECML passenger could not fail to recognize the importance of York as a railway junction. The station was provided with commodious waiting-rooms, dining-rooms, buffets and all the other facilities, and a great footbridge across the main lines. Passengers had less reason to complain of dirt and of cold than at any other ECML station, and moreover the Royal Station Hotel adjoining was a leading Railway hotel. As at other major stations on the former NER, passengers coming to take a train at York were instructed by a splendid map of the NER system featured in ceramic tiles on a wall of the entrance hall. They left the station at York through a glazed portico onto Station Road, busy with local buses and taxis that swept over the River Ouse

on Lendal Bridge into the city. Across the road was a stretch of York's famous mediaeval walls, and on the other side of these was the entrance to the LNER (later to become the National) Railway Museum, in its original location in the former York & North Midland Works and the earlier Old Station in Tanner Row.

After York the next major centre on the ECML likely to concern our ordinary traveller was *Darlington*. Darlington (Bank Top) station, albeit on a smaller scale than York or Newcastle, was also commodious and well-appointed. It featured a fine arched span over a great island platform - and a clock-tower, but the approach from the outside world was from a side entrance on Victoria Road or up a ramp from Parkgate, and was not too impressive. Nearly all ECML expresses stopped there - even the *SILVER JUBILEE*, for passengers for the important town of Darlington itself and more especially those bound to and from an extensive and populous hinterland that included the great industrial Tees-side conurbation of Stockton/Middlesbrough, also the seaside resorts of Redcar and Saltburn. On the other hand, to some extent passengers on the ECML for Tees-side, West Hartlepool and Sunderland were catered for by trains that diverged at Northallerton and missed Darlington, although some of the trains on this Coast line to Newcastle came from Leeds *via* Harrogate and impinged on the ECML only at Northallerton. As well as having a busy service of comfortable local trains to Tees-side, Bank Top was also the terminus of local services to Richmond, to Bishop Auckland, and up the West Durham valleys. Time-worn trains went *via* Barnard Castle right over the Pennines to Penrith and Tebay, in what is now Cumbria and in 1939 was the different world served by the LMSR.

From the railway angle, Darlington was a centre of the first rank, not only by virtue of the passenger traffic outlined above, and of a corresponding flow of freight, but also on account of the presence of major Locomotive and Wagon Works, with over 2,500 workers, rendering Darlington to the NER what Doncaster was to the GNR. Finally, the pioneering Stockton & Darlington Railway of 1825 had given Darlington a head-start in the railway business, the passing traveller being reminded of this by the presence of the preserved S&D locomotives, LOCOMOTION and DERWENT, set up on plinths at Bank Top.

Many expresses necessarily stopped next at *Durham*. The relatively modest station there was sited awkwardly on the side of a hill rather away from the town, and had only Down and Up main platforms and no overall roof. People alighted there for Durham City itself (Durham station issued 132,000 tickets in 1938) but it was a long, steep walk down from the station. It is unlikely they would be changing into one of the rather antiquated local trains that ran to Sunderland from Bishop Auckland, because the service to those places was better from Newcastle or Darlington respectively. If they were bound for the Lanchester valley, up to Consett, they had lost their local service earlier in 1939, but there might have been the odd soul who intended to catch the one early morning train to Waterhouses and he would have to get out at Durham.

Soon after Durham came *Newcastle-upon-Tyne*. The approaches to Newcastle Central station from the south, over either the King Edward or the High Level Bridge, were impressive, giving as they did lofty views of the River Tyne and its industry and shipping as well as the skyline of the city. The Central station, with its 15 platforms was large and impressive, but its overall roofs lacked the grandeur of York, and the ambience at Newcastle Central was in keeping with the heavy *(right)* **A 'period' Civil Engineering scene, at Thirsk in June 1932 during the widening and signal electrification work on the ECML north of York. A scissors crossing, weighing 25 tons, which was constructed by the side of the track, is being moved into position on ball-bearing rollers. The view is northward just north of the station and shows the extensive sidings on each side of the main line.** *K.Appleby coll.*

(below) **The revolutionary new Thirsk power signalbox, as new in 1933.** *K.Appleby coll.*

(right) **Darlington Bank Top, 19th July 1958, and the 08.05 Birmingham -Newcastle express stands at the Down side platform 4, with V2 No.60910 (LNER No.4881).** *M.Mensing.*

Newcastle: a particularly fine view - in April 1947 - of the classic ECML crossing at the east end of the Central station, where the lines across the High Level Bridge diverge to the right over the lines to Edinburgh and Tynemouth. With the Castle setting it off, an A4 approaches on the Up *FLYING SCOTSMAN*, and a Tyneside electric train (with front four coaches still in LNER blue-and-white livery) departs for Tynemouth. The prominent truss bridge on the right is the Tyne Bridge, built in the 1930s. *K.Appleby coll.*

Berwick-upon-Tweed, the Border station midway between Newcastle and Edinburgh: a view of the main Up side buildings (as rebuilt in 1927), bedecked with flags for the Coronation in 1953. *Henry Wilson coll.*

industry of the city and in which the railways had always played a major part. (As at Darlington, the close association of Newcastle with the earliest days of railways was commemorated, by a very early George Stephenson locomotive standing on a plinth on the platform). The station was essentially as built in 1850, but its public facilities were ample and had been recently modernized to a certain extent, and alongside was the prestigious Royal Station Hotel. The city's business district was close by, and Newcastle's yellow-and-white trams took passengers in all directions from the impressive portico of the station in Neville Street.

Newcastle being a large city and county in its own right - the largest intermediate city on the ECML - and having a hinterland with a population approaching a million, the majority of the long-distance trains terminated there. Thus most of the ECML passengers alighted, either for the city itself, or to go on to such places as Sunderland, South Shields or Tynemouth. In addition, Tyneside including Newcastle was a seaport of considerable importance, and trains ran regularly from London to the Tyne Commission Quay at North Shields to connect with passenger ships to Norway. Two other important services ran from Newcastle, largely independently of the ECML, that to Middlesbrough *via* West Hartlepool and Stockton, and that to Carlisle. These lines also catered for more local traffic than did the ECML itself, and there was also the oddity of an alternative but very slow service into Scotland, formerly provided by the NBR, which ran *via* Hexham through the depths of Northumberland over to lonely Riccarton Junction on the Waverley Route and on to Hawick. Dirty local steam services ran from Central to North Wylam, to Leamside *via* Ferryhill, and to Blackhill by two routes.

However, rather unusually in the 1930s for a Railway Company other than the Southern, the LNER ran *electric* trains from Newcastle Central, with an intensive service of multiple-unit trains. On the north side of the Tyne they were made up of modern articulated saloon stock painted red-and-cream, and ran on a circular service to Tynemouth *via* Jesmond, Benton and Backworth, and back *via* Wallsend (or vice-versa), also a less frequent service to Tynemouth by the Riverside route. To the south side of the Tyne there was a frequent electric service, using older (refurbished) stock although the line was electrified only in 1938, over the High Level Bridge to South Shields. However our hypothetical ECML traveller, if not a native of the area would have little reason to alight at Newcastle for pleasure, nor was Newcastle Central a great place of interchange, the non-ECML trains there serving primarily the rather close-knit people of the region.

In 1938, 2.72m. passengers bought tickets at Newcastle Central, and the seaside resorts in the District collected 4.11m. tickets - and this was a 'poor year' for the era. That year Newcastle District also dealt with 1.07m. parcels, 48,000 bicycles and prams, 97,000 items of Passengers' Luggage in Advance, 236,000 milk-cans, 1,761 horses, 58,000 (individual) fishes, and 330 tons of poultry and game. In 1958, no less than 14.5m. passengers were handled (*excluding* those merely changing trains), and Newcastle Central was the busiest provincial station in the country.

As Newcastle was a city of much heavy industry and the centre of a large industrial and mining hinterland, much of the freight as well as passenger traffic of the ECML southwards was generated in the area, and Newcastle was the repository of many of its locomotives and much of its rolling-stock. Moreover, all freight traffic across the Tyne - north - south or east - west, which

included much coal and other traffic of a local nature, had to pass through Newcastle Central. This, together with the intensive local passenger services, made Central extremely busy - and necessitated renewal of its famous diamond crossings every few years. On the other hand, northwards from Newcastle down the ECML, traffic - both passenger and freight - was considerably lighter than south of it. Apart from the rich coalfield around Bedlington and Ashington, there were few sources north of Newcastle to generate freight traffic for the ECML and most of the freight was Anglo-Scottish traffic passing through.

The rest of the journey down the ECML - at any rate after Morpeth, was through thinly populated country. Most ECML expresses to Edinburgh then stopped only at Berwick-upon-Tweed. In part they did so in respect of crossing the Border and entering the North British Railway system; Berwick itself was not a large place, but it was the railhead for a wide and prosperous area of North Northumberland and the Border country. Otherwise, as with the stop made by some expresses at Alnmouth, trains may have stopped partly for the local gentry to be collected by car to be taken to some estate in the area, or for passengers to join a branch train to historic Alnwick or Kelso.

So we come to the end of the ECML - as defined in this account. Let us try to imagine how our supposed foreign tourist would have reacted to arriving at Waverley station in *Edinburgh* - punctually at 5.0 p.m. of course. Discounting his probable compulsion, along with most of the other passengers at the merest hint of the end of the journey, to collect his coat and his bags and to crush into the vestibule in desperate readiness to get off the train as if it were on fire, he might already have had fleeting glimpses of Edinburgh's incomparable skyline. On alighting at Waverley, he would not see the skyline properly until he had laboriously climbed the renowned Waverley Steps out of the station to street level. (The only civilized way to leave Waverley was by taxi, that had come down the steep approach road to the station entrance off Waverley Bridge[9]). Then indeed it will have struck him: the Mound with the Scottish National Gallery, the Scott Monument, the Castle, the proud buildings along Princes Street, the majestic North British Hotel with its prominent clock-tower, the North Bridge striding across the station complex at a dizzy height, and the trams in their restrained maroon colour in keeping with the dignity of the United Kingdom's alternative Capital.

What of Waverley station itself, the focus of the LNER in Scotland? Waverley was one of the very *largest* stations in Britain, with 21 platforms the same as London's Waterloo. In spite of being down in the deep natural cleft separating the New from the Old Towns of Edinburgh, and therefore quite well hidden from the city's populace, it was relatively unsulphurous and clean. The greater bulk of the station and all its public and railway offices and facilities were incorporated in a wide island structure, which was flanked by the main through lines with their double-length platforms; in the centre of this was a very fine booking and waiting-hall illuminated through a dome and decorative iron screens. The dignity and splendour of this hall accorded with the ambience of the Scottish capital itself, a city like none other - if our foreign visitor was a Frenchman, he would find Edinburgh in its way more akin to Paris than to London.

The island arrangement worked well, because the great majority of passenger trains originated or terminated at Waverley, and most of the numerous through freight trains went round the city well away on the South Suburban line. From Waverley's many terminal platforms, trains set from either end of the great station out largely independently: they went to the suburbs of Edinburgh, and to destinations almost all over Scotland - to Glasgow (by two routes) and to the West Highland line, and over the Forth Bridge to Fife, to Perth and Inverness - even Dalnaspidal, and on over the Tay Bridge to Dundee and Aberdeen. The other way they went by the ECML back to Berwick and England or by the Waverley Route to the Border towns, Carlisle and eventually to London (St Pancras) *via* Leeds and Sheffield.

If our ECML traveller was not staying in Edinburgh, he would as likely as not have to change trains at Waverley. A passenger on the *FLYING SCOTSMAN* could stay on the train and continue over the Bridges to principal stations to Dundee and Aberdeen[10], but it would be a hardy traveller who made the whole trip, Aberdeen not being reached until 10hr 15min after leaving King's Cross. A number of through travellers would go on - by other trains - from Edinburgh to Glasgow (Queen Street), but most people from London and the South to Dundee and Aberdeen used the overnight sleeping-car trains.

The Scottish Area of the LNER with its headquarters at Edinburgh and the ambience of its forerunner, the NBR, was a world apart from the Southern Area, as was the Scottish nation from England. In spite of the telephone, and a mere seven hours travelling by *FLYING SCOTSMAN* - and the staff of ECML expresses 'commuting' several times a week to and from London, the English capital may have seemed then, as now, a degenerate and foreign place, where resided faceless Railway and Government bureaucrats seemingly unconcerned with Scottish affairs. It follows that a Scotsman venturing to London by the *FLYING SCOTSMAN*, reversing the part of our traveller from King's Cross, might journey up with certain prejudices and misgivings, and when he saw King's Cross station would find it a poor counterpart to Waverley, its environs reinforcing his ideas of London's debauchery. Waverley and its surroundings were a far better image of Scotland's capital than were those of King's Cross representative of London.

Finally it must not be forgotten that, as on other trunk routes in the Steam Age, the ECML had small wayside stations spaced every few miles throughout its length. In 1939 there were 108 stations between Hitchin and Edinburgh (Waverley); in 1993 there were just 21. However, the wayside stations generally had a very poor service, provided by a few extremely slow stopping-trains running over limited stretches of the line; many of these little stations had only three or four trains stopping each way per day. Life at one of these wayside stations, at least if they also had only one or two pick-up goods trains serving them, was therefore really rather a sinecure - but a poorly paid one. Often their staff occupied their time tending the station flower-beds, encouraged by an annual Competition with prizes - even after the war. The larger stations, where such efforts would have been justifiable economically, were not normally involved, but on the other hand there were competitions for the Prize Length of permanent way - often won by the men responsible for stretches of the ECML.

Unlike the larger stations, the little wayside ones would be passed almost unseen from an express, but not so the signals. The whole of the ECML main lines was of course worked on the Absolute Block system, much of it protected by track-circuiting at major stations and junctions. Signals were mostly semaphore, and in general worked manually, as were points at most locations. The GNR's 'somersault' signals, almost unique in the country, were still in use in 1939 - a few into the 1950s - in many places

down to Doncaster, and large gantries of these rather graceful structures were prominent especially in the London area. In main NE Area centres - notably at York and Newcastle - those great gantries characteristic of the NER, with their multitude of signal and repeater arms, were to be seen. The signals on the NB section, with their rather slender lattice posts made of old rails, also had their own character. However, at King's Cross, between Skelton Junction and Darlington South, and at Edinburgh Waverley, electrical power-signalling with colour-lights was installed, and the forests of semaphores had already gone.

That was the ECML in a nutshell. The line, its stations and what was to be seen at them - especially for 'Overgrown Train-Spotters', its locomotives - will be pored over later in detail in Part II.

POSTSCRIPT

Some may feel, with justification, that the ECML did not end at Edinburgh, but continued to Aberdeen. Be that as it may, this account goes no further than the Scottish capital. The journey on was quite enticing: the awesome Forth Bridge and the endless Tay Bridge were crossed, a great deal more of the real East Coast could be seen, and there was yet more to appeal in the locomotive and general railway scene. Indeed, the line from Edinburgh to Aberdeen was all so interesting and geographically complex that it merits a separate account on its own. In the Age of Steam it took over 10 hours to reach Aberdeen from London. It would have been extremely tiring to do the whole journey in the course of one day, and except around the Summer Solstice it would have been *dark* long before the end was reached. Today an IC125 (or IC225) whisks a traveller from London to Aberdeen in the time it took in Steam days to reach Edinburgh, but - apart from the scenery and the remains of forgotten stations and obliterated yards fleetingly glimpsed - what is there for the *railway* enthusiast to see out of the window?

1. Throughout this book, for the sake of clarity, tenses in the description are all in the Past, even if features described still exist.
2. To be precise, the end-on union was with the L&Y line to Knottingley, whence access was obtained to York by running-powers over the York & North Midland (later NER) through Ferrybridge, Burton Salmon and Church Fenton, until in 1871 the NER built its line down from York through Selby to connect with the GNR at Shaftholme Junction.
3. In practice the first two-track stretch was at least $3\frac{1}{4}$ miles long, because *passenger* trains had to turn onto the main line at New Barnet, short of Greenwood box.
4. Throughout this book prices are given in modern decimal currency, although prior to 1971 it was of course £.s.d.
5. Although second-class accommodation had been provided on London (GN and GE line) suburban services, it was abolished in January 1938, and in 1939 it was used only on certain Continental boat trains to and from the packet ports, mainly to conform to the three- (or occasional four-) class practice in Europe.
6. The GN was also the innovator of the side-corridor coach, in 1882.
7. A bottle of Niersteiner cost 25p, a Volnay 1923 $52\frac{1}{2}$p, and various champaignes £1.00.
8. Except the SILVER JUBILEE, on which it was not practicable for the staff to serve meals all along the train from only one kitchen.
9. If you were 'in the know', you could also use the staff lift into the North British Hotel.
10. In the Winter timetable, the *FLYING SCOTSMAN* also had through carriages to Perth - with the locomotives still carrying the head-board.

(above) **A study in NER signals, at Alnmouth: J39 No.64924 (LNER No.1563) comes off the Alnwick branch with a local train, 29th May 1962.** *M.Mensing.*

(right) **A very basic NBR wayside station, East Fortune: the view is towards Edinburgh, 2nd May 1964. (Only the flat-bottom rails are more modern than our period).** *J.L.Stevenson.*

GREEN ARROW SERVICE
for Urgent Orders

When clients demand immediate delivery, when the sender's reputation for Service is in danger—that's when the British Railways' Green Arrow facility saves the day. The "Green Arrow" is a system of Registered Transit for merchandise and livestock by goods train which ensures additional watchfulness over your goods throughout transit. The special "green arrow" label affixed to the consignment brings it immediately within a specialised control system. Every point along the route has warning of its coming, every railwayman handling the consignment is conscious of its urgency; and a trained staff keeps constant watch until the goods are safely delivered. The fee for this special service is only 2/6d. per consignment. Ring up your nearest Railway Station or Goods Office for further particulars of the "Green Arrow" Service.

G.W.R   **L M S**   **L·N·E·R**   **S.R**

GOOD NEWS FOR *Countrymen*

The British Railways provide fast motor lorry services to and from farm and village and nearest Railway Depot, thus bringing modern and efficient transport facilities within easy reach, even in the most outlying Country Districts. The British Railways Country Lorry Service is available for almost every kind of traffic and the rates are reasonable. Make sure of the quickest transport in future—insist on goods and materials being sent by Rail. Scales of charges and detailed information will be gladly supplied at your nearest Railway Station or Goods Office.

G.W.R   **L M S**   **L·N·E·R**   **S.R**

DARE WE LET THE RAILWAYS DIE?

It is for *you* to decide.

The Railway industry faces a grave crisis.

The prosperity of the Railways vitally affects *you*. It affects you as a trader, as a ratepayer, as a tax-payer, as a purchaser. It affects the housewife, the retailer, the wholesaler. It affects you in peacetime—but what if war should come?

Can any means of transport other than the Railways evacuate in 48 hours London's millions, Birmingham's millions, Liverpool's millions, and millions from other danger zones.

Only the RAILWAYS can cope with the vast quantities of supplies that the nation requires in peace or in war.

Essential in Peace, **vital in War**, *dare we let the Railways die?*

The danger signal shines red . . . the Railways have asked the Minister of Transport to *clear the lines.** They have asked for the right of way to that efficiency upon which the country depends—upon which *you* depend.

They have asked that the shackles of a century may be removed; that out-of-date rules applicable to long vanished conditions should go ; *that they should be given the freedom enjoyed by other forms of transport.*

Shall they have this freedom?

IT IS FOR YOU TO DECIDE.

THE RAILWAYS ASK FOR A SQUARE DEAL—NOW

> *ASK FOR A COPY OF "CLEAR THE LINES," FREE AT EVERY RAILWAY STATION IN BRITAIN. IT TELLS YOU HOW THE OUT-OF-DATE RAILWAY RESTRICTIONS AFFECT *YOU*

ISSUED BY THE RAILWAY COMPANIES' ASSOCIATION

"The Railways' response to the threat of losing goods traffic to road operators."

(top left) **Pre-war poster advertising Green Arrow goods services.** *(top right)* **Pre-war poster demonstrating** *integrated* **goods transport.** *(left)* **Pre-war "Square Deal" poster. Even after the great conflict of 1939-1945, in which the Railways' had shown how vital they had been in wartime, they were allowed to become second best to road transport in peacetime.**

Chapter III. THE HISTORICAL CONTEXT OF THE CHANGES ON THE ECML OVER THE YEARS 1939 - 1959

THE SITUATION OF THE RAILWAYS IN THE LATE 1930s

By the late 1930s the Railways no longer had the near monopoly that they had enjoyed before the First World War of inland transport - excluding purely local traffic, inland water transport and coastwise shipping traffic, and they were already in severe financial difficulties due to 'unfair' competition from nationwide road transport. Still in private hands, the Railways were at a disadvantage compared to road users in having to finance out of revenue not only their rolling stock but also their track, stations and other fixed assets. As we would say today, compared to the economics of road transport 'they were not operating on a level playing-field'. The private motor-car was already relentlessly creaming off especially the 'upper crust' of passenger travel, and in regard to freight the Railways were saddled with archaic regulations and systems of ratings imposed on them when they did have a monopoly. Between 1923 and 1938 personal *per capita* income in Britain had increased on average by over a third and the proportion of that spent on travel had risen significantly. But the Railways' share of the market was declining. Total passenger-miles by bus and coach, at 19,000m. nationwide in 1938, was almost the same as the rail figure of 20,000m.; tramway and trolley bus usage accounted for an additional 8,100m. passenger-miles. Meanwhile, travel by private car was estimated to be already in excess of 25,000m.

As for freight, haulage by road was seriously undermining the Railways' pre-eminence. There were about half a million independent commercial vehicles on the road, two-thirds of them 'C' licence lorries and vans carrying a firm's own goods, and ton-mileage by road was approaching that carried by the Railways. Legislation in 1930 had at least brought some control over private road hauliers, through regulation by licence - at a modest fee - of their vehicles and any common carrier service they provided. On the other hand, maximum railway fares and charges for the carriage of freight were fixed by statute. The statutory rates were aimed to enable the Railways to achieve a net 'Standard Revenue', calculated from the Railways' revenues *before* the First World War - before road motor transport was an alternative. Naturally, between the Wars the Railways never came near to achieving such a revenue. Moreover, railway charges were open to public scrutiny, and the Railway Companies were *obliged* to carry any goods offered to them however unprofitable. They also had to undertake to dispatch goods - however small the consignment - on the day it was received, which resulted in very poor average loading factors. They could not adjust their prices to true costs, which in any case were very difficult to determine. Charges had to be uniform across the country and the scope allowed for downward adjustment to meet the competition was limited. Freight charges set by the Railways were traditionally based on the value of the goods and not on the cost of carriage, whereas the road hauliers applied the latter - more realistic - criterion. Unlike those for users of road transport, rail charges had to take into account the interest that had been raised to build the track and stations - and to purchase the land they were built on, while road hauliers did not have these overheads, except in terms of fuel and vehicle taxes. Besides, their prices were

unpublished, and unregulated. They were often quicker[1], safer and more efficient in their handling and delivery of goods - and they moved goods from door to door without trans-shipment. The road operators were therefore able to cream off the most lucrative business. The only recourse open to the Railway Companies to counter the competition was to offer 'Exceptional' rates - that had to be between 5% and 40% *below* the Standard Rates, or (as from 1933) to negotiate 'Agreed' rates, *i.e.* flat rates, with particular traders - but still less than the Standard rate for the commodity, and still settled in open court with other traders able to object and demand identical treatment.

To limit their losses in the area of local passenger services, the Railways had themselves invested heavily in bus operations. Instead of running their own bus services, they bought substantial holdings (in most cases 49%) in the major operators, and found their investments profitable. The involvement of the Railway Companies with bus services led to some coordination of bus and rail services and fares before the Second World War, but these sensible arrangements were not perpetuated after Nationalization of the Railways. The road haulage industry on the other hand was too fragmented for the Railway Companies to invest in it in the way they did in the bus undertakings, other than in one or two larger Companies concerned mainly with parcels deliveries. These interests in road transport were handed over to the BTC on Nationalization, but the process of integration went into reverse before effective public control of road haulage was achieved, because the Conservative administration elected in 1951 lost no time in *de*-nationalizing road transport.

Definitely the year 1938 was *not* a good one, and almost all freight revenues were on an accelerating downward trend. In November 1938, Sir Ralph Wedgwood (Chief General Manager of the LNER, until succeeded by C.H.Newton in March 1939) led a movement, jointly with the other Railways and sponsored by the Railway Companies' Association, pressing the Government for a 'Square Deal' with respect to road competition and to relieve the Railways' obligation to maintain a published ceiling on charges. The hauliers, with a more powerful lobby, countered by asserting that vehicle and fuel taxes were not spent on roads. A compromise had not been achieved in those final months before the war came to alter everything - and very soon after the war a public demand for Nationalization of the Railways. In the first half of 1939 the downward trend in passenger receipts was accelerating, although freight receipts were improving rapidly by the outbreak of the war. Rearmament was no doubt the reason for this change and of course as soon as the war started the profitability of the Railways was transformed.

WARTIME (1939-1945)

The Second World War brought tremendous changes to the railway scene[2], as it did to every other aspect of life. The changes on the railways were basically of four kinds: Government control; major reductions in the frequency, speed and comfort of passenger services; a substantial increase in freight traffic; and lastly, damage - acute, due to air-raids, and chronic, due to reduction of standards of maintenance.

'The Darkest Hour': Anti-Invasion defences on the ECML, in the form of concrete blocks and Dragon's Teeth, Oakleigh Park, 1940 - and an *unofficial* picture at that. *J.Aylard.*

therefore of their costs. In effect, the Railways were 'hired' - for the duration of the war and for one year after its end. It was agreed that all revenues should be pooled, and a scheme was devised for the sharing of revenues and their taxation. A guaranteed net revenue of £43.5m. per year was to be distributed between the five principal bodies, in the proportions of 34% to the LMSR, 23% to the LNER, 16% each to the GWR and SR, and 11% to the LPTB; half of any further profits above the £43.5m. up to £56m. could be taken (in the same proportions) by the Railways, the other half and any profits above £56 m. would be retained by the Exchequer. The arrangement was designed to give the Railways some reward for their efforts and therefore encourage them to be efficient. But it soon transpired that the Railways were being called to take on more than enough traffic and to work to maximum capacity, while the Companies were open to criticism that they were 'profiteering from the war' because their competitors - chiefly road transport undertakings - were artificially handicapped by wartime restrictions. The need for people to travel and for goods to be transported was as great as ever and would quickly become greater, and the resources of the Railways became a major limiting factor in the prosecution of the war. Therefore the Government changed its mind and forced a new and more stringent financial agreement on the Companies in January 1941, whereby the Exchequer now kept *all* net revenues above the annual £43.5m., although it did set aside a special Trust Fund of £10m. a year for the Railways to draw on after the war to pay for arrears of maintenance. Meanwhile the Railway Companies agreed not to charge the cost of war damage and extra maintenance against revenue.

Based on their system of control of the Railways during the First World War, in the years between the rise of Nazi Germany and the outbreak of the Second World War, the Government had drawn up plans for similar direction in the event of another major war. When the Germans invaded Poland on 1st September 1939 the plans were activated. The Railways were taken over by the Ministry of Transport[3], and they remained under Government control until the end of 1947, the eve of Nationalization. In the Ministry the responsibility for railway matters was assigned to two Divisions, Traffic and Maintenance, the Heads of which were accountable to the Railway Control Officer. He provided the link with the Railway Executive Committee (REC). The REC, consisting - as will be described in Part II - of the Chief Executives of the Big Four Railways and the London Passenger Transport Board (LPTB), with G.Cole Deacon of the Railway Companies' Association as Secretary, was constituted in September 1938 and was in being as an advisory body from that date until the outbreak of war.

Meanwhile, early in 1939 detailed instructions were drawn up in secret and circulated to General Managers, for the 'Control of the Railways in the Event of Armed Conflict', and these included the appointment of liaison officers and long lists of addresses of officers responsible for all the military and other government agencies with whom the Railways would have to cooperate, while plans were drawn up well before the outbreak of hostilities to cope with immediate demands. These included evacuation of children and hospital patients - from London in particular, and of treasures, gold, and key Government and business departments, also the removal of naval ammunition from coastal depots[4] and of perishables from the docks to inland Cold Stores. Upon the outbreak of war, sixteen consultative Committees were set up to deal with different aspects of railway matters and reported to the main REC. The most important, and one which sat almost daily, was the Operating Superintendents' Committee, chaired by the LNER's V.M.Barrington-Ward. Naturally, a major aspect of the REC's work in preparation for the war was concerned with Air Raid Precautions.

The assumption of control of the Railways by the Minister of Transport entailed the negotiation by the Government of satisfactory financial arrangements with the Companies, and

The REC also had to take on the determination of pay levels with the Unions. Just before the war broke out, the Railway Companies had been in extensive discourse over pay and conditions with the railwaymen's Unions[5] (the NUR, the ASLEF and the RCA), and in November 1939 the Railway Staffs National Tribunal secured the men an increase in wages broadly of 5%. This in turn forced the Railway Rates Tribunal to agree to the Companies' request for increases in fares and charges. However, the Government was very anxious to avoid the Railways - or anyone else - passing on their wartime costs to the consumer and thereby fuelling inflation. For this reason they allowed only one limited increase in railway charges - in 1940, 10% in July extended to 16.7% in December. But further wage increases were conceded to the staff throughout the war, and thus the Railways had to foot the bill for these increases in costs. At the same time the Government negotiated reduced rates[6] for their own enormous freight traffic. Even so, in the event the profits made by the Railways during the war were very large. Net operating revenues advanced from £39.9m. in the last pre-war year to a peak of £105.6m. in 1943, prices having risen in the period by a mere 26%. The outbreak of war placed the Railways right away in the position of being able rapidly to increase their net revenues, because almost at a stroke their major competitor, private road transport, was stifled by the imposition of stringent restriction on the use of oil and later of rubber as well.

As a result of the unified Government control of the Railways, it was possible to alter radically the routing of traffic - especially freight - away from that benefiting individual Companies to routes that used the network most efficiently. Many streams of traffic were rearranged. For example, much traffic on the overloaded West Coast Main Line (WCML) was diverted to the ECML and the former GC main line, and special attention was paid to the increased traffic exchanged between the LMSR and LNER on the one hand and the GWR and SR on the other, especially by diverting it away from the overburdened exchange points in the London area. We shall see later how wartime necessities changed the traffic on the ECML. In any case, the demands of war enforced the coordination of all modes of inland transport, in order to make the best possible use of limited resources, such as had never before been attained in peacetime. Besides, in order to cope with the greatly increased freight traffic and the burgeoning needs of the Armed Forces in regard to special traffic in troops and military supplies, systems of operation by Working Timetable were frequently superseded by *ad hoc* control.

WARTIME PASSENGER TRAFFIC

The peacetime passenger services were pared to the minimum considered necessary for essential purposes. Private motoring almost had to cease yet more people than ever in peacetime, including the millions of Servicemen on duty and on leave, needed to travel - and to travel further; the demand was for *more* carrying capacity. The basic wartime timetable, established from December 1939, represented a coaching train-mileage of only 70% of the pre-war figure, and in light of the numbers of passengers travelling and the full loads conveyed the coaching stock was used much more 'efficiently'. Excursion trains and published seasonal holiday trains were abolished, but the REC did allow the Railways to provide relief trains to published services quite liberally during the first two years of the war - although they were *not* advertised in advance. Later on, the demand for rolling-stock and crews for extra freight and military traffic was so great that the running of unadvertised reliefs was rigorously curtailed, and almost all restaurant cars (and most sleeping-cars) were withdrawn.

In spite of the wartime discouragements and discomforts, passenger journeys fell only from 1,237m. in the last pre-war year to 989m. in 1940. After that they grew progressively to 1,335m. in 1943, and after a crescendo of *121 m. per month* in the summer of 1944, reached a peak of 1,377m. in 1945 (11% *above* pre-war). In terms of passenger-miles the rise was dramatic: from 19,000m. pre-war (1938) to 32,300 m. in 1943, and eventually to a climax of *35,248m.* (186% of pre-war) in 1945. About half of the wartime journeys were by Servicemen on duty or on leave, they (and many others) travelling free or at various concessionary rates. In July 1942, the number of Servicemen travelling on free warrants was 2m. while 6m. Servicemen and dependents travelled at concessionary rates, and these numbers

increased by 50% between 1942 and 1943. After that, to avoid overwhelming the capacity of the trains completely, the issue of free warrants for Servicemen and Civil Defence personnel had to be curtailed, as did the widespread distribution of concessionary fares. By 1943 the overall average distance a person travelled had risen to 25.4 miles from 15.9 miles immediately pre-war, an increase of 60%[7]; it rose further to as much as 26.9 miles in 1945, and was still 23.9 miles in 1946 and fell little thereafter. People - particularly Servicemen, whose average journey on warrant was 150 miles - were making far more long-distance journeys during the war than in peacetime. The number of Servicemen travelling on free warrants alone increased by 50% between 1942 and 1943. The figures for 1945 were so high because on top of the Service travel enormous numbers of people went on holiday that summer - and trains *were* provided for them, but the 1944 peak occurred during the OVERLORD period of restricted services and the overcrowding was unbelievable. Besides, it must be borne in mind that the statistics for passenger journeys were derived largely from ticket sales, and owing to 'fare-dodging' during the war and after it, the *true* number of passenger journeys may have been a great deal higher.

It was by no means only Servicemen who had to travel up and down the country because of the war. Dispersal of families, businesses and Government departments[8], and the widespread movement of non-military workers such as the Land Army, Irish immigrants, repair gangs, construction and munitions workers, and many other categories living away from home, entailed countless civilians travelling around for justifiable personal reasons. Except for the tiny minority who were allowed petrol, they *had* to go by train - or locally perhaps by bus. By the middle of the war petrol was allowed only to those who *really* needed it, with the result that car numbers fell from the August 1939 figure of 2.03m. to 0.72m. in 1943, - but they were already back to 1.49m. in August 1945. Although long-distance coach services were virtually abolished, bus numbers remained little changed (at about 90,000), and like the trains tended to be overcrowded, as they fulfilled the needs of most people for local transport - for work or recreation.

The authorities tried very hard to discourage non-essential travel, with 'Is Your Journey Really Necessary?' and other such exhortations widely proclaimed - and in February 1942 *THE PEOPLE* newspaper invited its readers to contribute ideas on ways to 'ration' travel for the war effort. Many of the readers' suggestions were much more unpleasant than the Orders and Restrictions that the Government did in fact impose. But these were bad enough: no seat reservation - except for First-Class passengers on Government business on some of the busiest routes (such as the ECML); fewer - and eventually no, restaurant cars; much fewer sleeping-cars - and reservation of first-class berths for those on Government business, and no towels, soap, rugs or pillows in them; no train heating except in the dead of winter; no heating in local station waiting-rooms - unless passengers were stranded in cold weather; and so on.

All excursion fares were abolished, including (from 1942) Cheap Day Returns. Still, it was comparatively *cheap* to travel by train. After having been unchanged for years and increased just by 5% in 1937, the only increment in the war was in July 1940 when Ordinary fares went up by 16.7% to 0.66p/mile (third-class), and this was hardly noticed. Indeed, any discouragement of non-essential travel during the war was on the whole unsuccessful - certainly with this author[9]. A threatened system of Travel Permits was - thank God - never implemented, not even one that would have applied only to certain designated routes - which included the ECML in particular. However, travel for purposes of 'holiday, pleasure or recreation' was banned to the 'restricted' East and South Coast resorts during the 1940-42 period when a German invasion was a possibility . Again, from mid-1943 to August 1944 when it was so vital to keep the Germans guessing about the Allied preparations for OVERLORD, a strip 10 miles inland from the Humber round to Penzance, the Bristol Channel and the Firths of Forth and Clyde was made into Regulated Areas[10], and for the four months April to July 1944 they were Restricted Areas. Nor was the ultimate brutality - total *abolition of first-class* - imposed, except on London Suburban services from October 1941. With the Services ordering their officers - but to the financial embarrassment of many a junior officer - to travel first-class, this was hardly a viable option anyway.

Trains of unprecedented length were run, most restaurant cars were used as ordinary passenger carriages, and in compartment stock the arm-rests were screwed back to allow more people to squeeze in. In 1943-44 when very few reliefs could be run, the demand for travel was so great - 18-coach trains on the ECML with seats for 500-600 were regularly conveying 1,200 (even up to *2,000*) passengers - that often hundreds of people were left stranded because it was physically impossible for them to get on to the trains. There were even instances where passengers had to be turned off trains because so many had jammed themselves in that coaches sank on their springs and their running-boards were fouling platform edges.

With long-distance trains often crowded to bursting, a long journey, especially the seemingly interminable journeys in the darkness of the Black-Out and with the delays caused by the awful weather of the first and second winters of the war, became an exhausting and depressing necessity. Without doubt, rail travel in wartime could be quite an ordeal. People and their baggage - and that of Servicemen tended to be singularly bulky - jammed the corridors and vestibules and made a visit to the lavatory a major undertaking. On the rare train that had a restaurant car you could not get to it, and conditions reverted to those of mid-Victorian times, with hordes of passengers - especially lively and vociferous young Servicemen - storming out of the train to the refreshment rooms at principal intermediate stops. Passenger train schedules were much slower than in peacetime, with longer station stops, a speed limit of 60 mph under normal conditions, and - at first - drastic slowing during air-raid alerts. Timekeeping was also very poor, for a number of reasons.

At the beginning of the war lighting restrictions for passengers were draconian - just a blue bulb. People could not stand that, and they were soon replaced either by shaded white lights or by full lighting with heavy blinds ferociously kept drawn down. Night-time journeys then became tolerable - and a lot safer. Travel after dark - never much fun for a railway enthusiast, was made very claustrophobic - even dangerous - by the minimal lighting allowed in carriages (extinguished during Alerts) and on stations, and confusion was confounded by the idiotic removal of station name boards (in August 1940). The pressures of war and the shortage of labour quickly led to stations, that had been well-kept before the war, becoming dirty and eventually decrepit, and their dinginess was accentuated by the necessity for the blacking-out or removal of all roof glazing. Moreover, the shortages that continued after the war resulted in the stations staying that way for many years.

MILITARY SPECIALS.

The special trains began even before the actual Declaration on 3rd September 1939. There was a certain degree of military mobilization before the Outbreak, and then in the few days before that date the long-planned programme of Evacuation of children from London and other large cities was carried out, in expectation of devastating air-raids as soon as the war began - but which did not occur for nearly another year. As the Forces were mobilized, industry was brought quickly to a high pitch of activity, and Allied Forces (especially from Canada and then the USA) were brought in to make Britain eventually 'one enormous armed camp', a steadily increasing number of troop specials and special freight trains of military equipment greatly overfilled the gaps in traffic left by the reduction in normal peacetime services.

The military traffic itself comprised special troop, and - after D-Day - ambulance and prisoner-of-war - trains on the one hand, and special trains of military equipment, ammunition, petrol and stores on the other. In addition, numerous non-military specials were run on Government Account, such as Evacuation Specials, trains to bring workers to London to repair Flying-Bomb damage - and to take rubble out to build airfields, and Ministry of Food fish and meat trains from Scotland.

A large bureaucratic system, Movement Control, was rapidly evolved during the war for the organization of military traffic. At the War Office, there was the Directorate of Movements[11] under the Deputy Quartermaster-General, with under him separate Directors of Personnel and of Freight Movements. Among the branches headed by each of these senior officers were Q(M)4 and Q(M)5, respectively responsible for movement within the U.K. and to and from the ports of personnel and stores. At the sharp end were the Railway Traffic Officers (RTO) with their assistants, established at the principal railway centres up and down the country. Working in liason with the Railway District Operating Superintendents, the RTO was responsible for the actual execution of the movements planned 'higher up' - by Movement Control at the War Office or at the HQs of the relevant Army Command[12] or District. This was for movement of relatively large bodies of troops in coach-loads or complete train-loads and of their stores, but the RTO's office also had to deal with countless journeys by individual Servicemen or of small groups. The RTO had other jobs as well, such as liasing with the Military Police on the station in their role of checking for men who were 'AWOL'[13] or misbehaving in other ways. The RAF and the Navy had corresponding Movement Control organizations, at the Admiralty and the Air Ministry (or Navy Division or RAF Command Group). When the US Army arrived from 1942 at first they sent Liaison Officers to work at British Army Movement Control Districts, but in July 1942 the Transportation Corps, ETOUSA[14] established their own Movement Control organization, modelled on the British and often sharing its offices.

There were mass movements of troops from the very first days of September 1939[15], when the British Expeditionary Force was being sent to France, and an indication of the scale of these operations is the fact that the movement of the personnel of just one Army Division would require *45 trains*. During the war the Railways ran on behalf of the Government no fewer than *258,624* special passenger trains, and *279,935* special freight trains; the peak year was 1944, with 82,205 and 96,157 trains respectively. Much of the mass movement of troops and supplies

York based K3 No.1307 heading towards Newcastle past Low Fell Junction with an ambulance train on 27th May 1940. Note that besides the red cross adorning each carriage side, there is also one painted on each roof, applied hopefully to deter attack from enemy aircraft. *W.B.Greenfield cty NELPG.*

for operations was to and from the principal ports, especially on the Bristol Channel, the Mersey, and above all the Clyde - where at Glasgow a new station solely devoted to troop movements was built at King George V Dock, and at Faslane on Gareloch a completely new port was constructed[16]. Then in 1945 almost as many troop specials as ever were needed for the men coming home on leave from abroad and later demobilization. The part played by the ECML in all this will be considered later in more detail.

Prior planning of special trains was naturally done as much in advance as possible and in great detail, although arrangements often had to be flexible, especially in relation to the traffic connected with the uncertain sailing and arrival dates of ships in incoming convoys that were delayed or re-routed. Sometimes, as in the military evacuation from France in 1940 ('DYNAMO' and 'AERIAL'), plans had to be improvised at very short notice and in those circumstances train orders were made by telephone and probably no permanent records were ever made.

However, as the war progressed and the requirement for military special trains grew inescapably, a standard schedule of paths between main military depots and the ports was evolved, although each train had to be scheduled in advance and the staff informed by means of Special Traffic Notices (STNs). The ports were divided into seven groups: North-West England, South Wales, South Coast, London Docks (including Tilbury), East Coast, North-East England, and Scotland. Each train was allocated a unique code, sometimes seen chalked on the first wagon, having four elements: date of departure, source, departure time, and destination. The despatches under this plan were normally scheduled at six-hour intervals, chosen to conform to a pattern of acceptance at the destination, and the schedules

were based on trains travelling at an average speed of 15 m.p.h. There was also a more long-standing coding system for train identification, which was displayed in a headboard on the locomotive and incorporated a designation of the originating Command and the date of the month. The 'paperwork' relating to all these military special trains would make fascinating reading, but seems not to have survived. Perhaps this is just as well considering that over half a million special trains were run for military and other purposes during the war.

WARTIME FREIGHT TRAFFIC

During the last two years or so of peace, rearmament had already been producing an increase in merchandise and minerals traffic, while the resulting resurgence of industry necessitated an expansion in the output and movement of coal. Right from the outbreak of the war freight traffic on the Railways began growing much more rapidly. One year into the war the tonnage of freight being carried by the Railways was 13% above that of the last three years of peace, while the average length of haul was up by no less than *33.1%*, and thus the really major increase was in ton-mileage. Mainly because of greater carryings of coal the figures tended to be highest in the autumn and winter months, when on the other hand severe weather, long hours of darkness and staff sickness combined to make operations all the more difficult.

The growth in freight traffic during the war was massive. Net ton-miles rose from 16,700m. (5,190m. merchandise, 3,182m. minerals, 8,300m. coal) in the last pre-war year to a peak in 1943 of 24,400m. (9,660m. merchandise - 86% above pre-war, 5,360m. minerals, 9,340m. coal). In 1944 the net ton-miles conveyed were almost the same as in 1943, and the traffic density persisted at only a slightly lesser level in the first half of 1945, 10,700m ton-miles being recorded in the first six months of that year.

The cardinal difficulty the railways had to tackle from the outbreak of the war - one they were already becoming aware of during the period of rearmament beforehand - was that of inadequate capacity to carry greatly increased freight class traffic, often by unusual routes or on lines and to destinations having relatively light traffic in peacetime. The limiting factors were: line capacity, wagon supply, availability of locomotives, and number of trained operating staff. Apart from the increased output of industry for war purposes, other factors that underlay the augmentation of railway freight traffic were the severe restriction of motor transport, the decline in the transport of freight - and especially of coal - by coastal shipping (due mainly to higher charges and greater delays of coastwise shipping under dangerous wartime conditions), the transfer of much import and export traffic from East to West Coast ports, and growth of traffic in military supplies.

Tremendous congestion occurred at times of severe winter weather, and at places particularly affected by the war. Usually it was relieved by clearing yards on Sundays - and even on Christmas Day. On a number of occasions partial or even total embargoes (Restriction Orders) had to be put on acceptances of traffic for a few days until the congestion had been relieved; indeed, on major routes such as the ECML, embargoes of some sort were in force for most of the time. Congestion was most frequent and severe at bottlenecks, such as the exits from South Wales, the ECML through Northallerton, through Carlisle, and at the points of exchange between the LMSR or LNER and the GWR (and SR), such as Bordesley, Banbury, Reading and in the London area. This was because in the free market circumstances of peacetime, facilities at the exchange points had not been designed for the transfer of more than the essential minimum of traffic between the Companies. Furthermore, it had been normal for wagons to be handed over to the receiving Company at these junctions not marshalled according to destination, leaving the marshalling to be done later. The great increase of exchange traffic in the war however called for the running of through pre-marshalled trains over these junctions, and the overall control exercised by the REC enabled through trains of this kind to be arranged.

The delays and congestion caused early in the war by working in the Black-Out - especially in shunting-yards, by gross speed restrictions imposed during Alerts, severe winter weather and by the Blitz, played havoc with schedules and rosters forcing widespread adoption of control of freight trains on an *ad hoc* basis. This was of long-term benefit in bringing about more efficient operation by Centralized Traffic Control. The strict limitations of the supply of oil and rubber prevented extensive use of road transport to relieve the railways. Nevertheless, in October 1943 the Ministry of War Transport were forced in desperation to relax a little the restrictions on the use of lorries. In the peak year of 1944, 64% of the freight moved was carried by rail, 20% by road (mainly on short hauls), 10% by coaster (mainly on hauls of over 200 miles), and 5% by canal.

The Inter-Company Rolling-Stock Control (ICRSC) was established pursuant to a Committee of Enquiry in March 1941, and undertook the gargantuan task of the day-to-day organization of the supply of empty wagons of the right type in the right numbers at the right place. (Until that date, the LNER had its own All-Line Freight Rolling Stock Control Office, at York). All private-owner wagons (and containers) had been requisitioned on the outbreak of the war, adding 589,000 to the total pool and bringing the wagon stock to over 1.2m. These measures improved wagon utilization and very few new wagons needed to be built during the war - although by the end an inordinate number of the requisitioned wagons were unusable. The ICRSC played a key role in organizing the pooling and distribution of special wagons, and it also kept an indent on nearly 0.5m. wagon sheets and over 0.25m. wagon ropes, which with a great shortage of covered wagons were vital for the protection and securing of manufactured goods from the weather and from pilferage. Every station and yard throughout the country sent daily records of its stock position to their headquarters offices, which passed summaries on to the ICRSC office. The task was achieved largely by the Railways' internal telephone and telegraph system, employing a comprehensive set of code words and phrases. Today it seems incredible that the system worked at all without computers, but it did, and it evidently enabled the much more efficient use of the wagon stock.

In other similar ways the REC through its subcommittees was able to expedite the flow of freight traffic by a number of measures. They arranged re-routing away from the worst bottlenecks - if they could. They cut marshalling delays by a great extension of the block-load system, and by adopting the system of 'Nominated Loading', in which the dispatch of goods from particular consignors was undertaken only on certain specified days and to specified destinations. They abolished wagon number-taking at all inter-Company exchange points, and they imposed much heavier demurrage charges - although not on Government depots and factories which (apart from collieries) were by far the worst offenders in delaying the turn-round of wagons. The Centralized Control of trains by telephone already in operation on parts of the Railway system was expanded, and as well as the installation of new Control Centres and emergency telephone networks, special telephone links were set up to allow daily conferences to be held between the four Chief Operating Superintendents simultaneously sitting at their respective Headquarters. Later, in August 1942 the LNER - the most decentralized Group - on its part established its own Central Traffic Office (at Marylebone), to provide an all-line operating organization responsible for controlling movements of traffic and the distribution of locomotive power between its three Areas. Such centralized control was essential when under wartime conditions the flows of traffic were also more varied and unpredictable.

On the outbreak of the war, a serious shortage quickly developed of available coaster capacity, due (at the beginning and end of the war) to the requirement to ship coal to European countries previously importing German coal, to German minelaying and bombing in the North Sea, and to the requisition of coasters for military operations. The coastwise transport of coal from the North-East to London and other ports in the South-East at one time fell by a third, two-thirds of the coal consumed by public utilities in this part of the country - about 10.5m. tons a year in London - being carried by sea in peacetime. There was therefore a vital need to divert to rail the coal shipments from Northumberland and Durham to the South. Moreover, the fall in exports was more than compensated by the increased home consumption for war industry. Coal that had normally left the country through ports in the North-East and South Wales was now dispatched inland, and for much longer distances than in peacetime, - a change that affected the LNER's ECML notably.

(above) **The LNER at War: a dramatic example of the immense and vital military traffic on the ECML - averaging nearly 40 special trains a day throughout the war. V2 No.3655 (BR No.60928) heads an Up train of 'Churchill' tanks near Askham Tunnel south of Retford on Sunday 19th September 1943.** *J.G.Dewing.*

(middle) **Working its way back to New England, C1 Atlantic No.4431 heads past Low Fell with an Up Goods on 15th June 1940. To the left of the picture can be seen the loading gauge guarding the exit to Team Valley exchange sidings. During the war period 4431 managed to have a couple of repairs at Doncaster works, even a 'general' in the summer of 1942 but in September 1944 its services were no longer required and it was withdrawn the following month.** *W.B.Greenfield cty NELPG.*

(right) **Wartime pictures of railway scenes, taken by private individuals, are not always of the best quality but they are nonetheless vital records of the period. In this Sunday afternoon scene at Low Fell, in May 1940, Doncaster based V2 No.4803 (BR No.60832), still with fully lined tender, overcomes gravity with the aid of a banking engine as it hauls the 3.40 pm Joppa - York No.2 Express Goods (with additional vehicles attached at Forth Goods) southbound having run via the Bensham diveunder bypass.** *W.B.Greenfield cty NELPG.*

Coal was absolutely vital, and the crisis that arose in January 1940 led the Government Departments concerned not only to introduce convoys of coastal shipping, but also to institute what were called 'Convoy' coal trains, the output of single collieries being routed right through without intermediate marshalling to single destinations or major consumers. These were run not

580,000 RAILWAYMEN
are maintaining
a Vital National Service

To the task of maintaining this service, the British Railways have brought the skilled assistance of more than half a million railwaymen and women, all animated by the spirit of service and the will to win ; they have also brought the mighty contribution of

50,000 Miles of Track	20,000 Locomotives
60,000 Passenger Vehicles	1,250,000 Freight Vehicles
76 Docks, Harbours and Wharves	11,000 Horses
25,000 Horse-Drawn Vehicles	10,000 Road Vehicles

Primarily this vast machine is harnessed to the tremendous requirements of the Forces and of Home Defence ; at the same time the British Railways continue to provide the public with the best services possible.

Issued by

THE RAILWAY EXECUTIVE COMMITTEE

**Stirring poster with 'macho' driver - albeit LMSR.
"Big Bill, your sturdy and reliable driver."**

only to London and the South-East and South-West but also to Lancashire, for there the growth of war industries had increased the consumption of coal well above the amount that could be mined locally. Paths from the North-East for 200 of these trains per week were arranged, although usually not more than 170 actually ran each week, and 5m. tons per year came south in Convoy trains - although in the mid-war years four or five times as much still came by sea. Naturally, the iron ore traffic - which increased by 150% in ton-mileage during the war - was also run in block trains, as were several other bulk commodities.

Throughout the war, mishaps that caused traffic disruption became more and more frequent, on account of the working difficulties, the extra burden of traffic, and later the arrears of maintenance. There were numerous minor collisions and derailments due to wartime causes, the more extraordinary being barrage-balloons coming down and fouling lines or signal wires, or even in one instance when a locomotive ran into a parachute, and so on. Direct enemy action disrupted traffic at times, but

rarely for more than a day or two. What is perhaps less well-known was the frequency with which Allied - and occasionally enemy - aircraft crashed on or very near railways. These amounted to about *200* - a remarkable figure until one realizes that many thousands of aircraft - only a small fraction being those of the Enemy - crashed somewhere in Britain during the conflict. Happily, more serious railway accidents - not attributable to enemy action - seem to have been no more common than in peacetime. (The effect of the air war on the ECML is recounted in Appendix H, and Appendix J is a compilation of traffic accidents on the ECML up to the end of 1959).

In the winters of the war the most disruptive factor was severe weather. Even in the absence of air-raids, exceptionally bad weather coupled with the very large increase in freight traffic added to the other wartime difficulties, and many temporary embargoes had to be imposed. Quite often total blocks were placed on certain sections of the system, affecting all freight traffic except perishables, certain essential traffics (collectively known as 'RECEX'), and that denoted as 'Government Priority'. Trains had to be stored wherever there was spare track[17] until they could be forwarded - usually on Sundays, and it became almost routine for hundreds of trains to be held up every day in this way without motive power.

Dislocation of railway operations was probably greatest during the earlier part of the war, especially in 1940 and 1941. In spite of the absence of air-raids, in January 1940 the worst winter weather of the century - snow, ice, and fog - coupled with the new difficulties of working under wartime conditions caused a reduction of up to a half in freight movement, bringing about a serious shortfall in the delivery of coal to London and the South, and for over a month this reached crisis proportions. (The effects of severe weather on ECML operations are recounted in Appendix K).

During the winter of the Blitz (September 1940 to May 1941) the disruption was not so much a consequence of air-raid damage, not inconsiderable as this was (see Appendix H), but was due more to the drastic speed restrictions imposed during the frequent air-raid warnings[18] and to interruptions and diversions caused by unexploded bombs, added to the difficulties already experienced during the previous winter. The throughput of freight traffic in the London area was diminished by 30-50% early in the Blitz, owing to drastic lighting restrictions during the prolonged Alerts making yard shunting extremely difficult, coupled with the enforced slowing of trains to 15 m.p.h. The problem was relieved to a considerable extent by changing Night Shifts to Double Day Shifts and by running trains in daylight hours as much as possible. In the autumn of 1940 the problems of the transport of vital coal to London and the South were so grave that the War Cabinet set up an all-powerful Coal Committee, headed by the Lord President (Sir John Anderson) to coordinate all aspects of the movement of coal and to devise all measures they could - some extremely unconventional - to ensure that public utilities and factories were kept going and the population did not freeze.

Air-raid damage in the London area - especially on the SR, was seriously holding up the movement and discharge of coal, and many collieries were having to curtail production on account of shortages of empty wagons. In November 1940 the average number of loaded coal wagons for the SR held up on the LNER on any one day was 2,000-3,500 on the GN Section and 500-700 on the GC Section, 1,500-3,000 for the South *via* Banbury, and 1,000-1,500 at London depots; figures for the

'Yes, I pulled the cord'

As the war went on new problems arose, with the progressive arming of the Forces - not least the vast programme of airfield construction and then the supply of fuel and armaments to the Air Force squadrons, the export of large amounts of raw materials, military equipment and supplies to Russia, and the commitment to ever greater military activities overseas. There was a relentless expansion in the needs of war industry and the Armed Services for all forms of transport continuing into 1942 - and all this to some extent before the build-up of the United States Army and its Air Force into Britain from May 1942 under the BOLERO plan. By late 1942 the pressure of traffic forced some relaxation of the lighting restrictions in marshalling yards, and at about this time an easement of the normal limits on freight train lengths.

Earlier in the war the critical factor had been the physical capacity of the railways to carry more traffic. That problem was addressed systematically by the REC in a March 1941 plan for spending £5m. in the next year - and a great deal more after that, to enhance traffic flow over principal routes including the ECML, and to provide extra facilities for marshalling freight and servicing locomotives. (Those relating to the ECML will be described in Part II). In the event, between 1941 and 1944 £11.5m. of public money was spent on additional running lines, loops - even bridges - on the bottleneck and overloaded sections of the system and effectively almost throughout the country. After most of this construction was completed, line capacity in the last two years of the war was then no longer a principal limitation to the Railways' ability to respond to the increasing demands.

By mid-1941 the rate of growth in total freight traffic on the Railways overall was running at about 5% per year, but during 1942 and 1943 the burdens on the railways grew even more, due to the accumulation of several factors. Already during the last ten weeks of 1942 - without difficulties due to the weather, except for fog at times - traffic congestion attributable to BOLERO forced both the LMSR and the LNER to put further embargoes on the acceptance of Anglo-Scottish freight traffic. Most of the mass influx of the men of the US Army from America

LMSR traffic through London were similar. The measures pursued by the Coal Committee included the use of diversionary rail routes, the slapping of heavy demurrage charges on coal consumers to speed up the turn-round of wagons, and the provision of special dumps of coal near the collieries and on the fringes of the London area.

The diversion of London's seaborne coal to rail was all the more inconvenient because the facilities at the major gas works and power stations on the Thames were geared to discharge from vessels on the river and not from rail wagons. This problem was circumvented to some extent by running coal trains to wharves on the Essex bank - much augmenting the traffic of coal from Ferme Park Yard to riverside destinations on the Tilbury line of the LMSR, to be tipped into barges for delivery upstream. Fortunately the enemy did not continue with major air-raids over Britain after May 1941, except for the V-weapon offensive - over London and the South-East - of June 1944 to March 1945, and the coal crisis of the 1940-41 winter did not recur. However, in the winter of 1943-44, serious shortfalls in deliveries of coal to London and the South were threatened as a result of the extra burden put upon the Railways by the removal of coasters for conversion for D-Day operations coming on top of unprecedented intensity of other traffic.

The clearance of import traffic from the West Coast ports - notably those on the Clyde - was a constant headache, partly as a consequence of the diversion of shipping from East Coast ports. Routes most frequently affected were those that converged on Carlisle, and the GWR main lines out of South Wales. To an extent because saturation of the WCML through Carlisle forced traffic onto the ECML but also because of the Convoy coal trains, congestion on the NER section of the ECML also came to threaten at times to bring inland transport in Britain to a halt; this problem is described in Chapter VI.

Poor photographically, but a *priceless* combination caught at the height of the war (29th March 1944) in York Shed Yard: the diminutive Y8 No.560 (BR No.68091), working as Shed Pilot, manoeuvres *Southern Railway* No.2068, one of the two ancient ex-LBSCR B4 4-4-0s that the SR lent to the LNER in November 1941, instead of scrapping them - the other was No.2051. The LNER actually *used* them, on stopping trains from Leeds or Bridlington but mainly for assisting overloaded Pacifics on expresses on the Leeds Northern and the ECML. They did well, running 40,000 miles in the first 18 months, but the effort wore them out and they never ran again after being returned to the Southern in December 1944. *Owen/Hoole coll.*

Thirsk: a view north on 15th April 1943, shortly after completion of the wartime widenings to four tracks and rebuilding of the station. The new Down and Up Slow lines are well shown, and in the station is what appears to be a D21 on an Up stopping train passing a Down stopping train. *LNER/H.G.Wilson coll.*

also entailed the running of an equivalent number of train-loads of equipment - including AFVs[19] - and supplies, which were usually dispatched on slower convoys in advance of the men. A measure of the impact on the railways is exemplified by the arrival in late August and early September 1942 of five US armoured Divisions, each bringing 390 light and medium tanks, 200 heavy tanks following in December 1942 to February 1943. We all know the reputation of the U.S. Army for its prolific use of motor transport: under BOLERO, 30,000 cased vehicles were shipped over to Britain, and a number of assembly depots were constructed to which these large cases had to be transported by rail on specially adapted wagons. By June 1944 there were 1.54m US Servicemen in Britain, and by April 1944 they alone were chartering 228 special trains of stores per day.

In the autumn of 1943, repeated and wider Restriction Orders had to be imposed affecting acceptance of the less immediately vital traffic on all the Railways except the SR. The Railways were threatening to break under the strain as they were now handling well over 900,000 loaded wagons a week. The necessity for embargoes at this time arose from the combination of enormous war demands, episodes of fog, and also a widespread epidemic of influenza. The major limiting factors by then were the number and availability of locomotives, of operating staff - especially footplate men - and of skilled workshop fitters.

The shortage of locomotives was eventually eased somewhat by the temporary use of British and American military freight engines, but until these were available new

Station names are now in small letters. If you can't see the name and can't hear the porter's voice – ask another traveller.

It is dangerous to raise the blind and make the train a target for bombers. If you know where you are – by local signs and sounds – please tell others in your carriage.

WE'LL BEAT THE BLITZKRIEG
BY HELPING ONE ANOTHER

BRITISH RAILWAYS

"And so they did"

construction of heavy freight locomotives, hampered by the commitment of the Companies' Workshops to the production of military hardware, was inadequate for the Railways' needs. Furthermore, an inordinate proportion of the existing locomotive stock was immobilized because of arrears of maintenance. Breakdowns were becoming increasingly frequent, and between November 1942 and March 1943 an average of 1,000 to 1,500 trains per week were being cancelled and 10,000 per week delayed owing to non-availability of locomotives.

The labour shortage became most acute towards the end of 1943 when it was aggravated by up to 10% of staff being off sick at any one time. Servicemen with railway experience were released for footplate and other duties, and also prisoners-of-war were brought in to do labouring work. The crisis continued into the first months of 1944, when men were needed more than ever for the extra traffic for the military build-up to OVERLORD. Poor and dirty working conditions[20], including the necessity for night and weekend shift work, along with rates of pay that compared unfavourably with those in war factories, led to slow rates of recruitment of boys leaving school. Some alleviation of the shortage had been achieved in mid-1942 by the complete reservation from military service of all railway 'Conciliation'[21] grades, and in early 1944 by concerted recruitment and redirection from less essential vacancies. (However, youths under 18 were 'non-directable' and could only be persuaded, not forced, to join the railways). Inevitably, with so many inexperienced and relatively unskilled men coming on to the Railways, standards of work declined, and

The Trains DO get through

The trains go through, whatever happens, thanks to the unremitting efforts of railway men and women. Occasionally bombs cause damage to railways but stations and tracks are functioning again within a few hours. Bridges are rebuilt, cuttings made good and repair records are broken over and over again.

RAILWAY EXECUTIVE COMMITTEE

Bomb damage holds up trains, takes you on roundabout routes, makes you late.

54,000 permanent-way men are doing a fighting front-line job—to repair damage quickly.

Your patience will assist them in their work.

Information services are being augmented at important stations, where details of alterations will be quickly available.

The Lines Behind the Lines

Government factories alone require 7,000 special trains a week for their people. Workmen's tickets are issued for 385,000,000 journeys each year. One war factory needs 58 trains a day for its workers.

That is just a glimpse of railway help to war production.

GWR · LMS **LNER · SR**

Facsimiles of posters designed to uplift railwaymen's morale and inform the public of the work being done by railway personnel and of the vaunting wartime freight burden.

overworked and poorly maintained engines deteriorated. Still, the long and irregular hours worked by footplate men and guards must undoubtedly have been off-putting, not least in the difficulty of getting something to eat when out on the job.

To plan the preparations for OVERLORD in 1944, a special Official Committee on Inland Transport was set up by the War Cabinet, and this met weekly from February until about September. It recognized at the outset that the railways were already carrying 46% more freight ton-miles than they were before the war and 70% more passenger-miles. In the peak month of September 1943, 940,000 *loaded* wagons were forwarded per week and although wagon supply was critical there simply were not enough staff or locomotives to operate any more trains than were already running. The earlier impediment - limited line capacity - had by then been mastered although further new works would be undertaken for BOLERO (as will be described in Part II), and with the timely help of the new military freight locomotives just enough motive power could be mustered. The most serious shortage was that of labour. The Ministry of Labour was in the event able, from March 1944, to divert to the Railways enough men from industry, recognizing that any likely disruption of industrial production would be far less harmful to the success of OVERLORD than would a failure of the railways to deliver men and supplies on schedule to the embarkation ports. Nevertheless, not only did the OVERLORD operation *itself* require 38-40,000 tons of freight to be moved *per day* in 1944 from February until several weeks after D-Day in June, but many of the small ships used for coastwise transport would be requisitioned from May for up to four months to deliver supplies to the Normandy beach-heads and therefore the traffic they carried had to be moved in other ways. Road transport was carrying about the same tonnage as the coasters, and could be

no more than doubled - and mainly for short-haul work. In addition, in order to free ports in the South of England for the OVERLORD operations, their import traffic would have to be diverted to more northerly ports, thereby leading to longer hauls by rail. As well, heavy movements of troop trains, particularly southwards from the Clyde and Mersey, would further delay freight traffic.

For all these reasons it was necessary to make cuts in normal (wartime) carriage of both passengers and freight, because during the build-up to D-Day and for some time afterwards no further traffic could be sustained. A 'Transport Balance Sheet' was drawn up in February 1944 and kept updated. The Balance Sheet, together with the projected needs for 'Operational Traffic' showed that in order to be able to carry the extra 1.25m. tons per month of military and munitions traffic (plus an increase of nearly as much coal) planned for about six months from March 1944, roughly equivalent reductions had to be made in the offerings of other traffic. Already measures had been taken by the Government to limit the *need* for transport, as by the Zoning Schemes such as adopted by the Ministry of Food, but now actual cuts in industrial production had to be planned to relieve the railways' freight burdens, and from May 1944 to make considerable reductions in long-distance passenger services. Sufficient locomotives and crews then became available for the build-up programme to be carried through largely as planned[22]. In the month or two before D-Day, although most lines were worked to the limit, the greatest burden fell on the routes to the South Coast ports and to London and the other Thames ports, even though traffic not related to OVERLORD through *all* these ports was drastically curtailed. On certain routes, the public services were taken off altogether at times - and, for security reasons, without notice[23].

The typical scene on the ECML in the 1940s, 27th July 1946: A3 No.521 (a number carried only between March and November 1946, previous LNER No.2552, BR No.60053) SANSOVINO on the 10.34 Leeds - King's Cross is overtaking, near Potters Bar, an Austerity 2-8-0, No.78673 (later LNER No.3153, BR No.90474), still with the Westinghouse brake pump and the number painted on the smoke-box provided for its work with the Liberation Armies on the Continent. *LCGB.*

Looking like something akin to 'war weary', V2 No.918 departs Northallerton with the 3.35 pm to Newcastle in August 1947. The reason for the locomotive's unkempt appearance stems from a lack of cleaning rather than wholesale neglect; it had, since the end of hostilities, been into 'shops' for a 'general' overhaul in 1946 when it was both renumbered and had LNER restored to its tender. Northallerton signal box has also had its nameboards restored to the ends of the building. *E.R.Wethersett.*

The movement of men and supplies to the south, to sustain the immense military operations in North-West Europe, slackened to a certain extent after September 1944 but continued still at a high level until Victory in Europe in May 1945, special freight trains falling only from 32,200 in June - September 1944 to 25,600 in January - March 1945. In the four months June - September 1944 no less than 866,200 loaded wagons were dispatched from War Department depots[24] and 404,670 from US Army depots, figures respectively up 17% and 173% on the same period in 1943.

After VE-Day, while the troop specials - now increasingly in the 'homeward' direction - continued to be numerous for some months, the military freight traffic tailed off quite rapidly. Throughout the winter of 1944-45, the amount of freight that had to be moved declined only slightly compared to the previous winter, whereas there was still a shortage of coasters, now needed for shipment of coal for the armies and the liberated populations in Europe, and this meant that more coal had to be moved by rail, and the railways did once again become congested to the extent of having to impose frequent embargoes on freight. Labour continued to be in short supply and the Railways could no longer depend on a supply of directed men, although Italian prisoners-of-war were employed extensively. At the same time there was much staff sickness, punctuated by spells of severe weather. There was again a dearth of locomotive power, because the military freight engines had gone to the Continent and inordinate numbers of locomotives were stopped for repair; mounting arrears of maintenance also exacerbated the chronic scarcity of wagons. Even in March - May 1945 total ton-mileage was still only 5% less than the very high level of a year before, and after the end of the war in Europe a lot of the traffic in military supplies was substituted by that for relief of the people of the liberated nations.

The effect of the war on the ECML in particular is described in Chapters IV and VI.

THE FORTUNES OF BRITISH RAILWAYS IN THE POST-WAR PERIOD UNTIL THE END OF THE 1950s

THE RETURN OF PEACETIME AND THE RUN-UP TO NATIONALIZATION

The end of the war in Europe on 8th May 1945 (VE-Day), followed by the end of the war with Japan on 15th August (VJ-Day), marked occasions of unimaginable relief and release for every adult person. Soon after VE-Day, the civilian population of Britain, exhausted to the limit by six long years of war, having suffered sometimes real danger, losses (or the fear thereof) of loved ones, hard work, long hours - including in addition night duties such as Fire-Watching, ARP work and above all the tedium and drabness of everyday life, all seemed to have one idea: to *go away*, preferably to the seaside, 'for a break'. Restrictions on travel to the seaside had been lifted by September 1944, but only after VE-Day were people provided with the extra trains. Of course they had to be *trains*, for severe petrol rationing was still cutting private car and long-distance coach travel to the irreducible

minimum. The result was again - as had occurred in 1944 - queues of half a mile long at London termini on Saturdays in the summer of 1945, and the *ad hoc* provision of train formations to clear the never-ending stream of would-be passengers. Yet there were still occasions - even after the war was over, when not enough trains could be provided and passengers were left behind.

As we have seen, the continuation of great movements of civilians and of Servicemen during the last months of the war in the first half of 1945 combined with the rush for holidays to produce an all-time peak of passenger-journeys that year on the Railways as a whole. After that - in spite of petrol rationing, there was a gradual falling off, all-line passenger-miles declining by 35% between 1945 and 1947. Meanwhile, fares were increased in July 1946 to 33.3% above pre-war and then in October 1947 to 55% above - increases still substantially less than inflation, which was 55.6% above pre-war in 1946, 73.4% in 1947. Freight rates were raised in July 1946 to 25% above 1937 rates, and finally to 55% above in October 1947. Subsequent increases were allowed, to 81% above 1937 rates in May 1950 and to 99% above in April 1951, which brought them up eventually in line with inflation - temporarily, and freight traffic remained well above the pre-war level. Therefore in the early post-war period the Railways' receipts from both passengers and freight remained buoyant.

Nevertheless, the *net* earnings of the Railways as a whole fell from £62.5m. in 1945 to £32.5m. in 1946 and *minus* £16.2m. in 1947, because costs had risen since before the war on average by about 80% while until July 1946 the Government had frozen charges. The most unsatisfactory statistics on the eve of Nationalization related to arrears of maintenance. The remarkable achievements of the Railway Companies during the war left them with large profits on operating revenue, even if much of the extra gains had had to be paid to the Exchequer under the wartime financial agreements. However, the Railways had been disinvesting capital already before the war, and now their burdens were redoubled by huge arrears of replacement compounded by excessive wear and tear during the war on rolling-stock, track and other equipment. The money set aside in the wartime Arrears of Maintenance Trust Fund was quite inadequate, because prices had gone up sharply while railway charges remained frozen. The Government - even a Labour Administration - decreed that resources had to be restricted to those current pre-war, *i.e.* no extra was allocated to catch up on arrears, let alone modernization[25]; by the first year of Nationalization arrears of maintenance amounted to no less than £179m. More particularly there were shortages of materials, and labour post-war was both lacking in numbers and in quality because young men joining the Railways tended to be less conscientious as well as less proficient than railwaymen had been before the war.

During the war the Railways lost only 637 passenger vehicles by enemy action, but over 12,436 were damaged, while about 1,000 coaches and vans had been converted for use in ambulance trains. There had been 3,375 wagons destroyed (including 636 requisitioned wagons) and 20,242 (including 4,062 requisitioned) were damaged[26]. For a number of reasons, repair and replacement was much delayed, and at December 1947 - well over two years after the end of the war, the proportion of the coaching stock under or awaiting repair was three times what it had been in December 1938, and the proportion of wagons 7.5 times the 1938 figure[27]. Most critically, although only seven had been destroyed and 450 damaged in the conflict, more than a third more locomotives (7.8% of the stock) than in December 1938 were at this time under or awaiting repair at Works. Locomotives were breaking down about once in every 50,000 train-miles (almost twice as frequently as before the war), and as well the quality of coal was much poorer and failures to make adequate steam were commonplace. Furthermore, no more mileage of track was being relaid than in 1938, so the wartime arrears were not yet being overcome and severe speed restrictions had to be imposed on most routes until they were. These conditions were to persist for several more years, and they were as bad on the LNER - the operators of the ECML - as on the other Railways. (As to how the LNER and its successor Regions of BR fared, the reader is referred to Appendix A).

The first five years or so after the war, both before and after Nationalization on 1st January 1948, were grossly abnormal in many ways, and although the management strove to restore the railway system and services to their pre-war condition this

---

Looking Ahead

The Main Line Railways' post-war plans include the introduction of the latest scientific improvements in new locomotives and in re-conditioning existing engines. Passenger rolling stock will include new designs with bright colours, new fabrics, plastics and other materials. The finest railway service in the world will be offered to the British public as soon as materials and manpower permit.

GWR · LMS   LNER · SR

"But was it...?"

was unrealistic. The nation was economically almost destitute as a result of the war and could only regain wealth by curbing imports - notably oil - and by concentrating all new investment on plant needed to manufacture goods for export. Thus shortages and rationing were at first even more severe than in the war. Motor fuel was rationed and its supply to owners of private road vehicles was curtailed, to a diminishing extent, until 1953. Traffic on the railways remained at a high level, but once road hauliers were released from Government control (from August 1946),

merchandise traffic began again to be lost to road. The problem however was not now that - as before the war - road transport was cheaper and often gave a better quality of service, but that due to their run-down state the Railways were incapable of carrying all the traffic on offer. The first post-war winters put a great strain on the Railways, and they were forced to resort to further restrictions on freight movements, their problems being aggravated by labour troubles, including dock workers' strikes in October 1945. In addition, early in 1947 the terrible weather and the consequent coal shortage forced temporary cuts in passenger train services, and also gave rise to a short-lived scheme for converting some locomotives to burn crude oil - not in fact pursued very far by the LNER (see Part II). The Ministry of Transport had to take special measures at those times to pass over freight to road haulage. These were still in force in the winter of 1947-48, when the weather turned out to be quite mild and the Railways could have coped, and as a result traffic became lost to road permanently.

Nevertheless, despite the Railways' shortcomings - temporary or inherent, with the steadily increasing industrial activity and a rise in real incomes the level of their traffic was in fact maintained through most of the 1950s. Net ton-miles of freight on British Railways (BR) in 1948 was 21,500m., reaching a peak in 1951 of 22,900m. (40% higher than in 1938) and remaining well above 20,000m. until 1957, after which the decline began. Meanwhile however, the proportion of total national ton-mileage carried by road rose from 37% in 1952 to 50.5% in 1959, while the Railways' share, which had been 41% in 1938 and 52% in 1946, fell in the 1950s from 43% to 32%. (The rest was by coastwise shipping, and this - about 6,900m. ton-miles - changed little).

The freight ton-mile figures were in part kept buoyant by the coal traffic. Although there was a fall in national coal output during the war of 25% from the 1938 figure of 231m. tons, and in the 1948-53 period it was still a little below pre-war, far less coal was being exported and instead it was being carried on longer hauls, the average journey of a wagon of coal being 28% longer than in 1938. Because they were needed to transport most of the coal to the generating stations, the railways also came to benefit from the post-war increase in coal consumed for electricity and gas generation. While household consumption of coal fell between 1938 and 1946 substantially, during the same period electricity consumption more than doubled.

THE TRANSPORT ACT 1947, THE RAILWAY EXECUTIVE PERIOD (1948-52) AND THE TRANSPORT ACT 1953

The benefits in efficiency gained by a planned distribution of traffic between rail and road, which had been attained by strict central control during the war, encouraged the idea of State ownership and control of all public transport. It was perhaps fortunate that the political swing to socialism at the end of the war led to the election of a Labour Government committed to public ownership of the Railways, for it is unlikely that it would have been possible for private capital to restore the run-down railway system. Nevertheless, the valuation placed on the railway undertakings was probably too high. As a result the nationalized British Railways were saddled with greater central charges on capital than might otherwise have been the case, and this burden was a root cause of their subsequent decline. Moreover, expectations for the nominally 'unified' transport system that the Transport Act 1947 envisaged were not in the event fulfilled,

The celebrated Locomotive Exchanges of 1948: one of the LMS locomotives tested on the former LNER main line was Rebuilt 'Royal Scot' No.46162 QUEEN'S WESTMINSTER RIFLEMAN, seen approaching Potters Bar on the 12.15 from Leeds - a heavy load for this engine, with dynamometer-car as well - 30th April 1948. *D.A.Dant.*

Possibly in consequence of the disorganization caused by the great Borders Floods of the day before, Class O7 Austerity No.63182 (ex-WD No.79185) heads a *local* towards Waverley past St Margarets Shed, Edinburgh, 13th August 1948. *Author.*

Excitement from the spotters as a sparkling blue-liveried A4, No.60027 (LNER No.4486) MERLIN, passes through Doncaster Central on the Up Non-Stop *CAPITALS LIMITED*, June 1949. *J.Davenport.*

The Up *QUEEN OF SCOTS* with brilliantly burnished Haymarket A1 No.60162 SAINT JOHNSTOUN waits to leave platform 1 at Edinburgh Waverley, late 1950s. At the adjoining platform 2 is another well-cleaned Pacific and in the gloom of the siding to the left can be glimpsed one of the J83 pilots. *Hepburn/RAS.*

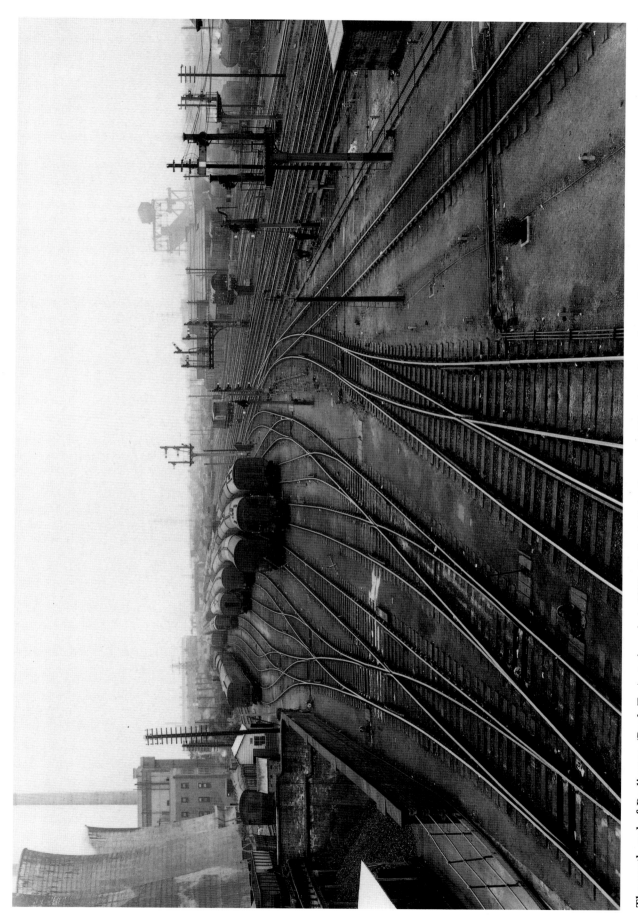

The north end of Darlington (Bank Top) station circa 1955. To the left, in the background, is the local power station with one of its cooling towers still showing the remains of wartime camouflage. Nearer is the coal yard with its staithes catering for the coal merchants. The nine-road carriage siding is well filled with stock but soon the area would be cleared to make way for a depot to service a diesel multiple unit fleet yet to be built. Across the main lines, to the right, is the engine shed which it will be noted, was playing host to a couple of the new 0-6-0 diesel-electric shunters by then being turned out in large numbers by the nearby BR Locomotive Works.

while the extent to which the shift to the private car and to road transport would so rapidly undermine the railways' profitability was not appreciated.

In fact, the 'Roads Lobby' (especially the British Road Federation) was already very powerful and managed to have even the socialist 1947 Act modified in the critical matter of 'C licence' lorries: instead of being restricted to 40-mile journeys as was originally intended, there was no mileage restriction enacted. As a consequence, these lorries carrying their owners' own goods, which already numbered 0.365m. or 60% of the national fleet of road goods vehicles, rapidly multiplied. Their use took away most of the gain in general merchandise traffic resulting from a steadily growing manufacturing output which might otherwise have been secured by the railways. The 1947 Act however did nationalize most of the road haulage industry, but this was highly profitable and at the time helped to 'balance the books' for the BTC as a whole, although the non-railway operations of the BTC were unable to wipe off more than a fraction of the losses that BR accumulated.

The 1947 Transport Act established the British Transport Commission (BTC), subservient to the Minister of Transport, a statutory public corporation for the control of 'all' national transport, *i.e.* all *except* private cars and 'C licence' vans and lorries. The philosophy behind the Act had been that State control with a public (*i.e.* State) obligation to provide transport services to all - whether or not they were profitable - was necessary both to provide the most efficient transport system and to avoid abuses of monopoly and 'wasteful competition' between modes of transport. The aims of integrating the rail and road spheres of public transport embraced in the Act could not however be achieved unless the true economic costs of both public and private transport - not to mention the environmental costs, such as the slaughter of over 5,000 people a year on the roads, were accepted by the consumer. They were not, nor indeed were they really known to the BTC. The Transport Act still required the BTC to cover *all* its costs, including central charges and depreciation, 'taking one year with another', and with the Government-controlled Transport Tribunal forbidding fare increases. Consequently from the outset it would appear that the BTC were obsessed with cost-cutting as opposed to enhancing efficiency by modernization. At the same time, throughout the 1950s - and also the 1960s - an inflated bureaucracy created desk jobs that cost far more than was saved by closing branch lines, the number of administrative staff employed per mile of railway operated by the BTC in 1958 growing to *twice* the pre-Nationalization figure.

Yet the latent pressure to shift to road transport was always present, and once the nation was able to afford unlimited imports of oil, while restoration of some national wealth brought the return of a Conservative Administration in 1951, the floodgates were opened. At that time (1951) BR were carrying 20,600m. passenger-miles and 22,900m. ton-miles of freight - almost their highest output ever - and were making a working profit that was very nearly enough to cover central charges on capital as well. The new Government briefly thought of making private road transport pay a levy to support the railways, but soon discarded the idea. Indeed - without even serious consultations with the BTC, the nationalized transport system was radically reformed, in the 1953 Transport Act. Little more than lip service had been paid anyway to integration of rail and road transport, *e.g.* running local bus services to connect with trains, or the widespread introduction of containerization of freight much

disliked by the Unions - as witness what happened over the Docks. Any possibility of achieving an integrated transport system under State planning was now lost by the denationalization of the road haulage industry, and by a general philosophy of allowing private industry and private and sectional interests to prevail. 'Integration' was substituted by 'competition', and by decentralization with abolition of the Railway Executive; it was not possible to denationalize the railways because *on their own* they were not financially viable.

While it is undoubtedly true that modernization of the railways was unduly delayed until the late 1950s and the 1960s, there were two major factors outside the control of the Railway Executive which worked against the financial viability of the railways. Firstly, the 1947 Act did not abolish the 'common carrier' duties of the railways referred to earlier. This was supposed to occur after the 1953 Act, but it took several years to implement and in the meantime the BTC was not able to begin to achieve a balance of charges in the face of relentlessly increasing costs - especially of wages, and of the restrictions imposed by the Government on the allocation of both finance and materials needed for modernization. The funds provided were not even sufficient for catching up on the arrears of maintenance, and the only new works of any magnitude undertaken before the mid-1950s were the completion of projects funded and begun before the war.

THE PROBLEMS OF BRITISH RAILWAYS AND THEIR CAUSES

Already in 1950 estimates could highlight the vastly greater fixed costs of the railways, and also the hidden subsidy of road services, underlying the carrying of passengers respectively by train and by bus. In terms of passenger-miles, costs of long-distance coaches were marginally higher than main-line express trains, but branch-line rail costs were over ten times those of country buses. Much of the problem with local passenger trains was that they often carried only a handful of passengers - less than a single-decker bus load. On the freight side, British Railways at that time were not doing so badly: it cost them £1.34 per net ton-mile to carry merchandise and £0.65 to move coal, but long-distance road costs still ranged from £0.81 to £1.17 per net ton-mile, and such advantage as the road haulier had was to a great extent due to his much better load-factors. But still, rail freight traffic entailed a great deal of empty wagon mileage, long-distance road hauliers usually securing a load in each direction while they could pick and choose their traffic and were not obliged to run to a fixed schedule. (In more recent years, after they had 'won' most of the traffic from their rail competitors, the measure of empty and inefficient mileage practised by road hauliers has tended to slip back to that previously common on the railways).

During the first five years or so of nationalization, the BTC was not only starved of materials - especially steel until it was decontrolled in 1953, to re-equip and modernize the railways but also of finance. It was unable to maintain the level of investment with which it began in 1948, when it was allocated 4.4% of total UK capital investment, for in 1951 this fraction was down to 3.3%[28]. Between 1948 and 1953 the capital value of BR remained static, while that of all UK industry and trade increased by 21% in real terms. Capital equipment costs rose by 35 to 55% during those five years, and average labour costs went up by 28% while 'productivity' rose by less than 10%. While the

Doncaster: the approaches from the south in 1949, soon after completion of the resignalling, with the new South power signalbox on the right, St James' ('Great Northern') Church and the goods station to the left. Gresley A4 No.60021 (LNER 4467) WILD SWAN runs through on the Down Main with an express. *J.Davenport.*

prices of materials and labour were constantly rising, the BTC was delayed for nearly a year by the deliberations of the Transport Tribunal before it was able to raise fares and charges in 1952 and even so was not allowed to match charges with costs.

At Nationalization on 1st January 1948, British Railways took over 19,639 route miles of railway (52,253 track miles), 20,148 locomotives (83.8% of the number in stock at Grouping in 1923), all but 110 being steam, plus 411 steam locomotives loaned from the Ministry of Supply - and soon to be taken into BR stock, 2,049 rail-motor vehicles (all electric except for three steam and four diesel railcars), 40,257 passenger vehicles and 1,223,700 freight wagons. Between 1948 and 1952 the BTC was provided with funds sufficient just to relay 9,475 miles of track (1,895 miles per year), and up to 1953 to build a mere 2,060 new locomotives, 9,900 coaches and 209,300 wagons; otherwise, superannuated rolling-stock had to be repaired and put back in service. Corrected to 1948 prices, capital expenditure on the railways was held to £30-£42.5m. per year (£5.0-£10.0m. on ways and structures) until 1952, although it then rose gradually to £98m. (£40m. on ways and structures) by 1959 as the Modernization Plan got under way.

The effects of the shortages of materials and funds was only too obvious in the shabbiness of the stations and the sloth of the trains. The bad image acquired by BR hampered recruitment of good staff - and has still to this day to be shaken off. Growing staff shortages in the early days of Nationalization were filled by imported - and later by immigrant - labour, until gradually mechanization and modernization of operations such as permanent way work - and eventually acceptance by the Unions of radically lower staffing levels, allowed substantial reductions in the labour force. Nevertheless, the impression remained that the *quality* of staff generally, from top management downwards, was not as high as it was in many industries in the private sector - or in other countries. The management staff on French and German Railways in particular were generally better qualified academically and technically than on BR. Furthermore, the standard of training on the Continent, right through from the bottom ranks to the top, was much more thorough and rigorous.

When in 1952 investment on the railways was only £40m. per year (just £11.6m. on ways and structures), investment on

road transport by contrast was already over £300m. per year (£100m. on private cars). Even in 1959, when the railway Modernization Plan was well under way, railway investment had risen only to a paltry £168m. (£62m. on ways and structures), while investment on road transport had risen to nearly £800m. of which £420m. was on private cars - and the motorway-building programme was only just beginning.

At the same time, the wide adoption of paid holidays as the norm after the war, the reduction in the working week with the gradual abandonment of Saturday morning working - and of shift working except in a few industries, led to an increase in leisure time. A growth in real personal wealth and in the proportion of *per capita* income spent on travel combined with other social factors to maintain constant the aggregate of passenger-miles by rail: 21,000m. in 1948 and 22,300m. in 1959, varying by less than 10% in the interim. This was so even though the proportion of all their travel expenditure that consumers spent on all *public* transport fell from 67.7% in 1950 to 35.9% in 1960.

THE TRANSPORT REVOLUTION OF THE 1950s AND ITS CONSEQUENCES FOR BRITISH RAILWAYS

Although in the 1953 Act many of the old restraints on railway charging were removed, the BTC still had to settle their maximum rates through a 'QUANGO', the Transport Tribunal. In the event the very prolonged process was extended for a further year by ministerial intervention. The Conservative Minister (Harold Watkinson) introduced in 1956 'deficit financing' by allowing substantial - but temporary - borrowing by the BTC to cover its losses, in exchange for the agreement by the Commission as an 'anti-inflationary measure' to postpone increases in charges already sanctioned, even though this ran counter to the Commission's obligation to make a profit. (At the same time the Government allowed the price of coal to rise at double the rate of inflation between 1956 and 1962). Therefore both bureaucracy and politics hampered the BTC's attempts to match charges with costs, and they were still obliged to maintain

Two of the 'Standard' locomotive types designed for BR: *(top)* **On the Down Goods line built during the war, a relatively rare BR Standard Class 3MT 2-6-0 No.77000 passes Pilmoor on a Down Class F freight. The Down side building erected at the time is visible on the island platform, formed with the branch from Knaresborough - by this time (1953) goods only. Pilmoor North (formerly Pilmoor Station) Box is on the left.** *D.V.Beeken.*
(bottom) **One of the strange and unprepossessing looking Crosti-fitted BR 9F 2-10-0s, No. 92026, on a Class C freight, somewhere north of York, late 1950s.** *E.Sanderson.*

years of BR to improve the profitability of the railway freight sector. Emphasis was placed on using more containers to get round the inherent advantage of the lorry in providing door-to-door transit; on building wagons with automatic brakes and running more braked freight trains at higher speeds and with minimal intermediate marshalling; on constructing wagons of 21 - or 24.5 ton capacity for coal and minerals - depending however on facilities for their handling being provided at collieries, power stations *etc.*; on providing special wagons for powders and liquids; and on rationalizing domestic coal distribution by building Coal Concentration Depots[29]. Really substantial progress in freight movement had to wait until the 1960s with the advent of diesel (or electric) haulage, as well as a consistent policy on the vacuum *vs.* air brake systems, by which time it was too late to recover much traffic lost to the roads.

Ordinary fares in October 1947 were 1.02p/mile third-class (0.68p/mile Monthly Return), but were reduced to 0.73p/mile when Monthly Returns were abolished in 1952, rising to 0.78p/mile in June 1955. In 1959 Ordinary fares (now second-class) were set at 0.83-0.94p/mile (depending on distance), an increase of only 34 - 38% since January 1948. These rates were thus *lower* than in 1947, although there were now no Monthly Returns - only Day Returns; in real terms passenger fares were *half* what they had been in 1938. (But while average rail fares had gone up by 130% since 1938, average *bus* fares went up by only 64%). Meanwhile, railway costs had risen much faster than their charges: it was calculated that whereas in 1949 passenger traffic contributed £30m. to track and other 'indirect' costs, by 1958 it contributed nothing to them.

Freight rates, in 1947 some 55% above pre-war, were raised subsequently in several stages so that by 1959 they were 144% above pre-war - roughly the same degree as average passenger fares. On the other hand, the consumer price index was by then 171% above the figure for 1938. Moreover, in Western Europe rail freight rates were generally much higher than in Britain, and more realistically set. It was calculated that at the end of the 1950s for £1 the railways of Britain produced an average of 60 ton-miles, but public road hauliers only 37 ton-miles. (The productivity of 'C' licence vehicles was about half that). Although the advantage of the Railways was to some extent due to the large tonnage of coal and minerals they conveyed at relatively low rates, it was evident that firms - and, even more, private

unremunerative services without Government subsidy. Repeated delays in the process of increasing charges after the concession of wage claims were believed to account in large measure for BR's deficits up to 1955. The delays were such that it was not until July 1957 that a new charges scheme came into operation and the railways were free at last to charge rates that were able to attract the type of traffic they were best able to carry and to discourage what they were not. Maximum charges were then still fixed, but at least they no longer had to be published. Meanwhile, rail freight ton-mileage fell between 1951-53 and 1960-61 by a quarter - most of the fall being after 1955. The market share fell from 45% to 29%, although the volume of freight carried remained above pre-war levels until 1962. Even the railways' traditional bulk traffics in coal and minerals were drifting away to the roads. Large privately-owned lorries were allowed on the roads after the 1953 Transport Act, and anyway Licensing Regulations and Road Traffic Laws were flagrantly breached, and the shift to road haulage accelerated when the many emergency arrangements for road haulage made during the Rail Strike of 1955 became permanent.

Within the limitations of their scarcity of funds, the Commission and the Executive did try to take steps in the early

42328, one of the two ex-LMS Fowler Class 4 2-6-4Ts (the other was 42374) which ran prolonged trials on the Outer Suburban services from King's Cross in the mid-1950s. With no indigenous locomotives in the scene, it may not seem quite so out of place as it really did, here beside the signalbox at King's Cross. Behind is York Road station with an Up local at the platform, and on the left can be seen the smoke-filled Gas Works Tunnels. *R.Barnard.*

Instead of the more usual NER or LNER type, we have here by the mid-1950s an LMS Ivatt 'Flying Pig' Class 4MT 2-6-0, No.43126, on an Up Class K goods coming round behind Newcastle Central station, 18th May 1954. These locomotives were sent to the North Eastern and Eastern Region in large numbers during the early period of BR and were amongst the last ones still working at the end of steam on BR. *J.Robertson.*

The LMS presence at the south end of York station: on Sunday 16th July 1950, Stanier Class 5 4-6-0 No.44963 at platform 8S is heading for the Sheffield Midland line with an Up express containing at least one GWR coach. A J71 pilot stands at platform 9, and what is probably the brake at the rear of an Engineers' train can be seen on the Down Through line. Note the new colour-light signals on the gantry - nearly a year before the final conversion, and - in spite of its being a Sunday - the crowd of train-spotters (all with their raincoats) at the end of platform 3/8. *E.R.Morten.*

individuals, were prepared to pay a lot more for road transport because of its 'other advantages'.

The Railways made a *working* surplus until 1955, but central charges were so high that the BTC suffered a deficit as a whole in every year after Nationalization except in 1951-53, and even this disappeared if the hidden subsidy of the wartime Arrears of Maintenance Fund was not counted as 'revenue'. The deficit reached the £100m. mark by the end of the 1950s - and was to rise still further, partly because of the interest charges on the further borrowing necessary. The trend for rail charges to lag behind costs continued into the early 1960s to represent a substantial *decrease* in real terms compared to pre-war, and the BR deficit widened further. From 1958 onwards BR lost money in both the passenger and freight sectors even with respect to direct costs; only the parcels sector made a profit. The average wagon load of merchandise was merely a little over four tons, and even though two-thirds of merchandise was still being loaded at private sidings, it is not hard to see the cost advantage of a *lorry* load of 10 tons - with probably little empty mileage. It was calculated that 30% of railway freight costs related to provision and repair of wagons and another 39% to marshalling *en route* and shunting and haulage at the terminal. These costs of railway merchandise traffic were being carried on the back of the much more profitable coal and minerals traffic, but with industrial recession in 1958 and a decline in heavy industry thereafter profits in the other sectors could no longer cover losses on merchandise traffic.

The outstanding problem that BR was suffering in the post-war period concerned labour costs. There was a chronic shortage of adequately skilled and motivated labour, because of the expectations aroused by the Welfare State together with the rather higher wages and generally better working conditions in private industry. As the result of a number of wage increases that had been granted, wage costs had become - for BR and for all industries, a relatively greater proportion of total costs. Under strong Railway Unions, labour costs had risen inexorably, while over-manning continued to be rife. By the end of 1959, average earnings for railway work were 77% above even those in 1948, whereas retail prices had risen by only 51%. The total railway labour force in 1954 had fallen by only 8% (to 577,000) and was to decline only to 519,000 by January 1960, still 80% of the total in 1948, yet 'productivity' was estimated to have risen by only 17%. Along with the many other failures of the state-owned monolith to improve efficiency, such as by bringing in diesel multiple units on branches or abolishing manual signalling and manned level-crossings, the overstaffing and antiquated work practices were fundamental causes of BR's afflictions.

THE 1955 MODERNIZATION PLAN AND ITS REAPPRAISAL: THE DECLINE OF BRITISH RAILWAYS IN THE LATER 1950s

The British Transport Commission, bereft from October 1953 of the Railway Executive - and taking over and expanding its premises at 222 Marylebone Road, was reconstituted as an interim organization in 1953, before being reorganized in January 1955 to take on more directly the responsibility for the railways. In practice this work was undertaken for the next year or so by several Committees. The new BTC, headed by General Sir Brian Robertson, was an elaborate set-up of military style under a 'General Staff', and in effect a substantial bureaucratic enlargement - under a *Conservative* Government - swelling the

BTC's administrative costs by more than was saved later by branch-line closures. The reorganization and decentralization of the control of BR resulting from the 1953 Act further delayed the preparation of plans for modernization, which had already been put off for far too long for the reasons alluded to above. The attitude of the Government - and the people - can be contrasted with that on the European Continent, where the post-war Governments, traditionally more directly involved with their railways than was the case in Britain, placed a much higher priority on the restoration of their war-ravaged railways than on the motor vehicle and the roads. Today, in France the proportion of rail-transported freight is four-times that in Britain, in Germany nearly five-times, and even in little Denmark and Belgium it is double. In France there are - in relation to the length of the network - five-times as many private sidings as in Britain.

The BTC's stated objective in the Modernization Plan was "to exploit the great natural advantages of railways as bulk transporters of passengers and goods and to revolutionize the character of the services provided for both, not only by the full utilization of modern equipment but also by purposeful concentration on those functions which the railways can be made to perform more efficiently than other forms of transport." The Plan was costed at £1,240m. (soon raised to £1,660m.) *over 15 years*, - but this was still a small investment compared with the £600m. *a year already* being spent on roads in Britain, or with the £200m. per year being spent by the Federal Railways (of comparable extent) in West Germany. More especially, the true value of this apparently large Government hand-out for modernization was much less than it seemed because half the sum would have had to be spent anyway just to cover arrears of maintenance and keep the railways going. Moreover, the costing of major modernization of the railways, such as of electrification, was made on a different basis from that applied to the costing of motorway construction, in which the time saved by drivers and hauliers switching to the motorways was set against the costs.

Although earlier Conservative Ministers of Transport, under the influence of the powerful Road Lobby, had been pressing the BTC to close unremunerative branch-lines, at this stage rationalization by the closure of lines and stations was not a major objective as it was calculated to save no more than £3m. The extent of the modernized railway system was still envisaged as essentially unchanged, and much greater savings were expected to be achieved from the new commercial freedom being negotiated. The planners imagined that the railways would break even financially by 1961-62, but the forecasts they made in 1954 when drawing up the Plan proved too optimistic; this was especially so in the freight sector, as we have seen. However, shackles on charging policies were only relieved when the Area Boards were set up under the 1962 Transport Act, with much more devolved executive authority. Yet the Government did seem to feel more positive towards the railways than it had been earlier in the 1950s, and introduced consecutive Railway Finance Acts of 1957 and 1959 empowering the BTC to borrow £1,200m. for the Plan and also up to £400m. to cover revenue deficits, - but in doing so burdened BR with even greater interest charges.

By 1958, annual deficits were growing, even though the widespread introduction of diesel multiple-units (DMUs) on secondary and branch-line services was radically cutting their operating costs (63% on average) and usually much improving passenger revenue (34% on average). It seems that a great opportunity was missed of attracting many more passengers,

The shape of modernization, Thirsk 1954: a brand-new Derby light-weight four-car DMU running down to take up work from Newcastle. *Beeken.*

(above) **There are two unrelated features of interest in this picture: the TPO on the 20.20 Down Mail from King's Cross is about to pick up mail-bags at Hitchin South on 10th July 1959. The train is headed by the new and extraordinary 'Deltic' on its trials from English Electric.** *J.Aylard.*

(right) **King's Cross, 1959: the prototype English-Electric 3,300 hp Type 5 DELTIC (in striped blue livery) and English Electric/ Napier 1,160 hp Type 2 'Baby Deltic' No.D5900, on Up trains.** *E.Sanderson.*

because when the DMUs were belatedly brought in there was at first no radical increase in the frequency, speed or convenience to passengers of many of these services. In the late evenings, on Sundays and at other leisure times they remained abysmal, and people continued to find it more convenient - and ultimately essential - to use their private cars.

Other benefits of modernization were slow to reveal themselves, and it seemed after all that BR could only be got 'out of the red' by cost-cutting. As a result the planned rates of scrapping of steam locomotives and of the introduction of main-line diesels were accelerated, and a great deal of money was wasted by a too rapid acceptance of inadequately tested diesels of types that were unreliable, having been built mainly by relatively inexperienced private contractors. Besides, with its high initial cost and mechanical complexity, the true economic advantage of the main-line diesel over the equivalent modern steam locomotive was far from overwhelming. *Electric* motive power was the outstanding winner, but that was economically justifiable only on routes of high traffic density.

The paralysis caused by the two-week ASLEF Strike in mid-1955 had accelerated the drift of freight to the roads - notably the traffic in essential perishables such as fish, and the new charging system when it finally began to operate in mid-1957 seemed to have come too late to reverse the downward trends in freight revenue. Net ton-miles rail-borne in 1959 of 17,700m. were the lowest since the war in spite of significant *reductions* in charges (in real terms), and road vehicles were carrying as many ton-miles - and five times the tonnage - as were the railways. (Since then freight transport, in ton-miles, by rail has more than halved again). The freight transport market became dominated by the costs of the firms carrying their own goods in 'C' licence vehicles, on *roads* for which the vehicle and fuel taxes they paid were orders of magnitude less than the cost of building and maintaining the roads to the standard needed for heavy lorries. This contention may be debatable because it depends upon the way these costs are calculated, but there is no doubt that the tax burden carried by the operation of heavy lorries is not commensurate with the damage they cause to the roads and motorways, let alone wider environmental harm[30]. In terms of such wider considerations the *real* cost of building new roads is probably double that ascribed at the time by the Ministry of Transport. Thus, it was impossible for BR to reduce its charges to compete, when it had to pay for its fixed assets, including track and signalling and ultimately for the land on which they were built - that together nonetheless made the railways infinitely *safer* than the roads. Apart from this, a blind eye was usually cast on constant flouting of speed limits on lorries, on their overloading and inadequate maintenance, and on excessive hours worked by their - often non-Unionized - drivers.

In the later 1950s the loss of freight from the railways was also an inevitable result of the relative decline of coal-mining and of the iron and steel industries in Britain. The 1952 Clean Air Act had already caused the disappearance of much of the traffic in domestic and industrial coal, and the average length of haul of coal was diminishing as more and more large electricity-generating stations were being built near the principal coalfields. Conversely, recent industrial growth in Britain had been largely in the higher-value manufactured products - *including motor cars,* for which road transport was usually more appropriate. Meanwhile, the efficiency of rail freight transport was improving only marginally.

In reaction to the mounting and accelerating deficits of

BR together with doubts about the ability of the Modernization Plan to restore its viability, a Parliamentary Select Committee on Nationalized Industries was examining the BTC and the fortunes of BR in depth (it reported in March 1960), while in the meantime the new - and still Conservative - Government was also rather secretly examining the problem with its own Special Advisory Group (headed by Sir Ivan Stedeford). The outcome of the two studies was a lot more new legislation, embodied in the 1962 Transport Act.

The history of British Railways in the 1960s is outside the period set in this book, however. Suffice it to say that the 1962 Act abolished the BTC and set up four autonomous Boards, the railways being under the aegis of the British Railways Board (BRB). As they were financially autonomous, cross-subsidization between transport modes was now no longer possible - if it ever had been. The new Minister of Transport (Ernest Marples) was very much a 'Roads' man, and the Select Committee's recommendation of subsidies to the railways for their 'social obligations' seemed to be ignored. The BRB was expected to devote themselves solely to managing the railway system to make it pay its way, yet they were still to be saddled with an element of 'common carrier' obligation. It was 1968 - and another Labour Government - before the principle was adopted, already widely accepted in most other countries (though not in the influential USA) of financing out of taxation the social service obligation of public transport.

The Select Committee had gone a long way towards identifying the sources of BR's losses. These were not yet, at that time, on the freight side, which was as a whole profitable, but on passenger operations - notably the stopping-trains although not particularly at that time the 'commuter' services. It was these parts of the passenger services that were candidates for subsidy. None was forthcoming, and instead in the light of the Modernization Plan the Government wrote off some £500m. of the accumulated debt and another £700m. of the debt was 'suspended' until the railways should begin to make a profit again, while powers were given for grants of up to £450m. during the next five years.

It has been argued by Henshaw and others that there was a conspiracy, to run down the railways deliberately, by the Ministry of Transport. In that Ministry, under the all-powerful influence of the motor and oil industries and their satellites, along with the motorway construction interests, the careers of most senior civil servants depended on furthering road transport. The case made by Henshaw to interpret the crushing of railways in Britain by an all-pervading Roads Lobby with enormous political power is a compelling one, but it needs to be understood in the context of the desire of every man to have his private transport and of the deep influence of democratic forces in Britain. The idea of a conspiracy is based mainly on the thesis that branch lines *could* have been made profitable, by quite modest cost-cutting and an expenditure on modernization of equipment that was miniscule compared with the cost of new roads. It is asserted that the BTC went out of its way to cut services until they were useless anyway and then distorted the statistics to make it appear that the lines were losing more money than they really were. In particular, there was a deliberate disregard of the *contributary revenue* produced by the branch (and secondary) lines towards the viability of the system as a whole. Indeed, it is axiomatic that the profitability of a transport *network* must break down if its branches are severed. However, it seems that in many cases the losses on remote branch lines and at wayside stations would have persisted

The New Order, 1958: English Electric 2,000 hp Type 4 No.D206 on an Up express at Crescent Junction, Peterborough. *A.C.Ingram.*

whichever way the calculations were made or whatever working economies were possible. The question of direct *subsidy* is another matter, but at least in the 1950s - if not after Marples and Beeching - the BTC and the Regions do not seem to have been whole-hearted in their apparent determination to cut services, and the Government was prepared to provide road bus services as an alternative - albeit this was not usually a viable one. (The first *major* closure, that of the M&GN system in March 1959, had come about following a hardening of the attitude of the Government, under a new Minister of Transport (Harold Watkinson) already unsympathetic to the idea of any 'social obligation' of the railways).

What was perhaps more sinister was the failure of the Government to publish the Stedeford Report, and their focussing down on the financial problems of the country branch-lines - which in terms of the overall deficits of the BTC were relatively minor; cynics would say that this was in order to force people to buy cars. In any case, the fundamental problem was the universal shift towards private transport, coupled with the political impossibility of making people pay, by adequately targeted taxation or by road pricing, the economic (and environmental) costs of their private transport - as has been mooted here in Chapter I. Besides these factors, there had been very great technological improvements in the performance, efficiency and comfort of road vehicles of all kinds, and concomitant reductions in the real costs of road transport. At the same time, while the cost to the BTC of diesel fuel was falling, relentlessly rising were the costs of coal (up 18% between 1956 and 1960), of materials, and above all - especially after the Guillebaud Report on the

Comparability of Railwaymen's Wages - of labour.

Certainly under Marples a more aggressively commercial philosophy prevailed[31]. Marples radically cut the investment in railway modernization, and he brought in a 'new broom' in the person of Dr.Richard Beeching to head the BRB from January 1963, replacing the 'pro-Rail' Sir Brian Robertson[32]. Beeching had been a member of the Stedeford Advisory Group, and his famous report *The Reshaping of British Railways* was published in March 1963. Although strictly coming after the end of this chronicle, the findings deserve to be recalled in light of their revelation of the situation as it existed at the close of the 1950s, when BR's share of national passenger traffic (passenger-miles) was still one-sixth, and of freight (ton-miles) one-third.

Broadly, Beeching reported that total railway traffic in 1961 was losing marginally even on *direct* costs, with stopping passenger services and wagon-load (and sundries) freight losing heavily. The small gains on operating fast and semi-fast passenger services, on parcels and mails, and on coal and minerals, were not bringing about a positive margin overall. Even the coal traffic - so suited to rail - was a lot less profitable than it should have been, mainly because terminal facilities were geared to the traditional 10 - or 12-ton wagons.

The railway network had been shortened since 1951 by a mere 2,000 miles, and it was still nearly 17,500 route miles. Half of this mileage carried 4% of the passenger-miles and 5% of freight ton-miles. Sixty percent of the goods stations handled less than 100 tons per week and accounted for only 9% of the tonnage. The average wagon load (including coal and minerals) was a mere 9.3 tons, and - surprisingly - half of the tonnage was

During their brief period in London - indeed their brief life, one of the less successful early main-line diesels, NB Loco/MAN Type 2 (later Class 21) No.D6103, is passing Harringay West with the Mail vans for turning on the Dalston Junction triangle, 2nd June 1959. *Author.*

carried less than 50 miles. There was evidently still much scope for the further incursion of the lorry into the business, but that transfer of freight to road had already gone far was evidenced by the fact that most of the siding-to-siding traffic was being moved through only a small proportion of all the sidings available.

What Beeching achieved and the revolution brought about by the Reshaping of British Railways is another tale, not to be recounted here. It is enough to remind the reader that *in spite of* Rationalization and Modernization, and *in spite of* direct Government grants for unremunerative services after the 1968 Transport Act, BR's working surplus remained relentlessly negative. The real savings in costs achieved by the massive closures of the 1960s, which were only *expected* to save less than a third of BR's current deficit, were matched by a fall in revenues due in part to the closures themselves. This was because Beeching's criteria of profitability were set way above the levels that would be set by far less biassed accountants today. He had entirely failed to take into consideration the contributory revenues from branch-line traffic or their often massive seasonal fluctuations, and of course he knew that little concerted effort had been made to operate branch lines more efficiently.

A very detailed analysis that Beeching made of most aspects of railway traffic and operations, mainly of data collected in 1961, showed how grossly inefficient was the handling not only of freight sundries traffic but also of wagon-load traffic. The chief factors contributing to their unprofitability were fairly obvious: labour-intensive transshipment between rail and road delivery services at terminals, transshipment *en route* of sundries between wagons, wagon marshalling, and the slow transit speed of unbraked freight trains. As is well known, Beeching not only recommended the closure of most of the small loss-making services, stations and depots, but also the revivifying of railway freight traffic by the introduction of Liner Trains. These would employ road-rail containers to avoid transshipment, and move rapidly between major centres in dedicated trains of continuously-braked wagons with minimal intermediate marshalling. But the Government of the day resolved instead on the building of a nationwide network of *Motorways*, and the Liner Train idea never came to fruition to any substantial extent.

By the end of 1959 nonetheless, considerable strides had been made since January 1955 with modernization. Long-welded track had been laid on 185 miles of main line, 630 miles had been resignalled, and 443 route miles were now fitted with the automatic warning system (AWS). A total of 1,490 diesel

locomotives (including 421 for main-line work) were in service and 4,386 steam locomotives had been displaced by these and by the 3,192 DMU and 2,012 electric (EMU) vehicles brought into use; 4,231 new coaches had replaced 10,815 old ones. Nearly one-third of the wagon fleet now had power brakes, but it had been decided to fit the less efficient *vacuum* brak e - at immense expense, only to incur further great expense when ten years later BR changed its mind and went over to the *air* brake. Plans to fit mineral wagons with these brakes (and automatic couplers) were frustrated by inadequacy of handling facilities, as was the building of wagons of larger capacity. The embedded idea that wagon-load - let alone sundries - traffic by rail could be made profitable in the face of a heavily subsidized road transport industry was long in dying - beyond the period in this narrative. Therefore the great sums that were spent on new mechanized marshalling yards[33] for this traffic were largely wasted, the yards becoming 'white elephants' ten years later. Another scheme of the period that came too late, and indeed hardly got off the ground before it was abandoned - in favour of motor ways, was the improvement of the Cambridge - Oxford - Reading - Redhill - Tonbridge ring as a freight route to by-pass London, a modernized version of the route employed for the same purpose in the war.

A measure of the situation on BR as the 1950s drew to a close is afforded by the following facts. In 1958 the BTC's freight traffic receipts were £370m. while private ('C' licence) transport was spending over £1,000m. a year on moving their own goods by road. Passengers on BR and London Transport rail services were contributing £162m. while buses drew in £109m., but private car owners were spending £1,100m. on their 4.5m. cars and 1.5m. motor-cycles. In 1958 BR were moving 19,400m. ton-miles of freight while 22,800m. were being moved on the roads. Public transport was conveying 70,700m. passenger-miles (25,000m. by rail), while private cars were carrying 50,000m. Expenditure on new railway vehicles was £116m. in 1958, but private individuals spent £130m. on goods vehicles and *£500m.* on cars - and this does *not* include enormous costs incurred by firms on the purchase and maintenance of 'Company Cars'.

The brief history just recounted of British Railways during its first 12 years until the end of 1959 is intended to provide an overview of the circumstances under which the ECML had to be operated. Having previously been all part of the LNER, the ECML after Nationalization came administratively into three separate Regions of the new BR and these differed somewhat in character. Nevertheless, for operating purposes it was natural to maintain the ECML much as it had been. Train services changed hardly at all for many years after Nationalization, and the links between the Eastern Region and the rather small North Eastern Region were so close that the two Regions were merged into a single Eastern Region in January 1967. The fortunes of the LNER until Nationalization, and of the ER, NER and ScR of BR in the early years after Nationalization (between 1948 and 1959) are summarized in Appendix A.

Having thus set the stage, a survey will now be made of the different components of the ECML, its management, services, motive power, and rolling-stock, and of the changes that occurred during the twenty-year period with which this account is concerned.

Notes:

1. But even in 1951 the speed limit for heavy vehicles was 20 mph, - which 45 years on now seems incredible.
2. Soon after the war, an interesting report circulated by the Railway Clearing House in January 1946 was prepared by the four Railway Chief Operating Superintendents, and in 1946 also the RAILWAY GAZETTE published an official history (Bell, 1946). Each of the Big Four soon brought out their own accounts thereafter, the one on the LNER (Crump, 1947) probably being the best. The authoritative account of Inland Transport in the war is by Savage (1957). A popular account (John, 1945) was published directly after the war, and a more informed general survey (Nock, 1971) more recently, but there is still a lack of detailed records of the wartime railway workings as they happened: a recent book on the GWR by Bryan (1995) represents a good start in this direction.
3. Ministry of War Transport, from May 1941 after incorporation of the Ministry of Shipping.
4. The LNER moved this ammunition to dumps at Haxey (Lincs.) and Leadburn (Midlothian). Other emergency needs provided for by the LNER alone included 34 Casualty Evacuation Trains, and a contribution of 21 trains to the pool needed for mobilization of the British Expeditionary Force, and also the establishment of railheads for the emergency stocks of coal, petrol, potatoes and fish.
5. See Part II.
6. Up to 20% off Standard rates for merchandise, 33% for explosives, - but in the First World War the Railways had to carry Government traffic free of charge.
7. To the author this seems still a very low figure, showing that the *average* passenger journey was nevertheless entirely a local one - say Knebworth to King's Cross, Thirsk to York, or North Berwick to Edinburgh. Still, in 1938 the average third-class journey (on ordinary fare) was a mere 7.0 miles while the average first-class one was 50.4 miles.
8. Harrogate, with its many hotels, was favoured for Government Departments evacuated from London, and so the relocation of these Departments entailed more traffic on the ECML in particular.
9. The author however considered himself fortunate, for he had a divided family and for much of the war he was away at boarding-schools. This gave him valid reasons for a good deal of travelling around the country - which he *enjoyed*. His secret, in order to get a better view out and see what was passing by, was to sit in the corridor on his bag, rather than in a stuffy compartment probably not even near the steamy and often partly netted-over windows.
10. Much of the Western Highlands of Scotland was already in this category.
11. For details, the reader is referred to the most interesting account written for the War Office in 1955 (available at the PRO at WO 277/17), *The Second World War 1939 - 1945*, *Army Movements*, by Major J.B.Higham and E.A.Knighton. For the American side, see *United States Army in World War II. The Technical Services. The Transportation Corps: Operations Overseas*, by J.Bykofsky and H.Larson. Office of the Chief of Military History, Department of the Army, Washington D.C., 1957.
12. For military traffic on the ECML, the Movement Control District HQs were in Eastern Command at Cambridge and at Dunstable (from August 1941, and mainly concerned with stores), in Northern Command at York and (from June 1940) at Darlington and Nottingham, and in Scottish Command at Edinburgh.
13. Absent Without Official Leave.
14. European Theatre of Operations, United States Army.
15. The very first train left, in great secrecy, early on the morning of 1st September - over 48 hours before war was actually declared - for Glasgow, from London's *Cannon Street* station, and went *via* Redhill, Guildford and Reading!
16. Military Port No.1 at Faslane was later supplemented by Military Port No.2, built at Cairnryan near Stranrear.
17. In the NE Area of the LNER one of the two tracks of the Picton - Battersby and of the Tadcaster - Wetherby lines was used for this purpose.
18. The enemy was well aware of the disruptive effect of air-raid warnings, and would send planes over in relays in order to keep a Red Alert in operation for hours on end.
19. Armoured fighting vehicles, carried on 'Warflats' or on 'Warwells'. The big tanks (Cromwells, Crusaders, Churchills, Shermans) were so wide that they were slightly out-of-gauge, and trains of them were a great nuisance and had to be meticulously planned.
20. Savage (1957) says that "lavatory accommodation [at railway depots] for women was inadequate and canteens were often non-existent or very poor" - as if *men* didn't need lavatories.
21. Constituting the manual railway workers, so called after the Conciliation Boards set up in 1907 to allow negotiation between the Railway Companies and the men's representatives.
22. Fortunately, the Luftwaffe was by then incapable of sending over any significant force of bombers. Their 'mini-Blitz' of February 1944 was ineffective, and the damage done to the railways by the Flying Bombs - in spite of the extraordinary fluke that one of the very first four fired by the Germans on 13th June 1944 cut the main line between Liverpool St. and Stratford - scarcely held up the great flow of OVERLORD traffic at all.
23. Lines on which passenger - and most normal goods - services were suspended included: Dalston Junction - Poplar, Palace Gates - Stratford - North Woolwich, and Didcot - Newbury - Southampton, also most services on the Kentish Town - Barking line.
24. Long Marston R.E. Stores Depot was the busiest, handling 10,027 wagons in its peak month of December 1944.
25. It has also been asserted in some quarters that the then Labour Government used the Fund for other purposes, unconnected with railways.
26. These figures are of course *miniscule* compared to those suffered by the enemy and by our European Allies.
27. This figure was high partly because of the necessity to repair so many of the run-down and antiquated former private-owner wagons in the 540,000 taken into public ownership at Nationalization, but of the Railways' own stock that of the LNER was the worst.
28. In 1959, under the Modernization Plan, it was back up to 4.1% - *temporarily*.
29. One of the first was built at Palace Gates, just off the ECML at Bounds Green, in July 1958.
30. Houghton, 1994 (*loc. cit.*)
31. Indeed Marples overruled a Central Transport Consultative Committee recommendation not to close the Westerham branch - which is now buried under the M25 motorway.
32. At 2.4 times Sir Brian's salary - shades of the 1990s privatizations.
33. The first one opened was at Thornton (Fife) in September 1957, and the only ones directly connected with the ECML - Millerhill near Edinburgh, Tees (Newport) and Tyne (Lamesley) - were not opened until the early 1960s.

BUTLIN'S EXPRESS (Skegness to King's Cross), with B1 No.61282, approaching Peterborough North at Spital Junction, 16th August 1958. Behind the B1 is part of Spital Yard beyond which is the new goods station under construction; the two independently moving light engines are on the lines to New England Shed, with Westwood Yard to the left of them, and the coaling plant visible in the distance beyond Westwood Bridge; the two tracks on the left are the reception roads for Crescent LMS Yard, the LMS line being out of sight to the left. *P.H.Groom.*

Chapter IV. PASSENGER SERVICES ON THE ECML IN SUMMER 1939 AND IN THE WAR, AND CHANGES THEREAFTER UNTIL THE END OF THE 1950S

SUMMER 1939

The basic pattern of ECML express services was one of quite fast trains between King's Cross and Leeds, Bradford and other West Yorkshire destinations, Hull and the Yorkshire coast resorts, Darlington and Newcastle, and on to Edinburgh, Glasgow, Perth, Dundee and Aberdeen. Subsidiary express services ran to Boston, Grimsby and Cleethorpes. The services to Glasgow, Perth and Aberdeen were in competition with those of the LMSR - which was quicker only to Glasgow. The West Yorkshire services were also quicker by a considerable margin than those of the LMSR from St Pancras, while the services to Newcastle and other East Coast destinations had no competition - other than from the embryonic air services. The principal expresses down the ECML and to intermediate destinations on it were therefore providing an essential service for travellers from London and the South-East to parts of England where some 15-20% of the population lived and at least a third of the population of Scotland. Moreover, at York the ECML tapped almost all the traffic to the North-East and about half that to Scotland from most of the rest of England and from much of Wales.

Thus passenger services provided by the LNER along the ECML in the last months of peace before the outbreak of the Second World War in September 1939 were comparable with those run by the LMSR on its corresponding trunk routes. Secondary and branch services that fed onto the ECML were also analogous, and they were typical of the era, one during which competition from the motor bus and to a certain extent the motor car in country districts was already serious. Branch services were being rendered unprofitable to the extent that such substantial cuts in services had been made in the 1930s, in comparison with their standard prior to the First World War, that their inadequacy was driving away custom and a vicious circle was being set up.

Road competition in the 1930s was hardly yet serious as far as the long-distance expresses were concerned. These remained profitable, and on the ECML as elsewhere they were arranged in the first place for the business community and received widespread support from it. No businessman or official expected to be able to travel up to London for a day's appointments and get back home the same day from more than about 100 miles, or for a half day's meetings from about 200 miles from the Capital. This meant that sleeping-car services from more than about 200 miles, *e.g.* Newcastle at 269 miles, were very popular for these purposes. Although luxury trains were provided in the form of the *YORKSHIRE PULLMAN* and the *QUEEN OF SCOTS PULLMAN*, there was a market for high-speed daytime services. Indeed by the mid-1930s travel by *air*[1], albeit unreliable and expensive, was becoming a genuine alternative for the Newcastle or Edinburgh business 'executive'. It is said that the *FLYING HAMBURGER* in Germany spurred Gresley and the LNER to introduce the *SILVER JUBILEE*, and later the *CORONATION* and *WEST RIDING LIMITED* high-speed trains - the Streamliners. As matters turned out, while the early

evening Down *SILVER JUBILEE* was a great success, the Up train was less so, the departure times of none of the three high-speed trains in the Up direction really being early enough in the morning to allow much time in London for business; anyway the Up *CORONATION* left Edinburgh at 16.30. Their operation over a line with largely 19th Century signalling was a problem: they could not come to a halt in one block section, and so two sections had to be kept clear ahead, *i.e.* double-block working.

The schedules of the ECML expresses in the late 1930s, even apart from those of the high-speed trains, were far from leisurely. The LNER had 23 daily runs, totalling 2,896 miles, timed at 60 m.p.h. or over in Summer 1939. This was very much the same total as attained by the GWR, and although less than the total of the (larger) LMSR their fastest run was 65 m.p.h., whereas the LNER had six runs at over 67 m.p.h. and three at over 70 m.p.h. Moreover, loadings were normally at least 14 coaches (or about 450 tare tons), and the policy was not to resort to piloting other than in emergencies except to a limited extent in the NE and Scottish Areas - albeit on a route with no really severe gradients. (Heavy trains - and important ones such as the *FLYING SCOTSMAN* - were regularly piloted in the Up direction from Edinburgh, because of Cockburnspath Bank).

In 1939 the pricipal motive power for the express services on the ECML was provided by the 100 or so Gresley Pacifics (Classes A1, A3 and A4). However, the Class C1 Ivatt Large Atlantics were still playing some part at the southern end, while the Raven Class C7 Atlantics and the Gresley Class D49 4-4-0s were employed to a limited extent along the northern part. The new Gresley Class V2 2-6-2s were also beginning to share in this work, presaging their comprehensive use alongside the Pacifics during and after the war.

The performance exploits of LNER steam locomotives, especially of Gresley's Pacifics, in terms of high speeds, the capability to make up time with heavy loads, and reliability, have been so professionally, exhaustively and frequently described by well-known and well-informed authors in so many publications, that no attempt is made here to discuss or even to summarize them. Suffice it to say that in the late 1930s the express passenger locomotives on the ECML were as capable - in some ways unequalled - in the handling of the quite exacting schedules and loads as were the equivalent modern locomotives of the other three Groups.

The services in Summer 1939 are summarized in Table 4.1, where all regularly scheduled ECML main-line, feeder and local services (other than those entering Edinburgh Waverley from the west and north) are collated. Perusal of the Table will give the reader an idea of the adequacy or otherwise of the services that were run. It provides a basis of comparison for the description later of the drastic changes that came about during the war and of the post-war recovery of services, as summarized in Tables 4.2 and 4.3. The operations of the London suburban services and of the secondary and local services feeding in and out of other ECML junctions will be covered in Part II, and details of all passenger class trains at some of the principal ECML centres

4419, the C1 Atlantic that had been fitted with a booster on the trailing pony truck for many years and also with extended frames and a side-window cab, assists another C1 out of Grantham, late 1930s. *Goslin coll*.

will be set out in Part II in an Appendix; the contributions of the various locomotive depots on the ECML are also portrayed in Part II.

What is immediately striking in the 1990s is not only the comparative snail's pace of express trains in Steam days, but also their relative infrequency. This was only partly compensated by the existence of many branch line services that are no longer available. On the other hand, compared to recent times, the number and variety of Summer Saturday extras and through workings were much greater. Conversely, the Sunday services were memorable for their sparseness and slowness on the main line, and their absence from many of the branches. This was a reflection of the quasi-religious proscription of Sunday work or travel in the Victorian era, leading later to the Trade Unions negotiating higher pay for Sunday work.

In 1939 there were still a large number of branch services feeding to the ECML - many in a terminal stage of dissolution. Several of these were withdrawn at the beginning of the war - to be quickly reinstated in most cases, but some for the Duration and two permanently, and 15 were taken off in the first ten years afterwards. Likewise in 1939 there were still exiguous services of slow trains calling at the many wayside stations on the ECML itself, the survival of many of which after the war was brief. (Details of the closures of branches and wayside stations are given in Part II).

However, we are not setting out to compare the ECML of Steam days with the electrified ECML of the 1990s, but rather to recollect the facilities for rail travel in the late 1930s and to compare the railway scene then with that in the war and in the early post-war years.

The 1939 lists also seem remarkable today in some other ways. There was the variety of different destinations served, by dividing and recombining sets of coaches *en route*. From King's Cross some 'unusual' destinations, such as Cromer and Horncastle (and on Sundays, Gainsborough), were served, and - by sleeping-car only - Nairn, Lossiemouth and North Berwick. Indeed, a feature of the main-line services down the ECML from King's Cross was the number of destinations reached by portions of any one train - amounting to three or even more, most often separated at Doncaster but also at Wakefield Westgate, York, Edinburgh, and elsewhere. Then there were some strange and most complex cross-country through services. Perhaps the most remarkable of these was the so-called 'Aberdeen - Penzance' service. At *24 hours* this was by far the longest regular service in Britain - but it was only available from Aberdeen in the southbound direction, as was the sleeping-car attached from Swindon on to Penzance. In the northbound direction the train ran from St Erth to Glasgow - and *no* sleeping-car. Still, the LNER was running on it one of its novel new buffet/restaurant cars each way between Newcastle and Swindon, returning next day from Swindon to York. So some crazy passenger had the chance of making in the same seat such unlikely journeys as from Laurencekirk to Marazion, or from Lostwithiel to Polmont.

Another strange pre-war service on the ECML was the Swansea (High Street) - Newcastle restaurant car express (with a portion for Hull). This took a curious route from the GWR to the LNER, in that it ran from Gloucester *via* Cheltenham South, Andoversford and Chipping Norton to Banbury - even conveying a restaurant car over this Cotswold backwater, part of which was closed as long ago as 1951. Thus one could travel in the same

TABLE 4.1: SUMMARY OF PASSENGER SERVICES ON THE ECML AND CONNECTING LINES, AUGUST 1939

Below are given the numbers of through trains (or through coaches - some being sleeping-cars only) in the public timetable, and terminating at the stated destinations[1]. The listed services are for the Down direction only on Monday - Saturday with any different totals on particular days - e.g. Saturdays (SO) and totals for Sundays (SuO) - if any. When trains ran *only* on certain days of the week, this is indicated by italics, *e.g. 'SO'*. It is assumed that Up services were very similar. The distance (m, miles) and the quickest journey times (minutes) is given. In general, the trains that ran Monday - Friday also ran Monday - Saturday all the year round, although there were a few exceptions. Journey times were usually longer on Saturdays in summer, and very definitely so on Sundays throughout the year because of delays and deviations due to track maintenance work.

Apart from the *FLYING SCOTSMAN* - non-stop from King's Cross to Edinburgh, all trains to Scotland stopped at Newcastle, and all stopped at York except for the *NIGHT SCOTSMAN* (nominally but *not actually* non-stop to Haymarket because it conveyed passengers to beyond Edinburgh only), the *SILVER JUBILEE*, and the *QUEEN OF SCOTS* (which went *via* Leeds and Harrogate) and a few *SO* trains. Other trains made stops also at Peterborough, Grantham, Doncaster, Darlington, or Durham, and a number stopped as well at other places such as Newark, Retford, Northallerton, and Berwick.

Main Line Departures from King's Cross:-

Edinburgh Waverley (393m, 417m *via Leeds and Ripon*) - 11 (360 min), 10 SO, 9 SuO (one Non-Stop, every day). **Via Edinburgh Waverley:** Glasgow Queen St. (440m, 464m *via Leeds and Ripon*) - 3 (527 min), 5 SO, 3 SuO; Aberdeen (524m) - 4 (615 min), 3 SO, 1 SuO; Perth (441m) - 1 (553 min), 1 SuO; Fort William (563m) - 1 (837 min), nil SO, 1 SuO; Inverness (559m) - 1 (800 min), nil SO, 1 SuO; Nairn, *via Dava* (569m) - 1 (891 min), nil SO, 1 SuO; Lossiemouth, *via Aberdeen, Craigellachie and Elgin* (610m) - 1 (887 min), 1 SuO; North Berwick (380m) - 1 *FO* (525 min). **Newcastle** (269m) - 6 (240 min) - 7 MFO, 4 SO, 3 SuO; Tyne Commission Quay *via Newcastle* (277m) - 2 (350 min). **York** (188m) - 1 (273 min), 1 SuO. **Via York:** Sunderland *via Stockton* (281m) - 1 *SO* (325 min); Saltburn *via Middlesbrough* (260m) - 1 *SO* (308 min); Scarborough *via Malton* (230m) - 1 (235 min), 2 SO, 1 SuO; Whitby (244m) - 1 (295 min), 3 SO, 1 SuO. **Via Selby:** Scarborough *via Bridlington* (240m) - 1 (330 min); Bridlington (217m) - 1 (290 min), 2 SO; Filey *via Bridlington* (223m) - 1 (315 min), 2 SO. **Doncaster** (156m) - 1 (218 min), 1 SuO. **Via Doncaster:** Leeds Central/Bradford Exchange (186/193m) - 5 (163/190 min), 9 SO, 5 SuO; Hull (197m) - 6, 7 *FO* (210 min), 9 SO, 5 SuO; Harrogate *via Leeds* (204m) - 3 (240 min), 4 SO, 2 SuO; Ripon *via Knottingley and Church Fenton* (220m) - 1 *SO* (282 min); Halifax Old (202m) - 1 (252 min). **Via Retford:** Sheffield Victoria (162m) - 1 (226 min). **Via Grantham:** Lincoln (130m) - 1 (167 min). **Via Peterborough North:** Cleethorpes (158m) - 1 (224 min), 1 SuO; Gainsborough Lea Road *via Lincoln* - 1 *SuO*; Boston (107m) - 1 (167 min); Skegness (131m) - 1 (185 min), 3 SO, 1 SuO; Horncastle (130m) - 1 *FO* (203 min), 1 *SO*; Cromer Beach (161m) - 1 (275 min); Kings Lynn (116m) - 1 *SO* (180 min).

Cambridge Line Trains, *via Hitchin*
King's Cross to: Letchworth (35m) - 1 (66 min), 2 SO, 4 SuO; Baldock (37m) - 7 (65 min); Royston (45m) - 3 (80 min), 2 SO, 2 SuO; Cambridge (58m) - 11 (75 min), 12 ThSO, 6 SuO.

Regular trains running over part of the ECML north of Peterborough:-
Harwich Parkeston Quay *via Ipswich, March, Lincoln, Doncaster, and Knottingley* to **York** (223m)[2] - 1 (347 min). Harwich Town (222m, 374 min)/Yarmouth Vauxhall (218m, 364 min)/Lowestoft Central (221m, 379 min) *via March, Lincoln and Doncaster* to **York** - 1[3]. **York** to: Newcastle *via Durham* (81m) - 1 (112 min), 6 *SuO*; **Newcastle** *via West Hartlepool and Sunderland* (90m) - 1 (165 min), 1 SuO; **Berwick-on-Tweed**/Saltburn[4] (148/64m) - 1 (226/100 min); Middlesbrough (51m) - 1 (91 min) (to Redcar East *SO*). **Via York:** Liverpool Exchange *via Durham* to **Newcastle** (187m) - 1 (276 min), 1 SuO (combined with a train from Sheffield Victoria); Southampton Terminus *via*

Newbury, Oxford, Sheffield Victoria to **Edinburgh** and Glasgow Queen St. (496m)[5] - 1 (865 min); Sheffield Victoria/Leeds City to **Edinburgh** and Glasgow Queen St. (299/278m) - 1 (413/373 min), 1 SuO (to **Newcastle** only); Scarborough Central[6] to **Edinburgh** and Glasgow Queen St. (294m) - 1 (413 min), 2 SO; Swansea High St. *via Gloucester, Andoversford, Banbury, Sheffield Victoria, and Doncaster*, and Bristol Temple Meads *via Birmingham New St. and Sheffield Midland* to **Newcastle via Durham**[7] (377m from Swansea in 600 min; 293m from Bristol in 450 min) - 1, 1 *each* SO; Scarborough Central to **Newcastle via Durham** (123m) - 1 (185 min), 2 MSO; Bournemouth Central *via Oxford, Banbury, Sheffield Victoria*, and Bristol Temple Meads *via Birmingham New St. and Sheffield Midland* to **Newcastle via Durham**[8] (360m from Bournemouth in 656 min, 293m from Bristol in 468 min) - 1, 1 *each* SO; St. Erth[9] *via Westbury, Swindon, Oxford, Sheffield Victoria* to **Edinburgh** and Glasgow Queen St. (706m) - 1 (1,104 min), nil SO, 1 SuO. Via *Northallerton*: Bradford Forster Sq. *via Harrogate* to **Newcastle via Durham** (103m) - 1 (186 min); Liverpool Lime St. *via Leeds City, Harrogate* to **Newcastle via Durham** (169m) - 1 (253 min), 1 SuO (combined with train from Sheffield Victoria). **Darlington** to: **Edinburgh Waverley** (161 m) - 1 (243 min). **Newcastle** to: **Berwick-on-Tweed** (67m) - 1 (112 min), 5 *SuO*; **Edinburgh Waverley** (125m) - 1 (163 min) (to Glasgow on *SO*; 2 to Glasgow on *SuO*, 1 each from Sunderland and from Whitley Bay, *also* 1 *SuO* from Whitley Bay to Edinburgh); **Edinburgh Waverley** *via Tweedmouth, St. Boswells, and Galashiels* - 1 *SuO*.

Main Line Stopping Trains - not necessarily stopping at *all* stations. (No Sunday trains, unless stated.)

King's Cross to: Peterborough North - 3, 1 SuO; Grantham - 1; Doncaster - 3, 1 SuO. **Hitchin** to: Biggleswade - 1; Sandy - 1; Huntingdon North - 1 *SuO*; Peterborough North, 1 *WThFO*, 1 *MO*; *via Grantham* to Derby Friargate[10] - 1, 1 SuO. **Peterborough North** to: Grantham - 3; Doncaster - 1. **Grantham** to: Doncaster - 1, 1 SuO. **Rossington** to: Doncaster - 1. **Doncaster** to: York - 3. **Selby** to: York - 4, 1 SO. **York** to: Sunderland *via Northallerton and Stockton* - 1; **Darlington** - 1; **Newcastle** *via Darlington and Durham* - 1. Leeds City *via Thirsk* to Stockton - 1. **Darlington** *via Durham* to Newcastle - 3. **Darlington** *via Leamside* to Newcastle - 1. **Durham** to Newcastle - 7, 8 SO. **Newcastle** to: Morpeth - 2, 1 SO; Alnmouth and Alnwick - 3, 4 SO; Belford - 1; Berwick-on-Tweed - 1, 2 SO, 2 SuO. Alnwick *via Alnmouth* to Tweedmouth - 1. **Alnmouth** to Berwick-on-Tweed - 2. **Berwick-on-Tweed** to: St. Boswells *via Reston* - 3; **Edinburgh Waverley** - 3.

London Area Suburban Trains (south of Hitchin), and Newcastle Electric Trains.
A detailed and accurate exposition of the numbers of suburban trains in the London area or of the Tyneside electric suburban trains would be difficult and tedious. In summary, the approximate numbers of suburban trains per day in the London area (Monday - Saturday) amounted to the following: about 60 to High Barnet (most connecting with a shuttle to Edgware at Finchley Church End) and about 50 to Alexandra Palace, nearly half starting from Finsbury Park and in the peak hours about 15 from Moorgate and a similar number were LMSR trains from Broad St. Some 35 ran to New Barnet, many of which were from Moorgate or LMS trains from Broad St. during the morning and evening rush-hours. In addition about 45 trains per day, mainly starting from King's Cross, terminated further down the main line towards and including Hitchin, apart from those listed above which continued onto the Cambridge branch. On the Hertford North line there were about 85 trains per day, more than half of which terminated intermediately (mainly at Gordon Hill); some 35 were from King's Cross and 25 started from Moorgate, but about 12 were LMSR trains starting at Broad St. although none of the LMSR trains went further than Gordon Hill. Naturally, the Down peak-hour trains on Saturdays were between 12.00 and 14.00 hr rather than in the evening. On Sundays, trains ran at only about hourly intervals on most of these lines, but with none from Moorgate or Broad St. and none to Alexandra Palace.

The Newcastle electric trains comprised about 75 trains each way per day (Monday - Saturday) on the circle service *via* Tynemouth (not necessarily all running right round), about 20 on the Riverside line, and about 55 on the South Shields line. On Sundays there were about 30 trains each way on the circular service and another 12 during the height of the summer to and from Whitley Bay *via* the Riverside line, also a restaurant-car train each from Glasgow and from Edinburgh. On the South Shields line there about 35 trains each way on Sundays, many of them high summer only.

Regular Non-ECML Express, Secondary and Branch Trains - *excluding those from King's Cross - that passed through or started from the stations listed:-*
(Destination stations given are *only* those where a service terminated. Originating stations, if different from the junction station, are stated only where noteworthy. Equivalent trains ran in the reverse direction. **No** Sunday services, unless stated. For trains through from or to other ECML stations, see above. Seasonal trains are listed in the next section).

Hatfield to: St. Albans Abbey - 9 MTWFO, 10 ThSO, 12 SO; Dunstable LMSR - 8 (plus 1 *SO* to Luton LNER only), 6 SuO to Dunstable Town only (plus 2 to Luton LNER only)[11]; Hertford North - 8, 9 WSO. Hertford North *via* **Hitchin** (steam railcars) to: Letchworth - 2, 1 SO; Baldock - 1; Royston - 1. **Hitchin** to: Baldock - 6; Royston - 4, 3 SO, 1 SuO; Cambridge - 1, 2 SO; Bedford Midland Rd.[12] - 4 WThFO, 5 MO, 6 TO, 7 SA. **Sandy**[13] to: Bletchley - 9, 2 SuO; Cambridge - 6, 7 SO (1 daily through from Oxford), 3 SuO; Gamlingay - 1 *SO*; Bedford St. Johns - 2 SuO; Potton - 1 SuO. **Holme** to: Ramsey North - 3.
Peterborough North to: March - 3, 4 SO, 1 SuO; Ely - 8, 2 SuO; Cambridge *via St. Ives* - 3, 2 SuO; Lincoln *via Spalding and Boston* - 3, 1 SuO; Grimsby/ Cleethorpes - 6, 7 FSO, 1 SuO; Skegness - 1 *SO*, 1 *SuO* (through from Peterborough East); Boston - 1 MThFO, 2 TWO, 3 SO, 1 SuO. M&GN trains: King's Lynn - 6; Melton Constable - 2; Yarmouth Beach - 2. Down LMS line trains passing or calling at **Peterborough N.**: Leicester London Rd. - Peterborough E. - 7, 8 SO; Nottingham LMS - Peterborough E. - 1; Luffenham - Peterborough E. - 1 *SO*.
Essendine to: Stamford - 11, 12 SO, 2 SuO; Bourne - 7, 8 ThO, 9 SO. **Grantham** to: Skegness - 3; Boston - 3, 4 SO; Lincoln - 5, 6 MO, 7 SO; Derby Friargate - 7, 8 SO; Nottingham Victoria - 7, 8 SO, 2 SuO; Pinxton *via Nottingham*, 2; Leicester Belgrave Rd. *via Melton Mowbray* - 5. **Newark** to: Nottingham Victoria - 3. **Via Retford**[14]:- Harwich Parkeston Quay *via Lincoln and March* to Liverpool Central *via Sheffield Victoria and Manchester Central* - 1; Yarmouth Vauxhall/Lowestoft Central *via March and Lincoln* to Liverpool Central *via Manchester Central* - 1 SuO. Cleethorpes *via Worksop* to: Leicester Central - 1; Sheffield Victoria - 1, 2 SuO; Manchester London Road or Central - 3; Skegness *via Lincoln and Worksop* to: Sheffield Victoria - 1, 1 SuO; Lincoln *via Worksop* to: Sheffield Victoria - 3, 2 SuO. **Retford** to: Lincoln - 3, 4 SO; Sheffield Victoria - 4.
Doncaster to: March - 2, 1 SuO; Spalding, *via Sleaford* - 1; Spalding *via Boston* - 1, 1 SuO (Boston only); Lincoln - 3, 4 SO; Cleethorpes - 3, 1 *SuO*; Barnetby - 1 *SO*, 1 SuO; Sheffield Victoria - 4, 1 SuO; Sheffield LMS[15] - 3; Penistone *via Barnsley*, 2, 1 SuO; Barnsley Court House, 1 *SO*; Leeds Central - 9, 11 SO (1 daily through from Sheffield Victoria); Hull - 4, 3 MO, 1 SuO. LMSR trains *via Knottingley* to Wakefield Kirkgate - 9 (1 to Knottingley only). **Via Doncaster (GC line)**[16]:- Sheffield Victoria to Cleethorpes - 3, 1 SuO *via Chapeltown*; Penistone *via Barnsley Court House* to Cleethorpes - 1; Barnsley Court House to Cleethorpes - 1 *SuO*; Manchester London Rd. to Hull - 1; Sheffield Victoria to Hull - 4, 3 SuO; Liverpool Central to Hull - 3; Swansea High St. *via Gloucester, Banbury and Sheffield Victoria*[17] to Hull[18] - 1; Penistone to Hull - 1.
Selby to: Bridlington - 4; Brough - 1; Hull - 1; Goole - 5; Church Fenton - 4; Micklefield - 1; Leeds City - 4; Normanton - 1 SuO. **Via Selby**[19]:- Leeds City to Bridlington - 3, 1 SuO[20]; Deepcar *via Sheffield Victoria and Swinton*[21] to Bridlington - 1 SuO; Leeds City to Hull - 7, 8 SO, 5 SuO; Sheffield LMS to Hull [LMS] - 1, 1 SuO; Bradford Forster Sq. to Hull - 1; Liverpool Lime St. to Hull - 2; Pontefract Baghill to Hull - 1; Normanton to Hull - 1; Church Fenton to Hull - 2.
York to: Bridlington *via Market Weighton* - 1, 2 SO, 2 SuO; Hull *via Market Weighton* - 8; Scarborough - 5, 6 FO, 8 SO, 4 SuO; Whitby Town - 1, 2 SO, 1 SuO; Harrogate - 10, 11WO, 12 SO, 6 SuO; Leeds City - 19, 21 SO, 8 SuO; Normanton - 1, 2 SuO; Church Fenton - 1 WO, 1 SO; **Selby** *via Church Fenton* - 1 SuO; Pickering - 4; Sheffield Victoria - 1 MX, 2 SuO. **Via York**:- Leeds City to Scarborough - 7, 10 SO, 3 SuO; Leeds City to Whitby Town - 2 Sheffield Victoria to Scarborough - 1 SO. Deepcar *via Sheffield Victoria* to Scarborough - 1 SuO; Leeds City and Sheffield Victoria to **Edinburgh** and Glasgow Queen St. - 1; Leeds City to **Newcastle** - 1, 1 SuO; Sheffield Victoria to **Newcastle**, 1 SuO; Scarborough to **Newcastle** - 1. LMSR trains:- **York** to: Sheffield LMS - 5, 4 SO; Bristol Temple Meads - 1, 2 FO; Worcester Shrub Hill - 1; Birmingham New St. - 1, 2 SO; Manchester Victoria - 3; Liverpool Exchange - 1; Wakefield Kirkgate - 1; Normanton - 2, 3 SO Bradford Forster Sq. *via York* to Scarborough - 2 *SO*; Manchester Victoria *via York* to Scarborough - 1; Liverpool (Exchange, Lime St.) *via York* to **Newcastle** - 1 each..

Alne to: Easingwold (Easingwold Railway) - 6, 7 SO. **Pilmoor** to: Harrogate - 2, 4 SO. **Thirsk** *via Melmerby* to: Harrogate - 1, 1 SuO. Leeds City *via Thirsk* to **Northallerton** - 3 *SuO*; **Northallerton**[23] to: Stockton/West Hartlepool - 3, 4 SO; Leyburn - 1 *SX*; Hawes - 1, 2 SO; Garsdale - 3. **Via Northallerton**[24]: Leeds City *via Thirsk* to **Darlington** - 1; Leeds City *via Wetherby and Pickhill* to **Darlington** - 1; Leeds City *via Ripon* to Stockton - 3; Leeds City *via Harrogate and Pickhill* to West Hartlepool - 2; Ripon to **Northallerton** *via Thirsk* - 1; Harrogate **via Thirsk** to **Darlington** - 1; Leeds City *via Harrogate and Thirsk* to **Northallerton** - 2; Leeds City *via Ripon and Pickhill* to Sunderland *via Stockton* - 1; Bradford Forster Sq. *via Ripon* to **Newcastle** - 1; Liverpool Lime St. *via Harrogate* to **Newcastle** via West Hartlepool - 2 (1 *via Wetherby*). Liverpool Exchange *via Leeds and Harrogate* to **Newcastle** via *Darlington* - 1.
Darlington to: Richmond - 9, 11 SO, 7 SuO; Saltburn - 35, 26 SuO (including one each through from Wearhead, Barnard Castle, Tow Law, and Crook); Scarborough *via Saltburn* - 1 *SuO*; Barnard Castle - 1 SO, 1 SuO; Penrith - 4, 2 SuO (one through from Sunderland, one from Saltburn); Kirkby Stephen - 3, 4 SO; Middleton-in-Teesdale - 2, 1 SO, 4 SuO (one through from Saltburn); Etherley - 1 SO; Crook - 3, 4 SuO (2 through from Saltburn); Tow Law - 5, 6 SO, 1 SuO; Wearhead - 4, 5 SO, 2 SuO (one through from Saltburn); Bishop Auckland - 3, 2 SuO. **Ferryhill** to: Bishop Auckland - 6, 7 SO, 2 (1 to Willington) SuO; Stockton - 6, 8 SO, 1 SuO (to Redcar); West Hartlepool - 9, 10 SO, 3 SuO (1 through to Redcar); Felling - 1 *SO*. **Durham** to: Sunderland - 11, 12 SO, 6 SuO (2 to South Shields); **Newcastle** *via Felling* - 2 *SO*; **Gateshead** *via Felling* - 1 *SX*; Felling - 1 *SO*; Middleton-in-Teesdale - 3; Bishop Auckland - 4; Barnard Castle - 1 *SO*; Waterhouses - 2, 1 SuO. Bishop Auckland: *via Durham* to **Newcastle** - 4, 5 SO, 3 SuO; Sunderland - 7, 5 SuO.
Newcastle Central to: Sunderland - 19, 20 SO, 4 SuO; Seaham Harbour - 1, 12 SuO; West Hartlepool - 1 *SuO*; Middlesbrough - 11, 4 SuO; Redcar - 1 SuO; Haverton Hill - 1; *via West Hartlepool* to: Leeds *via York* - 1; York - 1; Liverpool Lime St. *via Harrogate and Leeds* - 2; **King's Cross** *via York* - 1, 1 SuO; Leeds *via Harrogate* - 1; *via Scotswood* to: Blackhill - 11, 18 SO, 2 SuO; *via Birtley* to: Blackhill - 10, 14 SO, 2 SuO; *via Leamside* to: **Ferryhill** - 3 (1 through to Saltburn), 1 SuO (through to **York**); Leamside - 1, 2 SO; Carlisle - 14, 21 SO (1 to Silloth), 7 SuO (one each to Blackpool North and Keswick); *via Carlisle* to: Stranraer Harbour - 1; *via Prudhoe* to Hexham - 19, 20 ThO, 21 SO, 5 SuO; Haltwhistle - 1 SuO; Prudhoe - 2 *SX*; Wylam - 1 *SX*; Blaydon - 1, 2 ThO, 3 SO; North Wylam - 31, 33 SO, 12 SuO; *via Hexham* to: Riccarton Junction - 1; Hawick - 1; Reedsmouth - 1 (to Hawick on *SO*); **Morpeth** *via Newbiggin* - 1; Backworth - 1; Newbiggin *via Benton* - 3 *SuO*. (Also 17 (7 on SuO, one through to **Morpeth**) trains ran from **Manors North** to Newbiggin). **Morpeth** to: Rothbury - 4 (including 2 through from **Newcastle**), 1 SuO. **Alnmouth** to: Alnwick - 12, 15 SO (including 3 (4 SO) through from **Newcastle**), 13 SuO. **Chathill** to: Seahouses (North Sunderland Railway) - 4, 5 WSO, 4 SuO.
Berwick-upon-Tweed to: Coldstream - 1; Kelso - 4, 5 SO; Eyemouth - 5, 6 SO. **Burnmouth** to: Eyemouth - 3. **Reston** to: St. Boswells - 4 (3 through from Berwick); Duns - 1 *SO*. **Drem** to: North Berwick - 18, 17 ThO, 18 SO (14 through from **Edinburgh Waverley**, and 1 *SO* from Glasgow Queen St.).
Longniddry to: Haddington - 13[25], 14 ThO, 15 SO.

Trains for the Edinburgh Suburbs and the Waverley Route from the East End of Waverley Station. (Equivalent trains entered from the east).
Carlisle - 2; Bristol - 1; St. Pancras - 2, 1 SuO; Hawick - 3, 5 SO, 2 SuO; Kelso - 3, 4 MSO; Gorebridge - 2, 3 WO, 8 SO; **Newcastle** *via Kelso* - 1 SuO.
Dunbar - 2, 1 SuO; North Berwick *via* **Drem** - 9, 10 ThO, 11 SO (1 through from Glasgow); Galashiels *via Peebles* - 5, 6 SO; Polton - 6; Rosewell & Hawthornden - 1 *SO*; Penicuick - 5, 7 SO; Dalkeith - 4, 5 SO; Leith Central - 25 (1 through from Glasgow), 20 SO; Musselburgh - 33, 28 SO; North Leith - 11, 9 SO.

SEASONAL CROSS-COUNTRY TRAINS, RUNNING ON THE ECML OR THROUGH ITS MAJOR CENTRES
(Equivalent trains ran in the reverse direction. Many of the Summer *FO* and *SO* trains featured some interesting routes and nominally non-stop runs. Seasonal trains run on *Sundays* are incorporated in those listed in the previous sections).

Mondays Only
Heeley, *via Sheffield LMS, Pontefract Baghill,* **Selby**, *and Bridlington,* to Scarborough

Fridays Only

Harwich Parkeston Quay to **York**, *via Ipswich, March, Lincoln,* **Doncaster**, *and Knottingley* - also on Mondays.

Liverpool Central *via Sheffield Victoria,* **Doncaster** *and* **York** to Scarborough[26].

Liverpool Central *via Sheffield Victoria,* **Doncaster**, *Lincoln, and March,* to Yarmouth Vauxhall and Lowestoft Central.

Saturdays Only.

Via Retford[27]**:** Cambridge to Manchester Central *via March, Lincoln, and Sheffield Victoria.* Liverpool Central *via Manchester Central, Sheffield Victoria, Lincoln, and March,* to Yarmouth Vauxhall and Lowestoft Central - also ran on *Fridays.* Manchester Central *via Guide Bridge and Sheffield Victoria* to Skegness, and to Sutton-on-Sea and Mablethorpe *via Lincoln* (1 each). Manchester London Rd. *via Sheffield Victoria, Lincoln, March, and Ipswich* to Clacton-on-Sea. Manchester Central *via Sheffield Victoria* to Norwich and Yarmouth Vauxhall *via Lincoln and March.* Manchester London Rd. *via Sheffield Victoria and Barnetby* to Cleethorpes. Leicester Central *via Nottingham Victoria,* also Nottingham Victoria (1 each) *via Mansfield Central,* **Tuxford, Retford, Doncaster, and Selby,** to Bridlington, Filey, and Scarborough.

Doncaster *via Sheffield Victoria* to Liverpool Central and *via Gateacre* to Southport Lord St. **Via Doncaster (GC line)**[28]**:-** Barnsley Court House, also Deepcar *via Sheffield Victoria* (1 each) to Cleethorpes. Sheffield Victoria *via* **Selby** to Bridlington. Sheffield Victoria *via* **York** to Scarborough. Bradford Exchange and Leeds Central *via Lincoln* to Skegness (2 trains)[29], also (1 train) to Mablethorpe. Penistone *via Barnsley Court House,* to Skegness *via Grimsby.* Bradford Exchange and Leeds Central *via Scunthorpe* to Cleethorpes. Stockport Tiviot Dale *via Godley Junction,* also Manchester London Rd. (1 each) *via Sheffield Victoria and* **York** to Scarborough. Liverpool Central *via Manchester Central, Sheffield Victoria and* **York**, to Scarborough. Liverpool Central *via Stockport Tiviot Dale,* also Manchester London Rd. (1 each) to Bridlington and Filey *via* **Selby.** Leeds Central to Norwich and Yarmouth Vauxhall *via Lincoln and March.*

Via Selby:- Bradford Forster Sq. and Leeds City to Bridlington. Bradford Exchange *via Wakefield and Castleford* to Bridlington. Leeds City to Bridlington (*3*). Low Moor to Bridlington, Filey, and Scarborough. Leicester London Rd., Derby LMS, and Chesterfield LMS (1 each) *via Sheffield LMS and Pontefract Baghill* to Bridlington, Filey, and Scarborough. Blackburn *via Normanton* to Bridlington, Filey, and Scarborough. **York** to Bridlington, also *via Bridlington* (1 each) to Scarborough.

York to: Scarborough, direct (*4*); Whitby Town; Harwich Town *via* **Doncaster**, *Lincoln, March, and Ipswich* - also *MFO;* **Edinburgh** and Glasgow Queen St. (2); *via* **Northallerton** to Redcar East; Manchester Victoria (2); Birmingham New St. *via Sheffield LMS.* **Via York:-** Liverpool Lime St. *via Manchester Exchange and Leeds City* to **Newcastle.** Manchester Victoria *via Normanton* to Scarborough (2). Manchester London Rd., also Liverpool Central/Manchester Central *via Guide Bridge and Sheffield Victoria,* also Sheffield Victoria (1 each) *via Pontefract Baghill* to Scarborough. Birmingham New St., and Derby LMS (1 each) *via Sheffield LMS and Pontefract Baghill* to Scarborough. Southampton Terminus *via Newbury, Oxford, Banbury and Sheffield Victoria* to Scarborough. **Newcastle** to Scarborough (2). Bradford Forster Sq. and Leeds City to Scarborough (2). Leeds City to Scarborough (4). Leeds City to Whitby Town. Scarborough to Heeley *via Sheffield LMS*[30].

Via Pilmoor:- Glasgow Queen St. and **Edinburgh** *via Malton* to Scarborough (2). **Via Northallerton:-** Sunderland *via Stockton, Harrogate and Leeds City* to Manchester Exchange (2). **Via Durham:-** Liverpool Exchange and Blackpool Central *via Preston, Tebay, Kirkby Stephen and Bishop Auckland* to Sunderland.

Newcastle:- *via* **Doncaster**, *Lincoln, and March* to Lowestoft Central and Yarmouth Vauxhall. *Via* **Durham**, *Bishop Auckland, Kirkby Stephen, Tebay and Preston* to Blackpool North and Southport Chapel St. *Via* **York**, *Normanton, and Manchester Victoria* to Liverpool Exchange and Blackpool Central. *Via* **York** *and Sheffield LMS* to Derby LMS. *Via* **York**, *Sheffield LMS, Birmingham New St., and Bristol Temple Meads* to Paignton. *Via* **Edinburgh** to Glasgow Queen St.

Notes:-

1. Except in the case of Edinburgh, where *all* trains calling there are given, the numbers of trains terminating at intermediate points, such as Newcastle, are *in addition* to those going further.

2. In the reverse direction the train ran *via Selby*, and there were through carriages

(*SX*) from Glasgow Queen St. to Harwich (471 m in 747 min).

3. On Sundays, terminated at Doncaster.

4. Combined part of the way with a Bradford - Newcastle train.

5. This curious service from Southampton was noteworthy not only in running by the Didcot, Newbury and Winchester line, but also by using the 'normal' route *via* Reading West and Basingstoke in the other direction. Moreover the southbound service terminated at *Basingstoke*, only passengers for Cross-Channel steamers being conveyed - to Southampton Docks - beyond there. There was also a train, overnight on Saturday/Sunday to Bristol from Newcastle *via* Sheffield Victoria, Banbury and Oxford - but no corresponding Down service.

6. On SO commenced at Leeds City. On SX the Southampton - Glasgow and Scarborough - Glasgow trains were combined from York.

7. The Swansea and Bristol trains for Newcastle were combined at York (SX). In the reverse direction, the Swansea train ran *via Barry.*

8. The Bournemouth and Bristol trains combined at York (SX) with the 16.00 from King's Cross, entailing waits at York of *47 and 30 mins* respectively.

9. 'ABERDEEN - PENZANCE' service. Ran through to Penzance - from *Aberdeen* - in the *other* direction.

10. This was the King's Cross - Egginton Junction milk empties, which conveyed passengers part of the way.

11. Two to Dunstable LMS on weekdays and 5 to Dunstable Town on Sundays were through from King;s Cross.

12. LMSR trains.

13. LMSR trains.

14. Westbound trains; equivalent trains ran eastbound. GC trains *not calling* at Retford not listed here. For seasonal *SO* trains running on the GC through Retford, see below. Sundays only trains also included one each Wadsley Bridge to Firsby and Spalding and one Deepcar to Skegness (both *via Sheffield Victoria*) and return workings.

15. LMSR trains

16. Northbound; eastbound on GC line. Equivalent trains ran in the opposite direction.

17. Coaches attached at Sheffield to Liverpool - Hull express.

18. Conveyed in Swansea - Newcastle train as far as Doncaster.

19. Eastbound trains only; equivalent trains ran westbound.

20. Did not stop at Selby.

21. Not stopping at Selby.

22. *LMS* LMS workings.

23. Down trains given only.

24. Down trains given only.

25. One through from Edinburgh Waverley, *FO.*

26. Many of the summer seasonal trains to Scarborough used the Londesborough Road platforms near the Central station.

27. Trains also ran from Leicester Central and from Nottingham Victoria to Cleethorpes, *via Mansfield, Ollerton and Lincoln,* crossing the ECML at Dukeries Junction. A number of *SO* trains ran through Retford without stopping, by taking the 'straight line' over the Crossing.

28. Some trains not booked to stop at Doncaster used the Hexthorpe Junction - Bentley Junction avoiding line, or in the case of trains from the Leeds direction to Lincolnshire, the Adwick Junction - Applehurst Junction loop.

29. Either *via Grimsby,* or *via* **Doncaster** *and Lincoln,* but in the reverse direction one train called at **Newark**, so ran down the ECML from **Barkston North Junction**.

30. This train did not run in reverse direction.

57

coach from famed Bourton-on-the-Water to (say) Northallerton - *and* back. However, even more odd were the through coaches from Southampton (Terminus, for Docks) to Glasgow Queen Street - also Scarborough on Saturdays Only. These started out on a stopping train up the bucolic Didcot, Newbury & Southampton line, so it was possible for someone to climb into a carriage at Churn in the remote and isolated Berkshire Downs and not get out until he reached Lenzie Junction - for example. But the *return* journey could not be undertaken without a large number of changes, including crossing London, and anyway the southbound through coaches from Glasgow terminated at Basingstoke and conveyed Southampton passengers only if they were catching a Cross-Channel boat. In any case, anybody misguided enough to try to travel from Glasgow to Southampton by this service would be subjected to a wait in the train of nearly an hour at York on the way; it was quicker to go *via* London.

The through services using the ECML in parts on Summer Saturdays embraced a further extensive variety of through coaches and routes, as can be seen from Table 4.1. (Corresponding - but not necessarily identical - trains or through coaches were of course run in the opposite direction, and in the discussions and listings in the rest of this book this is tacitly implied). Many of these extra trains were third-class only and had no restaurant (or refreshment) car, particularly after the war.

There were regular, publicized Boat Trains on the ECML, notably the expresses from King's Cross to Newcastle Tyne Commission Quay - the *NORSEMAN*. These trains ran in connection with the steamship services of the B & N Line to Stavanger and Bergen, those of the Fred Olsen Line to Oslo and of Swedish Lloyd to Gothenburg. The several Continental services from Hull on the other hand were provided with Boat Trains as needed, rather as the SR serviced the Channel crossings. (Parenthetically, it should be recalled that in Summer 1939 you could go from London to Newcastle, Dundee or Aberdeen by perhaps a more relaxing mode even than the ECML - on regular twice-weekly services *by sea*).

You could also, for £20 (£500 in today's money), go for a week on the 'Land-Cruise' train, the *NORTHERN BELLE*. This first-class-only luxury train did trips in June (two in 1939) from King's Cross to the North of England and Scotland. Customers lived on the train, with the best shower-bath sleepers, hair-dressing saloon and even a 'wardrobe van', and of course the choicest food and wine. The varied itinerary included daytime coach and steamer trips, as well as covering such lines as the West Highland to Mallaig. (For the 'mountainous' stretches the train was divided into two parts, on account of the weight of the sleeping-cars). For humbler folk, there were the Camping Coaches, located at wayside stations near the sea or in the Dales; some of these were *movable* and set off from York on a week's tour of beauty spots. The LNER even offered 'Self-Catering Apartments' in closed stations, *e.g.* Castle Howard, Akeld, and Kirknewton.

The regular express services on the ECML were supplemented in peacetime by a host of special trains for public use, the timings of which were not given in the normal timetables but were provided in handbills and on posters. In addition to these - mostly run on Summer Saturdays only, the railways ran a large number of relief trains at times of heavy traffic - especially at Christmas and Easter - for passengers paying standard fares, as extra parts of regular trains to usual destinations. A few were regular from the operating point of view - designated 'Q' for 'when required' in the Working Timetables (WTT)[2]. The majority of reliefs were arranged at relatively short notice, and their details were set out only in Special Traffic Notices (STNs) provided for the staff.

Another category of (public) special trains were the Excursions, for passengers to be conveyed at greatly reduced fares, singly or as parties, the last often in chartered whole trains. The Excursions could be Period, Day, Half-Day or Evening Excursions, or there were also overnight trains at cheap fares such as the specials from London to Newcastle and Scotland. The Excursion trains (*see also* Appendix C) comprised firstly quite regular trains, often on Sundays, to major 'normal' destinations, but also to seaside resorts. (Many more of these trains were scheduled in 1939 than after the war). The most numerous Excursion trains were those that ran - again especially on Sundays - to seaside resorts, beauty spots, or to popular venues like Belle Vue Zoo at Manchester. (The takings on these depended very

From	To	Vehicles in order from Engine.	Class	Weight Tons.	Seats 1st.	Seats 3rd.	DOWN WORKING
		30					
		"THE HIGHLANDMAN"					
7.25 p.m. from King's Cross.		Saturdays and Sundays excepted.					
King's Cross	Inverness A (via Carr Bridge) (arr. 8.45 a.m.)	Brake Van		141	29		4.40 p.m. from Inverness. 9.35 p.m. from Perth and 11.17 p.m. from Edinburgh.
		Convertible Third }		1241	35	28 berths or 42 seats	
		First Class Sleeping Car }		1673	43	10 berths	
	Inverness (via Forres) (arr. 10.38 a.m.)	Compo		1066	34	15 berths	30
		Sleeping Compo E		1088	37	6 berths	8 berths or 12 seats
		Brake Compo E (South End)		1083	34	12	12	See E Note.
	Perth (arr. 4.56 a.m.)	Brake Van		153	27		Locally 2.5 p.m. Perth to Edinburgh 10.30 p.m. from Edinburgh.
	Glasgow (arr. 5.29 a.m.)	Brake Van C		153	27		2.25 a.m. from Glasgow. 4.15 a.m. from Edinburgh 4.20 a.m. from St. Boswells. 12.7 p.m. from Berwick 7.52 p.m. from York.
	Fort William (arr. 9.22 a.m.)	First Class C Sleeping Car }		1673	43	10 berths	5.10 p.m. from Fort William 11.17 p.m. from Edinburgh.
		Convertible Third C }		1241	35	28 berths or 42 seats	
		Brake Compo B (South End)		1083	34	12	12	
	York (arr. 11.6 p.m.)	Rest. Car	G.N. 42782	43	30 (unclassed)		3.0 a.m. from York Tues. to Sats. (Ety.)
	Edinburgh (arr. 3.35 a.m.)	Brake Van		141	29		10.30 p.m. from Edinburgh.
		Brake Van C		163	31		7.50 p.m. from Edinburgh.
	Leaving King's Cross				481	65	150	

All vehicles must be fitted with vestibule at each end. **A** When Inverness via Carr Bridge portion exceeds 4 vehicles rear vehicle must be Brake Third or Brake Compo. When Carr Bridge portion is run separate from Forres portion Perth brake Van should work rear of front portion. **B** Gangway to be kept clear for passengers using Restaurant Car between Cowlairs and Fort William. **C** Formed in 7.33 p.m. when run. **E** Empty by 3.20 p.m. from Inverness to Perth. Loaded 9.35 p.m. from Perth and attached to 11.17 p.m. from Edinburgh July 4th to Aug. 12th. From Aug. 14th works from Inverness, departing 3.20 p.m.

Extract from LNER Carriage Workings (1939)

much on the weather, but the NE Region of BR - with public spirit - displayed the Weather Forecast on blackboards at stations such as York and Newcastle). Then, there were the numerous Excursions run to take the crowds to major Events: to soccer and Rugby football matches, culminating in the Cup Finals in London; to horse-race meetings - Newmarket, Doncaster, York, Thirsk, Catterick, Sedgefield, Stockton, and Gosforth Park (Newcastle), producing much traffic of this kind for the ECML. Finally, there were special trains, often chartered, for a variety of other events and occasions, from the Eclipse of the Sun to the Coronation. Lastly, in 1939 even before the war broke out, the railways were called upon to provide a number of military specials; naturally, these were *not* advertised at all.

Many of the Excursions and other special trains ran from unfamiliar stations - even in some cases originating at places such as collieries or factories where there was no normal passenger station. There were a great number of combinations of routes taken by special traffic on the railway network, many of which were followed throughout the year by freight trains. Their use served to widen the experience of train crews, and came to be especially useful in the war, when strange routes and destinations naturally figured very much in the case of military specials. In regard to the ECML, the various routes to Scarborough serve to exemplify the complexities. From the north, trains could run either from Pilmoor *via* Gilling (with double reversal at Malton), or *via* York (with one reversal). From the west the usual route was *via* Leeds and York, but trains from places such as Blackburn or Burnley might come over the Pennines to Skipton and reach York *via* Ilkley and Harrogate. From the south, apart from taking the direct route from York *via* Malton, many trains ran *via* Bridlington, following the routes of trains that terminated there. They came principally through Selby, Selby in turn being reached from Doncaster or from Gascoigne Wood Junction on the line from Leeds. Trains from the Sheffield direction reached Gascoigne Wood Junction by the loop off the Swinton & Knottingley Joint line at Milford Junction - and the S&K led at Dearne Junction from the GC system, either from the west *via* Wath or from the south *via* Mexborough; again, at Burton Salmon on the S&K, trains came from West Yorkshire *via* Lofthouse and Castleford or off the L&Y *via* Wakefield and Normanton.

Nevertheless, even when one recognizes that before the war only a small minority had their own cars, the *regular* passenger

services provided by the Railway Companies - here exemplified by the LNER's ECML, for either short- or long-distance journeys seem very inadequate by the standards of mobility we have come to expect in recent decades. The long-distance trains may have been as comfortable as today - and of course infinitely *safer* than travelling by road, but how sparse were the services! On Sundays, the sole day when most people were free to travel any distance, they were quite exasperatingly insufficient. In the 1950s they were scarcely any different, British Railways signally failing to confront the advance of private transport by providing services - even on the electrified lines of the South-East, that would encourage people to use the train for their leisuretime needs; rather, they gave up and *withdrew* most of such services. Seen the other way round, the cessation on most lines of local services after about 9.00 in the evening - even on Saturdays, and their total absence on Sundays, reflects the Way of Life of the Working Man and his family which existed in the 1930s and still to a great extent prevailed in the 1950s. Perhaps it was the eventual ready availability of the private car, then of *free* motorways, which so radically altered that Way of Life.

If we take Doncaster as an example on the ECML of a major Working Man's town, the last stopping trains - alike in 1939 and 1955 - on any of the six lines radiating from the Central station left well before the pubs or the cinemas closed - even on Saturdays, and it was much the same at York, Darlington, Newcastle or Edinburgh. We know that bus services were very little better, and the conclusion once again is that people were much less mobile than they are today. Fundamentally, they could not afford much more mobility in those days, and they had to stay at home - before the war without even Television, or go to the *local* pub or cinema.

WORLD WAR TWO

The August 1939 timetable - reflecting the days of peace, and seeming to deny that the most terrible war in history was about to burst on the world - was adhered to until 10th September. Thus a final Summer Saturday service remained on 2nd and 9th September - for holiday-makers and others to get home,

An extraordinary sight even for those extraordinary days: GWR diesel railcar No.19 running trials at Blackhill near Consett, 25th April 1944. Note the tablet-catcher beside the signalbox. *Hoole coll.*

except that many trains from London and other large cities were cancelled during the period 1st to 4th September for the Evacuation trains. Nevertheless, a major feature of the timetable plans for the outbreak of war, affecting the ECML as much as any other line, was the programme of evacuation of children from London and other major industrial cities, planned many months in advance. It was put into effect on 1st September and completed during the ensuing three days, very extensive cancellation even of freight services being required to furnish the crews and locomotives needed. (The REC must also be admired for the detailed and quite explicit plans and instructions that they drew up, from May 1940, for the action to be taken by Railway staff, including immobilization of locomotives, demolitions and the evacuation of non-essential civilians, 'In the Event of a German Invasion').

Providing you

TRAVEL ONLY WHEN YOU MUST

it doesn't matter how you say

IS *your journey really necessary?*

★

is **YOUR** *journey really necessary?*

★

is your **JOURNEY** *really necessary?*

★

is your journey **REALLY** *necessary?*

★

is your journey really **NECESSARY?**

★

RAILWAY EXECUTIVE COMMITTEE

From London a staggering *1,577* Evacuation specials were run, of which about 120 ran down the ECML, albeit mainly for relatively short distances - no further than Peterborough and Spalding. Because it was feared that main-line termini might be bombed, a lot of the children were entrained at suburban stations (Bowes Park or New Barnet for the ECML), to which they were taken by bus from the nearest Tube station. In addition, in the first ten days of the war a similar number of LNER special trains took Evacuees from Tyneside, Sunderland and Tees-side - again mainly not for any distance along the ECML, and from Leeds and Hull. Overall the ECML was heavily involved in this great operation[3]. In July 1940, when there was a real threat of a

German invasion, and again in 1941, further programmes of evacuation of children were carried out from the North-East industrial area and from certain coastal towns in East Anglia and Kent. Then in July - August 1944 during the V1 offensive, 1,400 officially sponsored special trains were run from London to evacuate children and also hospital patients, while many more special trains were put on during this period by the District Officers to carry away the large numbers of 'self-evacuees' - people who on their own wanted to get away from the Flying Bomb menace, and a certain number of these Evacuation trains ran down the ECML. Special trains were run on Sundays for relatives to visit the evacuees, travelling at concessionary fares, but nearly all the evacuees had drifted back to the big cities by the end of the war, and for the Return of Evacuees only a mere 115 trains were needed for the whole of London.

The services on the ECML, like the other main line services all over the country, were savagely cut by half and decelerated in the emergency timetables first brought into operation on 11th September 1939. The train frequencies approximated to those of a Sunday service - and at an average speed of 45 m.p.h. Indeed in the ECML emergency timetable of 2nd October the Sunday service was now for once *the same* as on weekdays - an excellent principle that was normal practice on the Continent but has never prevailed in Britain. Just one day and one night train was provided to Edinburgh (9hr. 45min.), two day and two night trains to Newcastle, one day train to Leeds and York (combined to Doncaster), and one overnight train to Aberdeen (14hr.).

All reduced fare facilities were withdrawn[4] at first, as were seat reservations and restaurant cars - and ECML 'expresses' reverted briefly to the practice of mid-Victorian times of making stops of about 20 minutes at Peterborough or Grantham for people to rush out and get some food. Peacetime through services to coastal resorts were almost completely eliminated, and these remained served only by a residuum of connecting trains. Swingeing reductions were also made in local and branch line services. However, the dire air-raids, gas attacks and the rest that were expected did not happen. It was realized almost immediately that the cuts had been rather overdone, and as early as 16th October on the LNER many trains and restaurant cars were reinstated, while the limit for average speeds was set at a more acceptable 50 m.p.h. On 4th December a more adequate train service in terms of both frequency and speed was re-introduced. However, sleeping-car accommodation was severely restricted and from 1942 drastic cuts were again made in restaurant cars.

On the introduction of the great programme of Convoy coal trains on the ECML in February 1940, severe cuts in express services had to be made again. Still, by the summer of 1943 and after representations to the REC from C.H.Newton, some improvements of passenger services were allowed for a while,

---

Notes on Table 4.2 opposite:-

1. Including the Aberdeen service.
2. One was fast to Morpeth and Acklington.
3. LMSR trains.
4. LMSR trains.
5. Westbound trains only; equivalent trains ran eastbound.
6. Equivalent trains ran in the opposite direction.
7. Eastbound trains only; equivalent trains ran westbound.
8. Down trains only.
9. Also shown above as Main Line Stopping train.

TABLE 4.2: SUMMARY OF PASSENGER SERVICES ON THE ECML
AND CONNECTING LINES, SUMMER 1942

This Table is drawn on the same basis as Table 4.1, and allows comparison of the summer services in the middle of the war with those in the last pre-war summer.

In general, the trains ran Monday - Saturday all the year round, and there were no advertised seasonal trains. Unlike in peacetime, all trains to Scotland stopped not only at York and Newcastle, but also made other stops, such as at Peterborough, Grantham, Doncaster, York, Darlington, and Durham, and there were a number of other trains which stopped as well at places such as Newark, Retford, Selby, and Northallerton.

Main Line departures from King's Cross:- Edinburgh Waverley[1] (393m) - 5 (525 min), 5 SuO; **via Edinburgh:** Aberdeen (524m) - 1 (792 min); **Newcastle** (269m) - 4 (370 min), 2 SuO; **York** (188m) - 1 (325 min); **via Doncaster:** Leeds Central/Bradford Exchange (186/193m) - 7 (259/275 min), 6 SO, 1 SuO; Harrogate (203m) - 1 (332 min). **Doncaster** (156m) (228 min) *SuO;* **via Peterborough North:** Cleethorpes (158m) - 1 (281 min).

Cambridge Line Trains, *via Hitchin.* King's Cross to: Letchworth - 1, 1 SuO; Baldock - 2; Royston - 3, 2 SO, 2 SuO; Cambridge (58m) - 11 (113 min), 5 SuO.

Regular trains running over part of the ECML north of Peterborough
Colchester *via Ipswich, March, Lincoln, and Doncaster* to York (216m) - 1 (380 min). Colchester *via Ipswich, March and* **Peterborough North** to: Leeds Central (208m) - 1 (421 min); **Edinburgh Waverley** (415m) - 1 (745 min), 1 SuO. Ashford *via Tonbridge, Redhill, Guildford, Reading, Oxford, Banbury, Sheffield Victoria and York* (387m) - 1 (720 min). **York** to:- **Newcastle** *via* **Durham** (81m) - 2 (125 min) (one *via Stockton*), 4 SuO (one *via Stockton*); **Newcastle** *via* **Northallerton, Stockton and Sunderland** (90m) - 1 (200 min), 1 SuO; *via* **Edinburgh** to Glasgow Queen St. (253m) - 1 (390 min); **Edinburgh Waverley** (205m) - 1 (330 min); Liverpool Lime St. *via Leeds City, Harrogate, Northallerton and Durham* (172m) to Newcastle - 1 (314 min), 1 SuO. Leeds City *via York and Durham* (106m) to **Newcastle** - 1 (195 min). Leeds City *via Harrogate and Thirsk* to Darlington (61m) - 1 (142 min) *SuO.* **Darlington** to: Newcastle (37m) - 1 (73 min); **Edinburgh Waverley** (161m) - 1 (252 min). **Newcastle** to Edinburgh Waverley (125m) - 1 (188 min).

Main Line Stopping Trains - not necessarily stopping at *all* station. (No Sunday trains, unless stated). **King's Cross** to: Peterborough North - 3, 4 SO, 2 SuO; Grantham - 2, 1 SuO. **Finsbury Park** to Doncaster - 1, 1 SuO (to Grantham only). **Hitchin** to Sandy - 1. **Peterborough** to Grantham - 1, 1 SuO. **Grantham** to Doncaster - 1, 1 SuO. **Doncaster** to York - 2, 1 SuO. Doncaster *via Selby* to Hull - 1. **Selby** to York - 3, 1 SuO (non-stop). **York** to:- Newcastle - 1, 1 SuO; Darlington - 1. Leeds City *via Harrogate and Thirsk* to **Northallerton** - 2, 1 SuO. **Darlington** to Newcastle - 1. **Durham** to Newcastle - 6, 8 SO. **Newcastle** to:- Berwick-on-Tweed - 2[2], 3 SuO; **Alnmouth** and Alnwick - 1. **Manors North** *via Benton* to:- **Alnmouth** and Alnwick - 3; Morpeth - 1. **Berwick-on-Tweed** to:- **Edinburgh Waverley** - 1, 2 SO; St. Boswells *via Reston* - 3.

London Area Suburban Trains (south of Hitchin), and Newcastle Electric Trains. After the electrification to High Barnet and Mill Hill East in 1940/41, the approximate numbers of suburban trains per day in the London area (Monday - Saturday) amounted to: about 30 Finsbury Park - Alexandra Palace; a similar number King's Cross - New Barnet; in addition about 45 trains per day, starting from King's Cross, terminated further down the main line towards and including Hitchin, many of which continued onto the Cambridge branch (see above). On the Hertford North line there were about 45 trains per day, about half of which terminated intermediately (mainly at Gordon Hill), starting at King's Cross or from Finsbury Park. There were no trains from Moorgate or Broad St. after October 1940, due to war damage. Naturally, the Down rush-hour trains on Saturdays were between 12.00 and 14.00 rather than in the evening. On Sundays, the services were about one-third of those on weekdays, with none to Alexandra Palace.

The Newcastle electric trains comprised about 60 trains per day Mon-Sat on the circle service *via Tynemouth* (not all running right round), about 15 on the Riverside line, and about 45 on the South Shields line. Sundays saw about 17 trains on the Tynemouth circuit and to South Shields, but none on the Riverside line.

Regular Non-ECML Express, Secondary and Branch Trains - *excluding* those **from King's Cross** - that passed through or started from the stations listed:- (Destination stations given are *only* those where a service terminated. Originating stations, if different from the junction station, are stated only where noteworthy. Equivalent trains ran in the reverse direction. **No Sunday services,** unless stated. For trains through from or to other ECML stations, see above).

Hatfield to: St. Albans Abbey - 4, 5 SO; Luton LNER - 1; Dunstable Town - 2 *SuO;* Dunstable LMSR - 5 (one was through from King's Cross); Hertford North - 4, 6 SO. **Hitchin** to: Baldock - 3, 4 SO; Royston - 4; Cambridge - 1 *SuO;* Bedford Midland Road[3] - 4. **Sandy**[4] to: Bletchley - 5, 2 SuO; Cambridge - 6, 2 SuO. **Holme** to: Ramsey North - 3. **Peterborough North** to: Peterborough East - 3, 2 SuO; March - 1; Ely - 2, 2 SuO; Cambridge *via St. Ives* - 1; Boston - 1, 2 SuO; Lincoln *via Spalding and Boston* - 2; Grimsby/Cleethorpes - 4, 2 SuO. M&GN trains:- Yarmouth Beach - 4. <u>Down LMS line trains passing or calling at</u> **Peterborough North:-** Leicester London Rd. - Peterborough East - 5, 2 SuO. **Essendine** to: Stamford - 6; Bourne - 4. **Grantham** to: Boston - 5; Lincoln - 6; Derby Friargate - 7, 2 SuO; Nottingham Victoria - 4, 2 SuO. **Via Retford**[5]**:-** Cleethorpes to Manchester London Rd. - 2; Lincoln to Sheffield Victoria - 2, 1 SuO; Cleethorpes to Sheffield Victoria - 2, 3 SuO. **Retford** to: Lincoln - 2, 1 SuO; Sheffield Victoria - 2, 3 SO, 1 SuO.

Doncaster to: March - 2; Spalding *via Lincoln and Boston* - 1, 1 SuO; Cleethorpes - 5 (plus 1 to Barnetby), 3 SuO; Sheffield Victoria - 3, 2 SuO; Penistone *via Barnsley Court House* - 1, 2 SuO, 2 SuO; Barnsley Court House - 1; Leeds Central - 6; Hull - 7, 2 SuO. **Via Doncaster**[6]**:-** Penistone *via Barnsley Court House* to Cleethorpes - 1. Liverpool Central to Hull - 2, 2 SuO. **Selby** to:- Bridlington - 3; Goole - 6; Leeds City - 2; Sheffield LMS *via Pontefract Baghill* - 1; Normanton - 1, 1 SuO. **Via Selby**[7] **:-** Leeds City to Hull - 8, 9 SO, 4 SuO; Liverpool Lime St. to Hull - 2; Normanton to Hull - 2 *SuO;* **York** to Hull - 1; **Doncaster** to Hull - 1. **York** *via Market Weighton* to Hull - 7. **York** *via Sheffield Victoria, Banbury and Oxford* to Swindon - 1. **York** to: Scarborough - 5, 6 SO, 3 SuO; Harrogate - 7, 8 SO; Leeds City - 13, 14 SO, 5 SuO; Church Fenton - 1; Sheffield Victoria - 1 *SuO.* LMSR trains:- Sheffield LMS - 3, 2 SuO; Bristol Temple Meads - 4; Manchester Victoria - 1; Liverpool Exchange - 2; Normanton - 3, 4 SO, 4 SuO. **Via York:-** Leeds City to Scarborough - 1.

Alne to: Easingwold (Easingwold Railway) - 2, 3 SO. **Pilmoor** to:- Pickering - 2; Harrogate - 2, 4 SO. **Thirsk** to: Melmerby - 1; Leeds City - 1 *SuO.* **Northallerton** to:- Leeds City - 4; Stockton/West Hartlepool - 2; Leyburn - 1; Garsdale - 3. **Via Northallerton**[8] **:-** Liverpool Lime St. to **Newcastle** *via* **Darlington** - 1; Leeds City *via Harrogate and Thirsk* to Stockton - 1; Leeds City *via Harrogate and Pickhill* to Middlesbrough - 1.

Darlington to: Richmond - 10, 9 SuO; Saltburn - 20, 10 SuO; Thornaby - 1 *SuO;* Penrith - 3; Appleby LNE - 1 *SuO;* Middleton-in-Teesdale - 3, 1 SuO; Barnard Castle - 1 *SuO;* Tow Law - 5, 6 SO; Wearhead - 1; Bishop Auckland - 7, 5 SuO; Etherley - 1 *SX.* **Ferryhill** to: Spennymoor - 5; Stockton - 4; West Hartlepool - 3, 4 SO, 1 SuO. **Durham** to: Sunderland - 10, 11 SO; Bishop Auckland - 9, 3 SuO; Waterhouses - 1. **Via Durham:-** Bishop Auckland to **Newcastle** *via Low Fell*[9] - 2, *via Felling* - 1 *SO,* 1 *SuO;* Bishop Auckland to Sunderland - 1, 1 SuO.

Newcastle Central to: Sunderland - 18, 19 SO; *via West Hartlepool, Northallerton, Harrogate and Leeds* to Liverpool (L. St.) - 1; **Middlesbrough** - 11, 12 SO, 4 SuO; West Hartlepool - 1 *SuO;* Pelaw - 1 *SO;* Leamside - 1 *SX; via Leamside* to:- **Durham** - 1; Penshaw - 2; *via Scotswood* to: Blackhill - 5, 6 SO, 1 SuO; Rowlands Gill - 1; Lintz Green - 1 *SX;* North Wylam - 22, 23 SO, 9 SuO; *via Prudhoe* to: Carlisle - 11, 12 SO, 4 SuO; Haltwhistle - 3, 4 SO, 1 SuO; Haydon Bridge - 1 *SX;* Hexham - 10, 13 SO, 4 SuO; *via Hexham* to: Riccarton Junction - 1; Hawick - 1; *via Newbiggin* to: Morpeth - 1. (Also 10 trains ran from **Manors North** to Newbiggin). **Morpeth** to: Rothbury - 2, 3 SO. **Alnmouth** to: Alnwick (including through trains from **Newcastle**, see above) - 14, 8 SuO. **Chathill** to: Seahouses (North Sunderland Railway) - 5. **Berwick-on-Tweed** to: Coldstream - 1; Kelso - 3; Eyemouth - 1 *SO.* **Burnmouth** to: Eyemouth - 7. **Reston** to: St. Boswells - 1; Duns - 1. **Drem** to: North Berwick - 10, 12 SO (including 4 through from Edinburgh). **Longniddry** - Haddington - 9, 11 SO.

Trains for the Edinburgh Suburbs and the Waverley Route from the East End of Waverley Station. (Equivalent trains entered from the east). Carlisle - 3; St. Pancras - 2, 1 SuO; Hawick - 3, 4 SO, 2 SuO; Gorebridge - 2, 3 SO.
Dunbar - 2, 3 SO; North Berwick - 4; Galashiels *via Peebles* - 3, 4 SO; Polton - 5; Penicuick - 4, 5 SO; Leith Central - 11, 8 SO; Musselburgh - 20, 16 SO; North Leith - 6, 3 SO.

A wartime picture - no doubt secretively snapped - of an extraordinary combination on a passenger train crossing a viaduct - believed to be on the Leeds Northern Line: the C1 leading, No.4424 (BR No.2854 - never 62854), was a York engine at the time as was the *Southern Railway* B4 4-4-0 behind, either 2051 or 2068 both of which were on loan to the LNER (NE Area) between November 1941 and December 1944. Note also the elderly NER clerestory as leading vehicle. A picture that is by no means photographically perfect, but offset by its curiosity value. *Hoole coll.*

Edinburgh, and of relief night trains on the route. This was possible because of the widening of the line between York and Thirsk, less block coal traffic to carry on the ECML after partial revival of North Sea coastal shipping, and the drafting in of many WD and USA locomotives. Then from May to October 1944 services were cut even more drastically, and the scant remaining restaurant cars were taken off, to release stock, crew and paths for the huge extra burden of military traffic associated with OVERLORD, the Allied invasion of Europe. Between 22nd May and 31st July 1944 - the period of the 'Stand To' programme, from King's Cross there was only one through Leeds/Bradford train (passengers otherwise had to change at Doncaster), two to Newcastle and three to Edinburgh[5]. The worst of the cuts had been restored by October 1944, and then the services were improved gradually as the war in Europe came to an end. Thus the new timetable in June 1945, after VE-Day on 8th May, showed a tentative beginning of a revival from the stringencies of the war.

The wartime services on the ECML (at August 1942) are summarized in Table 4.2. It can be seen that on Mondays to Saturdays (and including overnight trains) there were a mere seven services to the West Riding, one to Hull, one to Cleethorpes, nine to Newcastle, five to Edinburgh, and one to Aberdeen. Many of them made more intermediate stops than in peacetime, and there were a good deal fewer through coaches. In the NE Area, this sparse service of main line expresses was supplemented only by a morning service from Darlington to Edinburgh, one each from York to Glasgow Queen Street and to Edinburgh, and also expresses from Leeds to Newcastle *via* York, from York to Newcastle (two), and from Liverpool to Newcastle *via* Leeds, Harrogate and Ripon.

On the other hand, wartime on the ECML saw the birth in 1940-41 of four new regular cross-country services, primarily for the benefit of Servicemen on leave. Three ran from Colchester, to York, to Leeds and to Edinburgh (overnight); the York train ran *via* the GN&GE Joint, the other two *via* Peterborough. The fourth train was the celebrated 'Ashford Belle', introduced in September 1940 - but until December 1940 only for Servicemen, and publicly advertised very soon after. Envisaged as a means

for soldiers on leave from their camps in the South-East to avoid going through Blitz-torn London, the train followed routes so intensively used by wartime special trains, including the former GC main line, and took a *nominal* 12 hours - heaven knows how long often in practice (up to *two hours* more during the Blitz) - with two reversals and four changes of locomotive, to reach Newcastle from Ashford (Kent) *via* Redhill, Reading, Banbury, Sheffield and York. Sometimes it was found necessary to run reliefs from North Camp northwards, but the 'Ashford Belle' was withdrawn in the May 1944 cuts. It was replaced in September 1944 by a train - *not* in the public timetable but freely available - from Southampton to Newcastle by the same route (from Reading West Junction), on which however the SR locomotive worked to Woodford. Coaching stock was provided by both the LNER and SR, and there was a buffet car - with NAAFI[6] prices, also a travelling RTO[7].

The contrast in wartime with the frequency and speed of trains in peacetime on the ECML was stark, and looking back it seems incredible that on the whole - but not quite always - this meagre service sufficed, carrying as it did quite as many passengers as in peacetime. The decelerations are exemplified by the almost *nine hours* the *FLYING SCOTSMAN* took during the war to reach Edinburgh from London, or the best time of nearly six hours of an express to Newcastle. To allow more passengers to be conveyed, the restaurant-car facilities were radically reduced, especially after May 1942 when also sleeping-car bookings were controlled in order to ensure that priority was given to people on urgent Government business.

Local services for getting people to and from work had to be maintained much as in peacetime - even greatly increased where workers needed to be conveyed to war factories, notably the 44 Royal Ordnance Factories that worked round the clock in three shifts and seven days in the week, and for which special new lines and stations were built. The enormous ROFs established at a number of places across the country had to be served by fleets of trains to convey thousands of workers from large centres of population often some distance away. Relatively few ROFs were in the eastern part of the country, but the ECML was concerned directly with the Engineering ROF at Birtley in

Co. Durham and the Explosives ROF at Ranskill in Nottinghamshire, and slightly indirectly with the Filling ROFs at Thorp Arch and at Aycliffe and the Engineering ROFs at Spennymoor and at Maltby, also with a number of large wartime depots[8] (see Appendix E). At Thorp Arch, opened in May 1941 and where 18,000 people were employed, a ring line with stations at Walton, Roman Road, Ranges, and River was built off the Church Fenton-Wetherby line. The normal services on the lines through Harrogate and on the Leeds-Hull line through Selby were radically cut in 1942, partly to make more paths available for ECML freight by-passing York, but also partly to allow enough trains to serve Thorp Arch ROF, some of which also came from York. (Thorp Arch ROF resumed production early in the 1950s, so some of the munitions workers' trains continued to run until the end of 1958). For Aycliffe ROF, stations were built at Simpasture and Demon's Bridge on the Shildon-Tees-side line. Thus some of the 25 or so trains daily to Aycliffe ROF impinged on the ECML at Ferryhill - and the *public* service between Spennymoor and Bishop Auckland was withdrawn permanently from December 1939 and that between Ferryhill and Leamside in July 1941. A big aircraft factory (used for breaking up damaged aircraft) was built beside the Darlington-Eaglescliffe line at Urlay Nook, and a new Halt was built to serve it which survives today as Allens West. Ranskill ROF, built just to the east of the ECML south of the station, was served by a number of trains from the Leeds direction through Doncaster (some of which picked up workers at Bentley, a stop not in the public timetable), from Gainsborough *via* Retford and from Mansfield *via* Tuxford. Down south, the vital De Havilland aircraft factory acquired its own (unadvertised) Halt, Lemsford Road, on the Hatfield - St Albans branch.

Cuts in local services were made mainly at off-peak times, especially late in the evening. In the London area, services were radically altered after April 1940, when the Northern Line 'Tube' extensions were opened, and after October 1940 when the through trains from Moorgate and from Broad Street ceased on account of Blitz damage[9]. On the Cambridge line virtually all trains now called at all stations. Certain services feeding to the ECML were suspended in September 1939 altogether, if for only two or three months: Moorgate-King's Cross, Broad Street-Finsbury Park, Hatfield-St Albans, Finchley Central-Edgware, Hertford North-Langley Junction (not restored until 1962), also Newcastle-Tyne Commission Quay.

In the first half of the war, relief trains were put on freely at weekends and other peak times. Indeed some trains such as the *FLYING SCOTSMAN* had a relief almost daily - but they were mostly not advertised except on blackboards at the stations. For example, no less than 200 extras were run down the ECML from King's Cross over the Christmas 1939 period, and 37 extras were still run on Maundy Thursday in 1940. Some holiday trains were run that summer and Camping Coaches were still available, but there was *no* Bank Holiday in August 1940. By 1942 the demand for locomotives and crews of the inexorably burgeoning freight and military traffic forced the REC to impose severe controls, and this kind of provision became out of the question even if a few relief trains were put on at the last minute at times of the heaviest pressure such as Christmas.

There was indeed grievous overcrowding, the ECML expresses being among the most severely affected. Statistics on tickets[10] issued and collected at particular stations show that passenger traffic fell off a little in 1939 compared to 1938 - and no wonder when one recalls those stringent cuts in services in

September/October 1939 and the appalling delays before the speed restrictions were eased, but then it grew enormously. In the peak month of 1942 (August) passenger receipts nationwide were 23% above those of August 1941, and at Easter 1943 the LNER reported that passengers from its London termini were *41%* above those at Easter 1942. The establishment of a standard bomber station was 2,500 persons, so it can be imagined how many RAF and USAAF personnel used the ECML trains on postings and leave, and how the resulting movement of countless thousands of airmen greatly added to the overcrowding of the ECML passenger trains. At Grantham, a fairly typical ECML station but with an inordinate number of airfields in the vicinity, passenger-journeys increased by 55% between 1941 and 1942, and by the peak year of 1945 were 158% above the 1938 figure.

The withdrawal of Cheap Day fares in October 1942 probably led to some easing of the civilian pressure, and a redistribution of the stops made by the exiguous service of ECML expresses relieved the overcrowding a little, but it was more than compensated by the persistent growth in the numbers of Service passengers. Already by the middle of the war the majority of the passengers on long-distance trains - and 80% of those travelling over 200 miles - had come to be Servicemen, and this was so as much on the ECML as anywhere. For example, on the ordinary Friday of 23rd January 1942, when five relief trains were put on from King's Cross down at least to Doncaster, 65-90% of the passengers were Servicemen. In fact, when from mid-April 1944 Service leave was drastically curtailed until D-Day there was a decline compared with a year before of 22% in LNER passenger receipts, but this lasted for only two to three months and then the numbers continued to increase well into 1945.

The feeding of the great numbers of Servicemen making long rail journeys presented special difficulties, and in the Winter of the Blitz the LNER ran one of its buffet cars exclusively for them in the 13.00 King's Cross - Edinburgh (13.05 return), staffed by the WVS[11], but the experiment resulted in even worse blockage of corridors and was not perpetuated. Instead, at stations such as York, Darlington, and Newcastle large semi-movable refreshment stalls were set up on the main platforms to supplement the station buffets and the small trolleys that were wheeled around. Apart from these extra refreshment facilities provided by the Railway, the Salvation Army, WVS and other voluntary organizations built hostels for Servicemen - where bed & breakfast cost just 7.5p - at King's Cross, York (former Parcels Depot) and Edinburgh Waverley stations, as well as 24-hour canteens[12] there and at Grantham, Retford[13], Doncaster, Darlington, and Newcastle.

King's Cross, at least as much as any other main-line London terminus, was vital for essential (civilian and military) purposes in the war. Innumerable soldiers and sailors passed through, but on account of the large number of Bomber Command airfields served by the ECML (see Appendix E), King's Cross also became poignantly for many air crew the last they ever saw of London before they flew to their death on missions over Europe. Countless thousands of airmen thronged Peterborough, Grantham and York[14] stations, and wayside stations handled unprecedented numbers of them, even expresses stopping at the little station of Heck for Snaith and Burn Airfields. Large numbers of US Army airmen also used the terminus, coming up to London from their bomber bases in the East Midlands and from some of those in East Anglia, and as well (during 1944) men of the IXth US Troop Carrier Command from their bases near Grantham and Newark.

Although many unadvertised reliefs were run at busy times, the LNER's chief response to the burgeoning passenger traffic was not so much to duplicate timetabled trains as to double their length, the result being trains of 20 or more coaches[15]. Such gargantuan trains were far too long for the platforms at King's Cross, where 14 coaches was the maximum capacity, and so they had to be divided. Thus Down trains were loaded at two platforms, joined up and then drawn out through the tunnels up the 1-in-107, *without a pilot* and without more than a brief shove from the tank engine that had brought in the empty stock. Likewise, Up expresses coming into King's Cross - often already very late and out of course, had to be divided by a pilot engine on arrival and placed in two platforms; in the process many impatient passengers in the rear half of the train would have climbed down onto the ballast. It was of course very difficult for these enormous trains to run to time, not least because they had to 'draw up' at most intermediate stops, often twice or even sometimes three times, but Gresley's magnificent Big Engines were usually on top of the job. On the other hand, failures were not infrequent, especially later in the war and in the first few years after it, because of maintenance arrears and poor coal, and these failures caused havoc to the free flow of traffic - even occasionally to serious accidents (Appendix J).

The problem of 'time lost to locomotive' became progressively more serious, and from May 1943 a strict limit of 18 coaches was set for ECML expresses, by which time anyway almost all restaurant cars were being used as seating vehicles. However much schedules were extended, punctuality was abysmal. This was especially so when air-raids began in 1940. From August 1940, the *average* lateness of Down ECML expresses at Newcastle jumped from about 20 to 60 minutes - or even in November 1940 to 90 minutes, with a similar degree of deterioration for all Up expresses into King's Cross. More specifically, in July 1940 the *FLYING SCOTSMAN* was achieving on average almost a punctual arrival in Edinburgh, but this average fell to 45 - 55 minutes late in September - October 1940, and continued to average about 20 minutes late even after the Blitz and for much of the rest of the war. The 17.25 King's Cross to Newcastle deteriorated from an average of about 15 minutes late at Newcastle to averages approaching *two hours* late in November 1940. In the Up direction, things were even worse and the 13.05 from Edinburgh (allowed nine hours) found itself arriving almost every night at King's Cross in an air-raid; its average lateness plummeted from 10 minutes in August 1940 to *three hours* in some weeks of September and October 1940. (No wonder passenger carryings did not increase in 1940 - in spite of the swelling number of Servicemen and other 'displaced persons' having to travel). The problem in the autumn of 1940 was not so much air-raid damage as such but the draconian speed restriction of 15 m.p.h. during an Alert - even in daylight. However, even when the speed restrictions during Alerts were relaxed - and after the Blitz Alerts themselves became much less frequent, punctuality still left a great deal to be desired. The average lateness of principal ECML expresses was about 20 minutes during the summer and fell to an hour or more in the winter. There were many reasons for this, but the basic problems were congestion (near overloading of line capacity), increasingly frequent locomotive breakdowns and poor steaming, and recurring traffic mishaps. Compounding these were the over-long over-crowded trains - and the inordinate numbers of parcels to be handled - prolonging station times, and in winter the usual problems with fog and frozen points. All this bore very heavily on the overworked staff, and there was an unusual prevalence of staff sickness - especially in late 1943. A sample (for October 1944) of the recorded causes of serious delay to individual major ECML expresses is listed in Appendix B.

The part played by the LNER - and its ECML - in conveying special military traffic was tremendous. In fact throughout the war the LNER was involved with no less than 127,000 trains on Government Account, passenger (mainly troop) trains and freight trains each accounting for about a half of this total. In 1944 alone it ran 41,500 (or *114 a day*) of these specials; in the first six months of 1945 the figure was 20,000, falling to 14,000 in the second six months. If it is assumed that two-thirds of these LNER trains used the ECML in whole or in part, we have for the ECML all-war figures of about 42,000 passenger *and* 42,000 freight trains - *an average of 19 trains a day* in each category. Such an estimate corresponds with the number in 1944 (26 per day, of the two categories combined) reported to have run in the NE Area, because the great majority of these latter presumably ran on the ECML. As early as April 1940 many of the 202 train-loads of the Expeditionary Force to Norway which sailed from Leith and Glasgow must have passed along the ECML[16]. Then, in the great improvised operations, DYNAMO and AERIAL, for distributing the retreating armies brought back from France in June 1940, the LNER played a major part in bringing numerous train-loads of exhausted troops up to camps in the North, down the ECML at least from York. It provided 47 out of the total of 186 trains collected for the Dunkirk Evacuation, in which a total number of 572 train-loads were conveyed from South Coast ports during the nine days of the Operation Dynamo and another 226 in Operation Aerial.

The great majority of the airfields of Bomber Command and many of other Commands of the RAF, and subsequently of the Eighth and Ninth US Army Air Forces, were located in territory that constituted the 'catchment area' of the ECML and thus produced immense traffic to the line in personnel and in military supplies. Indeed, in June 1944, over 60 airfields of Bomber Command Nos.1, 3, 4, 5, 6 and 8 Groups, plus seven of the USAAF 1st Bombardment Division, were more or less directly served off the ECML. In addition, airfields of the RAF and USAAF catering for Fighter, Troop-Carrying, Army Cooperation, Coastal, Maintenance *etc.* Groups accounted for half as many airfields again providing traffic for the ECML. There were a number of major Army establishments as well served by the ECML, such as the great Army Garrison complex at Catterick and in the wide spaces of Lincolnshire, Yorkshire (for the Tank Corps, especially in East Yorkshire), and Northumberland. From these camps tens of thousands of troops were conveyed to other parts of the country and to embarkation ports in the South and in Scotland. (Airfields and other military and supply depots served in the war by the ECML are listed in Appendix E).

For Operation TORCH - the invasion of North West Africa in November 1942, 440 troop specials and 680 special trains of supplies were needed. They ran mainly to Merseyside and Clyde ports - and about half from entraining areas connected with the ECML, between late October and early December 1942, most being run between 7th and 12th and between 21st and 26th November. For BOLERO and then OVERLORD, the LNER was called upon to cope with an *average* of eight troop trains and four supplies trains *per day* from Scotland to the South and East of England throughout 1943 and much of 1944. As well as with the troops being brought in through Glasgow but also with those entering at Liverpool, the LNER assisted the LMSR to a

Illustrative of the difficult times just after the war, C1 No.2840 (LNER No.4410) assists A3 No.110 (LNER No.4479) ROBERT THE DEVIL on an Up Newcastle express approaching Finsbury Park, 5th October 1946. (Note the missing headlamp and bent buffer beam on the Atlantic). *LCGB*.

Haymarket based A4 No.12 (later No.60012; ex-LNER No.4491) COMMONWEALTH OF AUSTRALIA (resplendent in blue livery and with pre-war head-board) leaves a grimy Newcastle Central on the Down *FLYING SCOTSMAN*, July 1948. *E.Oldham*.

The ex-GN D3 No.2000 (previously LNER No.4075), which was modified in 1944, for hauling the Inspection Saloon for Directors and Officers of the LNER, being given a roomy cab and painted in fully lined-out LNER green livery. Here it is hauling a Down local comprising an articulated twin set and what appears to be an ex-GCR coach, approaching Peascliff Tunnel, 18th May 1948. *Hepburn/RAS*.

A rare view of the 'Ally Pally' push-pull as it was during the war and for a few years afterwards. For several years the motive power was an ex-GC F2 2-4-2T, and here E7111 (LNER No.5783, never becoming 67111) stands at Platform 10 at Finsbury Park waiting to return to Alexandra Palace, 22nd April 1948. *J.Aylard.*

considerable extent. Many of the US Forces that came in through the Clyde, and later through Hull or Immingham, were also carried on the ECML.

The assembly of the Field Force for OVERLORD began on 26th March 1944, and in five weeks 796 troop specials were run from the ports[17] (mainly West Coast), and in April 1944 nearly 200 train-loads of troops were dispatched from Scotland alone to the South, and in the same period internal movements of British Army units[18] between Scottish and Northern Command and South-East Command required 241 special trains. Nearly half of these probably came by the ECML at least as far as York, although in the NE Area troop trains were often routed *via* Leamside, Ripon and Church Fenton. South of York a great many specials were routed up the former GC main line, reached either *via* Mexborough West Junction or *via* Tuxford, the latter Junction in turn offering alternative routing including the ex-LD&EC line through Langwith Junction. Eastbound trains were brought from Liverpool over the Cheshire Lines system, joined at Hunts Cross West by means of the loop from the LMSR at Allerton Junction, then *via* Godley Junction onto the LNER proper (GC section). After going over Woodhead to Sheffield Victoria, these trains would either go northwards *via* York, or - more often - south up the GC main line, or *via* Retford onto the ECML, and in some cases to the Eastern Counties *via* Nottingham Victoria and the Allington Junction - Barkston East Junction cut-off, Sleaford and Spalding (for the M&GN) and March, or *via* Peterborough East.

By the end of 1944, each day an average of 3,000 British servicemen alone were coming home on leave, and from 5th January 1945 a regular BLA (British Liberation Army) Leave train - originating at Dover - was run down the ECML, initially with often highly-polished Pacifics carrying a name-board. Then from about April 1945, the Dieppe - Newhaven cross-channel service having recommenced in January, this train ran from Newhaven *via* Kensington - and it also sometimes carried a Nazi flag at the rear. Two regular Leave trains were put on from Parkeston Quay, one to Glasgow (with buffet-car) *via* Peterborough and the ECML and the other to Manchester *via* Peterborough East and Rugby; there was also one from Southampton, *via* the GC line to York and on to Newcastle *via* Stockton. After the end of the war in Europe, from October 1945 Leave trains were run from Hull[19] to King's Cross in connection with a boat from Cuxhaven. None of these trains appeared in the public timetables. At the same time, numerous specials to Hull were conveying German Servicemen released from British prisoner-of-war camps.

As early as October 1941, the Government selected Dispersal Centres throughout the length of Britain, and began to draw up plans for Demobilization of Servicemen but of course it was only after VE-Day that they began to be implemented. In general the men were expected to make their way home from the Dispersal Centres by ordinary train services, but in June 1945 it was found necessary to institute a daily (including Sundays) special overnight train from *Euston* to York (*via* Northampton), balanced by a return working and complemented by a train from Taunton to Edinburgh (and reverse) which connected with the first train at York. Indeed, on the LNER Southern Area passenger-journeys in the 12 weeks ending 20th October 1945 were 8.0% higher than in the same period in 1944. That summer there was also the Rush to the Seaside, and as early as June 1945 a great military camp at Filey was partially handed over to Billy Butlin, to restart his famed Holiday Camp, for which the LNER built a brand new branch and station in May 1947.

MAIN-LINE PASSENGER SERVICES AFTER THE WAR UNTIL THE END OF THE 1950s

The great ECML trains of the LNER were gradually restored between 1946 and 1950 to some of their pre-war glory and certainly to peacetime frequency. Cheap fares that had been abolished in the war were reintroduced for party travel in August 1946, but not for individuals until late 1947 or early 1948. The holiday crowds in 1945 were dealt with by numerous reliefs - mainly unadvertised. Some of these appeared in the timetable as 'Saturdays Only', but in practice ran in the summer virtually every day; others were put on as required, often at the last minute. However, both track and locomotives were, as already noted, in a poor state after six long years of war. A great backlog of track relaying had accumulated, and this necessitated the continuation of a 75 m.p.h. overall speed limit, which in March 1947 was curtailed to 60 m.p.h. because of waterlogging of the formation. Meanwhile the incidence of locomotive failures due to mechanical problems had risen to double the pre-war level and the proportion of locomotives under or awaiting repairs mounted steadily, having many causes which on the LNER included design weaknesses in Gresley engines built with high standards of maintenance in mind. Another constant cause of trouble just after the war was 'lack of steam due to inferior coal', with over British Railways as a whole the incidence of serious delays due to 'bad steaming' being three times in 1947 the level it had been in 1939. This led to gross delays and frequent requirements to 'stop for assistant engine'. (Why the coal should be so much inferior to its pre-war quality is not clear to the author). Thus Christmas - always a difficult time - was chaotic at King's Cross in 1946, with trains leaving one or two hours late for reasons by no means wholly due to the weather. In the four weeks ending 25th January 1947, 49% of ECML expresses were more than 45 minutes late, but worse was to come with the Fuel Crisis caused by the frightful weather early in 1947 (see Appendix K). Along with a shortage of locomotives owing to so many being under or in need of repair, radical cuts had to be made in passenger services between February and June and even the Summer timetable had 10% less passenger train-miles than in 1946 - and the Railways were prohibited from running any more reliefs. Passenger-journeys originating on the LNER Southern Area actually fell by 16%

in 1947 compared to 1946, but at least the punctuality of the principal expresses improved - modestly, from an average lateness of 40 minutes to 26 minutes.

Loads on the ECML remained heavy in the early post-war years, some trains again including portions for three destinations as well as individual through coaches, although both loads and destinations varied somewhat with the seasons. Some but not all of the variety of subsidiary destinations served before the war by the LNER came back on the notices under BR. Thus by 1955 were added: Lincoln, Ripon, Halifax, Scarborough, Saltburn, Fort William (by sleeping-car), and Newcastle Tyne Commission Quay, also on Summer Saturdays Skegness, Bridlington, and Filey Holiday Camp.

As before the war, scores of reliefs were run at exceptionally busy times such as Christmas, Easter and Whitsun, on Summer Saturdays[20] and on special occasions like the Cup Final and other major football events, the St Leger, the Grand National and other race-meetings. Many Excursions were also run for the Festival of Britain in 1951 and for the Coronation in 1953. In the pre-Motorway days of the 1950s, major football events could require

(*top*) **The earliest BR liveries are shown here, on B1 No.61084 with the 17.00 Newcastle - Liverpool express made up of an LMS set, leaving Thirsk 7th July 1948.** *D.V.Beeken.*

(*above*) **The NBR in the NER stronghold of Newcastle Central: D30 No.62428 (LNER No.9419) THE TALISMAN, in its first BR livery, leaves platform 13 on the 16.30 to Hawick *via* Hexham and the Border Counties line, 21st September 1950.** *A.G.Ellis coll.*

The LNER ran 'push-and-pull' trains on many of its branches, but few off the ECML, and this was one that lasted into BR days: the Goole service seen here at Selby, with G5 No.67250 (LNER No.1837), 16th August 1952. *J.Robertson.*

the running of phenomenal numbers of specials for the fans - and they *did not* vandalize the trains in those days. To give one example: for the Cup Semi-Finals on 26th March 1955 no less than *52* excursions were run from the Newcastle/Sunderland area to Birmingham. Reliefs and excursions would bring to King's Cross locomotives from depots otherwise rarely seen in the terminus - although some were common enough on fast freight, fish trains, *etc.* - sheds such as March, Retford, Ardsley, Bradford, Colwick, Darnall, Lincoln, Neville Hill, Darlington, Dairycoates, or Hull Botanic Gardens. In the 1940s, when these non-ECML sheds had old GN, GC and NE types on their books, the variety of locomotives was wide, but by the 1950s the specials rarely brought anything more extraordinary than a B16, otherwise the usual B1 or perhaps a K2 or K3.

It was common for conditions to become quite chaotic at King's Cross at times of pressure, and the *Railway Observer* relates how at Christmas 1950 - "Scenes [at King's Cross] of such confusion and congestion were witnessed as have never before been known in the history of the East Coast Route." The writer went on to describe the congestion of 24 engines queuing to get into Top Shed, and to list a number of late departures of well over an hour. It was little better at Christmas 1954 for example, when there were three derailments and ten engine failures. Again, at Christmas 1957 services were totally disorganized, this time by severe fog as well as exceptionally heavy traffic on account of the return of a modicum of petrol rationing. Innumerable reliefs were run, and 21 extra diagrams were operated from King's Cross on 21st December and on 22nd December no less than 27; Down expresses - and some Outer Suburban trains - were delayed for over an hour, and Up expresses for over two hours. At Newcastle they had fog as well, also a derailment on the High Level Bridge which blocked all its lines for over an hour at the busiest time.

The Summer timetable of 1945 showed little overt change - after all the war was not yet over in the Far East. It was the Winter timetable that year which first announced the reintroduction of several more through expresses. Also with the

introduction of regular sailings from the Tyne to Norway in January 1946 the Boat Trains to Tyne Commission Quay from King's Cross ran once again. The London - Edinburgh time of the *FLYING SCOTSMAN* (on which the restaurant car was restored) was cut by 50 minutes to 8 hours 5 minutes, and commensurate reductions were made in the scheduled times of many other expresses. Nevertheless, another four years elapsed before any substantial accelerations were possible, although - apart from the constraints in 1947 already mentioned - the *frequency* of scheduled trains down the ECML was increased successively each summer, but especially in 1949. With Summer Saturday through trains to the seaside gradually reintroduced on a scale eventually exceeding those of 1939, and abundant reliefs run at peak times, the passenger services down the ECML became perhaps more interesting than the freight.

The *FLYING SCOTSMAN*, the *ABERDONIAN* and the *NIGHT SCOTSMAN* had never lost their names throughout the war, and other named trains soon reappeared after it: the *YORKSHIRE PULLMAN* was reinstated in Winter 1946 (*via* Leeds) when through King's Cross - Leeds locomotive workings were restored. Summer 1948 saw the first post-war King's Cross - Edinburgh *non-stop* schedule (by the *FLYING SCOTSMAN* in 7hr. 50min.), and the reappearance of the *QUEEN OF SCOTS PULLMAN* to Glasgow Queen Street *via* Leeds and Harrogate. In Winter 1948 a new *TEES-TYNE PULLMAN* was introduced, and the *WEST RIDING* came back - albeit not as a streamlined train, for none of the pre-war luxury trains ever came back. In Summer 1949 the *FLYING SCOTSMAN* became no longer the Non-Stop and instead a new Non-Stop - the *CAPITALS LIMITED* - was put on, allowed 8 hrs; the *WHITE ROSE*, non-stop King's Cross to Wakefield, was also instituted that Summer. In Winter 1949, the 12.20 King's Cross - Newcastle was named the *NORTHUMBRIAN*, and the 08.48 Leeds City - Glasgow *via* York the *NORTH BRITON*. The Summer timetable of 1950 reintroduced the *SCARBOROUGH FLYER*, the name the *NORSEMAN* for the thrice-weekly Boat Express from King's Cross to Tyne Commission Quay, and the *TYNESIDER* for the

Seen from the York Road platform, *THE ELIZABETHAN* leaves King's Cross on its non-stop run to Edinburgh, with A4 No.60017 (LNER No.2512) SILVER FOX, 11th July 1953. The limited spread of the station's throat is displayed, from the signalbox at the end of platforms 6/7 on the left to the locomotive yard on the right; L1 No.67741 is clearly seen and A3 No.60049 can be glimpsed. Note also the theatre-type indicators beckoning Up trains into platforms 1 and 5. *B.K.B.Green.*

Newark North Gate, 16th May 1953: a view north along the Up platform, animated by the throng of enthusiasts off the Special standing in the bay, headed by N5 No.69313 (LNER No.5773), which was run that day on the Bottesford line - soon to be closed to passengers. A Down express is at the Down platform, and on the right is the Up yard with what appears to be a J69 working in it. *Nottingham County Library.*

A photographer's delight - capturing two trains converging: A4 No.60011 EMPIRE OF INDIA on the Up *ELIZABETHAN* meets A1 No.60117 BOIS ROUSSEL on a Down express as they pass Potters Bar Golf Course, Summer 1953. *Goslin.*

A typical train of Gresley non-corridor twins, headed by A5/2 No.69832 (LNER No.1738) enters Darlington Bank Top from the Saltburn line, 11th August 1956. (The large Cowans-Sheldon Engineering Works is behind the train, and Darlington South Box is on the right). *P.Hay.*

The 15.00 King's Cross - Newcastle express, diverted over the Hertford Loop (to allow a new four-track bridge to be put into place at Potters Bar) passes the then-closed Watton-at-Stone station, Sunday 13th September 1953, headed by A4 No.60028 WALTER K. WHIGHAM (ex-LNER No.4487 'SEA EAGLE). *J.Aylard.*

Northallerton in the rain: D20 No.62373 (LNER No.708) on an Up stopping train (with an old NBR coach at the front), 9th August 1952. *Beeken.*

23.30 King's Cross - Newcastle sleeping-car express. On Sunday 15th July 1950, a Special was run from King's Cross to York and back (outward by the 'Towns' route *via* Boston, Lincoln and Knottingley), hauled by rebuilt Pacific 60113 GREAT NORTHERN, to celebrate the centenary of the opening of the GN main line[21].

For Winter 1950, there were further modest accelerations: the *FLYING SCOTSMAN* now took 7hr. 45min. for its journey - with stops at Grantham and Newcastle, but high-speed expresses from King's Cross there certainly were *not* - not yet, a speed trial in May 1946 having shown that a great deal of work on the track had to be done before pre-war high-speed schedules could be contemplated. Thus 90 m.p.h. was prohibited anywhere until 1951. The first post-war 60 m.p.h. booking (of the *NORTH BRITON* between Darlington and York) was effected in 1949, but it was several years before mile-a-minute schedules became common again on the ECML. Innovations in 1950 however included the beginnings of the standardization of departure times from King's Cross, and of the turn-round there of Up expresses without leaving their platforms of arrival - although it was 1956 before the practice was adopted extensively.

Changing engines of London expresses at Peterborough, Grantham, Doncaster, or York was phased out after the war. Many locomotive rosters through from London to York and Newcastle were brought back from May 1946, but the main change in this regard came in Summer 1950. However, this was not for long. On account of poor timekeeping on long-distance through runs, the rather poor mechanical condition of the Pacifics and V2s and inferior standards of maintenance, forced a complete rearrangement of rosters in 1951 to give locomotives and crews relatively short runs. Nearly all trains were again re-engined and re-manned at Peterborough or Grantham. Meanwhile however, in the 1948-51 period there were many London - Newcastle (and Edinburgh) through locomotive rosters - the Edinburgh engines being from Haymarket and not confined only to the Non-Stops. Accordingly there were a considerable number of lodging-turns for the footplate-men - albeit unpopular especially with Tyneside men. The Haymarket A4s, along with Pacifics and V2s from Gateshead, Heaton, York and Copley Hill as well as from Doncaster, Grantham and New England, now came up to London regularly. The two new series of Pacifics - the 6' 2" A2s and the 6' 8" A1s - became prominent in this period on the ECML, the former being unpopular on expresses and therefore employed more often on fast freight. In addition, from March 1950 through working was restored of Immingham engines to King's Cross, but now they were almost always B1s[22] and not the GN Atlantics or the variety of GC 4-6-0s seen before the war.

The diagrams on which the ECML Pacifics (helped by the V2s) were operated have been documented elsewhere so often and so fully that it would be superfluous to repeat them here. Noteworthy nonetheless were the alterations in 1951, for at that time there was an influx of the new A1 Pacifics and a considerable rearrangement of allocations, including the return of A3s to the GC main line. In spite of the changes in diagrams however, a very considerable degree of long-distance light engine working became necessary, and this continued for many years; the sight of a Pacific running light at speed down the southern half of the ECML became a daily - if slightly odd - experience. At all events, the Gresley Pacifics of both the non-streamlined (now all Class A3) and streamlined (A4) classes, the Thompson and Peppercorn Pacifics and the indomitable V2 2-6-2s, had many more years of hard work and remained the staple motive power of the fast trains on the ECML throughout the 1940s and 1950s.

Summer 1951 saw the introduction of another new named express, the *HEART OF MIDLOTHIAN*, an afternoon London - Edinburgh train. There were also some minor accelerations, and six runs (totalling 265 miles) were scheduled at over 60 m.p.h. In Summer 1952 the crack *CAPITALS LIMITED* was accelerated to reach Edinburgh in 7 hrs 6 mins. That Summer a daily through service was introduced: Newcastle - Swansea, not seen since before the war except briefly in Winter 1946 and subsequently as a Summer Saturdays Only service - and unlike pre-war, running *via* Oxford and Swindon. From 1951 the through coaches were routed *via* Birmingham and Gloucester, and by Summer 1957 had developed into a complete Newcastle - Cardiff train, the two sets of coaching stock being shared between the NE and Western Regions.

In October 1952 the centenary of King's Cross station was celebrated with an Exhibition including locomotives, and in the Winter 1952 timetable the first faint sign of real accelerations on the ECML was shown by the introduction of a new King's Cross - Leeds express, leaving London at 08.00 and taking 168 minutes (with one stop) to cover the 156 miles to Doncaster - seeming at the time quite an achievement.

In April 1953 the pre-war overnight reliefs from Marylebone to Newcastle were reinstated and ran through to Edinburgh, running throughout the summer season. They ran

TABLE 4.3: **SUMMARY OF PASSENGER SERVICES ON THE ECML AND CONNECTING LINES, SUMMER 1955**

This Table is drawn up on the same basis as Table 4.1, and allows comparison of the summer services 10 years after the end of the war with those in the last pre-war summer. Apart from the absence of the pre-war Streamliners, the ECML services under BR in the mid-1950s had recovered a comparability with those offered by the LNER in 1939: Pullman services were restored - with some new names, the general level of speed and comfort was now adequate and frequency on the main line was improved, but motive power was still entirely steam and great improvements were soon to follow with the advent of main-line diesel traction; the volume of traffic at the summer weekends was at the highest level ever attained, but was soon to fall away. At wayside stations in the country and on branch lines, however, traffic was already vanishing - and the introduction of diesel multiple-units failed to restore it to a semblance of the pre-war level.

In general, the trains that ran Monday-Friday also ran (Monday-Saturday) all the year round, although there were exceptions - notably the *ELIZABETHAN*. Apart from the latter being non-stop between King's Cross and Edinburgh, all trains to Scotland called at Newcastle, and all called at York except the *FLYING SCOTSMAN*, the *NIGHT SCOTSMAN* (nominally but not actually non-stop to Edinburgh, also the 22.35 King's Cross - Edinburgh (and the *QUEEN OF SCOTS*, that went *via* Leeds). Other trains made stops also at Peterborough, Grantham, Doncaster, Darlington or Durham, and a number stopped as well at other places such as Newark, Retford, Northallerton and Berwick.

Main Line Departures from King's Cross.
Edinburgh Waverley (393m, 417m *via Leeds and Ripon*)[1] - 7 (390 min), 8 MO, 9 FO, 10 SO, 7 SuO. **Via Edinburgh Waverley:-** Glasgow Queen St. (440m, 464m *via Leeds and Ripon*) - 2 (534 min[2]), 3 SO, 1 SuO; Aberdeen (524m) - 3, 4 FO, 2 SuO; Dundee (452m) - 1 (617 min), 1 SuO; Fort William (563m) - 1 (912 min), nil SO, 1 SuO. **Newcastle** (269m) - 9 (280 min), 12 FO, 8 SO, 9 SuO (*1 via Stockton*); Tyne Commission Quay *via Newcastle* - 2. **Via Northallerton:-** Sunderland *via Stockton* (281m) - 1 (354 min); Saltburn *via Middlesbrough* (260m) - 1 FSO (353 min). **York** (188m) - 2 (249), 1 SO, 1 SuO. **Via York:-** Scarborough (230m) - 1 FSO (273 min); Whitby (244m) - 1 FSO (353 min). **Via Doncaster:-** Leeds Central and/or Bradford Exchange (186/193m) - 7, 9 MFO (213/227 min), 15 SO, 8 SuO; Hull (197m) - 3, 4 FO, 7 SO, 3 SuO; Harrogate *via Leeds* (204m) - 3, 4 MO, 1 SO, 2 SuO; Ripon *via Leeds* (215m) - 1, 2 MO; Halifax (202m) - 1 (292 min). **Via Grantham:-** Lincoln (130m) - 1 (194 min). **Via Peterborough:-** Cleethorpes (158m) - 2 (244 min), 1 SuO; Lincoln *via Spalding and Sleaford* (133m) - 1 SuO (197 min); Skegness (131m) - 4 SO (172 min).

Cambridge Line Trains, via Hitchin. King's Cross to: Baldock (37m) - 4 (64 min), 5 SO, 2 SuO; Royston (45m) - 3 (77 min) (1 from Broad St. *SO*), 3 SuO; Cambridge (58m) - 13 (88 min) (2 from Broad St. *SO*), 8 SuO.

Regular Trains running over part of the ECML North of Peterborough:- **Via Doncaster:-** Colchester *via Ipswich, March, and Peterborough North* to **Edinburgh Waverley** (415m) - 1 (726 min), 1 SuO; Colchester *via Ipswich, March, Lincoln* to **Newcastle** (296m) - 1 (481 min); Yarmouth Vauxhall (218m, 375 min)/Lowestoft Central (221m, 385 min) *via March, Lincoln* to **York** - 1 (**Newcastle** FSO, *via Knottingley and Church Fenton* on *SO*). Ely *via March and Lincoln* to York (144m) - 1 SuO (240 min); Sheffield Victoria to **York** (43m) - 1 (100 min). **Doncaster** to **Newcastle** - 1 SuO.
York to:- **Edinburgh Waverley** (205m) - 2 (321 min) - 2 (1 carried through coaches from Tyne Commission Quay), 1 SuO; **Newcastle** *via Durham* (80m) - 1 (133 min), 1 SuO; *via Northallerton:-* Stockton (48m) - 1 (82 min); West Hartlepool (59m) - 1 (94 min); **Newcastle** (90m) 1 SuO. **Via York:-** Leeds City to:- **Edinburgh** and Glasgow Queen St. (278m) 1, 2 MSO (335 min); **Newcastle** *via Stockton* (131m) - 2 (206min); **Newcastle** *via Durham* (115m) - 1 SuO (173 min); Sheffield Midland to **Darlington** (91m) - 1 MO (128 min), 1 SuO; Leeds City to **Darlington** (70m) - 1 SuO (109 min); Birmingham New St. *via Sheffield Midland* to **Darlington** (168m) - 1 MO (285 min); Bristol Temple Meads *via Birmingham New St. and Sheffield Midland* to **Newcastle** *via Durham* (293m) - 2 (492 min), 1 SuO; Bristol Temple Meads to **Newcastle** *via Stockton* (490 min); Cardiff General *via Gloucester, Birmingham New St. and Sheffield Midland* to Newcastle *via Durham* (312m) - 1 (507 min); Paignton *via Bristol Temple Meads, Birmingham New St. and Sheffield Midland* to **Newcastle** *via Durham* (397m) - 1 SuO (683 min); Liverpool Lime St. to **Newcastle** *via Durham* (181m) - 1 (297 min), 2 SuO; Liverpool Exchange *via Normanton* to **Newcastle** *via Stockton* (187m) - 1; Bournemouth West *via Gloucester, Birmingham New St. and Sheffield Midland* to **Newcastle** *via Durham* (369m) - 1. **Via Northallerton:-**

Liverpool Lime St. *via Leeds and Harrogate* to **Newcastle** *via Durham* (169m) - 2 (276 min); Manchester Exchange *via Leeds and Harrogate* to **Newcastle** *via Durham* (137m) - 1 SuO (243 min). Richmond *via Darlington and Edinburgh* to Glasgow Queen St. (223m) - 1 FO (324 min). **Newcastle** *via Edinburgh* to Glasgow Queen St. (171m) - 1 MO (219 min). **Newcastle** to **Edinburgh Waverley** (125m) - 1 SuO[3] (155 min).

Main Line Stopping Trains - not necessarily stopping at all stations. (No Sunday trains, unless stated). **King's Cross** to: **Sandy** - 1 *SO*; Peterborough North - 6 (1 started from Broad St. on *SO*), 2 SuO; **Grantham** - 1, 1 SuO; **Doncaster** 1. **Hitchin** to **Sandy** - 1, 1 SuO; Peterborough North - 1 *SX*. **Peterborough North** to: **Grantham** - 4; **Doncaster** - 1. **Grantham** to: **Newark** - 1; **Doncaster** - 1 SuO[4]. **Doncaster** to **York**[5] - 6, 5 SO, 1 SuO[6]. **York** to **Darlington**, then *express* to **Edinburgh** - 1. **Darlington** to **Newcastle** - 1. **Newcastle** to: **Alnmouth** and Alnwick - 2, 3 SO; **Berwick-on-Tweed** - 3, 2 SuO. **Berwick-on-Tweed** to **Edinburgh Waverley** - 2.

London Area Suburban Trains (south of Hitchin), and Newcastle Electric Trains. The numbers of Monday - Saturday suburban trains per day in 1955 in the London area were somewhat fewer than even in the war. Apart from those listed above which continued onto the Cambridge branch, about 25 trains per day from King's Cross went down the main line to Hatfield or Welwyn Garden City, 4 - 5 continuing to Hitchin, and only another 3 - 4 went just to New Barnet. On the Hertford North line there were about 35 trains per day, of which only 3 - 4 terminated at Gordon Hill or Cuffley; some 20 (in rush-hours only) started from Moorgate, about 10 rush-hour trains - mainly for the Hertford line - came from Broad St. and about 7 commenced at Finsbury Park. A half day was still being worked on Saturday, and the Down peak-hour trains on Saturdays were still between 12.00 and 14.00 hr rather than in the evening. As in 1939, on Sundays trains ran at only about hourly intervals on the main and Hertford lines. The Alexandra Palace branch had been closed the previous year.

Except on the South Shields line, where still about 55 ran each way on Mondays - Saturdays and 32 on Sundays, the Newcastle electric trains in 1955 were down to about 35 - 40 each way per day (Monday - Saturday) on the circle service *via* Tynemouth (most running right round), and just 8 (2 on Saturdays) on the Riverside line. On Sundays there were about 25 trains each way on the Tynemouth circular service.

Regular Non-ECML Express, Secondary and Branch Trains - *excluding those from King's Cross* - that passed through or started from the stations listed. (Destination stations given are *only* those where a service terminated. Originating stations, if different from the junction station, are stated only where noteworthy. Equivalent trains ran in the reverse direction. **No** Sunday services, unless stated. For trains through from or to other ECML stations, see above. Seasonal trains are listed in the next section.)
Hatfield to: Luton Bute St. - 4, 1 SO; Dunstable North - 3, 7 SO. **Hitchin** to: Shepreth - 1; Baldock - 1, 2 SO (1 *SO* started from Welwyn North). **Sandy**[7] to:- Bletchley - 6, 7 SO, 2 SuO; Cambridge - 6, 7 SO, 2 SuO. **Peterborough North** to:- Harwich Town - 1; March - 1 *SuO*; Ely - 1, 2 SuO; Hunstanton - 1 *SuO*; Grimsby/Cleethorpes - 4, 6 SO, 1 SuO; Skegness - 1, 2 ThO, 1 SuO[8] ; Boston - 1, 2 SO; Firsby - 1. M&GN line: King's Lynn - 2, 3 SO; Hunstanton - 1 ThSO; Melton Constable - 1; Yarmouth Beach - 2, 3 SO. Down LMR line trains passing or calling at **Peterborough North:-** Leicester London Rd. to Peterborough East - 5, 4 SuO[9]; Oakham to Peterborough East - 1; Birmingham New St. to Ely - 1, 1 SuO[10].
Essendine to: Stamford East - 6, 7 SO. **Grantham** to:- Skegness - 1; Lincoln - 8 (one *via Sleaford*); Boston - 4, 5 SO; Derby Friargate - 8, 1 SuO; Nottingham Victoria - 10, 11 SO, 3 SuO. **Retford** to:- Cleethorpes - 1, 2 SO; Ulceby - 1 *SuO*; Lincoln - 5, 1 SuO; Sheffield Victoria - 3[11]. **Via Retford**[12] **:-** Cleethorpes to Manchester London Rd. *via Sheffield Victoria* - 2, Cleethorpes to Sheffield Victoria 3, 3 SuO; Harwich Parkeston Quay *via March and Lincon* to Liverpool Central *via Sheffield Victoria and Manchester Central* - 1; Lincoln to Sheffield Victoria - 5, 4 SO, 2 SuO[13].
Doncaster to:- March - 2, 3 SO; Spalding *via Boston* - 1; Lincoln - 1 *SO*; Cleethorpes - 8, 7 SO, 5 SuO; Barnetby - 1, 2 SO; Scunthorpe - 1 *SuO*; Bridlington - 1; Leeds Central - 7, 1 SuO; Hull - 4, 4 SuO; Sheffield Victoria - 5, 5 SuO; Penistone *via Barnsley Court House* - 2, 2 SuO; Barnsley Court House - 1, 2 SO. **Via Doncaster**[14] **:-** Yarmouth Vauxhall/Lowestoft Central *via March and Lincoln* to York[15]; Sheffield Victoria to:- Scunthorpe - 1 SuO; Cleethorpes - 1 SuO; Bridlington - 1; Hull - 3; Sheffield Midland to Hull - 1; Liverpool Central *via Manchester Central and Sheffield Victoria* to Hull - 2, 2 SuO.
Selby to:- Bridlington - 1; Goole - 5; Leeds City - 1. **Via Selby**[16] **:-** Leeds City to: Bridlington - 3, 1 SuO; Hull - 9, 10 SO, 5 SuO. Bradford Forster Sq. to Hull - 1. Liverpool Lime St. to Hull - 1. **York** *via Church Fenton* to:- Hull - 1, 2 SuO; Scarborough *via Bridlington* - 1. Wakefield Westgate *via Normanton* to: **York** - 1 *SuO;* Bridlington[17] - 1 *SuO*.

York to:- Hull *via Market Weighton* - 8; Scarborough - 4, 7 SO, 6 SuO; Whitby Town - 2, 1 SO; Harrogate - 7, 8 SO; Leeds City - 3, 4 SO, 1 SuO; Church Fenton - 1; Normanton - 1, 2 SuO; Banbury *via Sheffield Victoria* - 1; Sheffield Victoria - 1 *SuO*. LMSR trains:- Sheffield Midland - 3, 4 SO; *via Sheffield Midland* to: Bristol Temple Meads - 1, 2 FO, 1 SuO; Gloucester Eastgate - 1 SuO; Birmingham New St. - 1; *via Leeds and Manchester Exchange* to Liverpool Lime St. and *via Stockport, Crewe and Shrewsbury* to Swansea Victoria[18] - 1, 1 SuO; *via Normanton* to: Manchester Victoria - 2; Liverpool Exchange - 1, 1 SuO; Wakefield Westgate - 2 *SuO*. **Via York:-**[19] Leeds City to Scarborough - 7, 8 FO, 9 SO; Bradford Forster Sq. to Scarborough 1, 1 SuO; Normanton to Scarborough - 1; Sheffield Victoria to Scarborough - 1; Selby to Whitby Town - 1; Leeds City to Whitby Town - 1 *SuO*.
Via Thirsk[20]**:-** Leeds City *via Harrogate* to: Northallerton - 3, 4 SO, 2 SuO; Middlesbrough - 1; Harrogate to: **Northallerton** - 1 *SX;* **Darlington** - 1. **Northallerton** to: West Hartlepool 1 *SX*; Leeds City *via* **Thirsk** - 5. **Via Northallerton**[21] :- Leeds City to:- West Hartlepool - 1; Middlesbrough - 1. **Darlington** to:- Richmond - 12, 13 SO, 10 SuO; Saltburn - 35 (2 through from Tow Law), 20 SuO[22] ; Crook - 1 *SX* (through from Middlesbrough); Scarborough *via Middlesbrough* - 1, 1 SuO; West Hartlepool *via Eaglescliffe* - 1 *SuO*; Penrith - 3; Kirkby Stephen - 1; Saltburn[22] *via Darlington* to: Barnard Castle - 3 *SuO*; Penrith - 1 *SuO*; Middleton-in-Teesdale - 3; Tow Law - 6, 7 SO (1 through from Saltburn); Crook - 6, 5 SO (1 through from Middlesbrough); Bishop Auckland - 3, 4 SO (1 through to Newcastle *SO*), 7 SuO (5 through from Saltburn, and 1 through to **Durham**). **Durham** to: Sunderland - 4, 1 SuO; **Via Durham**:- Bishop Auckland to Sunderland - 9, 3 SuO[23].
Newcastle Central to: Middlesbrough - 11 (2 through to Redcar *SO*), 6 SuO (2 through to Saltburn, 1 to Redcar); Sunderland - 19, 18 SO, 10 SuO; West Hartlepool - 1 *SuO*; Washington - 1; Barnard Castle *via Washington and* **Durham** - 1; Carlisle - 8, 10 SO, 6 SuO; *via Carlisle* to: Glasgow St. Enoch - 1; Haltwhistle - 3; *via Hexham* to: Riccarton Junction - 1; Hawick - 2; Hexham, *via Prudhoe* - 6, 7 SO, 6 SuO; Hexham *via North Wylam* - 4, 3 SO, 6 SuO; Newbiggin *via Benton* - 1. **Manors North** *via Benton* to Newbiggin - 1, 3 SO. **Alnmouth** to Alnwick - 12 (including 3 through from Newcastle).
Berwick-on-Tweed to: St. Boswells - 2; Eyemouth - 1. **Burnmouth** to Eyemouth - 3. **Drem** to North Berwick - 7, 6 SO.

Trains for the Edinburgh Suburbs and the Waverley Route from the East End of Waverley Station. (Equivalent trains entered from the east). Carlisle - 2; Sheffield Midland - 1 SO; St. Pancras - 2, 1 SuO; Hawick - 3, 5 SO, 3 SuO; Riccarton Junction - 1 *MWO*; Newcastleton - 1 *SO*.
Dunbar - 1; North Berwick *via* **Drem** - 2, 3 ThO, 5 SO; Galashiels *via Gorebridge* - 1; Galashiels *via Peebles* - 3, 5 SO; Bonnyrigg - 3; Rosewell & Hawthornden - 1, 2 SO; Musselburgh - 15, 10 SO; Joppa - 3, 2 SO; **Edinburgh Waverley** *via Duddingston* - 6, 5 SO; Gorgie East *via Duddingston* 1 SO.

SEASONAL CROSS-COUNTRY TRAINS RUNNING ON THE ECML OR THROUGH ITS MAJOR CENTRES (Equivalent trains ran in the reverse direction. Many of the Summer *FO* and *SO* trains featured some interesting routes and nominally non-stop runs).

Fridays Only.
Harwich Town *via Ipswich, March and* **Peterborough North** to Doncaster. Leeds City *via* **Selby** to Filey Holiday Camp. Leeds City *via* **York** to Scarborough. Manchester Exchange *via Leeds, Harrogate,* **Northallerton** *and Stockton* to **Newcastle** (2, 1 also *MO*). Newcastle to Swansea High St. *via York* (also *MO*). **York** to Birmingham New St. (also *MO*). **York** to Scarborough. Bradford Exchange *via* **Doncaster, Lincoln and March** to Yarmouth Vauxhall (overnight). Glasgow Queen St. *via Edinburgh and York* to Scarborough (overnight). Hull *via* **Doncaster** *and Sheffield Midland* to Paignton (overnight). **Newcastle** *via York and Sheffield Midland* to:- Birmingham New St. (overnight); *via Birmingham and Bristol* to Paignton (overnight). **Newcastle** *via York, Sheffield Victoria, Banbury, Reading West and Basingstoke* to Bournemouth Central (overnight). **Newcastle** *via Carlisle* to Stranraer Harbour (overnight).
Saturdays Only
Via Peterborough North:- Harwich Town *via Ipswich and March* to **Doncaster**. LMR train: Leicester London Rd., Nottingham Midland and Derby Midland to Lowestoft Central and Gorleston-on-Sea[24] . **Grantham** to Scarborough[25].
Via Retford[26]**:-** Sheffield Victoria to:- Boston (2); Skegness; Yarmouth Vauxhall; Hucknall *via Mansfield* to Skegness *via Lincoln*. Manchester London Rd. *via Sheffield Victoria* to:- Skegness *via Lincoln*; Sutton-on-Sea and Mablethorpe *via Lincoln*; Cleethorpes; Manchester Central *via Guide Bridge and Sheffield Victoria* to:-

Yarmouth Vauxhall *via Lincoln and March*; Bury St. Edmunds *via Lincoln and March*. **Doncaster to:-** Yarmouth Vauxhall *via Lincoln and March*; Bridlington (2, one on to Filey Holiday Camp). **Via Doncaster (GC line)**[27] **:-** Sheffield Victoria to Cleethorpes; Rotherham Central to Cleethorpes; Blackpool North *via Todmorden, Normanton and Barnsley*, also Barnsley Court House, to Cleethorpes *via Carcroft and Skellow Junction*; Blackpool Central *via Todmorden, Normanton and Barnsley* to Lincoln; Leeds Central to Skegness *via Grimsby*; Leeds Central/Bradford Exchange to Yarmouth Vauxhall *via Lincoln and March* (2). Sheffield Victoria to Lincoln; Basford North *via Mansfield Central and* **Tuxford** to Scarborough *via Goole and Bridlington*; Manchester London Rd./Stockport Tiviot Dale *via Godley Junction and Sheffield Victoria* to Scarborough *via Goole and Bridlington*; Liverpool Central *via Manchester Central and Sheffield Victoria* to Gainsborough Lea Road.
Via Selby:- Leeds City to Bridlington (2, one on to Filey Holiday Camp); Manchester Exchange *via Leeds*, Gloucester Eastgate, and Chesterfield Midland *via Sheffield Midland and Pontefract* (1 each) to Bridlington and Filey Holiday Camp; Sheffield Victoria *via Pontefract* to Filey Holiday Camp; Manchester London Rd. *via Barnsley Court House and Pontefract* to Scarborough *via Bridlington*; York, Stalybridge *via Leeds*, and Liverpool Exchange *via Normanton* (1 each) to Scarborough *via Bridlington*.
York *via Normanton*[28] to:- Blackpool Central (2). York to Scarborough. **Via York:-** Hull *via* **Edinburgh Waverley** to Glasgow Queen St.; Leeds City to **Edinburgh Waverley**; **Edinburgh Waverley** to Filey Holiday Camp; **Newcastle** *via Stockton* to Bridlington and Filey Holiday Camp; Leicester Central *via Sheffield Victoria* to Bridlington, Filey and Scarborough; Manchester Victoria *via Normanton*, Kings Norton, Leicester London Rd. and Derby Midland *via Sheffield Midland*, and Sheffield Victoria *via Pontefract*, and Bradford Forster Sq. *via Leeds* (1 each) to Scarborough. **Via Pilmoor** and **Gilling:-** Glasgow Queen St. *via* **Edinburgh**, and Newcastle 1 each to Scarborough.
Darlington to:- **Edinburgh Waverley**; *via Barnard Castle, Tebay and Preston* to Blackpool North. Saltburn *via Stockton,* **Newcastle and Edinburgh** to Glasgow Queen St. Leeds City *via Harrogate and* **Northallerton** to:- Newcastle *via* **Durham**; Saltburn *via Stockton,* **Northallerton**, Harrogate, Ilkley, Skipton and Preston to Blackpool North. South Shields *via Sunderland, also* Newcastle *via Durham (1 each)*, Bishop Auckland, Barnard Castle, Tebay and Preston to Blackpool North.
Newcastle to:- Heads of Ayr *via Carlisle and Dumfries*; *via* **Durham**, Harrogate, Leeds, Manchester and Chester to Llandudno; *via* **York**, Banbury and Basingstoke to Bournemouth Central; Paignton, also Newquay (1 each) *via* **York**, Birmingham New St. and Bristol. Sunderland *via Stockton,* **Northallerton, York, Doncaster,** Lincoln and March to Yarmouth Vauxhall.

1. The totals *include* the trains continuing beyond Edinburgh. One train (Monday - Friday) was non-stop.
2. The quickest time was by the *QUEEN OF SCOTS via Leeds*.
3. This train, and many Sundays Only trains to the seaside ran only in the summer peak.
4. Called only at Crow Park, Newark and Retford.
5. One was through from Lincoln.
6. Called only at Selby.
7. LMR trains.
8. Through from Peterborough East.
9. One train terminated at Peterborough North.
10. Through to Cambridge.
11. One through from Gainsborough Central.
12. Westbound trains; equivalent trains ran eastbound. GC trains *not calling* at Retford not listed here. For seasonal *SO* trains running on the GC through Retford, see below. Sundays only trains also included one each Wadsley Bridge (*via Sheffield Victoria*) to Swineshead and to Boston and return workings.
13. Not stopping at Retford.
14. Northbound; eastbound on the GC lines. Equivalent trains ran in the opposite direction.
15. Extended to **Newcastle** on *FSO*.
16. Eastbound only: equivalent trains ran westbound.
17. Not stopping at Selby.
18. Hereford on Saturday night/Sunday morning.
19. Down direction only; equivalent trains ran in the Up direction.
20. Down trains listed only.
21. Down trains listed only.
22. Six were not after 4th September. Included through trains from Barnard Castle, Tow Law, Durham/Bishop Auckland, and Penrith.
23. Not after 4th September.
24. Several were through from Barnard Castle, Middleton-in-Teesdale, Middlesbrough or Saltburn, and through to South Shields — especially on Sundays.
25. LMR train not calling at Peterborough North.
26. Many of the summer seasonal trains to Scarborough used the Londesborough Road platforms near the Central station.
27. A number of *SO* trains ran through Retford without stopping.
28. Certain trains used the Doncaster avoiding-line, Hexthorpe Junction - Bentley Junction. LM. LMR trains.

(left) **Headed by Haymarket D34 No.62494 (LNER No.9492) GLEN GOUR and Doncaster based V2, No.60889 (LNER No.4860), the 15.40 Edinburgh - Berwick stopping train emerges from Penmanshiel Tunnel and passes under the Great North Rd, 31st August 1956.** *C.J.B.Sanderson*.

(left) **London Inner Suburban: N2/1 No.69495 (LNER No.4611) pulls a pair of 'quad-arts' out of the sidings at Hatfield to work a local up to King's Cross as the destination board indicates, 21st April 1956.** *F.Hornby*.

(below) **A panoramic view at Selby, with A1 No.60122 CURLEW pulling away on a Down express. Selby Abbey is prominent behind the train. The tall double telegraph poles, as seen here, on the ECML carried the vital telephone circuits between Control Offices.** *E.Sanderson*.

(right) **Not quite on the ECML, but will soon meet it at Chaloners Whin, this early morning Leeds - Scarborough relief rattles past Osmondthorpe station near Leeds, headed by D49/2 No.62761(LNER No.353) THE DERWENT piloting B16/1 No.61428 (LNER No.933), 15th June 1957.** *B.K.B.Green.*

(centre) **Hitchin: an evening view up the line towards London, from by the South Box, 29th July 1950; an L1 2-6-4T is crossing from the Up Slow to the Up Fast on the 19.19 SO Royston - King's Cross.** *G.W.Goslin.*

(below) **The Forces Leave train that ran regularly on Fridays from Henlow Camp on the ex-MR Bedford branch to King's Cross is seen here in the Up main platform at Hitchin, hauled rather unusually by J68 No.68654 (LNER No.7028) on 5th October 1957, the train being made up of two 'quad-arts'.** *F.Hornby.*

continued from page 71.

down the former GC main line but avoiding Sheffield Victoria by the Darnall loop, thence to York and onwards. Called 'Starlight Specials', they proved very popular for a few years. The Starlight Return fare to Edinburgh was only £3.50 in 1955 and £4.25 in 1958, compared with the Ordinary Return fare (third-class) in 1955 of £5.73; many of the trains conveyed a cafeteria car, but they had no sleeping-cars. Summer 1953 saw some really substantial accelerations. In particular the Non-Stop - the former *CAPITALS LIMITED* now renamed the *ELIZABETHAN* in honour of the Queen's Coronation - was speeded up to reach Edinburgh in 6hr. 45min., but it ran in the summer only; it kept its non-stop schedule every summer until 1961. Also from June 1953 the new morning express to Leeds and Bradford (unofficially the 'Bradford Flyer') now had to run from Hitchin to Doncaster at 65.8 m.p.h., while the Up *TEES-TYNE PULLMAN* was scheduled non-stop from Darlington at 62.3 m.p.h. The Coronation itself on 2nd June 1953 naturally brought a number of reliefs and Excursions up to King's Cross. The most noteworthy Excursions were overnight runs of the *TEES-TYNE PULLMAN* from Newcastle and the *YORKSHIRE PULLMAN* from Leeds and Bradford[23]. The ECML line speed limit having been relaxed to 90 m.p.h., in the Summer 1953 timetable there were 15 mile-a-minute runs, totalling 1,883 miles and no less than 89% of the total for the whole country. The Winter 1953 timetable was heralded by the running in late September of the two preserved GN Atlantics (No.990 HENRY OAKLEY and No.251) on Outer Suburban trains and then twice on the 'Plant Centenarian' Specials to Doncaster and Leeds. The 'Bradford Flyer' - now also with a Newcastle portion - was speeded up further, to cover Hitchin to Retford start-to-stop at 66.7 m.p.h.

Summer 1954 brought some further accelerations, notably of the *ELIZABETHAN* to 6 hrs 30 mins, and a few additions to the ECML timetable. The daily aggregate of mile-a-minute runs was now 22 (2,098 miles), although other Regions were doing better and this distance represented only 48% of the national total. The Winter timetable of 1954 brought little further change, but the Summer timetable of 1955 - delayed because of the

ASLEF Strike - showed some more welcome accelerations on the ECML. For example, the London - Edinburgh time of the *FLYING SCOTSMAN* was cut to 7 hrs, and near 60 m.p.h. averages for the hard Newcastle - Edinburgh stretch were attained by several trains, while on the York - Darlington 'speedway' as many as 14 trains were scheduled at over a mile-a-minute. (The 17-day ASLEF Strike did not paralyse BR completely, because enough NUR footplate-men were available for a few trains still to be run. After the first 10 days skeleton timetables were issued, which on the ECML provided for example a day and a night train from King's Cross to Edinburgh and for two trains to Newcastle).

A portentous development that Summer was the *CAR-SLEEPER LIMITED*, BR's belated response to the 'Love Affair with the Motor Car'. A service was put on from King's Cross to Perth on Wednesday and Sunday nights, and these by-passed Edinburgh Waverley, locomotives being changed at Niddrie West. It was very popular, and in Summer 1956 it ran every night. The motor vehicles were end-loaded into covered vans which had a total capacity for 20 cars, and passengers travelled either in third-class sleepers or in open saloons. The charge was set at £15 for car plus driver and £4.50 for each additional passenger. (This compares with a third-class London - Edinburgh Return fare of £5.73 and a charge of 80p for a third-class berth). The popularity of the service soon necessitated the running of several motor-car vans on each train, and further car-sleeper trains were introduced in the following summer. One ran (Wednesdays and Saturdays only) Newcastle - Dover *via* York, Sheffield and the GC line to Northolt Junction thence *via* Greenford and Kensington onto the SR, and connecting with a car-ferry at Dover. Another ran (Mondays only) Newcastle - Exeter St Davids *via* Birmingham and Bristol, and a third (Sundays only) York - Inverness. In Summer 1957 several more car-sleeper sets were in operation on the ECML, the services of 1956 being augmented by three services a week Marylebone - Perth. The facilities were further expanded in Summer 1958, with a King's Cross - Perth service now running every night (Fridays excepted).

Perhaps the most 'ominous' innovation of Summer 1954 was the very first wholesale operation on BR of a passenger service by diesel multiple-units (DMUs). Indirectly associated with the ECML, this radical change involved the local trains between Bradford Exchange, Leeds Central and Harrogate. It was followed by the introduction in 1955 of DMUs (based at Lincoln and Norwich) on East Anglian and Lincolnshire services, thus bringing them to Grantham and later to Peterborough, the transformation being largely completed in 1956. In Winter 1955 the Newcastle - Middlesbrough service went over to DMUs, maintained at the modernized and adapted South Gosforth electric train depot.

Selby: the north end, 5th April 1957, with D49/2 No.62761 (LNER No.353) THE DERWENT coming off the swing-bridge on a stopping train of very mixed stock from Hull. *Author.*

A splendid view - looking south - of the flyover just north of Wood Green station, with N2/4 No.69593 (LNER No.2687) crossing on a Down Hertford local, 14th September 1957. Bounds Green carriage depot can be seen on the left. *B.K.B.Green.*

As 1955 was the last year before the Modernization Plan began to come into effect, before the extensive introduction of DMUs on local services, and perhaps a peak year for Summer Saturday travel, it can be taken as an 'index year' of this early period of BR. Moreover, the demand for rail passenger travel in 1955 was still healthy, as is exemplified by the passenger counts (including Season Ticket journeys) for July 1955 at King's Cross (241,000), Finsbury Park (53,000), Hatfield (27,000) and Hitchin (46,000). Therefore in Table 4.3 are summarized the passenger services timetabled in August 1955. Full lists of passenger trains in August 1955 at the principal ECML centres are provided in an Appendix in Part II, and these include unadvertised 'Q' trains, and will enable comparisons to be made with those for pre-war (August 1939) and for wartime (August 1942) in their respective Tables.

In Summer 1956 a considerable expansion of the long-distance services - over those listed in Table 4.3 for the previous Summer - was attained by extension of the regular-interval principle, with quick turn-round at King's Cross. Loads were restricted to 12 bogies and reservations suspended on Saturdays. This was very useful on Summer Saturdays, when there were expresses every hour between 08.40 and 15.40 to Newcastle and every *half* hour to West Yorkshire, but if anything went wrong chaos could result in the cramped and awkward confines of King's Cross.

In Winter 1956 a new King's Cross - Edinburgh express - *THE TALISMAN* - was introduced, leaving London at 16.00 hrs. and taking only 6hr. 40min. Then, in the Summer timetable of 1957, another Edinburgh express was put on, leaving King's Cross at 07.45, and named the *MORNING TALISMAN*, the 16.00 departure now being called the *AFTERNOON TALISMAN*; both

ran non-stop to Newcastle, as did three more expresses. The *AFTERNOON TALISMAN* was a successor in a way to the pre-war *CORONATION*, but took 40 minutes longer to get to Edinburgh.

In Winter 1957 the *MORNING TALISMAN* was renamed the *FAIR MAID* and extended to Perth - as was also the *HEART OF MIDLOTHIAN*, the latter being routed by the former LMS line *via* Larbert and Stirling. (These extensions to Perth were however cancelled a year later, and the *MORNING TALISMAN* got its name back again). The *FLYING SCOTSMAN* was further accelerated, its King's Cross - Edinburgh time being cut by 37 minutes to 6hr. 58min. The *ABERDONIAN* was much altered, to leave King's Cross at 22.15 instead of 19.00, and was 50 minutes faster throughout, having no *public* stops before Inverkeithing. The new 19.45 from King's Cross now had through carriages for Elgin, and the *NIGHT SCOTSMAN* - all first-class sleeping-cars and no seating accommodation at all, was no less than *2hrs 24mins* quicker to Edinburgh. Many other expresses were speeded up by omitting former stops, while more through King's Cross - Hull trains were put on, running independently of those to West Yorkshire and making intermediate stops missed by the others. Finally, the through Lincolnshire services were much improved. At the end of 1957, the number of mile-a-minute runs over the York - Darlington 'speedway' had risen steeply to 24 - the fastest being 66.2 m.p.h., and it should be noted that all these improvements antedated the introduction of main-line diesel locomotives on the ECML by at least a year.

In Summer 1958 there were some further accelerations of ECML expresses and the addition of more night expresses. The number of regular 60 m.p.h. runs had now risen to 35 (2,436 miles, 25% of the national total). The accelerations were still

The Up *ANGLO-SCOTTISH CAR-CARRIER* south of Peascliff Tunnel, headed by a filthy A2/3, No.60522 **STRAIGHT DEAL, 21st June 1960. The train has ten motor car vans at the head and passenger coaches at the rear.** *Hepburn/RAS.*

Hornsey: the north end of the station with its booking office (free from Council rates) on the footbridge, and No.2 (Up) Box on the left. A3 No.60109 (LNER No.4478) HERMIT, in its latter days with a double chimney, speeds through on the Down *TALISMAN*', passing a local on Down Slow No.1, 8th May 1959. *P.H.Groom*.

A lot rarer on the GN section then than they had been in earlier years, this York based B16/1 (No.61436, LNER No.2365) was caught as it left Grantham on an Up empty stock train in August 1958. *P.H.Groom*.

Colwick K2 No.61749 (LNER No.4659) stands at the Western platform at Grantham on a Nottingham train, 11th September 1957. Behind is part of the locomotive yard. *B.K.B.Green.*

TABLE 4.4: SUMMARY OF MAIN LINE PASSENGER SERVICES
FROM KING'S CROSS, SUMMER 1959

This Table is drawn up on the same basis as the first section of Tables 4.1 - 4.3, to demonstrate the changes brought about during the later 1950s to the ECML express services, when quicker turn-round at King's Cross and then the introduction of main-line diesel locomotives allowed more frequent and faster trains. As before, distances and fastest times are given, the number of trains (or through coaches) being those to the stated destinations - except that the figures for Edinburgh include *all* trains going beyond there.

King's Cross to:-
Edinburgh Waverley (393m, 417m *via Leeds and Ripon*) - 14 (one non-stop; 395 min), 16 FO, 13 SO, 10 SuO. **Via Edinburgh Waverley:-** Glasgow Queen St. (440m, 464m *via Leeds and Ripon*) - 2 (533 min), 3 SO, 1 SuO; Aberdeen (524m) - 4 (629 min), 5 FO, 4 SO, 3 SuO; Elgin *via Aberdeen* (604m) - 1 (862 min), nil SO; Dundee (452m) - 1 (647 min), nil SO, 1 SuO; Fort William (563m) - 1 (882 min), nil SO, 1 SuO. **Newcastle** (269m) - 11 MO, 10 TThO, 9 WO (282 min), 11 FO, 13 SO, 7 SuO (1 SO, 1 SuO *via Stockton*); Tyne Commission Quay *via Newcastle* - 2. **Darlington** (232m) - 1 *SuO* (313 min). *Via Northallerton:-* Sunderland *via Stockton* (281m) - 1 (354 min), 2 FO, 1 SO; Saltburn *via Middlesbrough* (260m) - 1 (353 min). **York** (188m) - 1 (246 min), 2 SO. **Via York:-** Scarborough (230m) - 1 (273 min), 1 SuO; Whitby (244m) - 1 *FSO* (353 min). **Doncaster** (156m) - 1 (192 min), nil SO. **Via Doncaster:-** Wakefield Kirkgate (176m) - 1 *SO* (228 min); Leeds Central/Bradford Exchange (186/193m) - 10 (223/247 min), 12 MFO, 19 SO, 8 SuO; Hull (197m) - 6 249 min), 7 FSO, 2 SuO; Harrogate (204m) - 1 (270 min), 2 SuO; Ripon (213m) - 1 (308 min); Halifax (202m) - 1 (293 min). **Via Retford:** Sheffield Victoria (162m) - 2 (165 min), 1 SO. **Via Peterborough North:-** Cleethorpes (158m) - 2 (249 min), 4 SO, 1 SuO; Lincoln *via Spalding and Sleaford*- 1 *SuO* (132m); Skegness (131m) - 5 *SO*.

In the first days of the diesels on the ECML in 1958-59, English Electric Type 4 No.D201 passes Lolham Crossing (south of Tallington) with an Up express. It is said that the gates of these crossings on the descent of Stoke Bank once-in-a-while succumbed to speeding expresses. *A.C.Ingram.*

not however attributable to the introduction of main-line diesels, although the new 2,000 hp Type 4 diesel-electric No. D200 first ran trials on the ECML in March 1958, and one of these locomotives first worked the *FLYING SCOTSMAN* - as far as Newcastle, on 21st June 1958. Regular diagrams for the diesels began in July 1958, on the *WHITE ROSE* as far as Doncaster, and on the *HEART OF MIDLOTHIAN* as far as Peterborough; in September 1958 the Type 4s were put to work on the new Pullman train, 19.20 King's Cross - Sheffield Victoria *via* Retford, the *MASTER CUTLER* - a name previously given to a Sheffield express from Marylebone. Winter 1958 also saw the introduction of yet another fast 'business' train, the *TEES-THAMES LINK* (06.48 Middlesbrough to Doncaster), operated by a DMU set and connecting at Doncaster with a locomotive-hauled non-stop express to King's Cross - but the service did not run in the opposite direction. At last in the Winter 1958 timetable five very intensive Class 40 diesel diagrams from King's Cross to Newcastle and Sheffield were introduced, each of about 4,500 miles per week, Pacific diagrams from King's Cross being cut drastically as a consequence. The ER celebrated its introduction of the new diesels onto the ECML with an Exhibition, held on 14-15th September 1958 in Noel Park goods yard on the Palace Gates branch, displaying the latest main-line diesel locomotives and the DMUs alongside modern and not-so-modern steam locomotives associated with the GN Line.

However, the reliability of the diesels left a lot to be desired, and substitution by a steam locomotive was a very common occurrence. In spite of the operation now of a sizeable proportion of ECML expresses by diesel power, neither the Summer nor the Winter 1959 timetable (which did not begin until November) yet showed any dramatic changes, although another new named express was introduced - the *TEES-THAMES*, which was a

necessary development of the previous year's *TEES-THAMES LINK* into a through express, 07.05 Saltburn to King's Cross returning at 14.00. Examination of Table 4.4 will show the extent to which the *frequency* of ECML expresses had been enhanced in the later 1950s. (Main-line departures from King's Cross in August 1959 are listed in the Appendix in Part II).

Major *accelerations* however were not possible until the diesels were both more numerous and more reliable. Moreover, the original BR Mark I standard coaches gave a poor ride at more than about 60 m.p.h. and were not improving BR's faded public image - until later when the Commonwealth bogie was introduced. At the end of 1959, when Gateshead was acquiring a considerable stud of Type 4s they were allotted regular diagrams, most of which took them in the Edinburgh direction. Nevertheless, no mass movements of ECML Pacifics had yet taken place: the A3s previously on the former GC section had been returned to the GN lines and King's Cross had gained nine (and lost one by withdrawal), New England two, Grantham four, and Gateshead five, while Doncaster had lost four, Copley Hill three, and Heaton three. A1s had been moved, in that Doncaster had gained twelve (ten from Grantham and one each from Ardsley and Copley Hill); lastly, one A2 had moved from Grantham to New England.

During the late 1950s, the 'Swan-Song of Steam' was sung by the running of a number of steam-hauled Enthusiasts' Specials on the ECML. Speed restrictions were relaxed where it was safe, and Gresley's Pacifics were 'given their head'. Notably, on 23rd May 1959, No.60007 SIR NIGEL GRESLEY on the Stephenson Locomotive Society '*Golden Jubilee Special*' achieved an official post-war record for steam of 112 m.p.h. - descending Stoke Bank of course. (This run, and a number of others, are described fully in P.Semmens' (1990) *Speed on the East Coast Main Line*).

Notes:

1. North Eastern Airways ran a *daily* service from London (Croydon) to Perth and Dundee, 'calling' at Doncaster and Newcastle. Connecting services flew from Doncaster to Hull, Grimsby, and Leeds, and *by request*(!) to Manchester, and Liverpool. There was also a flight on many days from Newcastle to Glasgow.

2. Those along the ECML are shown in the tables for 1939, 1942, 1955 and 1959 in Part II in an Appendix.

3. However, in the plans for the *complete* evacuation of East Coast towns, drawn up in case of a German invasion - that mercifully never had to be implemented, the ECML was specifically excluded, to keep it clear for military traffic.

4. Cheap Day Returns were reintroduced almost right away in October 1939, only to be rescinded again in October 1942.

5. Even one of these was taken off on 19th June.

6. Navy, Army and Air Force Institutes.

7. Railway Traffic Office(r).

8. For example, passenger trains took workers into the large RAOC depot at Barlow, on the Goole branch near Selby.

9. Officially, services from Moorgate were abolished on 6th January 1941 "to allow additional coal traffic to be carried by the Widened Lines" - *i.e.* without restriction during the rush-hours.

10. But see the comment on bilking, made earlier.

11. Women's Voluntary Services.

12. The York canteen alone, during the 6 years and 10 months it was open, served 10 m. customers. The Army Council Instructions specified precisely what refreshments should be available, and their price, for troops on the move (*e.g.* tea 0.25p a cup, sandwiches 1p each).

13. A plaque remains to this day at Retford station commemorating the serving by the WVS of "2,284,000 meals to HM and Allied Forces during the Second World War."

14. Near York were some dozen bomber airfields, and the HQ of 4 Group at Heslington Hall (from April 1940) and of 6 Group (RCAF) at Allerton Park Castle; Grantham (St. Vincents) was the HQ of 5 Group, until November 1943 when as Spitalgate it became the HQ of 9 Troop Carrier Command USAAF, 5 Group moving to Moreton Hall, Swinderby; HQ 2 Group was at Huntingdon (Castle Hill House) from October 1939, and later HQ 8 (Pathfinder) Group was near there at Brampton Grange - as was later the HQ of 1 Bombardment Division, USAAF; HQ 1 Group was at yet another ECML location - Bawtry Hall. For the Army, York was the HQ of Northern Command and HQ Scottish Command was at Edinburgh.

15. The record claimed was 26 coaches - including some vans (estimated at a gross load of 850 tons), hauled from Peterborough to King's Cross on 31st March 1940 by V2 No.4800.

16. The details of these trains, of those more 'innocent days', were actually documented - even the number of men and nature of stores conveyed, and can be studied in PRO AN2/1027. Most of the trains using the ECML were destined for Rosyth, Dunfermline or Leith, and the great majority joined the ECML at York (having gone up the ex-GC main line) or else originated in the NE Area.

17. On 17th April no less than 400 empty coaches were sent up to Glasgow from the SR, and the peak day for dispatch of arriving overseas troops was on 19th April, when 82 specials were forwarded from all the ports.

18. 11th Armoured, 3rd Infantry and 15th Infantry Divisions, with 8th and 27th Armoured Brigades and 6th Guards Tank Brigade.

19. The line from Hessle Road Junction, Dairycoates, to Riverside Quay was upgraded in 1946 for passenger train working

20. About 20,000 passengers left King's Cross on peak Summer Saturdays.

21. This trip was noteworthy in that on the return leg the locomotive collided with a crossing-gate near Balne - without serious damage to anything but the gate.

22. One of these B1s, No.61379, was named MAYFLOWER, because it passed through Boston, whence the Pilgrim Fathers had sailed.

23. Other overnight Excursion trains were: one each from Aberdeen, Dundee, Edinburgh, Newcastle, East Boldon, Scarborough and Bridlington, Bradford, Cleethorpes and Lincoln, and Grantham, and there was a daytime one from Cranwell by the RAF branch to Sleaford. For the Coronation also many major stations on BR enjoyed a much overdue *repainting*, and the frontage at King's Cross was cleaned and renovated.

(below) **The ECML in all its glory; a King's Cross - Edinburgh express formed of splendid new BR stock headed by 60034 LORD FARINGDON (LNER No.4903 PEREGRINE) shows off well in stormy weather at Brayton, south of Selby, late 1950s.** *E.Sanderson.*

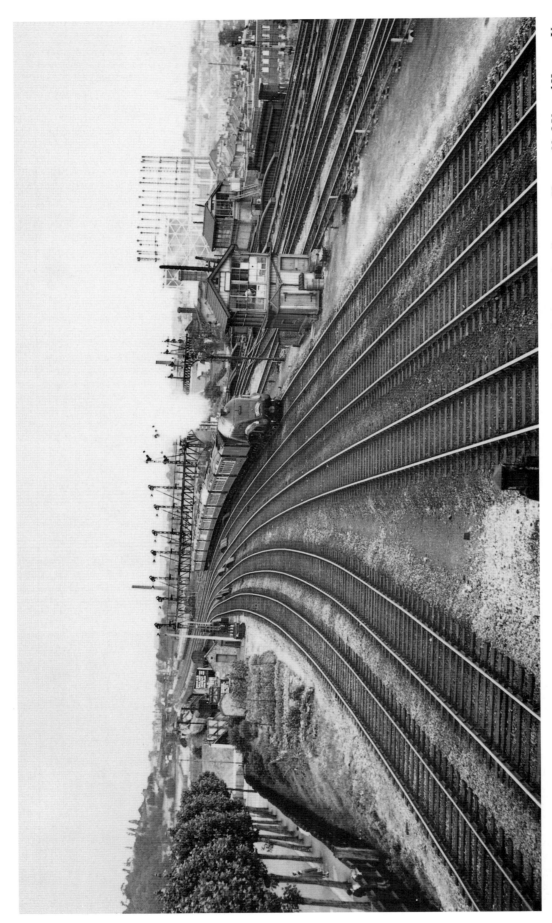

The Up *TEES-TYNE PULLMAN*, headed by A4 No.60028 WALTER K. WHIGHAM (LNER No.4487 SEA EAGLE), approaches Hornsey station, 31st July 1956. In this panoramic view northwards, the two signalboxes are Hornsey No.2 Up and Hornsey Up Goods, and beyond are the extensive sidings of No.1 Carriage Yard. *J.Aylard coll.*

Chapter V. RESTAURANT, PULLMAN and SLEEPING-CAR FACILITIES, POST OFFICE SERVICES, ROYAL TRAINS, and HOTELS ON THE ECML, 1939-1959.

RESTAURANT CARS and BUFFET CARS.

In 1939 restaurant car meals were provided on the great majority of ECML expresses. On Mondays to Fridays about 15 regular departures from King's Cross had restaurant cars. They also ran on many of the Saturday extras and the relatively infrequent Sunday services. Although a number of trains, notably the Cambridge and the Cleethorpes expresses from King's Cross and the 08.45 to Doncaster, had buffet cars instead; meal facilities were proffered also on the principal ECML expresses not emanating from London. The catering vehicles plied mainly between the major ECML centres, with the staff - of six men - often doing the double journey (*e.g.* to and from Leeds) in one working day, but the vehicles also worked through to Ripon and to Scarborough. On the Newcastle and Edinburgh runs the staff lodged overnight, as they did often on long-distance Excursions when they slept in hammocks on the train. Buffet cars were definitely considered 'modish', and they were especially favoured by those who liked to drink at all times of the day, for - like the restaurant cars - they were unaffected by Licensing Laws.

Catering vehicles were built to last, and on the ECML before the war there were still a number of pre-Grouping sets running, although the majority were Gresley LNER vehicles. They had to be solidly built - especially the kitchen cars, for not only was much heavy equipment carried but the staff needed a steady vehicle in which to cook, serve and wash-up, also there was a large store for 'bonded goods' which needed to be secure from pilfering in sidings. The Gresley cars included his articulated triplets in which the kitchen car was attached permanently to restaurant saloons at each end, one for 1st-class the other for 3rd-class. Then there was also the unique quintuplet, which had ordinary compartment seating vehicles permanently attached at each end of a triplet catering set. This normally ran on the 10.15 King's Cross-Leeds and 17.30 return, and was probably more nuisance than it was worth because a defect in any one part effectively put five whole vehicles out of action. During the war the set was stored at Nottingham, and in 1950 was returned to the Leeds run, but only for two years after which it was broken up. On the ECML in the 1930s a kitchen car had to have the equipment and food for up to 500 meals. Thus having a restaurant on each side of the kitchen facilitated the waiters' work by 'swing service', as also did their practice of 'silver service' - serving passengers from dishes rather than trying to carry bowls of soup on a swaying train.

Unlike on most other Railways, where oil gas was employed for cooking, Gresley's kitchen cars were all-electric. The all-electric kitchens needed to be supported by a system of charging the batteries from electrical supplies to allow some cooking to be done while the kitchen car was not on the move. But the batteries could not carry the whole load, and therefore not only did charging facilities have to be available at the main carriage yards (such as Holloway, Hornsey, Heaton and Craigentinny), but also a range of mains electrical points had to be provided at some principal ECML stations. To prevent the cooks being embarrassed by unplanned cooling of hot-plates and ovens while they were in the middle of preparing dozens of meals, men rushed to plug in the kitchen to the mains when the train stopped and unplug it before the guard blew his whistle. Therefore the more modern electric kitchen cars running on the ECML in the 1930s were fitted as well with anthracite stoves to keep the ovens and hot-plates going. The anthracite/electric kitchen car was perpetuated in the new stock built for the ECML services directly after the war, and it was only under the BR regime that electricity and anthracite for cooking were eventually abandoned and the standard fuel for kitchen cars became propane gas. In the meantime on the celebrated Aberdeen - Penzance service, in 1939 a new type of vehicle had been introduced - a car with both a restaurant and a buffet section served from an integral kitchen. The sets ran between Newcastle and Swindon, yet still somehow managed to run on electricity only; after the war they too were converted to use propane gas.

The LNER had indeed been the foremost of the Big Four in the development of buffet cars, and it had some 70 in service just before the war. Some 25 of these had been Open 3rds, one end having been converted by the installation of a small kitchen and a service counter, leaving seating for about 24 passengers in a 2-to-1 arrangement with tables. The rest were purpose-built cars to the same basic design, either typical Gresley in varnished teak or with plywood panels in green and cream for incorporation into the Tourist train sets. The first buffet-car trains were used for the King's Cross-Cambridge fast service introduced in 1932, but by 1939 the majority of the buffet cars were employed in the NE Area, mainly on the services from Newcastle to Middlesbrough and to Carlisle.

During the war there were no changes in catering stock, except a large reduction in the number in use. For a month or so after the outbreak of war, restaurant cars were taken off entirely. But they were soon restored, and in 1940-41 there were still about ten regular restaurant services from King's Cross, and many other ECML trains had buffet cars - some for Servicemen only. In March 1941, the LNER was still running daily 36 restaurant cars and 21 buffet cars on the ECML - and on the midday King's Cross-Edinburgh service one of each. Like so much else in wartime, there was now a 'standard' restaurant-car lunch and dinner (each at 12.5p) and tea (at 5p) - even the service charge was regulated (at 1.5p). In 1942 the services were cut down again to three, to two in 1943[1] and to none at all in Summer 1944. Thereafter there were none until Winter 1945, when the *FLYING SCOTSMAN* alone acquired a restaurant car and one Newcastle service a buffet car.

Generally, the number of restaurant services - if not their quality - were back to pre-war levels by 1948, although the Cambridge line services did not return until late in that year, and many buffet car services that had run from Newcastle to Middlesbrough and to Carlisle before the war (surviving until 1941) came back only very briefly in the late 1940s although

King's Cross: the classic pre-war scene, as Gresley A1 No.2555 CENTENARY leaves from No.10 on the *QUEEN OF SCOTS* Pullman. Numerous N2s are visible too, from the Milk Dock on the right (St Pancras station behind it), in the Suburban station and at platform 8, and an Atlantic stands in platform 6, late 1930s. *G.Tidey, Lens.*

one or two were perpetuated in the 1950s on the Carlisle trains. Likewise the buffet-car services between Leeds and Scarborough had a very transitory post-war revival. After the war Thompson built two buffet-lounge cars, which were employed on the ECML Non-Stops. Later, in 1958, many of the standard buffet cars were rebuilt as restaurant-buffet cars to the design of those introduced in 1939 mentioned above. During the 1950s therefore buffet cars came to be employed on a number of ECML services, including King's Cross to Edinburgh, Grantham, Peterborough and Cleethorpes as well as to Cambridge, and Newcastle to Liverpool, York and Colchester.

In the 1950s snacks were more in vogue, supplied often in new buffet-pantry cars, and full meal services were definitely a lot less sumptuous than pre-war - and by 1952 restaurant cars were called 'refreshment cars'. The trend established in the war towards self-service feeding was perpetuated, and on the ECML cafeteria cars were first introduced in 1952 on the Starlight Specials to Scotland. The food in cafeteria cars was very largely prepared before the journey, and minimal cooking facilities were needed. Much preliminary cooking for ECML catering was done in the large kitchen under platforms 6-10 at King's Cross. There followed 'miniature buffet' cars, 'griddle' cars and more such

(left) **The interior of the third-class restaurant car of the 1938 *FLYING SCOTSMAN* set.** *Newsome/Hughes.*

The Up *CORONATION* flashes past the junctions at Low Fell in early July 1939, headed by A4 No.4492 (BR No.60013) **DOMINION OF NEW ZEALAND.** *G.J.Hughes collection.*

The rural panorama at Ganwick between Hadley North and Potters Bar tunnels, with the Down *SILVER JUBILEE* (4498 at the front - according to the *Gresley Observer*) speeding out of London in the evening, 3rd August 1938. The wide strip of railway land to the left, between the lines and the fence, was owned by the LNER in anticipation of the widening to four tracks eventually achieved in 1959. *E.R.Wethersett.*

labour-saving arrangements. For a while soon after Nationalization, one of the new 'tavern cars' - named 'The Salutation' - ran on the ECML, and in January 1958 a 'miniature buffet' car was incorporated - in addition to the usual restaurant-car set - on the *FLYING SCOTSMAN*. The reorganization resulting from the Transport Act of 1953, when catering was passed from regional control to a new British Transport Hotels & Catering Services, did little to improve standards of catering on the move and the high pre-war standards never returned.

New catering vehicles introduced by BR in 1951 conformed to the new Mark I series of coaching stock, and comprised open 1st and 3rd-class restaurant cars with loose seating, and kitchen cars with anthracite stoves combined with electrical heating as on the later LNER cars. A limited number of these vehicles worked on the ECML in combination with LNER vehicles, until the introduction in 1956 of an entirely new series of (Mark I) catering vehicles on BR. The series included: a kitchen-buffet with a bar section with seats, a kitchen-restaurant (unclassed) car (33 seats) with full cooking facilities, and a kitchen-buffet car capable of providing full meals to 23 seats and light refreshments from a self-service area. The cooking in all these vehicles was with propane gas, electricity being used only for refrigeration. With minor modifications these 1956 cars were built in substantial numbers between 1957 and 1963, and were employed extensively on the ECML.

Life for travelling catering staff was not easy, and is well described by Wooler (1987): "On the restaurant cars a crew is always out on its own, and at the mercy of unforeseen hitches and delays, for up to 13 or 14 hours at a stretch. In that time, its members will cook, serve and wash up for many hundreds of hungry and demanding travellers, not to mention the continuous coming and going at the buffet counter. Nearly everything is freshly cooked on board - and cooked in a kitchen smaller than that in the average suburban three-bedroom house, which by contrast would seldom prepare meals for more than six people. Much skill is needed by cooks and waiters working on a swaying train. It is a life of challenge, responsibility and variety. They are often called on to care for as well as cope with passengers, and must be able to tackle equipment failures *en route*. There are no changeovers on the way, as for locomotive men or guards, for restaurant-car staff have a very long stint - preparing, cooking and serving two or three sittings per meal, then washing up, cashing up and clearing up. Catering cars are at once a grocer's store, wine merchant's cellar, tobacconist, hotel kitchen, store room, and pantry. They must carry a refuse-bin area, and have a wardrobe, locker, and dressing space for up to eight staff, plus a toilet."

PULLMANS

Just before the war there were two regular Pullman expresses running down the ECML on weekdays: the *QUEEN OF SCOTS* to Leeds, Harrogate, Newcastle, Edinburgh and Glasgow, and the *YORKSHIRE PULLMAN* to Leeds, Harrogate[2], Bradford, Halifax and Hull, and one, the *HARROGATE SUNDAY PULLMAN*, on Sundays to Leeds, Bradford and Harrogate[3]. (The LNER also ran Pullman-restaurant cars on certain trains in Scotland, including Perth-Edinburgh, Glasgow-Edinburgh, Carlisle-Edinburgh, and Glasgow-Dundee). These luxury trains vied with the Streamliners for comfort, and like them they called for a supplementary charge (30p 1st-class, 15p 3rd-class, to Leeds in 1939) for which passengers enjoyed meals at their seats and other gratifications. The coaches belonged to the Pullman Car Company, which also provided the 'cabin' staff. Dressed in their distinctive uniforms and with an ingrained civility, the latter were more highly selected and probably even more skilled than the Railway restaurant-car staff. Each train had a Conductor, who had under him one attendant for each coach and in addition the staff working in the kitchen compartments situated in each alternate car, and this team of men tended to remain with their own train set. The trains running on the LNER were made up from 31 all-steel cars built by the Metropolitan-Cammell Carriage & Wagon Co. in 1928.

During the war the Pullman trains were withdrawn, and after being stored for a while most of the coaches (repainted brown) were employed by the LNER as ordinary 1st-saloons in service trains. Some of the coaches however were used in the special trains provided for the Prime Minister, for the Military Chiefs, and at times for the King and Queen.

The *YORKSHIRE PULLMAN* was reinstated in November 1946, with a portion again for Harrogate and for Hull, but the pre-war Halifax coaches went no further than Bradford. The *QUEEN OF SCOTS* was restored in July 1948 - again to Glasgow via Leeds - while in September 1948 a new service was introduced: the *TEES-TYNE PULLMAN*, to Newcastle calling at Darlington (also at York in the Down direction). Eventually, in September 1958 a fourth Pullman service was brought to the ECML, the *MASTER CUTLER PULLMAN*. This ran up from Sheffield Victoria early in the morning - and back in the evening - quite quickly (58.7 m.p.h. with one stop, at Retford). One of the first trains on the ECML to be scheduled from the outset to be worked by diesels (the new Type 4s), the *MASTER CUTLER* set was worked intensively for in the middle of the day the same train, now unnamed, made another return trip to Sheffield - on a slower schedule with more stops.

The all-steel Metro-Cammell cars of 1928 comprised the following: ten kitchen-1sts, with names female of course ('Belinda', 'Evadne', 'Ione', 'Joan', 'Loraine', 'Nilar', 'Penelope', 'Philomel', 'Phyllis' and 'Thelma'), seven parlour-1sts ('Agatha', 'Eunice', 'Juana', 'Lucille', 'Sheila', 'Ursula' and 'Zena'), four parlour-3rds (Nos.73-76) and 10 brake-3rds (Nos.67-72/7-80). Description of the fine appointments of the Pullman cars would be superfluous here, but it is of note that, unlike in the more modern LNER kitchen cars, cooking was still being done by oil gas, but this was superseded by propane gas when the Pullman Car Co. pioneered the use of this safer fuel in the 1950s.

The consist of the *YORKSHIRE PULLMAN* was 11 cars as far as Doncaster, where two 1sts and two 3rds were detached for Hull, two 1sts and three 3rds ran through to Harrogate *via* Leeds, and at Wakefield one 1st and one 3rd were detached for Bradford. The *QUEEN OF SCOTS* had two sets of coaches, each comprising ten cars (four 1sts and six 3rds), two of each class being detached at Leeds and the remainder continuing to Glasgow. The new *TEES-TYNE PULLMAN* was made up of eight cars of mixed origin including some still with wooden bodies: one kitchen-1st, two parlour-1sts, two kitchen-3rds, one brake-3rd, one composite, and a newly-converted 1st-class bar car named the 'Hadrian Bar'. The *MASTER CUTLER* had just six cars (three kitchen-1sts, one kitchen-2nd and two brake-2nds), initially still cars from the 1920s until the new cars built to the BR Standard design were brought into service in 1960. In the meantime the BTC had bought themselves a controlling interest in the Pullman Car Company in 1954, and in 1959 the BRB bought up the rest of the shares.

60084 (LNER No.2595) TRIGO passes Northallerton on the Down *QUEEN OF SCOTS* Pullman having just come off the Leeds Northern line. The view is south from the Down island platform, with the Up platform and bay on the left, 2nd August 1953. *B.K.B.Green.*

The rear end of the YORKSHIRE PULLMAN as it enters smoky Gas Works Tunnel, King's Cross, 1950. *K.Oldham.*

Getting into its stride, the Down *YORKSHIRE PULLMAN*', with A3 No.60062 (LNER No.2561) MINORU passes Hadley Wood, emerging from Hadley South Tunnel on what is shortly to become the *Up* Fast after completion of the New Barnet - Potters Bar widening. The date is 8th April 1959, and the lines through the new Hadley South Tunnel (on the left) were brought into use on 3rd May 1959. *J.Aylard.*

SLEEPING-CAR FACILITIES

On account of the long distances involved, especially to Scotland, the sleeping-car trains on the ECML were of primary importance. Just before the war there were six[4] regular sleeping-car services from King's Cross, including one (the *NIGHT SCOTSMAN*) that had very little seating accommodation at all. The *HIGHLANDMAN* conveyed sleeping-cars to Inverness, Nairn (*via* Forres) and Fort William, and the *ABERDONIAN* included a car to Lossiemouth as well as those just to Aberdeen. On Friday nights, the 22.35 from King's Cross conveyed a 1st-class car to North Berwick, which returned on Monday nights.

Apart from a period in the second half of 1940 when Edinburgh sleeping-car services were diverted to the LMSR and Princes Street, during the war there were three on the ECML (one each to Aberdeen, Edinburgh and Newcastle), and these services remained unchanged throughout the war - and until 1946. At the beginning of the war the REC stipulated a limit of one sleeping-car of each class per train, but the demand for 1st-class berths was so heavy that the limit soon had to be relaxed. Nevertheless from the middle of the war, the "number available to the general public is strictly limited", because most berths (including all 1st-class) were reserved for civilian and military 'Top Brass' on Government business.

Interior of a modern 1930s LNER first-class sleeping-car.
A.Newsome.

By April 1947 four[5] services to Scotland (including Edinburgh, Fort William, and Aberdeen) and the one to Newcastle - named the *TYNESIDER* in 1950 - had been restored, with a relief (with 1st-class car to Darlington) on Fridays which became nightly by 1949. In 1955 there was one more regular service to Edinburgh, by 1957 one more again, and in 1958 the

TYNESIDER formation - sleeping-cars only - contained two cars that were transferred at Newcastle to the 07.05 semi-fast to Edinburgh, returning on the 20.00 Up Mail train. That made seven sleeping-car services to Scotland and one to Darlington and Newcastle. First-class berths from King's Cross to Edinburgh cost £1.05 in 1939, rising to £2.00 by 1959. Several of these sleeping-car trains to Scotland in peacetime made no stops on the way other than for locomotive and crew changes - usually at Newcastle - and the *ABERDONIAN* would not even deign to deposit passengers at Edinburgh. The long non-stop runs made them all the more comfortable for their sleeping passengers.

The oldest sleeping-cars in the 1930s were pre-Grouping - albeit renovated - 1st-class single-berth[6] vehicles, but by 1939 most were of LNER vintage, some being articulated vehicles. They had single-berth 1st-class compartments - and one shower compartment per car, or in 3rd-class four-berth compartments in some of which the upper berths were capable of being folded back to give normal seating for daytime use. Naturally the 3rd-class had more primitive facilities, only the modern ones even having mattresses, and neither class in those days had 'en suite facilities', but the more modern 1st-class cars had full pressure-ventilation with ducts leading warm or cool air by nozzles above the bed-heads. First- and 3rd-class accommodation was usually - but not always - in separate vehicles, and there were two articulated sets (one half for each class) running on the ECML. Wash-basins, with electrically heated water and a self-flushing '*pot de chambre*' beneath, were usual before the war only in 1st-class, but were introduced in the two-berth 3rd-class sleepers built by the LNER soon after the war.

Sleeping-cars built to BR Standard Mark I design in 1957 were 1st-class only, composites or 2nd-class only, both classes having full bedding and wash-basins with hot and cold water. First-class was now single-berth and 3rd/2nd-class twin-berth, but the charges for berths in the two-berth 2nd-class cars were higher than for those in the older four-berth cars.

POST OFFICE MAIL SERVICES ON THE ECML

The ECML had no 'Down Special' equivalent to that on the WCML. The principal Mail service was the North-Eastern Down Travelling Post Office (TPO), comprising three carriages attached to the *NIGHT SCOTSMAN*, two of which came off at Newcastle, the third continuing to Edinburgh. The other TPO from London ran as part of the 20.25 express parcels, newspapers and mail train from King's Cross to Edinburgh. In addition there was the Bristol-Newcastle 'Midland' TPO, and also - before the war only - daytime (04.45) King's Cross-Leeds and York-Edinburgh TPOs. Only the London TPOs employed - mainly in the Down direction - automatic exchange apparatus, situated at New Barnet, Hatfield, Welwyn Garden City, Langley Junction, Hitchin, Biggleswade, Sandy, St Neots, Huntingdon, Peterborough, Pegswood, Alnmouth, Tweedmouth, Ayton, Dunbar, and Drem. After the war there were some changes in these locations, and of course like so much else they eventually disappeared. The TPO workings were taken off during the war in September 1940 and restored in May 1946, then remained essentially unchanged through the 1950s. Before coming south again on corresponding Up workings, the TPO vans had to be turned, at Newcastle by running them over the Bridges round by Gateshead, at Edinburgh round the South Suburban line or the triangle at Niddrie; at the London end they were turned on the North London line Dalston triangle.

Newspaper trains ran overnight from King's Cross to Edinburgh and from Manchester to Glasgow, some of the papers being sorted on the trains by travelling newspaper staff, who completed their sorting on trestle tables provided on the platforms.

TRAINS FOR ROYALTY AND OTHER 'VERY IMPORTANT PERSONS' ON THE ECML

ROYAL TRAINS

The LNER Royal Train, used in peacetime principally for Their Majesties to travel to and from Sandringham - normally down the ECML and *via* Cambridge[7], and not for overnight journeys, dated from ECJS days. It consisted of one or both principal saloons, up to four 'semi-Royal' saloons and two full brakes (as staff accommodation and luggage vans). There was no dedicated dining-car as such - but the LNER kept one of their 1st-class ones under cover at Bounds Green for Royal use when needed, and there was no sleeping-car. The two splendid 12-wheel saloons were built in 1908-09 (one each by the GNR and the NER) for King Edward VII and Queen Alexandra, but in 1926 the King's saloon was converted for Queen Mary's day use, and was run either in the Royal Train or attached to a service train; it was later made use of by Queen Elizabeth (the Queen Mother). The Queen's saloon in 1926 became the King's principal saloon and had two separate dressing-rooms.

The LNER Royal Train made numerous journeys along the ECML between King's Cross and Hitchin on its way to and from Wolferton (for Sandringham). (Journeys from London to Wolferton or elsewhere in East Anglia were made from King's Cross, because if the Monarch used Liverpool Street, He or She would have to get ceremonial 'permission' to enter the City of London). Probably the most memorable - and sombre - journey made during our period was on 11th February 1952, when (hauled by Britannia No.70000 from Kings Lynn) after the death of King George VI it conveyed the King's body from Wolferton to King's Cross. The train last ran in 1961, to York for the Duke of Kent's wedding, after which it was disbanded. Normally a pair of locomotives on Cambridge Shed's allocation was maintained in tip-top and sparkling condition as 'Royal Engines', to cover the Royal Journeys to Sandringham, each manned by its own picked crew. In LNER days they were D16/3s Nos.8783 and 8787, until superseded in March 1946 by the B2 (rebuilt B17) 4-6-0 No.2871 ROYAL SOVEREIGN (formerly MANCHESTER CITY), with B2 No.61617 FORD CASTLE as stand-by. The two D16/3s were then transferred to Kings Lynn and employed when necessary on the Kings Lynn-Wolferton leg of Royal Train journeys.

During the war, King George VI and Queen Elizabeth made numerous journeys in one of the Royal Trains all over the country - 44 on the LNER alone. On most journeys an overnight sleep was involved and therefore they employed the LMSR Train ('*GROVE*') rather than the LNER Train described above.

The resplendent 'Royal Engine', B2 No.1671 ROYAL SOVEREIGN (LNER No.2871 MANCHESTER CITY) leaves King's Cross on 20th May 1948 with the LNER Royal Train for Wolferton. Note, however, the head-code is not that carried when the Sovereign was on board. *Herbert/Goslin coll.*

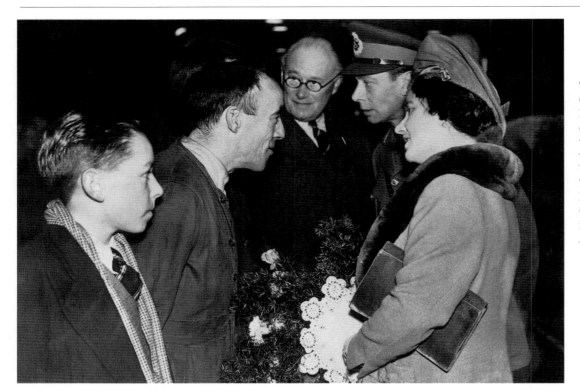

Their Majesties King George VI and Queen Elizabeth chatting with deferential Plant workers during their visit to Doncaster Works during the war. The Chief General Manager LNER, Sir Charles Newton joins in behind. *Doncaster MBC Library.*

Although Euston was used most often for journeys to Scotland, many trips to Scotland and other places involved running over the ECML at least in part. Later, in the reign of the present Queen, Their Majesties sometimes travelled in other special coaches hired from BR and then these trains ran under what were known as 'Deepdene conditions'. (*see* Appendix D for details of the journeys).

The LMSR Royal Train of 10 (or 11) cars comprised the King's saloon, the Queen's saloon, one (or two) saloon-sleepers, three other saloons, a dining saloon, a dining-car, and a 1st-brake at each end. In the early part of the war the LMSR Train remained that inherited from the LNWR, but in 1941, on account of justifiable concern about Their Majesties' safety, three completely new all-steel armour-plated 12-wheel cars were built. Two were saloon-sleepers, one for the King ('Mr Grove') and one for the Queen ('Mrs Grove'); they not only had double-glazed windows and air-conditioning but the windows were fitted with sliding armour-plate shutters. The third vehicle was a composite comprising generator, brake and staff sleeping compartments. When the King travelled without the Queen the latter's saloon was left out of the consist, whereas when one or both of the Princesses (the 'Misses Grove') were travelling the extra saloon-sleeper was added. In 1942 the LMSR also built two saloons (not armoured) for the LMSR Chairman and other VIPs, equipped as self-contained mobile office/saloon/sleeping cars. After the war these two cars were converted into a lounge-sleeper and dining-sleeper for the use of Princess Elizabeth and Prince Philip.

On all these journeys the Royal Party included at least one Private Secretary, Equerry, Lady-in-Waiting, maid, dresser, and valet, plus two footmen, and a chauffeur. Normally also various other VIPs, often in the war - military, would be travelling with the Royal Party. The Railway provided several Senior Officers (Mr. Barrington-Ward - Divisional General Manager, Southern Area, often accompanied on LNER journeys), two Senior Police

Officers, and a number of attendants and engineering staff. Naturally, Railway 'Top Management' were closely concerned with the supervision of the preparation, operation and safeguarding of the Royal Train and its occupants. (Before the war the driver of the Royal Train got a gratuity of £1, his fireman 50p - and the officers concerned were sent pheasants at Christmas).

In peacetime the most detailed Instructions and Schedules were distributed in advance, and in wartime the instructions were much the same but not quite so widely circulated. Early in the war there was a great deal of concern - and discussion between the Palace, the Railways, the REC and the Home Office - as to whether the plans for Royal Journeys should as in peacetime be printed and distributed to Railway and other staff formally several days in advance - the 'Grove' Plan, favoured by the LMSR, GWR and SR, or whether the schedules should be distributed as were those for an 'ordinary' special, the staff needed for checking the route and ensuring the safety of the Royal Train being informed only three hours ahead by *telephone* - the 'Secrecy' Plan, favoured by the LNER. Eventually, the 'Grove' Plan, ensuring better physical security for Their Majesties but also less secret and more open to terrorism, was adopted.

Most of the instructions were aimed at the avoidance of any possible delay by other traffic, but Their Majesties' safety and comfort had to be safeguarded as well, by double-block signalling, by forbidding other trains to pass where they might come to a stand beside the Royal Train - or splash it on water-troughs, and of course sites of possible terrorism such as bridges and crossings had to be guarded. Loud-speakers on stations were not to be used as the train passed through, and - in peacetime - Air authorities were informed in advance, presumably to prevent disturbance of TM by low-flying aircraft. The Royal Train and its staff had to be as self-sufficient as possible, but detailed arrangements were made for its servicing - and heating, during stops. Provision had to be made for replenishing the supply of

Her Royal Highness Princess Elizabeth, before she became HM The Queeen, looks perhaps uncertain about joining her train at King's Cross. Behind, Prince Philip looks displeased, the officials look anxious and the Royal corgi seems disinterested; date probably late 1940s. *National Railway Museum.*

gas for cooking and water for drinking[8], but also ice for the pressure-ventilation system - which did not always work correctly. Also, some other 'little essentials' had to be specially arranged:- "a supply of sanitary pans and steps will be required to be dispatched to York (addressed to R.M. Rutter, Esq., Superintendent, London & North-Eastern Railway, York) by the 2.12 p.m. train from Wolverton *via* Peterborough ..." Charges made by the Railway were remarkably low: thus in 1959 HRH Princess Margaret was not charged more than the normal fares to attach her coaches to a service train, and only just under 10p/mile for her Special working from Newcastle to Barnard Castle. Any amount of trouble was taken to look after Their Majesties: in the Darkest Days, in July 1940, telegrams flew to Top Management of the LNER because the Queen had mislaid a book that slipped behind her bed on the Train; and on another occasion the present Queen caused the Train to be stopped twice in the night for examination because she heard an unusual noise under her compartment.

The LMSR Royal Train was kept at their Wolverton Works, and for ECML journeys it was worked over *via* Bletchley and Sandy (reverse) to King's Cross[9], to reach there some two hours before the scheduled departure. This was either soon after 7 p.m. to allow dinner to be served *en route*, or departure was much later and the Royal Party slept while moving. Usually, at least the later part of the night was spent parked in some secluded - and well-guarded - siding, but preferably where Their Majesties could take a walk in the countryside. On journeys to East Anglia - other than Sandringham, the 'Night Halt' was made at Warren Hill (Newmarket), but on longer ECML journeys the site was quite often just north of Hertford on the Loop, or at Leadenham (Grantham - Lincoln line). Further north, Night Halts were made at Crimple or at Ripley Valley (both near Harrogate), or (after the war) at Baldersby (Melmerby - Thirsk line), Sledmere (Malton - Driffield line) or on the Wensleydale line from Northallerton. In Scotland, a favoured spot off the ECML was at Aberlady (on the goods-only branch east of Edinburgh); on the Royal Family's return from Balmoral in September 1944, they all ate and slept there on the Royal Train for two consecutive nights - although no doubt popping into Edinburgh for a few

hours. On that occasion also, two Royal Trains were assembled on 23rd September, the main one to bring 'Mr and Mrs Grove' back to King's Cross and the other to take the 'Misses Grove' back to Ballater.

After the war and when Princess Elizabeth married Prince Philip they used a smaller set of LMSR Royal Coaches, made up into a train referred to as 'Deepdene', which comprised some of the 'Grove' stock together with the converted LMS saloons mentioned above, and for the less complicated journeys this train was also used after Elizabeth became Queen. Again, when one of the somewhat lesser Royal Personages such as Princess Margaret made a journey, just two or three of the Royal Coaches were run at the head of a service train, for example a night express from King's Cross to Edinburgh. On the other hand, while staying at Balmoral, the Queen several times used the whole Royal Train to pay a quick visit to friends at Bawtry, coming up from Ballater overnight and returning the next night; the Train was parked on the Misson branch and sent to Doncaster for servicing after Her Majesty had alighted. Nonetheless, in peacetime some prolonged and elaborate tours were made by Their Majesties in the Royal Train, as when they toured in it - also in the Royal Yacht - around Scotland from 23rd June until 7th July 1948. This and other journeys are listed in Appendix D, from which list it is evident that most of the wartime journeys involved visits by Their Majesties to military bases and war factories[10] for the vital purpose of boosting morale.

OTHER TRAINS FOR VERY IMPORTANT PERSONS

During the war, the Prime Minister had his own train, supplied at first by the LNER and then by the LMSR, which included two spare vehicles from the LMSR Royal Train. Then in the latter part of the war, two special trains were assembled for the operational use in Britain of Commanders-in-Chief. The train 'ALIVE', a very heavy train of nine coaches, included two armour-plated cars (LNE No.1591 and GW No.574) as well as three

The ex-LNER Royal Train, conveying HM the Queen and the royal party to the Wedding of the Duke of Kent in York Minster on 8th June 1961, passing Harringay West. The locomotive is 60028 WALTER K. WHIGHAM (LNER No.4487 SEA EAGLE).

Main-line diesels - albeit NBL Type 2s used only for empty stock work - are already in the background, as N2/4 No.69579 (LNER No.2673) hauls out of the carriage yards towards Hornsey station a mixed rake of coaches, the first a restaurant car, next a Thompson First (with Ladies' Retiring Room - see two small oblong frosted windows), then two kitchen cars and finally an assortment of vans, 6th June 1959. *Hornby.*

sleeping-cars, two carriage-trucks and up to eight vans, was assembled by the GWR at Swindon but incorporated an LNER sleeping-car partly converted into a saloon and called 'Bayonet'. *'ALIVE'* was created for the US Army, and from January 1944 when he took over as Supreme Commander Allied Expeditionary Forces the train was dedicated to General Eisenhower and his Headquarters Staff. It was kept at Old Oak Common and normally set off from Kensington Addison Road, until it was shipped over to the Continent in December 1944[11]. After the victory in Europe, *'ALIVE'* was relinquished by the Americans and taken over in July 1945 by the War Office as Field Marshall Montgomery's special train, returned to England and disbanded during the winter of 1945-46.

The other train, assembled in October 1941, was *'RAPIER'*. It was made up of six coaches and three vans, comprising (in 1943): a 1st-class sleeper with 10 berths and a shower, two 1st-brakes for Other Ranks, a composite-sleeper, a 1st-saloon, a 3rd-restaurant with one saloon converted to an office - all LNER vehicles, an LNER generator van and two LMS motor-car vans. *'RAPIER'* was used by the C-in-C. Home Forces and his team, and was normally kept at King's Cross. The eight staff were all but one from the Army (including two ATS[12]). It ran 100,000 miles before it was disbanded in July 1945, and it would be most interesting to be able to detail the journeys made by both these trains, but records have not come to light.

RAILWAY HOTELS ON THE ECML

For the best-heeled ECML travellers - and for the 'Expense Account' ones - there were five major Hotels run by the LNER, the supervision of which came under a Hotel Committee appointed by the Board of Directors. All have survived to the present day, albeit since 1982 sold off by British Transport Hotels.

The Great Northern Hotel at King's Cross, like the station a Lewis Cubitt product, in spite of its five floors and an attic storey - making it unusually tall for its period, is yet almost dwarfed by the adjoining King's Cross and St Pancras stations. With a mere 69 bedrooms it was never one of London's best hotels, and as recently as 1950 a single bed & breakfast could be had for 95p - and even now 'no more than' £65. The Great Northern Hotel at Peterborough is likewise undistinguished, again in the severe style of GN station architecture of the 1850s.

Altogether much more superior were - and still are - the NER's Royal Station Hotels at York and at Newcastle, and lastly there was the NBR's magnificent edifice adjoining Edinburgh Waverley and connected directly with it by lifts, the North British Hotel. All of these three great hotels were the principal and most prestigious in their respective cities. The North British, built by W.H.Beattie in 1902, a magnificent pile of five storeys each with its own elaborate architecture had no less than 400 rooms. Its palatial public rooms had splendid views over the sights of Edinburgh - and its own well-known clock-tower adding to them. Three of the storeys were below street level, and it had its own sidings off Waverley station. In 1939, bed, breakfast, luncheon and afternoon tea cost 92.5p at the Newcastle Royal Station Hotel, while a double-room with breakfast at the North British Hotel would set you back £1.50 (a single room, £1.00 - about £25 in today's money, or about *one-third* of today's price).

These York, Newcastle, and Edinburgh LNER Hotels were the general meeting places for Society and Business, renowned for their good food and wine, the resorts indeed of 'bon viveurs'. With their banqueting rooms, ballrooms, and tea-rooms of the 'Palm Court' variety, they were - and again to a large extent still are - the venue of countless Dinners, Conferences and other major Events, and for innumerable important private assignations. In pre-war days and well into the 1960s, York and Newcastle boasted restaurants on the concourse - surely ideal for the railway enthusiast? - but even in 1914 the Hotels were catering for the 'opposition' by advertising their 'garages for motor-cars'. In the Second World War these great Hotels played a vital service to the myriad Commissioned Officers of the Services, especially to those from the USA with their bottomless purses, the Royal Station Hotel at York being crowded with the more wealthy of the RAF officers from the numerous Bomber Command stations in the vicinity.

In LNER days, the hotels were managed by Area Hotel Superintendents responsible to the three Area General Managers. After Nationalization, they came under the aegis of the BTC Hotels Executive (Chairman, Lord Inman until 1951, then Sir H.Methuen), which also ran BR's refreshment rooms and restaurant cars. When the Executives were abolished in 1953 they were taken over by the British Transport Hotels & Catering Services with its Board of Management (Chairman, Frank Hole). After the abolition of the BTC in turn in 1962, they were run by the nominally independent British Transport Hotels Ltd. - still headed by Frank Hole.

1. These were the 09.30 and 17.50 from King's Cross to Leeds (and back), noted in peacetime for their good meals, especially the 'Yorkshire Breakfast' served on the 07.50 up from Leeds.

2. In the Up direction, the Harrogate portion ran *via* York

3. The *HARROGATE SUNDAY PULLMAN* ran *via* York before the war, but *via* Knottingley when reinstated in 1946 - but only for a year, after which it - like the *QUEEN OF SCOTS* - went *via* Leeds.

4. Four on Saturdays and five on Sundays, as the HIGHLANDMAN and ABERDONIAN were *SX*, and the 01.05 Edinburgh was *SuX*.

5. Five on Friday nights.

6. Convertible however, if necessary, to twins by opening communicating doors.

7. However, on at least one occasion - after the great floods of 31st January 1953 - the route taken to London was *via* South Lynn, the M&GN and Peterborough.

8. On one occasion, water of doubtful quality was provided at Ballater, and complaints were made.

9. Sometimes, individual coaches were worked up *via* Willesden Junction and Canonbury.

10. Including Doncaster Locomotive Works, in 1941.

11. A second 'Bayonet' coach was sent over in April 1945.

12. Auxilary Territorial Service.

Unmistakably on the Scottish section of the ECML, a fine view of a J37, No.64558 (LNER No.9123), pulling away from Dunbar on an Up Class J empties, 1950s. *J.Robertson.*

Chapter VI. FREIGHT TRAFFIC ON THE ECML IN 1939, IN THE WAR, & IN THE POST-WAR PERIOD UNTIL THE END OF THE 1950s

PRE-WAR, SUMMER 1939

Stations and Yards

In commercial terms the freight traffic (in its broadest sense[1]) on the ECML was undoubtedly of equal value to that of passengers, but unlike on the other northern main lines probably not exceeding that of the passenger traffic. As a principal trunk route, the ECML had always been of great importance for the long-distance carriage of the urgent traffic of parcels, mail and newspapers.

Yet it may not be appropriate to generalize about ECML freight because even more than was the case with passenger traffic the flow was uneven along the length of the ECML. The middle section, Doncaster - Newcastle, passed through major industrial and coal-mining regions and connected with many other such areas and with East Coast ports. That section therefore carried the greatest flow, while north of Newcastle freight flow was the least. Indeed, by far the greater part of the freight passing along the ECML originated elsewhere than at the places directly served by the line. The possible flow of freight traffic along the ECML was also limited - a situation that arose originally from perhaps modest initial expectations of its 19th Century builders, in that most of the route was only double-track, and moreover the four-track sectors were interrupted by stretches of double track which acted as bottlenecks and caused serious operating difficulties. When in the Grouping period the LNER wanted to speed up its expresses it had not the financial resources necessary for the elimination of these bottlenecks. Little more could be afforded than the breaking up of sections with automatic signalling, although with the assistance of a Government Loan Guarantee scheme parts of the busy section between York and Northallerton had been widened in the 1930s. Still, the elimination of the worst of the bottlenecks on this section was only carried out later, with Government funding, to cope with the great increase of freight traffic in the war.

The nature of the freight traffic in general varied somewhat along the ECML (*see* Table 6.1). Through trains for the conveyance of high-class general merchandise, which was approximately equal in volume in each direction, ran between London and the major cities of Yorkshire, the North-East and Scotland, matching the primary flows of passenger traffic between these centres. One of its major predecessors (the GNR) having pioneered them, the LNER by the late 1930s was making major strides towards the provision of a regular and comprehensive service of fast braked freight trains - run mainly during the night, to cater for this important traffic that was already threatened by - and actually being lost to - road transport. As can be seen from Table 6.1, in 1939 there were already about 75 partially or fully braked services running regularly on weekdays[2] each way on all or part of the ECML. The Class V2 2-6-2 locomotives were introduced specifically for these trains, and named the 'Green Arrow' class after the new designation of the premium, registered service provided on the No.1 Express Goods (fully braked) trains.

In the 1930s, merchandise - and livestock - was handled at the vast majority of stations, however small, on the ECML as in Britain generally. On a trunk line such as the ECML, on which many fast express trains were run and there was a dearth of relief lines, it was most unsatisfactory to try to operate slow goods trains that had to be backed out of the way into refuge sidings or stopping trains which needed to do shunting movements onto the through lines. Often the goods yards were only on one side of the main line, and at some places wagons from the conflicting direction had to be worked past to the next major yard and then back the other way. Moreover, at some small sidings operated by a ground-frame, the guard had to get a key to unlock it from the preceding signalbox and arrange for the return of the key. After shunting was completed he had to ensure that all points and signals were restored for the main line. Operation of such sidings was normally forbidden at night or in fog or snow.

The only stations on the ECML which in 1939 did *not* cater for goods traffic were: the 'suburban' stations at Brookmans Park, Low Fell, Bensham, and Gateshead West, and the country stations at Dukeries Junction, Barnby Moor & Sutton, Moss, and Croft Spa. The goods traffic handled varied widely. Thus in the NE Area, while the several Newcastle goods stations between them forwarded (in 1938) 170,000 tons of merchandise (Classes 7 - 21) and received 511,000 tons, Bradbury forwarded just *one* ton and received *eight* tons[3]. The Goods station for Durham was not on the ECML at all, but across the city at Gilesgate, on a branch off the Leamside line; likewise, Croft Spa traffic was sent to the depot at the terminus of the Croft branch.

In the major cities there were of course large goods stations, providing employment for an army of men (*see* Appendix O in Part II) for the loading and unloading of many scores or hundreds of wagons each weekday, and to process piles of documentation relating to the smallest consignment. Scores of other men drove Railway-owned carts, hauled by live horses or the three-wheeled motor variety, which were driven round the town to collect or deliver, the LNER having in 1938 3,800 motor- and 4,300 horse-drawn cartage vehicles.

Horse-power for shunting, at Welwyn North: this is 1938, but the practice continued at least into the war. *G.Halls/Goslin coll.*

The major goods stations on or adjoining the ECML were the following:-

King's Cross. By far the largest, this was located on a spur from Copenhagen Junction on the Down side between Gas Works and Copenhagen tunnels, next to the 'Top' Locomotive depot. It comprised separate Inwards (high-level) and Outwards depots and two satellite sheds on the south side of the Locomotive depot. On the other side were substantial Empties and Coal yards; in the latter coal was dropped into delivery vehicles parked beneath the railway wagons, which were turned by capstans - as were merchandise wagons in the goods sheds. On the Up side, a great Potato depot and Market adjoined the main line.

In 1939 over 1,100 men were employed in King's Cross Goods. They were supervised by the Goods Agent, F.C.Robbins (salary £650 a year), about 10 other managerial staff and over 45 Foremen - some being 'Working Foremen'. In the Inwards shed 11 Foremen controlled - on different shifts - 123 porters, one 'underman', two lad porters and 57 loaders (who did the hardest work), 5 tracers, 60 checkers and 57 callers-off - all concerned with keeping tabs on the myriads of 'smalls' merchandise, while three number-takers checked the wagons for unloading. In the Outwards shed, where work was even more complex, 17 Foremen controlled 235 porters and 66 loaders who beavered away while the goods were checked by 72 checkers and but two callers-off, the wagons being recorded by five number-takers; there were also three 'undermen' and just one lad messenger - who must have been constantly on the run. Further similar men toiled away in the Potato and Granary sheds. Outside in the yards, six Inspectors and 10 Foremen oversaw the making up and breaking down of trains by 70 shunters and the marshalling of wagons by over 30 capstan-men, while 10 or so number-takers identified the wagons and containers - and of course work went on night and day. Finally, 152 King's Cross goods guards were in charge of trains on the move. Behind the scenes, a mere 35 or so clerks (one working all alone in the Fish office) - less than 10 being women, documented all these operations, and just one time-keeper and one 'working foreman' kept order in the depot. Other goods depots had comparable but less numerous teams of men and the establishments of some are given in Appendix O, Part II.

Continuing down the line, at **Peterborough**: Goods station - also including a large Tranship shed, on the Up side, just south of Peterborough North station; **Grantham**: on the Up side just south of the station; **Newark**: on the Down side just north of the station; **Retford**: on the Up side north of the station; **Doncaster**: on the Up side just south of the Central station. **Selby**: on the Up side next to the station; **York**: Leeman Road, just north of the station on the Down side; **Darlington**: on the Up side of the Goods lines passing Bank Top station on its east side; **Gateshead**: Eldon Street (also called Park Lane), on a spur from the Sunderland line west of Felling station; **Newcastle**: Forth Goods, adjoining King Edward Bridge but on a spur from Forth Goods Junction off the Scotswood line[4]; New Bridge Street Goods, adjoining Manors North station but on a spur from New Bridge Street Goods Junction on the Jesmond Loop; **Tweedmouth**: on the Up side, opposite the station. **Edinburgh**: South Leith, on the branch from Portobello; Leith Walk Goods, on a spur off the North Leith branch just west of Easter Road station; Waverley (New Street) Goods, adjoining the east end of Waverley station on the south side.

In the London area there were a number of other goods stations between which traffic was tripped in wagon-loads to and from the main ECML yards at Finsbury Park (Clarence Yard and East Goods Yard) and at Ferme Park (between Harringay and Hornsey). Most of them belonged to other Railways, but traffic also came from the LNER goods depots at Farringdon Street[5] (on the Metropolitan 'Widened Lines'), Royal Mint Street North (near Fenchurch Street station), Blackwall, Poplar, and Stratford Market.

In addition to the covered goods stations there were of course numerous goods and coal yards, usually serving a particular purpose, most commonly the discharge of coal. Subsidiary yards directly off the ECML in the London area included those before Finsbury Park at Caledonian Road, Ashburton Grove, and Highbury Vale. Wagons were distributed between the main ECML yards in London and a range of yards belonging to the LNER in East London, their coal yards on the SR at Elephant & Castle and at Brockley, and a number of small yards in the GN Suburban area. In the London area, as will be described later, there was also a great deal of interchange with the yards on the LMSR, GWR and SR.

In Steam days, when there were relatively few fully-fitted freight trains running on the ECML - or on any other line, average freight train speeds were low (of the order of 25 mph for loose-coupled coal trains), and a round trip of about 75 miles out and back was a day's work for both locomotives and men. Therefore, quite apart from the necessity of having large marshalling yards (or sorting sidings) at major traffic centres, where wagons from many different outlets were assembled and sorted, it was necessary to have yards where engines and crews could be changed at key points roughly 75 miles apart on a main route. As the trains also had to be thoroughly examined - for safety of load, and especially for hot axle-boxes - it was convenient to combine these needs with remarshalling of trains at key junctions.

On the ECML, the principal marshalling and staging yards of this nature were at: Hornsey (Ferme Park), Peterborough (New England), Doncaster (Decoy and Mineral Yards), York (Dringhouses Yard, York Yard Down and Up, Skelton Sidings), Darlington (Croft Junction), Newcastle (Low Fell, and Heaton Down and Up Yards), Tweedmouth (superseding Berwick Yard, closed in 1939), Edinburgh (Niddrie West - supplemented by Meadows Yard from the beginning of the war until the late 1950s). Most of the above yards also served the vital parallel function of assembling and distributing wagon-load traffic brought from or dispatched to other yards, goods stations, collieries *etc.* in their corresponding districts. Unlike at Whitemoor Yard at March or the yards at Woodford (Northants.) and elsewhere, their function was not in the first instance that of staging or remarshalling through traffic; only at New England (one yard) and at York Down Yard were there humps[6], and none had the wagon retarders and other modern equipment of Whitemoor. Smaller marshalling yards were situated at: Tuxford Exchange Sidings, Doncaster area, Selby, Darlington (Bank Top), Ferryhill, and Portobello. The war brought into use the installations at Connington (between Abbots Ripton and Holme) and the reopening of Thirsk Yard and of Meadows Yard in Edinburgh, as well as a considerable expansion of many of the major yards. After the war Dringhouses Yard at York was enlarged, and arranged specially for the preparation of braked trains.

Apart from Whitemoor, other major marshalling yards not far from the ECML which were the source of much ECML freight traffic were located at: Colwick, Welham, Annesley, Lincoln (Pyewipe and Holmes), Mansfield, Warsop, Worksop,

An evocative 1930s picture of N1 No.4583 still blowing off as it struggles up out of the steep Hotel Curve at King's Cross with a Class K freight from the SR *via* the Widened Lines. To the left are other King's Cross Suburban platforms, at which an N2 can just be seen, while the other N2 on the right is on one of the lines of the locomotive yard. *Lens.*

Coal traffic up to London was the mainstay of this southern stretch of the ECML from the day it was opened in 1850, and this is a characteristic pre-war scene, with an Up Class J coal train hauled by a Gresley two-cylinder Class O1 - a class rarely seen south of Peterborough after the war. It is passing Abbots Ripton, another of the mean little wayside stations of the GNR, the view being northward, with the Up platform behind the photographer. *D.Thompson.*

New England Yards, Peterborough: little changed since LNER days, this is the northward view in the early 1960s from Spital Bridge. To the left are the lines to the Old Coal and North yards, in the centre behind Eastfield Box is the West Yard and to the right the East Yard. The water-tower and coaling plant at New England shed are on the horizon - and this gives a measure of the extent of the yards. *R.Townsin*.

The interior of a typical large goods station, Leeman Road, York - in the 1950s and not yet modernised. This building eventually became part of the National Railway Museum. *Hoole coll.*

Hitchin: a general view from the north end of the Up platform. Hitchin Yard Box is on the left and beyond is the ex-GN Down Yard; on the right stretches the larger Up Yard, where a 204 hp 0-6-0 diesel shunter can be glimpsed, and Cambridge Junction Box, 18th July 1958. *M. Joyce.*

Hexthorpe, Wath, Frodingham, Hull (Hessle Haven and Inwards), Gascoigne Wood (near Selby), Normanton, Lofthouse, Healey Mills (near Horbury & Ossett), Newport (between Thornaby and Middlesbrough), North Stockton, West Hartlepool, South Dock (Sunderland), Stella Gill, Consett, Gateshead (Park Lane and Norwood), Addison[7] (Blaydon), Tyne Dock (South Shields), and various yards in Central Scotland beyond Edinburgh.

At the larger towns down the length of the ECML, the following goods and coal yards - in addition to the principal marshalling yards named above, needed a shunting pilot at least for part of the day, a need that reflected the existence of a substantial amount of goods traffic:-

Hatfield, Welwyn Garden City, Hitchin (South Yard for Civil Engineer's depot, Cambridge Junction), Biggleswade, St Neots, Huntingdon North; Peterborough (Yaxley, Fletton, South Yard, Westwood, Spital); Grantham (Down and Ambergate Yards); Newark, Retford (Low Yard, Whisker Hill, and North Yard); Doncaster (Belmont, West, and South Yards, and Cattle Dock Sidings, Carr Wagon Works, Locomotive Plant and Carriage Works, Cherry Tree, Marshgate and Wheatley Park Goods Depots); Selby (Canal, Old, New, and Barlby Junction Yards); York (Holgate Dock, Branches Yard, Carriage and Wagon Works and Civil Engineer's Yard, also Foss Islands goods and coal yards

at the end of a branch off the Scarborough line at Burton Lane); Thirsk Junction Sidings - Yard from 1940, Thirsk Town Goods; Northallerton (Low and Castle Hills Yards); Darlington (Croft and Darlington coal depots, West, Albert Hill, Northgate, Nestfield, Hope Town and Haughton Bridge Yards, and various yards associated with the Locomotive and Wagon Works); Ferryhill (Old and New Sidings); Gateshead (Chaytors Bank, Oakwellgate, Lobley Hill, Hawks Siding, Park Lane Sidings, and Gateshead Warehouse, Redheugh and Redheugh Bank Foot, Dunston Staiths, West Dunston, Norwood and Blaydon West and North); Newcastle (Forth Cattle Dock and Infirmary Yard, Trafalgar North and South, and Quayside Yards); Morpeth, Alnmouth, Tweedmouth (Town Yard and Tweed Dock), Berwick (Goods and Cattle Yards), Dunbar, Prestonpans; Edinburgh (Rose Lane, between St Margarets and Abbeyhill Junction; Duddingston, Gorgie Sidings and Cattle Yard on the Suburban line, and St Leonards off it; several yards in the North and South Leith and Granton Dock areas, Lochend, Scotland Street, Heriothill).

Up and down the line, and especially in industrialized areas, factories, mills and plants sited - deliberately - near the railway were served by their own sidings. At these sidings raw materials and components could be directly off-loaded and outgoing products on-loaded by men employed by the concerns

TABLE 6.1: TIMETABLED THROUGH FREIGHT TRAINS ON THE ECML, SUMMER 1939

In order to provide an overall picture of the ECML freight services, presented below is a summary, collated from the contemporary WTTs, of booked freight trains on the ECML in the Down direction. Broadly equivalent trains ran in the Up direction, although of course loaded coal trains ran mainly in the Up direction and they exceeded the number of Down empties trains. Important exceptions were also the fish and meat trains: running up to London in 1939 they comprised two fish trains from Grimsby, three from Hull, two from Aberdeen and one from Cowlairs (mainly Mallaig traffic), one meat each from Aberdeen and York, and a fish and meat from Berwick; there were also two No.1 Express Goods from Niddrie West to Marylebone, but no corresponding Down trains.

The list is only of trains running on most weekdays, and seasonal and 'Q' trains are not listed. Each entry represents one train and when more than one train was run daily this is shown by the figures in brackets. Routes are indicated only where this seems necessary for clarification.

Not included are freight trains running from connecting lines for short distances to or through Peterborough, Grantham, Retford, Doncaster, Selby, York, Darlington, Ferryhill, Durham, Newcastle Central or other ECML stations but not otherwise running on the ECML, nor those from Starbeck and other Yards in West Yorkshire which passed through Northallerton (some also through Thirsk) to Tees-side. Also not listed are trains running west and north through Edinburgh, off the Waverley Route or originating from Leith Walk, Meadows, Portobello and Niddrie Yards for destinations such as Glasgow (Sighthill, High St. or Cadder), Shettlestone, Bathgate, Falkirk Grahamston, Grangemouth, Thornton Junction, Townhill, Dundee, Perth, Montrose, or Aberdeen Craiginches. Some of these, especially at night, passed through Waverley but most went round the South Suburban line.

CLASSES BRAKED Nos.1 and 2

King's Cross Goods to: Edinburgh Niddrie; York Yard (3); York Dringhouses (2); Heaton (2, one being *meat empties*); Leeds (3); Ardsley; Liverpool Huskisson; Manchester Deansgate (2, one being *Fruit & Veg.*); Nottingham; Grimsby; New Clee (*fish empties*); Doncaster Decoy (2, one being *fish empties*); Peterborough Westwood; Peterborough Eastfield.
Clarence Yard to: Doncaster Decoy.
Peterborough Westwood to: Doncaster Decoy (2).
New England to: Doncaster Decoy (*empties*).
Burton-on-Trent *via Newark and Doncaster* to: Hull Hessle Haven.
Colwick *via Newark and Doncaster* to: Hull Hessle Haven.
Whitemoor *via Lincoln and Doncaster* to: York.
Newark to: Doncaster Decoy.
Doncaster Decoy to: York.
York to: Edinburgh Niddrie; Gateshead Park Lane (6, *4 via Stockton, 2 via Leamside*); Newcastle New Bridge St. and Forth; Newcastle Heaton and Forth (5); Newcastle Forth (2); Heaton (5); Croft; Newport (3).
York Dringhouses to: Newcastle Forth *via Stockton* (*meat*); Newcastle Forth and Heaton.
Hull to: Heaton *via Sherburn, York, and Leamside*; Monkwearmouth *via Sherburn, York and Stockton*; Edinburgh Waverley *via York (reverse)* (*fish*).
Normanton *via York* to: Newcastle Forth.
Leeds Armley to: Newcastle Forth *via Ripon and Darlington*.
Croft to: Tyne Dock *via Leamside*.
Heaton to: Aberdeen (2); Thornton; Glasgow High St. (2); Glasgow Sighthill; Cadder; Niddrie (2); Leith Walk (3)

CLASSES A - C

King's Cross Goods to: New England *via Hertford North*.
Ferme Park to: New England (17, *2 via Hertford North*); Peterborough Eastfield.
Hatfield to: New England.
Hitchin to: Huntingdon North
Holme to: New England.
Fletton to: New England (2, *bricks*).
Peterborough Westwood to: Essendine; Colwick *via Grantham*.
New England to: Colwick *via Grantham* (8); Tuxford North (2); Whisker Hill; Worksop; Doncaster Decoy (4); Doncaster Mineral (4). (In addition, there were 7 trains from **New England**, and a brick train from **Yaxley**, to Doncaster (one to Hexthorpe) *via the Joint line* and one to Colwick *via Spalding and Sleaford*).
Highdyke to: Frodingham (4, *1 via Doncaster, 3 via Lincoln*); Colwick *via Grantham*; Parkgate *via Retford* (2).
Grantham to: Doncaster Decoy.
Sleaford to: Newark *via Barkston North Junction*.
Colwick *via Newark* to: York (2); Doncaster Decoy (3); Doncaster Mineral (2); Scrooby.
Mansfield Concentration Sidings *via Tuxford* to: Hull Hessle Haven.
Immingham *via Retford* to: Doncaster Mineral.
New Clee *via Retford* to: Doncaster Mineral.
Doncaster Decoy or Mineral to: York (7); Gascoigne Wood.
Hexthorpe *via Doncaster* to: Gascoigne Wood.
Whitemoor *via Lincoln and Doncaster* to: York Yard.
Bentley Colliery *via Selby* to: Hull Hessle Haven (2); Gascoigne Wood.
York Dringhouses to: Newport.
York Yard to: Newport (9); Stockton Oxbridge Sidings (4); Port Clarence; Croft (5).
Gascoigne Wood *via York* to: Newport.
Starbeck *via Ripon* to: Croft (2).
Croft *via Ferryhill* to: Gateshead Park Lane; Newcastle Forth; Heaton (2); Monkwearmouth; Tyne Dock Bottom; Consett (2).
Newport *via Ferryhill and Low Fell* to: Carlisle; Blaydon Mineral; Heaton.
Darlington Haughton Bridge *via Ferryhill* to: Spennymoor.
Chester-le-Street to: Gateshead Park Lane.
Birtley to: Newcastle Forth.
Heaton to: Tweedmouth (3); Morpeth; Amble; Niddrie.
Tweedmouth to: Dunbar; Niddrie; Portobello.
Dunbar to: Portobello.

CLASS 'D' (Pick-Ups, main-line beyond New Barnet only)
(Scottish Area not recorded).

King's Cross Goods to: New England.
Ashburton Grove to: Peterborough Eastfield.
Ferme Park to: Sandy (*manure*).
Grantham to: Doncaster Decoy.
Scrooby to: Misson, then Doncaster Decoy.
York Yard to: Thirsk; Thirsk Town.
Starbeck *via Pilmoor* to: Thirsk.
Ripon *via Thirsk* to: Newport.
Leyburn *via Northallerton* to: Croft.
Richmond to: Darlington.
Kimblesworth Colliery Junction *via Birtley* to: Gateshead Park Lane.
Heaton to: Stannington; Morpeth.
Belford to: Tweedmouth.

Knebworth, looking south in 1959, shortly before the general goods yard was closed; it seems that agricultural machinery was amongst the last loads dealt with. Note the vast chimneys of the Down station buildings — possibly connected with the Knebworth Control Office there, which can just be discerned beyond the station on the Down side. *G.Goslin*.

Coal class traffic 1955. This is Newcastle Forth Coal Depot in October of that year - little changed from North Eastern Railway days except for the BR steel sided 21-ton hopper wagons. This is domestic coal, hundreds of tons of the stuff bagged and ready for delivery. Household coal was still big business in the 1950s but it was a market that would virtually disappear over the next couple of decades along with delivery facilities such as these. *Author's collection*.

involved. Otherwise, in the case of coal-mines and the largest industrial plants, branch railways were built to connect them with the main railway. Moreover, the general provision of rail access to industry, - wantonly removed since the 1960s, went a long way towards avoiding the necessity for rail-to-road transshipment of goods, and the loss of them has been a major factor causing almost total transfer of freight from rail to road in recent times. Indeed, in the NE Area of the LNER (later to become the NE Region of BR), the tradition established by the NE Railway at the turn of the Century of transporting coal in high-capacity (20-ton) hopper wagons, enabling bottom-discharge at coal-drops and staiths, was noteworthy for its relative efficiency - in an area where coal production and consumption was so great. In addition to the principal marshalling yards named above, at numerous places down the length of the ECML there were groups of sidings either belonging to the Railway or to other industrial concerns, and in the war military and other Government depots. (The latter, as they were in the middle of the war, are set out in Appendix E; private sidings are listed in Appendix F).

Although the ECML for parts of its length carried a great deal of coal, iron ore, and other raw materials destined for the heavy industrial plants of Humberside, South Yorkshire, Tees-side and Tyneside, and of the output of these plants and of the coal-mines in the North Midlands, South Yorkshire, Co. Durham, Northumberland and East Lothian, very few of the mines and plants involved were directly on the ECML itself. Even in the Tyneside area none of the great Shipyards and Works such as Vickers-Armstrong's actually had access directly to the ECML. Naturally, there was a wide variety of medium-size factories at principal towns down the ECML, such as engineering works at Peterborough, Grantham, Doncaster, York and Darlington, and sugar-beet factories, breweries, flour-mills *etc.* at Newark, Selby and Edinburgh. Nevertheless, the great bulk of merchandise on the ECML came onto it from its connecting lines.

Notable major industrial installations with their own sidings and (usually) private shunting locomotives, which were actually on or very close to the ECML included:-

Shredded Wheat Co. and Norton Grinding Wheel Co., Welwyn Garden City; Little Barford (Tempsford) electricity generating station; London Brick Co. brickworks at Three Counties, and the complex of 15 brickworks at Fletton and Yaxley just south of Peterborough, British Sugar-Beet Corp., Fletton; Ransome & Marles Bearing Co, Newark; General Refractories, Bawtry; at Doncaster, Logan & Hemingway, British Bamberg Ltd. and Crompton Parkinson Small Arms, Wheatley Park, and Doncaster Gas Works; at Darlington, Cleveland Bridge & Engineering Co., English Steel Corp., Robert Stephenson & Hawthorn's and several other engineering works; a variety of factories at the extensive Team Valley Estate at Low Fell; Birtley Iron Co, Birtley; at Gateshead/Newcastle, United Alkali Co., Vickers Armstrong's Elswick Works, Robert Stephenson & Hawthorn's Forth Bank Works and various others.

In addition to the large independent locomotive works at Darlington (Robert Stephenson), and at Newcastle (R. & W. Hawthorn-Leslie), the LNER's own locomotive, carriage and wagon works at Doncaster, York and Darlington, and the locomotive repair shops at Gateshead, together with wagon, engineering and masonry depots, were themselves major industrial installations.

The majority of collieries, including many quite close to the ECML, were served by lateral lines - usually built by the Colliery Companies and made connection only indirectly with the ECML itself, but during the war and after it provided tremendous coal traffic onto the ECML in Co. Durham and Northumberland. Coal mines adjoining and connecting directly with the ECML included the following:- Harworth (Bawtry) and Rossington; Bentley Colliery near Doncaster; Mainsforth, Thrislington and Tursdale near Ferryhill; Browney and Littleburn between Ferryhill and Durham; Kimblesworth south of Plawsworth, and Chester South Moor north of it; in Northumberland, several collieries near Killingworth, and at Dudley, Pegswood, Widdrington, and Scremerston (Nesthill); in Lothian, at Seton, West Mains, Thornton, Walleyford and Preston Links near Prestonpans, and Monktonhall. In addition, during the war an open-cast site was opened at Cramlington, and soon after the war one at Widdrington. There were quarries and/or lime or cement works near the ECML at Aycliffe, Ferryhill, between Alnmouth and Little Mill, and at Oxwellmains (near Dunbar).

There were several electricity generating stations very near the ECML, including Little Barford (between Tempsford and St Neots), Peterborough, Darlington, Portobello, *etc.* These consumed large amounts of coal, as also did the numerous gas works up and down the country, but it was only after the war - mainly after 1959 - that very large electricity generating stations furnished substantial and continuous new traffic in coal on certain sections of the ECML, although only one - Cockenzie, near Prestonpans - actually had its extensive sidings beside the main line.

Apart from the transport of general merchandise and of coal and other minerals, the ECML - notably north of Doncaster, the GN&GE Joint line being a parallel artery south of there - was a trunk route for the exchange on the one hand of agricultural products (including livestock) from the highly productive lands of the eastern side of England, with on the other coal, fertilizers and farm equipment from the industrial regions further north. Naturally, agricultural traffic varied with the seasons, the ECML being concerned with one particular peak traffic during the winter, that of seed potatoes southwards from Scotland. The massive winter traffic in sugar-beet was also borne on the ECML to a certain extent. North of York and especially between York and Northallerton, the ECML was virtually the sole carrier of the traffic in iron and steel from the great plants of Tees-side and Co. Durham to the consumers of steel - not least the motor-car industry - of the Midlands. Furthermore, much of the enormous output of bulk chemicals produced at ICI Billingham (and in the 1950s also ICI Wilton) came away onto the ECML.

FREIGHT FLOWS, SERVICES and ROUTES

Focusing down on the Working Timetables (WTTs) of the period, interesting details of the operation of freight traffic on the ECML become apparent. Details of the freight trains and other comments given below refer - unless otherwise stated - to those given in the WTTs as scheduled to run on Tuesdays to Fridays. Schedules, and to an extent the number of trains, were often different on Mondays and Saturdays - especially at the peak summer weekends. Very few were scheduled to run after about 06.00 on Sundays. Furthermore it must be emphasized that this is in a *peacetime* context, whereas during the war large numbers of freight trains ran also on Sundays. Moreover, numerous freight trains were not scheduled in the WTTs but

A Down Class B Goods runs through Tuxford North in about 1937, with J6 No.3606 (BR 64255) at the junction with the important loop from the GC (LD&EC) line, which is just visible crossing in the distance at Dukeries Junction; Tuxford Exchange Sidings, and also Tuxford shed, are to the right. *E.R.Morten.*

For some historic reasons, Southern Railway locomotives did not turn up at Ferme Park until the latter part of the 1950s, but here in 1960, Q1 No.33023 (SR No.C23) is bringing a freight to the yard and passing Harringay Up Goods Box, having come round by the North London and Tottenham & Hampstead lines and the loop off the latter. The train would have arrived on the Down side, gone forward to beyond Ferme Park North Down Box near Hornsey station and then, assisted by a J50 at the other end, backed over the flyover. *Loveday/Goslin coll.*

Selby, June 1946: Hull Dairycoates based Q6 No.3448 heads south through the station with a train of empty mineral wagons bound for the South Yorkshire coalfield. The locomotive had recently come back into traffic (renumbered from 2291) after a much needed overhaul from its wartime exertions. *Author's collection.*

were run *ad hoc* under orders from Control. This applied particularly to the seasonal traffic, and above all to the special trains in *wartime*.

Parcels, mail and newspaper traffic was a major source of income. Yet on the ECML most of the packages, bags and bundles were conveyed in brake compartments or in vans attached to passenger trains, and there were few trains wholly devoted to this traffic. However, such trains ran at express train speeds. For instance, in 1939, there was the 21.30 *SX* Express Parcels from King's Cross to York, while the 22.50 King's Cross to York and Leeds was virtually a parcels and mails train, as it conveyed passengers only as far as Huntingdon. There was a daily early morning newspaper train to Grantham, and over Saturday night the 23.25 King's Cross Goods to York took the *NEWS OF THE WORLD etc.* to the North of England. From York, on the other hand, there was one Express Parcels through to Edinburgh and four more of the same to Newcastle[8], while Newcastle sent one down to Morpeth as well as to Edinburgh. At Christmas time, these regular parcels trains were supplemented by many extra trains - and main platforms such as No.1 at King's Cross and No.8 at Newcastle Central were piled high with GPO parcels mail.

In addition, in the express but non-passenger category (Class C under BR), there were regular long-distance empty coaching stock trains on the ECML. Before the war these were: Hornsey (Waterworks Sidings) to York (Clifton Sidings) and to Doncaster (both 'Q' trains), and King's Cross to Doncaster, with corresponding Up workings. After the war the principal regular train was the Newcastle (Delaval Sidings)-Holloway and the King's Cross-York trains. All these Class C trains were worked largely by the Pacifics and V2s, but often also by K3s. The importance of these regular parcels and other Class C trains not conveying passengers is underlined by the fact that many continued to run during the war; afterwards they were all restored virtually as in 1939.

Before further description, a few words about train classification are necessary. In the LNER system, No.1 Express Goods trains were made up with vacuum-piped wagons only, 75% of the train being fully braked, and could run at an average of 50 m.p.h.; under BR these trains came under the C classification that included parcels and other fully-fitted non-passenger trains. LNER No.2 Express Goods trains were one-third braked, up to a maximum of 20 braked wagons behind the engine, and could run at an average of 40 mph; under BR these became Class D. The LNER also had two No.3 Express Goods classes, braked (20% of load) and unbraked (two or three wagons braked if possible), average speed 35 m.p.h. No.3 class was quite rare, the unbraked virtually overlapping with the Class A Express Freight (unbraked); average speed was 30 m.p.h., and under BR they became Classes E and F. The other unbraked trains on the LNER were: Through Goods (Class B) - average speed 25 m.p.h., and Class H under BR; Mineral or Empty Wagon (Class C) - average speed 20-25 m.p.h., and Class J under BR; finally, Stopping Freight (Class D) - Class K under BR.

Timetabled freight trains on the ECML in Summer 1939 are summarized in Table 6.1, with which the wartime *booked* freight services (Summer 1942) and those run after the war in the 1950s can be compared, in Tables 6.2 and 6.3 respectively. From Table 6.1 it can be seen that there were scheduled times for 20 to 25 fully or partially fitted freights (Nos.1 and 2 Express Goods) down and up the ECML from/to London, including three or four conditional. The majority of these trains ran in the night at times when the line was relatively free of passenger trains, but this was not so for some of them in the Down direction - all from King's Cross Goods. Representative of the rest, but varying between summer and winter, the Down day trains included: **321** 09.45 Fish Empties to New Clee, **389** 11.30 to Peterborough (Westwood), **527** 14.00 to York (Dringhouses), **584** 15.00 'Fruit & Veg.' to Manchester (Deansgate), **562** 15.35 to Niddrie West, **577** 16.05 to York (Dringhouses), **625** 17.15 to

York Yard, and **669** 18.00 to Leeds. Train **562**, the 'Scotch Goods', was booked to stop only at Hitchin South (for water), Arlesey, Sandy, and St Neots (to be passed at each), Peterborough Westwood (for change of crews, not necessarily of engine), then to run non-stop to York Yard North, Newcastle Central, Tweedmouth, Berwick, and Niddrie West (arriving 02.40); in the 1950s this train was further accelerated - see below. (Train **827** 23.00 King's Cross to York, which actually conveyed traffic only for Scotland, was also telegraphed as 'Scotch Goods').

Nearly all the Nos.1 and 2 braked trains from and to London - with certain exceptions, like the 'Scotch Goods' - had to stop at both Peterborough (Westwood for Down or Spital for Up trains, or New England) and Doncaster, to change engines and/or take water. Unbraked trains stopped also at Hitchin (South Box on the Down, Cambridge Junction on the Up), Grantham and Newark, at least for water. Optional stops for water were designated at Offord, Essendine and Retford, also at Biggleswade in the Up direction, but stops for water at other places were strongly discouraged. Wagon examinations had to be made at both Peterborough and Doncaster.

Specific instructions laid down for many of the freight trains concerning conditional stops, shunting *en route*, make-up, load and traffic to be attached or detached, make interesting reading, for example:-

366 10.50 Class A Goods and Fish Empties, King's Cross to Peterborough Westwood and No.2 Braked from there to Doncaster Decoy: "Worked by engine capable of hauling 60 wagons. May run at No.2 speed by Control orders and if run main line may convey 75 wagons of goods and empties between London and Peterboro' when worked by a K3 engine. Stops Crews Hill[9] when required to attach cattle for West Riding District. Crews Hill advise Control not later than 10.0 a.m. number of wagons. Room to be left accordingly. To be held Huntingdon North on Mondays for cattle from St Ives, on train due 4.11 p.m. On Mondays to Fridays inclusive to attach at Arlesey and Langford traffic for Manchester and the North which must be put off at Biggleswade for re-forwarding on **584**, **625** and **669** down. May attach at Biggleswade[10] vegetable traffic for Doncaster. Convey from St Neots, when necessary, Mondays to Fridays fitted wagons containing market traffic for Huddersfield and West Riding, which must be detached Peterboro' the former for connection with **625** and latter for connection with **669**. Stops St Neots on Saturdays when necessary to attach traffic for Glasgow. When conveying tanks of petroleum pitch for Botolph Bridge Siding or important traffic for Fletton, train must stop at Fletton to detach."

527 14.00 No.1 Braked Goods, King's Cross to Dringhouses, Saturdays excepted: "Worked by "K3" engine. Load 60 wagons. Convey from King's Cross and Clarence Yard all Scotch wagons available. Load to be made up at Clarence Yard if necessary, with wagons for N.E. Area. Attach at Clarence Yard wagons off:- 1.49 p.m. from Farringdon Street, 1.0 p.m. from Victoria Dock, 1.5 p.m. from Royal Mint Street, 12.50 p.m. from Poplar Dock."

584[11] 15.00 No.2 Braked Fruit and Vegetable, King's Cross to Manchester, Saturdays excepted: "Worked by Engine capable of handling 60 wagons London to Colwick. Traffic for Blast Lane, Sheffield, loaded in fitted wagon and attached next engine. Convey vegetable traffic for Deansgate, C.L.C., Liverpool, Sheffield, Nottingham and West of Colwick. Convey from Biggleswade, Doncaster (Decoy) road van which must be transferred to **669** down at Peterboro' Westwood. Also wagon for Chesterfield Central and road van for Peterboro' containing traffic for latter and L.M. & S. line. Convey from St Neots vegetable traffic for West Riding, to be transferred at Peterboro' to **669**. St Neots to advise Control nightly number of wagons for north of Peterboro'. Guards to give St Neots necessary information. Stop Tempsford, when required, for perishable traffic for Deansgate and Liverpool. Perishable traffic from Tempsford for Deansgate and Liverpool is sent St Neots by suitable empties train which must reach latter by not later than 6.15 p.m., otherwise **584** must stop Tempsford to attach. Transships for Sheffield, Manchester, Liverpool and Cheshire Lines from Tempsford are forwarded from St Neots on **465** down passenger, which must not be delayed in consequence."

Of some interest also was that **23** 00.27 King's Cross Goods to Grimsby "conveys mails, parcels and post hampers for Hitchin, Letchworth, Baldock, Royston, and Huntingdon."

In the Up direction, with all the coal, fish, meat and vegetable needs of London and the South-East to be satisfied, the nature of the freight traffic was somewhat different from that on the Down, many of the Down trains being made up largely of empty wagons. The fast fish and meat trains with their specially equipped insulated wagons were a very important traffic all the year up the ECML, and in the winter so were the seed-potato trains from Scotland to East Anglia. These traffics survived but little curtailed throughout the 1950s. In 1939 there were two booked Express Fish trains from Aberdeen, three from Hull and two from Grimsby, also one from Cowlairs (conveying Mallaig traffic), and there was an Express Meat train from Aberdeen and another from York. All these were No.1 Braked trains with fast schedules, and the motive power in 1939 was usually a K3. However, current new construction of V2s allowed a rapidly expanding utilization of this more powerful class, which could take a load of 525 tons whereas a K3 was limited to 420 tons. One train at least, the 10.45 Meat Aberdeen to King's Cross,

A rather unusual sight - but not so in the war: C1 No.4447 (one of those with boiler mountings cut down for trials in the Scottish Area) brings an Up No.1 Express Goods through York station, actually back on 27th July 1937. *Goslin coll.*

had "to be given the same precedence over other trains as given express passenger trains." (Similar special attention was given to the seed-potato trains, from fear of frost damage). In addition, there were two regular vegetable trains from Lincolnshire, one starting from Sibsey, the other from Old Leake, and in the sugar-beet season - especially during and after the war, many special trains were run out of the Eastern Counties to the beet factories in the Midlands, four of which were on the ECML at Peterborough, Newark, Selby and York.

Lastly, an interesting train that joined the ECML at Grantham was the overnight Milk train from Stafford Common via Egginton Junction, Derby Friargate and Nottingham Victoria to King's Cross. This train ran up at near express speed, but the empties went down (05.02 King's Cross to Derby) in more leisurely fashion - and also conveyed passengers after Hitchin. During the war the Milk train started from Derby, and continued to do so until withdrawn in 1951.

As for coal, just the LNER and private coal terminals on the GN line in the London area received about 32,000 tons of coal per month before the war, and many times more was consigned to other terminals in London or passed over to the SR for further transit to places in the South-East. Therefore, from New England Yard about 18 coal trains came up to Ferme Park - plus two to East Goods Yard, each Tuesday to Friday (slightly fewer on Mondays and Saturdays), and there was a corresponding number of empties trains on the Down. In addition, about five brick trains came up daily. Because of the constraints on line occupation, trains were usually made as long as possible, the 2-8-0s (2-10-0s in the 1950s) normally employed being allowed 80 loaded 10-ton wagons while 2-6-0s could take 70 (56 when running at Class A speeds). For the brick trains from Fletton, the distinctive 50-ton bogie wagons were used; these were rated as equivalent to four 10-ton wagons when loaded, to three when empty. (The two Gresley P1 2-8-2s were capable of hauling 100 loaded coal wagons, but by 1939 such long trains were no longer run - on account of the dearth of loops of sufficient length; nor were they run during the war).

The standage in the sidings at both New England and Ferme Park was large (about 3,000 wagons), but this nevertheless did not allow for any great accumulation of traffic, 3,000 wagons corresponding to about 35 - 50 trains or only two to three days' traffic. The main limitation lay in the speed with which the coal traffic could be distributed when it got to Ferme Park, for each 80-wagon coal train required four transfer trips to take the traffic on further. It was vital therefore to keep the essential flows moving constantly, and to organize the marshalling in such a way as to keep shunting to the minimum. The latter was achieved by laying down for Up trains a fairly rigidly ordered grouping of wagons according to their destinations in the London area and on the SR beyond it.

Although severe gradients were not really a problem, the ruling gradient being 1-in-200[12], it was not easy to work - along with many expresses including the high-speed Streamliners - the slow, heavy loose-coupled trains on a main line with several two-track bottlenecks. Running times therefore had to be adhered to, and points where the trains had to stop and wait - sometimes for an hour or more - were clearly laid down. Running speeds and therefore overall times between New England and Ferme Park depended on the class of train and proportion (if any) of braked wagons. Running times varied between about 3½ hours for Class A and 5 hours for Class C trains. All these trains stopped at Hitchin, where normally New England crews

changed over with Hornsey men, but some trains were scheduled not only to stop to detach/attach but also to shunt at certain other places on the way. Intermediate traffic however was largely catered for by the pick-up goods trains, which took anything up to 15 hours between King's Cross Goods and New England.

The Hertford Loop (Wood Green - Hertford North - Langley Junction) was used by several of the goods and coal trains, as a relief line avoiding the Greenwood - Potters Bar and Digswell - Woolmer Green bottlenecks. However, it suffered from a lack of refuge sidings and from a consequent restriction of its usefulness mainly to times outside that of the peaks of the important residential traffic on the stretch between Wood Green and Cuffley. Moreover, there was also the daunting 1-in-57 of the Wood Green flyover to be surmounted by Down trains.

Apart from all the high-value merchandise, the food and the coal and brick trains that ran on the ECML into London, livestock was also carried in great numbers, varying according to Market Days. Cattle wagons had to be booked if possible by station-masters in advance, and trains conveying the wagons when loaded were instructed to limit their shunting to a minimum; nevertheless, the unfortunate animals were often much buffeted around. Before and during the war, horses were still employed in large numbers as motive power for shunting and especially for delivery work to and from the Goods stations. There were so many horses around King's Cross that a manure train was run daily at 03.55 from Ferme Park to Sandy - where the load was presumably distributed to numerous farms in the region, and other trains were scheduled to take odd wagons of manure to other country stations. But lasting into the 1960s was the daily 'dust train' - latterly of great 50-ton wagons, of household refuse, from Ashburton Grove to Blackbridge or Holwell Sidings on the branches from Welwyn Garden City.

The traffic each way over the ECML between Peterborough, Grantham and Doncaster included firstly the Express Goods trains from London already mentioned, some of which turned off at Grantham for Nottingham and further west. Secondly, there were a considerable number of trains that joined the ECML at Newark or at Tuxford and ran on down it to Doncaster and beyond, and vice versa. Thirdly, there was a sizeable flow of coal (or empties) and goods trains to and from New England Yard via Grantham to Colwick Yard or to Doncaster, and also one or two brick trains northwards from Fletton.

The New England loose-coupled trains were principally for the staging of the London and South-East coal traffic in transit from and to the collieries of the North Midlands (collected principally at Colwick) and South Yorkshire (collected mainly at Doncaster). Eight or so a day of these trains rumbled up and down the ECML, but owing to the limited capacity of the mainly double-track line north of Stoke Summit, almost as many trains were sent round via Spalding, Sleaford (or Boston in the war), and Lincoln[13]. These trains round the Loop were much increased during the war and its aftermath. The time taken on the relatively roundabout routes was only about 20 minutes more than straight down the ECML to Doncaster, but trains rarely had to be stopped to allow passenger trains to overtake, and there were no banks like Stoke to climb. Moreover on the Joint Line coal trains of 80 wagons and empties trains of 100 wagons could be run, because not only were the gradients negligible but also many of the loops were long enough; O4 or other 2-8-0s could manage them, not only in terms of haulage power but also of braking. On the main line a stop for water was mandatory in either direction at Newark - even for fast freight trains if they were slowed too much to pick

Essendine: a view southwards on the Down side of this minor junction in Rutland, May 1956. The absence of an Up Slow line platform is evident; the corresponding Down platform (to the right of the North Box) was for branch trains from Bourne and Stamford. Further to the right are the Down Goods line, and the sidings put in during the war. *Author's coll.*

Huntingdon North: a May 1956 view up the line towards London. On the right is the main goods yard, and an elderly 0-6-0 is shunting in the Down yard. Beyond the Down island platform can be seen the main station building beside the Up platform. The loop leading to Huntingdon East can be seen curving away before the No.1 Box. *D.Thompson.*

Tallington, Lincs: a view northwards in May 1956. This first wayside station after Peterborough had only the two platforms on the main lines, there was no Down Goods line, and the Up Goods line ran behind the Up platform line on the right. The extensive goods facilities can be clearly seen. *Author's coll.*

V2 No.60887 (LNER 4858) on a Down Class C freight comes off the Royal Border Bridge into Berwick-upon-Tweed, 17th July 1951. The tarpaulins on the front few wagons look to pose a threat to passing trains, perhaps. *E.R.Morten.*

A Class E partially fitted freight passing through Doncaster on the Up Main, with Heaton based K3 No.61818 (LNER No.52); it is mid-1950s - judging by the flat-bottom track. *J.Davenport.*

Goods at Ferme Park, with J6 No.64253 (LNER No.3604), and J50 No.68971 (LNER No.1086) on the flyover, 14th May 1960. *F.Hornby.*

up at Muskham Troughs, and trains might be scheduled to wait there for an hour or so, also at Retford (Babworth). With through trains, prolonged stops were usually made at Doncaster Decoy for locomotive and crew purposes and for wagon examination.

Coal traffic between Mansfield Concentration Sidings and New England used the route *via* Lincoln in order to avoid Nottingham. Most trains between New England and Colwick went on the ECML over Stoke as far as Grantham, but some went instead *via* Sleaford. The line that joined the ECML at Newark South Junction from Bottesford West Junction brought in about 15 regular daily trains to and from further north - Doncaster, Hull, York *etc.*, a similar number to those leaving the ECML at Grantham. Both groups were mainly on their way to/from Colwick, but not least were the ale trains from Burton-on-Trent to Hull and to Newcastle. During and after the war, a number of trains - mainly of ironstone, off the GN & LNW Joint line also joined the ECML at Newark. Through Grantham passed also the ironstone trains from Highdyke, to Frodingham (for Appleby-Frodingham Steelworks at Scunthorpe) *via* Lincoln or *via* Doncaster, or to Parkgate & Aldwarke (for the Don Valley blast-furnaces) *via* Retford[14], or to Colwick (for onward working to Stanton Ironworks). During and after the war ironstone trains also ran to Tees-Side and to Scotland.

Joining the ECML at Tuxford North was a flow of coal traffic to Hull, originating from Nottinghamshire collieries and marshalled at Mansfield Concentration Sidings or at Warsop Junction, and also the principal through freight and fish trains to/from the GC system at Kirkby South Junction by the LD&EC line through Mansfield. Two Express Fish trains ran daily from Hull southbound through Doncaster and by this route to Banbury, conveying fish consigned to destinations on the GWR as far afield as Swansea, Bristol and Penzance.

The ECML between Doncaster and York, the section linking the Southern Area with the North-Eastern Area of the LNER, was heavily utilized for freight as well as passenger trains. As well as many of the through Express Goods to York and beyond already mentioned, trains from Whitemoor (joining the ECML south of Doncaster) and those from Grimsby and Frodingham (joining at Joan Croft Junction), ran over most of this stretch of the ECML, and it had 25 to 30 scheduled goods and coal trains each way per day. The line was very largely plain double track, and most extra trains - especially during the war, along with coal trains to Gascoigne Wood Yard assembled at Hexthorpe Sidings or from Bentley Colliery, had to be sent round *via* Knottingley and Church Fenton.

At Chaloner's Whin Junction, the ECML traffic joined all that coming into York from the Leeds, Normanton and Sheffield directions (also Hull *via* Selby), including the LMS trains. In 1939 this traffic comprised about 40 - 45 daily scheduled goods trains, of which about 15 were Nos.1 and 2 Express Goods. The LNE trains originated principally from: Neville Hill (Leeds), Gascoigne Wood, Wath, (and *via* Woodhead, Mottram, Dewsnap, Brunswick (Liverpool) and Birkenhead), Sheffield, Mexborough, Colwick, Staveley, Annesley, Woodford, Neasden, Banbury and Park Royal (London, GW). The limited number of LMS trains came mainly from Wakefield, Masborough or Toton. Before the war, nearly all freights from the Church Fenton direction terminated at either Dringhouses or York Yards, although two braked trains from Hull went on respectively to Heaton and Monkwearmouth and one ran through from Normanton to Forth (Newcastle)[15]. Notable were three No.1 Express Meat trains from Huskisson (Liverpool) to Dringhouses,

also three (conditional) cattle trains from Holyhead on the LMSR. One braked and two unbraked trains came from as far away as Woodford Yard, but as stated already the pre-war pattern was generally based on loose-coupled trains running between yards not more than about 75 miles apart. During and after the war there were many more workings from yards south of York through to points in the North-East and Scotland. Northward destinations included: Newcastle (New Bridge Street and Forth Goods, Low Fell, Heaton, Addison (from 1942), and Park Lane Yards), Edinburgh (Niddrie West Yard), West Hartlepool, Stockton, Darlington (Croft), and above all Newport Yard on Tees-side.

The freight traffic north from York, before the war consisting on the Down mainly of trains remarshalled there - but on the Up also the Express Meat and Fish trains from Scotland to London already mentioned - all had to be funnelled along the line through Northallerton, which was four-track for only part of the way at that time. Nevertheless, about 60 goods trains were *scheduled* over this stretch each weekday, the majority running at night, and no doubt as elsewhere this number was considerably swollen by various other trains running more or less *ad hoc* under the orders of Control. A substantial proportion of scheduled trains north of York in peacetime were No.1 or No.2 Braked Goods, otherwise almost all were either Class A or Class B, and thus timed to avoid holding up express trains. Nevertheless many of the freight trains were booked to stop at Pilmoor on the Down and at Thirsk (where they often watered) on the Up, to be passed by fast trains.

Many of the above, especially the unbraked trains serving the Tees-side industrial area *via* Newport Yard, but also including such braked trains as the 00.01 and 12.10 York Yard to Park Lane Yard, the 23.00 Hull to Monkwearmouth, and 01.15 Dringhouses to Forth (and equivalent trains in the Up direction), turned off at Northallerton to be joined by others coming up the Leeds Northern line through Ripon, leaving 25 to 30 braked and only about five unbraked goods trains to continue down the ECML to Croft Yard, Darlington, and beyond. Before the war there were just two goods trains in the WTT that joined at Northallerton from the Ripon line: the 18.51 No.2 Braked goods Armley (Leeds) to Forth, and the 22.00 Class A Starbeck to Croft, but during the war maximum use was made of the Leeds Northern line to relieve the main line through York, including traffic towards Darlington. Before the war the few freight trains passing through York stopped in the York Yards for examination or for water and crew and/or locomotive change, but during and after the war the situation was quite otherwise with the majority running through York. Then the principal Down through trains were mainly handled at the expanded Holgate Reception Sidings. On the Up side they were usually stopped at Clifton, used the new Up loop and passed through the passenger station. From 1942 also, with the Skelton New Sidings in operation, through unbraked goods trains made prolonged stops there, in both directions. Between York and Newcastle there were few if any prolonged stops laid down, and crew changes, if they took place at all, were made at Croft Yard or Darlington.

Quite a number of freight trains started and ended their journeys at Croft Yard, which dealt not only with Darlington traffic but that to and from many of the branches of West Durham, and it was therefore much more than a staging point on the ECML. Thus on the ECML north of Darlington the total number of timetabled trains (and the small proportion of unbraked goods) were very much the same as south of Darlington. Of these 30 to 35 trains, before the war only four braked trains (22.35 Hull to Heaton, 05.05 Croft to Tyne Dock Bottom, and 04.10 and 07.55 York Yard to Park Lane) were booked to turn off at Ferryhill onto the Leamside line; the great majority continued to and through Newcastle *via* Durham. The Leamside line catered mainly for the loose-coupled coal and steel traffic between Tees-side (Newport and Croft Yards) and South Dock (Sunderland), Tyne Dock, Park Lane, and Heaton, so only using the ECML through Ferryhill. During the war the Leamside line was used a great deal more - notably for Convoy coal trains, and continued to be in the 1950s.

North of Newcastle, Heaton Yard was a major staging and marshalling yard and in 1939 nearly all freight trains on the ECML began or ended their journeys there. In Edinburgh, ECML freight ended up (or originated at) Niddrie West, Leith Walk, Portobello, or - during the war and after - Meadows, but as many trains were to or from yards beyond Edinburgh, i.e. High St. or Sighthill in Glasgow, Cadder, Townhill (Dunfermline), Thornton, or Craiginches (Aberdeen). The Summer 1939 WTT shows 16 Express (Braked) trains running down to Berwick and Edinburgh, of which only four (one conditional) were No.1 Braked, namely the famed 'Scotch Goods' - and its 16.05 'Q' relief, from King's Cross, the 21.40 from York to Niddrie West, and the 19.15 Express Fish Hull to Edinburgh. In the Up direction there were however 12 (two conditional) Express Goods passing Heaton daily, including fish and meat trains: the 22.35 High Street (Glasgow) to Dringhouses, 20.35 Aberdeen to East Goods Yard, 03.40 'Q' Joppa to Dringhouses, 10.45 Aberdeen and 14.53 'Q' Edinburgh to East Goods Yard meat trains, 13.45 and 14.10 Aberdeen and 19.25 Edinburgh to King's Cross, 17.19 Leith Walk to York, 17.18 and 18.22 Niddrie West to Marylebone, and the 18.25 Niddrie West to Dringhouses. Tweedmouth was a staging point, and there or at Berwick Heaton crews changed over with men from St Margarets. There were some crew changes arranged at Alnmouth or Dunbar (a regular stop for water), and with the line before the war very much lacking refuge loops there were a number of stations where goods trains were scheduled to shunt off the main line and wait to be overtaken. This, and much else, changed radically in the war.

ECML FREIGHT TRAFFIC DURING THE WAR

The effects of the war on ECML freight traffic reflected the changes on the Railways as a whole which have been outlined in Chapter III, but there were factors peculiar to this particular trunk route and to the regions it served. On the LNER the most marked change in traffic pattern arose from a very great reduction in the export through East Coast ports of coal, steel and the products of heavy industry and the diversion of these traffics to long inland hauls.

The ECML was naturally recognized as absolutely vital to the prosecution of the war. When in May 1940 the German Blitzkrieg in the West raised the real threat of a German invasion of Britain, the major bridges, tunnels, junctions, yards and depots along the whole length of the line were designated as Vulnerable Points (VPs) - as were those on the other Key Routes across the country, susceptible to attack by enemy airborne troops or to saboteurs. The VPs were therefore assigned armed guards, initially from the Field Army but soon taken over by the Home Guard - especially at night-time. Moreover, from mid-May 1940 - when the menace of a German invasion on the East Coast was

taken quite seriously - until the instructions were rescinded in mid-November 1940, locomotives (and breakdown cranes) in steam were moved inland at night from places on the East Coast. Railwaymen were anyway given quite precise instructions about what to do with trains on the move and with locomotives if the enemy came, instructions that included derailing locomotives to block the exits from sheds and their immobilization. It is not clear what effect these desperate measures had on the ECML in particular, but one report mentions 99 locomotives being moved from the coast every night on the GE section.

Nevertheless, the ECML - directly or indirectly - was affected by wartime conditions in certain respects particularly. It served some of the greatest concentrations of the iron and steel industry (in South Yorkshire, Humberside, Tees-side, Tyneside and Clydeside) on which all war production ultimately depended, and the traffic on the NE section of the ECML was probably the most radically affected. In peacetime most of the huge coal output of Northumberland and Co. Durham was consumed by heavy industry in the region or shipped from local ports. Freight traffic in general on the main line north of Northallerton was relatively light, but this was to change notably from the outbreak of the war as the short-haul traffic diminished and that on the main line expanded.

As related in Chapter III, the Convoy coal train plan introduced on 26th February 1940 entailed a programme of up to 200 block coal trains per week from Northumberland and Durham, and 71,500 tons of coal was to be conveyed to London and the South-East each week. (Gas works alone needed 51 train loads weekly, and electricity generating stations, 49). All the block coal trains as well as everything else had to run on the ECML certainly through Northallerton and mostly along the whole stretch between Ferryhill and York. Most Convoy trains joined the ECML at Ferryhill, but some went *via* West Hartlepool and Stockton. The number of freight trains passing daily through Northallerton in March 1941 was *56 more* than in March 1938, and the capacity of the main line through York was already overstretched, especially by the traffic to and from the heavy industries of Tees-side, that of the Leeds Northern line down to Harrogate being limited by its rather severe gradients. The programme still involved running 94 extra coal trains per week south of Doncaster, 54 up the GN&GE Joint line and still 30 up the ECML all the way. The remaining ten were routed *via* Newark, Bottesford and the GN&LNW Joint line onto the WCML. A mere four were sent up the GC London Extension main line, the capacity of which had yet to be radically enhanced before it could carry the great extra wartime traffic that had to be sent that way as the war progressed. This massive programme meant that quite drastic cuts had to be made in passenger services, as related in Chapter IV. The demand for paths, wagons, men and locomotives resulting from the Convoy coal trains and other wartime freight traffic on the ECML was alleviated little by the decline in the traffic through East Coast ports. In any case, later in the war these ports came back fully into use for traffic in troops and war equipment from America.

Indeed the enormous production by the Tees-side plants of semi-finished iron and steel sometimes overwhelmed the railways. The number of wagons dealt with daily at Newport Yard doubled, to 4,500 in each direction, and hundreds of wagon-loads had to be held back, or else the ECML relieved by dispatching output over to Manchester (by rail) to be forwarded from there to South Wales by sea. Fertilizer output from ICI Billingham was very large, although varying according to season,

Wartime freight being hauled by passenger locomotives: C7 No.718 on a Down No.2 Express Goods on the busy - even on Sunday - main line north of York, Sunday 8th June 1941. *K.Oldham.*

while over 15,000 tons per week of Durham coke were sent south *in addition to* the Convoy coal. The output of Consett Ironworks in 1942 amounted to an average of 230 wagons per day, and that of Vickers-Armstrong in Newcastle to 60 a day. The NE Area coped in part by bringing in its scheme of rewarding men with bonuses for speedy working, hard as this was on the locomotives, which had to work flat-out almost continuously, seven days a week and 24 hours a day with boiler wash-outs delayed often until the engines almost broke down. Further south, the steelworks of Lysaght, Appleby-Frodingham, and Richard Thomas in the Scunthorpe area were turning out (in 1942) *1,000 wagons a day*, as were the steelworks in the Sheffield - Rotherham area *onto the LNER alone*, and much of this output was carried onto the ECML.

From the beginning of the war, there was a very great increase in freight traffic to and from Scotland by the ECML, which by mid-1942 - *i.e.* even before BOLERO (*see* Chapter III) - was about double that carried before the war. Under BOLERO the LNER was called upon to cope with an *average* of eight troop trains and four supplies trains *per day* from Scotland to the South and East of England throughout 1943 and much of 1944. With the transfer of much import traffic from East Coast to West Coast ports, extensive use was made of over-side discharge of ships in the Clyde and landing from lighters at Craigendoran (together with traffic from the Faslane Military Port No.1) led to great increases in freight traffic on the LNER at Glasgow. There was consequently a large expansion on the ECML of English traffic to and from Clydeside which could not be carried by the LMSR because of the bottleneck at Carlisle. (This was an inter-Company

arrangement begun during the Great Freeze of January 1940). About five trains a day from the Glasgow area to Lancashire which would normally have come up by the LMSR were handed over to the LNER and run *via* Berwick, York, and Leeds or Woodhead, and two a day for London and one for Birmingham were sent over the LNER from Carlisle to Newcastle and thence south. In the Down direction, trains of iron ore and dolomite for the steel works at Rutherglen were carried on the ECML. In a May 1941 report it is recorded that while on one day 5,940 wagons from Scotland were awaiting acceptance by the LMSR, in addition as many as 4,326 were to come south by the LNER *via* Berwick. The average diversion of traffic across the Border from the LMSR to the LNER in 1941 was 5,600 wagons per month[16]. In addition to this extra traffic from Glasgow, the ECML also had to handle a great deal more traffic to and from Leith Docks, which were heavily engaged in military traffic[17]. As well, from October 1941 Leith became a major port for shipping supplies to Russia[18].

The LNER also relieved the LMSR of some of its traffic to London and the South-East from Merseyside *via* the CLC and from Manchester. In Winter 1940-41 four goods trains a day and three meat and one train of whale oil which previously ran up the WCML to Willesden were routed *via* Woodhead and Colwick to King's Cross instead. Also, by the use of the GW/GC axis through Banbury and Woodford, the LNER relieved the LMSR to a similar degree by taking over traffic from the South-West to Scotland normally routed by the WCML - but this traffic also still came on to the ECML at York. In Winter 1941-42 the ECML was overloaded, and some of the iron ore trains from Highdyke (and some that had been taken off the LMSR at Codnor Park) to Rutherglen, coke and dolomite trains to Scotland from Co. Durham, and meat trains from Scotland to London had to be routed by the LMSR Settle & Carlisle line, while straw trains from the GE section to Leith were now handed over to the LMSR at Peterborough. This situation persisted, and even in the autumn of 1946 - well over a year after the end of hostilities - traffic to Scotland was being diverted from the LNER to the LMSR.

In 1944 the ECML carried an extra burden because as well as military supplies from Scotland additional coal was once again being moved from the North-East, and most of the East Coast ports were now being used as points of entry for US military supplies, and after D-Day for stores shipments to the Normandy beaches[19]. Moreover, by this time the route over the GC main line, Woodford and Banbury was saturated and supplies for the American Army in the south and west were already having to be diverted over the ECML and through London. At the beginning of 1944, imports through Immingham - mainly of steel and military supplies from America, was three times those of a year before and continued at that rate until September 1944. In May 1944, compared with the previous peak month of November 1943 the *extra* traffic southwards up the ECML balanced out as follows.

Through Berwick about 280 wagons a day extra of military stores and 30 a day of coal had to be passed south, and this was offset only by a reduction of 230 wagons a day (100 of timber, 15 of iron and steel, 65 empty lime wagons, plus the equivalent of 50 wagons by withdrawal of passenger trains). Between Newcastle and Northallerton, 2,350 extra wagons per day had to be moved south (made up of the 310 coming from Scotland, 390 of imports through North-East Coast ports, and 1,650 extra wagons of Northumberland and Durham coal), the extra being offset by a reduction of a mere 645 wagons (230 from Scotland, 145 of iron and steel, 235 empty ore wagons, 10 of basic slag and 25 of lime from Billingham). Through Northallerton a maximum of 5,850 wagons could pass per day, but the above extra burden coming from the north was further increased by 25 wagons a day of fertilizer from Billingham. Southwards from Doncaster the new burden amounted to a *net* increase of 1,115 wagons a day: 750 from north of York, swollen by 365 of imports through the Humber, and mitigated only by reductions of passenger services equivalent to 100 wagons per day. Up from Doncaster all the three principal routes were already working to full capacity. Earlier in the war the GN&GE Joint line had some spare capacity, but in 1944 this line was fully occupied with the heavy traffic to the Eastern Counties Air Force Bases, and the GC main line south was also working to the full. The LNER was therefore obliged not only to cut passenger services severely but also to reduce movements south of the less essential freight and it was compelled to apply extensive embargoes. Thus about 25 regular trains (passenger and freight) per day had to be cancelled on the ECML to allow the extra OVERLORD traffic to get through.

During the first six months of 1943, British and American Army depots dealt with 2.1m. wagons, but in the first half of 1944 the figure rose to a staggering *3.1m.* In the three months April - June 1944 the railways ran 45,538 special trains (passenger and freight) on Government Account, and in the period July - September 1944 55,787; 3,150 trains were handled by the NE Area in this period - which gives a measure of the number on the ECML. Despite the reduction of Convoy coal trains after the winter of 1941/42, the total wagon-miles on the LNER Southern

Area - of which *at least* half would be on the ECML, reached peaks of 89m. in September 1942, 88m. in November 1943 and 94m. in July 1944. The climax in traffic came in June 1944, total traffic moved nationwide in the four weeks after D-Day (6th June 1944) at 2,027m. ton-miles exceeding even the previous peak in September 1943 of 1,977m., and in the week ending 9th June 1944 884,000 loaded wagons were dispatched. The peak week for special trains was that ending 17th June 1944, when the Railways ran 3,063 special trains for troops and stores, and *also* 86 ambulance, 21 military postal and 25 prisoner-of-war trains. Of the specials, 180 troop trains and 364 supplies trains originated on the LNER, while 528 troop and 932 supplies trains travelled at least in part over the LNER. It seems likely therefore that about *1,000* military specials ran on the ECML or part of it that week, and it would be interesting to know the figures for traffic passing major ECML junctions[20] - let alone details of trains, but these can now only be imagined. Crump (1947) described how the special trains were meticulously organized, and details the 29 trains arranged by Cambridge District Control office just on D-Day itself; they make fascinating reading, but 50 years later this kind of record does not seem to have survived. The extra OVERLORD traffic continued for at least three months *after* D-Day, and even in October 1944 the LNER was still running twice as many military specials as in the same already busy period a year before. The net ton-miles of freight remained near 2,000m. per month until the end of 1944, and the number of military specials did not fall off appreciably until the end of the war in Europe in May 1945. Indeed freight traffic in general on the LNER did not decline until after VE-Day, for during the first six months of 1945 it was *10% above* even the 1944 level.

The stretch of the ECML from Northallerton to York was a major worry. After two extremely difficult years of working greatly augmented wartime traffic through two exceptionally severe winters and the Blitz, a Government Central Transport Committee (CTC) produced a special report in January 1942 on North-East Area traffic. Earlier, a systematic traffic count on a typical day in March 1941 - one of many made at key points up and down the country - revealed that at Thirsk (Green Lane) a total of 57 passenger trains - and *no* troop trains on that day, 184 freight trains and 49 light engines (with/without brake-van) passed in the 24 hours. Such an intensity over a still partially two-track stretch was unmatched anywhere else in the country. (At Stevenage on the same day there were 97 passenger and 88 freight trains in the 24 hours). This drew attention to a 70% increase over peacetime levels of main-line freight through the NE Area. The total number of freight trains passing through Northallerton per week *each way* was 722 in June 1941 and 796 in December 1941[21], the larger number in winter being attributable to greater traffic of coal, seed potatoes, sugar-beet and fertilisers[22]. The figures of 100 to 110 freight trains each way per day on the line through York[23] did not increase further during the war, despite line widenings increasing capacity, because other factors - availability of locomotives and crews - became limiting. The Tees-side yards alone (in October 1942) dispatched no fewer than 66 trains every weekday (49 from Newport Yard), and the majority of these would run on the ECML. Besides, fewer fast braked freight trains were being run in wartime and average speeds were very low - 20 m.p.h. for Convoy coal trains.

The latter presented a major problem. The report spelled out the existing limitations of the lines south through York or

TABLE 6.2: TIMETABLED THROUGH FREIGHT TRAINS ON THE ECML, SUMMER 1942
(Excluding trains running entirely within the NE Area)

The same limitations to genuine ECML trains apply as in Table 6.1. However, the list is incomplete because the author was unable to see a contemporary — wartime — WTT for the NE Area, although some indication of Convoy coal train paths was obtained from the Southern Area WTT.

Some of the important Up fish and meat trains to London and elsewhere that ran before the war were also scheduled during the war; in the Summer 1942 WTT the minimum remaining was one fish train from Aberdeen and one from Grimsby, with more (including meat trains) designated as 'suspended'. Nearly all the Braked Goods train, in both directions, were No.2, but these no doubt conveyed most of the perishables traffic.

CLASSES BRAKED Nos.1 and 2
King's Cross Goods to: Edinburgh Leith Walk and Glasgow High St.; York Yard (4, 1 *via Hunslet and Neville Hill*); York Dringhouses (2); Leeds (3); Liverpool Huskisson; Manchester Deansgate (*Fruit & Veg.*); Nottingham; Grimsby; New Clee (*fish empties*); Doncaster Decoy (2, *1 being fish empties via Hertford North*); Retford; Peterborough Westwood (*via Hertford North*).
Clarence Yard to: Doncaster Decoy.
Peterborough Westwood to: Doncaster Decoy (2).
Whitemoor *via Lincoln and Doncaster* to: York (3, *1 via Hunslet and Neville Hill*).
Newark to: Doncaster Decoy.
Colwick *via Newark and Doncaster* to: Hull Hessle Haven.
York Yard to: Niddrie.
Heaton to: Aberdeen (2); Thornton; Glasgow High St. (2); Glasgow Sighthill; Cadder (2); Niddrie; Leith Walk (3); Meadows (2).
Berwick to: Townhill; Aberdeen; Thornton.

CLASSES A - C
King's Cross Goods to: New England *via Hertford North* (2); Hitchin.
Clarence Yard to: New England.
Ashburton Grove to: New England.
Ferme Park to: New England (17, *4 via Hertford North*); Connington; Yaxley; Whitemoor *via Cambridge*.
Hatfield to: New England (3).
Hitchin to: New England.
Holme to: New England.
Fletton to: New England (2, *bricks*).
Peterborough Westwood to: Bourne *via Essendine*.
New England to: Colwick *via Grantham* (9); Tuxford North (3); Whisker Hill; Worksop; Scrooby; Doncaster Decoy (4); Doncaster Mineral (2); Ardsley; NE Area[1] (4). (In addition, in 1942 there were 9 paths scheduled from New England to Doncaster (one to Hexthorpe), 8 of them *via Boston*) and one *via the Joint line*, and one to Colwick *via Spalding and Sleaford*).
Highdyke to: Frodingham *via Lincoln* (5); Colwick *via Grantham* (2); Parkgate *via Retford*; NE Area (2); Whifflet (2).
Grantham to: Doncaster Decoy.
Sleaford *via Barkston North Junction* to: Newark.
Colwick *via Newark* to: York (2, *1 via Neville Hill*); Doncaster Decoy (3); Doncaster Mineral (2).
Harby & Stathern *via Newark* to: Doncaster Mineral.
Mansfield Concentration Sidings *via Tuxford* to: Hull Hessle Haven.
Retford to: Doncaster Decoy.
Immingham *via Retford* to: Doncaster Mineral.
Doncaster Decoy or Mineral to: York (9); Gascoigne Wood.
Hexthorpe *via Doncaster* to: Gascoigne Wood (2).
Whitemoor *via Retford and Doncaster* to: NE Area. Whitemoor *via Gainsborough and Doncaster* to: York Dringhouses; York Yard; Neville Hill; Newport.
Bentley Colliery to: Gascoigne Wood (2); Neville Hill.
Tibshelf *via York* to: Whifflet.
Stella Gill *via Newcastle* to: Whifflet.
Low Fell *via Newcastle* to: Whifflet.
Heaton to: Niddrie (2); Meadows (2); Whifflet.
Tweedmouth to: Dunbar; Niddrie; Portobello.
Dunbar to: Portobello.

CLASS D (Pick-Ups, main-line beyond New Barnet only)
King's Cross Goods to: New England; Hatfield.
Ashburton Grove to: Peterborough Eastfield.
Hitchin to: New England.
Ranskill to: Misson, and Doncaster Decoy.

1. These 'NE Area' paths were no doubt for empties of Convoy coal workings.

through Harrogate, with 72% using the former and 28% the latter (double the pre-war level), although by concentrating on bulk train-loads, the LNER had been able to ensure that 63% of the traffic passing through York did not have to be remarshalled there. By passing traffic through Harrogate - to Leeds or to Church Fenton, York could be by-passed altogether, but the Harrogate route was hampered by severe gradients: maximum loads were 32% less than on the York route and/or double-heading was necessary. South and west of Harrogate or York, traffic dispersed to various routes. About 40% of the coal went to Lancashire, but 32% came south to Doncaster (much of it *via* Church Fenton and Knottingley), but in doing so it conflicted with other flows across Yorkshire and the North Midlands. Further south, there was a heavy flow of coal from the

Nottinghamshire coalfield joining at Grantham, but the ECML south of Doncaster was relieved to some extent by sending traffic down the GN&GE Joint main line not only for East Anglia but also for London *via* Whitemoor or New England. In turn, *this* route was relieved by running trains all the way round from Lincoln to Spalding *via* Boston. Of course, the capacity of all these lines had to be expanded by the building of new and longer loops, as was done at innumerable places all over the country. The WTT for Summer 1942, for example, lists paths for 23 Up Convoy coal trains on the ECML through Doncaster - only four of which were routed to Whitemoor, seven days a week (*i.e.* 161 per week) with just as many on Sundays as on weekdays[24]. Routes and destinations were not specified, except that four were designated "Whitemoor coal" and 19 "South coal", this imprecision typifying the way most freight trains were run on an *ad hoc* basis during the war.

When the coal eventually got to London at Ferme Park Yard, there was then the problem of distributing it in small trips onto the other Railways, the trips to the SR alone amounting to over 60 per day (and at least 20 on *Sundays*) in 1940, compared with 34 a day pre-war. By the beginning of 1941, 1,000 wagons each way per day were being exchanged with the SR over the Widened Lines, and 120 with the GWR at Acton. The problem became acute in the Blitz[25] and was tackled by extensive diversions, in part making use of the ex-GC lines, the traffic through the Woodford Yards at the end of 1940 being 32% up on pre-war. Eventually, in 1944 the burden on Ferme Park Yard was relieved to a small extent by the link put in between the GN Hertford Loop and GE Section at Bounds Green, and some coal trains were then diverted that way to Temple Mills Yard - although that yard was already handling an abundance of coal traffic routed through Whitemoor Yard. (In July 1944, on *Sundays alone*, four coal trains - and return empties - were scheduled to use the new link).

The Arctic weather of the first and second winters of the war has been noted in Chapter III. In 1940, the first of several Restriction Orders during the ensuing month was put on ECML traffic through York and Doncaster on 22nd January. After that the weather and other troubles forced the LNER to restrict coal

traffic for the South through Peterborough intermittently during the next ten days, and to apply a complete embargo from 1st February for five days. Then the cumulative effect of diversion of Scottish traffic due to blockage by snow of the WCML and the Settle - Carlisle line at the end of the month, coupled with the LNER's own difficulties that included much staff sickness, led on 14th February 1940 to a three-day embargo being put on the loading of all but food and the most essential Government traffic from Scotland and the North-East to the GN and GE sections. During a period when there was flooding due to a sudden thaw and then more snowstorms followed by more flooding - this time in the south of the country, severe restrictions were again put on traffic over the southern portion of the ECML on 29th February and for four days from 4th March. Flooding was particularly bad in the lower Trent Valley - Gainsborough was under several feet of water for a week[26].

The dislocation during the 1940-41 winter was compounded by another spell of very severe weather in February 1941, bringing about congestion of crisis dimensions. Even in early October 1940 about 300 coal trains were already immobilized in yards owing to interruption of SR lines in London by the Blitz - without any snow. Then blizzards on 19th - 21st February and the extensive damage caused to signalling installations brought about complete paralysis on the ECML from north of Newcastle down to Darlington for a week (*see* Appendix K). This disaster naturally caused immense disruption of goods traffic along the ECML and elsewhere, in a period when the Blitz was in progress. During the next winter heavy snow again caused congestion of Anglo-Scottish traffic sufficient for at least a brief imposition of loading and/or acceptance restrictions by both the WCML and the ECML in the third week of January 1942, the first week of February and on 7th March, also on the ECML southwards from York a week later. The last three winters of the war were not particularly severe. This was just as well because in spite of the restrictions on the use of coal and mineral wagons for merchandise there was a shortage of wagons for the coal, as well as of locomotives and above all of staff. Therefore the greatly increased calls for the movement of merchandise made it impossible to run anything approaching the number of Convoy coal trains that had been dispatched out of the NE Area in the first three winters.

The weekly output of coal from Northumberland and Co. Durham mines in the winter of 1941 was running at 735,000 tons (about 20% of national output), of which about 105,000 tons was sent south

Wartime freight being hauled by passenger locomotives: D2 No.4377 pounding along on a Class B Goods near Ranskill, June 1941. *K.Oldham.*

by rail (mainly in Convoy trains) and over 210,000 tons per week by sea. Up to 30 train-loads a week were also sent up to Scotland[27]. The CTC believed that coal consumption for electricity generation would increase by over 20% in the coming year, and therefore more coal would have to be conveyed, mainly by rail, out of the NE Area. They concluded that, even on the assumption that the physical enhancements of line capacity currently in hand were completed by the following winter, the routes south from Northallerton could take a maximum of 595 trains per week through York, and 230 per week *via* Harrogate. It was estimated that 'demand' might reach 5,500 wagons per week - 10% above the calculated capacity, and therefore at times the capacity of the lines might be exceeded after either abrupt increases in forwardings or problems with severe weather. In practice, over 200 Convoy trains per week were run in 1941, but thereafter they fell markedly to 115 per week in 1942 and 87 in 1943, rose to 104 in 1944, and then fell away to 78 in the first six months of 1945. The widenings completed in 1942 between Northallerton and York eased the congestion a certain amount, but then - despite the installation of new loops - the mainly two-track section between Ferryhill and Northallerton through Darlington became a bottleneck, and many Convoy coal trains had to be re-routed to start from West Hartlepool and run *via* Eaglescliffe. In fact, but for the continuing limitations of the ECML, even more industrial expansion would have taken place in the North-East, because the labour needed was indeed available. 'Convoy' coal trains did not end with the war, for there were 60 per week in the second half of 1945, and still 41 per week in 1946. After the war, on occasions demand over the critical stretch of the ECML still exceeded capacity, and temporary embargoes had then to be applied. (A documented sample of just five Convoy trains in mid-March 1941 is reproduced in Appendix G, which is of interest because it specifies not only their origins and but also the actual locomotives used and the time they took to reach their destinations).

So there were a number of occasions during the war when the capacity of the railways for one reason or another reached saturation, and temporary restrictions - total or partial - had to be imposed on acceptances, and this situation arose especially on the LNER's ECML. Firstly - as we have seen, there were the problems caused by the very severe weather in early 1940, 1941 and 1942 (also less so in early 1944), and of course the Blitz in 1940-41. Then there was the burden imposed by the large new requirement to relieve the LMSR of some of its greatly swollen Anglo-Scottish traffic and to some extent its traffic from Merseyside, - also to help the LMSR during the Blitz. There were occasions when LMSR Scottish traffic had to be transferred to the ECML, notably during the great blizzards of early 1940, but also at other times such as on 15th May 1944 when a major derailment at Mossband (between Carlisle and Gretna) blocked the WCML completely.

The construction and operation of the numerous new airfields in Eastern England added to the burden of the ECML. It resulted in much heavier traffic entering East Anglia through Whitemoor and Peterborough, and quite often during 1943 and early 1944 led to the imposition of embargoes on acceptances of general goods that way. In fact, there was an abrupt increase of traffic in October 1942 which overburdened Whitemoor Yard to the extent that Convoy coal trains to East London and the LT&S section had to be diverted thenceforth *onto* the ECML. Finally, the ECML was of course heavily engaged in the traffic for OVERLORD, and this demanded severe cut-backs not only

in ECML passenger trains but also a reduction in regular freight movements - including coal trains. The LNER somehow managed in the first three years of the war with a reduced number of freight locomotives, by employing passenger locomotives on freight work probably more than any of the other Groups. The loan from early 1943 of substantial numbers of the British and American 2-8-0s built for military purposes alone made possible the satisfaction of the imperative additional demands for freight motive power in 1943-44, and in the end the limit to the amount of traffic that could be moved was set by the shortage of enginemen.

The importation of iron ore was curtailed in the war, and the requirements were made up by great expansion of home production. This came from Oxfordshire, Northamptonshire and Leicestershire. Therefore great tonnages of ore had to be carried from the Midlands not only to the blast-furnaces of the Rotherham and Scunthorpe areas but down the ECML north of York, at the rate of 75 trains per week to those on Tees-side and in Co. Durham, and also even up to Whifflet in Scotland. Earlier in the war, three-quarters of these trains came off the LMSR and joined at York, but by 1943 a third of them were from points on the LNER and running mainly down the ECML. They continued to run in the first years after the war, if at a lesser frequency and more predominantly from the LMSR. To save shipping space, the importation of foreign timber also was radically reduced in the war. As a result the felling of British woodlands was accelerated, and gave rise to especially heavy traffic in softwoods from Scotland up the ECML, for building work, pit-props, *etc.* and for paper-making. (The last also gave rise to a remarkable traffic in *straw* from East Anglia to mills in Scotland).

Wartime rail traffic in farm products was greatly augmented, on account of curtailment of imports and increased home production, as well as diversion from road and from sea. Nationwide, railway traffic in agricultural commodities rose by 70% between 1938 and 1945, to 1.85m. tons. Vegetables and potatoes figured largely, of which latter 3½ times as many tons were conveyed in the war period. Even between 1939 and 1940 the tonnage of East Anglian potatoes conveyed was doubled and that of grain multiplied four-fold, much of it on the ECML. Although perhaps less than in peacetime, each winter of the war up to 250,000 tons of seed potatoes were carried - under *two* sheets per wagon - down from Scotland, and 130,000 tons of sugar-beet came out of the Eastern Counties. Much of all this must have been conveyed on the ECML. Nevertheless, the ECML was relieved to some extent of this traffic during the war: normally thought too precious to shovel into boats, they were now transported partly by coaster - and coasters were also loaded with apples on their return from the South.

As mentioned in Chapter IV, between 1939 and the end of 1944 the number of military airfields in Britain rose from 158 to no less than 623 including 133 built for the USAAF in 1942-44. By February 1944 they covered in all 250,000 acres and had cost £615m. A high proportion were located in the eastern half of England and Scotland and therefore would be served at least in part by the ECML. The total area of paved runways, perimeter tracks and hard standings laid during 1940-44 (the peak being in 1942) was 175m. sq. yds. - equivalent to about 10,000 miles of 30 ft. roads[28]. Numerous wayside station goods yards on and off the ECML became their railheads and so dealt with unprecedented traffic, for the construction of *each* standard bomber station consumed 90,000 cu. yds. of hardcore and 18,000 tons of cement, and together with prodigious amounts of sand, bricks, timber and steel most of all this was brought to the locality by rail. A five-fold multiplication in the goods traffic of country stations supplying airfields was *average*, and at some stations the increase was 20-fold. After the airfields were in operation, the supply of armaments and fuel entailed the running of hundreds of special freight trains that had to pass over parts of the ECML and especially also over the GN&GE Joint line[29]. A 1,000-bomber raid was estimated to require the equivalent of 28 trains of petrol and eight of bombs. Raids by the RAF and the USAAF with over 250 aircraft were mounted at least twice a week from late 1942, from March 1943 the sizes of the armadas were usually well over 500 aircraft and during 1944 and early 1945 operations with up to 1,000 planes were mounted frequently. The explosive stocks for the RAF were held underground in main Reserve Depots, in remote but rail-served sites each having a planned turnover of 60,000 tons per month (84 wagons per day). Then, especially in Eastern England and near the Bomber Bases - and served by the ECML, were the Forward Ammunition Depots and Air Ammunition Parks (AAPs), which mainly received by rail and issued by road but still required to handle over 100 rail wagons per day. From late 1943 this traffic soared as the number of AAPs mushroomed and the turnover of the RAF No.42 Maintenance Group, responsible for the supply, rose to over 3m. tons in 1944[30] - and meanwhile the traffic in ordnance for the VIII and IX USAAF would have been of the same order. The airfields and the numerous depots for military stores and ordnance tended to be situated in rural areas and to be served by rail on branch lines, but several airfields and ordnance dumps were sited not far from the ECML - notwithstanding the potential danger; in any case their traffic would be on or off the main line at some point. The Doncaster - York section, with three airfields (Snaith, Burn and Riccall) and a large bomb depot (Escrick) very close to the main line, was particularly vulnerable and apart from the several occasions when aircraft crashed on the line it was closed - to passenger trains - for 10 days in 1943 after the bomb dump at Snaith Airfield blew up. (*see* Appendix H - on the impact of the air war - for more details).

There were a large number and variety of Government depots served by the ECML - many being close to it, and in Appendix E there is a list of most of them. Probably the largest military installation entirely dependent on the ECML for rail-borne traffic was Catterick Camp, on a steeply-graded military branch off the Eryhome - Richmond line, while not far off the ECML at Prudhoe (between Blaydon and Hexham) there was a huge Ministry of Supply depot turning out about 150 wagons a day. Although of necessity supplied principally by road, there was a great RAF Maintenance Unit (No.60) beside the ECML at Beningbrough, to which were brought the remains of most of the 1,500-2,000 aircraft that crashed in Yorkshire; the same Maintenance Unit had a factory nearby at York (Clifton) Airfield, where up to 4,000 people were employed repairing damaged Halifax bombers. The Ministry of Aircraft Production (MAP) had a factory (engaged in breaking up damaged aircraft) at Urlay Nook near Darlington and this dealt with several trains a day. Of the many huge storage depots built up and down the country for the BOLERO supplies, those feeding traffic more or less directly onto the ECML were at Bottesford, Boughton (near Ollerton) and at Histon (Cambs.), while the VIII USAAF had its 2nd Strategic Air Depot served by a branch from Abbots Ripton and dealt with an average of 45 wagons a day from December 1943. Lastly, it must be remembered that much of

the traffic to and from Naval bases in Scotland and on the East Coast was conveyed on the ECML; the Admiralty depots at Rosyth and Charlestown alone dispatched 200 wagons a day[31]. At the end of the war, stored ammunition was disposed of by sending it all the way up from the south to the military ports in Scotland to be dumped out at sea, and the vast surplus stores of the US Army had to be sent to the ports for export back to North America, and so on.

Another new major source of traffic during the war were the vast Royal Ordnance Factories, for the manufacture of guns, shells, bombs, mines and other armaments, the manufacture of explosives and the filling and assembly of explosive devices. There were eventually 44 ROFs up and down the country, and the transportation of many thousands of tons of explosives and ordnance was a vital but hazardous task taken on by the Railways. The principal ROFs on or near the ECML were as follows: in Co.Durham, Birtley (engineering, used in World War One and reopened in 1937), Aycliffe (filling, opened 1941) and Spennymoor (opened 1938); in Yorkshire, Thorp Arch (near Wetherby, filling, opened 1941), Barnbow (near Garforth), and Maltby (near Doncaster), and in Nottinghamshire at Ranskill (explosives - cordite, opened 1941). These added very considerably to the ECML freight traffic, with hundreds of wagon-loads per week at each, both inwards and outwards. In February 1944, *per day* Birtley was turning out about 30 wagon-loads, Aycliffe 70, Thorp Arch 45, and Ranskill 20. Most of the factories very quickly ceased work after the war, but maintained a modicum of traffic for the railway as they were transformed eventually to civilian Trading Estates; however, Thorp Arch remained in use - on a much reduced scale, as a military stores depot.

Trains of petrol tank-wagons were a major traffic. They were almost as dangerous as those of bombs and presented their own operating problems. During 1940 the British Railways as a whole ran 1,158 special trains of aviation spirit, but this tally rose to no less than 9,235 in 1944. Because so many of the operational airfields lay in Eastern England the LNER carried a high proportion, but to minimize enemy strafing they were kept if possible 30 miles away from the East Coast and not allowed to stand overnight in that area. During the early years of the war, much of the aviation fuel was sent from Stanlow and from Avonmouth through Peterborough to a stabling and distribution point at Whittlesea. The burden on the ECML of petrol traffic was eased to some extent when a major distribution depot was built at Sandy Heath (on the LMSR line between Sandy and Potton) in September 1943, and this was supplied by *pipelines* from Stanlow, from Avonmouth and later from Thames Haven. In the three months after D-Day, 634 train-loads of petrol were sent from Sandy to railheads all over East Anglia, but the latter also *still* received another 498 train-loads from the ports in that period. The ECML also continued to handle petrol coming in through Hull to the Air Force depot at Ripon. Moreover from 1943 at certain airfields across the country the fog-dispersal system, FIDO, was installed, and this used such enormous quantities of petrol that special sidings for its supply were put in at the local railway station; on the ECML, one at St Neots supplied Graveley airfield.

The movement of other military traffic, notably that of armoured fighting vehicles (AFV), also presented particular problems. British tanks had to be designed to fit the restricted British loading-gauge and required special Warflat and Warwell wagons, on which they had to be loaded with extreme care. The

'Over Here!' When the US Army Transportation Corps S160 2-8-0s first appeared in Britain in December 1942 they seemed like illusions tranported by Hollywood, but they became quite familiar for nearly two years, and were intensively employed on the ECML from Heaton, St Margarets and other depots. Here No.1834 waits in Edinburgh's Princes St. Gardens with an eastbound Class A Goods, 1943. *K.Oldham.*

An unidentifiable Austerity 2-8-0, on loan to the LNER and recently returned from war service on the Continent with Westinghouse brake pump, heads an Up Class C slow coal train south of Potters Bar, 1946. *R.E.Batten.*

- WARTIME WAGON LABELS -

WD wagon label: the centre strip would have been coloured as:- Red - ammunition; Green - ordnance; Blue - RASC supplies; Brown- stores; Yellow - RE stores; Yellow/Black alternate - petrol, oil & lubricants (POL); no strip - miscellaneous.

WD wagon label for urgent shipment traffic.

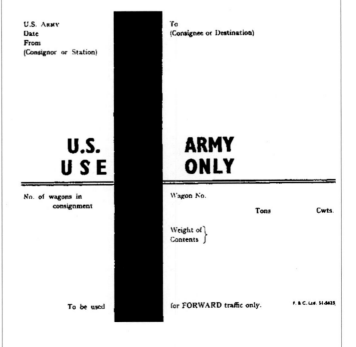

RAF wagon label for "Essential Traffic."

US Army wagon label: colour coding was as for WD.

loaded wagons were barred from branch lines with weak bridges, and there was a long list of places where they could not pass anything on an adjacent line - partly because at a considerable height above the rail they were in fact too wide. Trains dedicated to the transport of AFVs were assembled and stationed at many places up and down the country, usually adjacent to Army depots[32]. There was also a chronic shortage of bolster wagons, used for carrying steel plate and other large loads - including small naval craft and (from 1943) the large crates of vehicles sent over for the US Army. The transport of explosives - full of potential danger - required elaborate regulations and instructions, not least when wagon-loads of ordnance were stored - as they often were - on the railway. The requirement for special dedicated wagons was not large, but an example on the ECML was the provision of designated wagons (with supports for protective sheets), for transporting corrosive nitre-cake in large quantities away from Ranskill ROF.

Thus direct military needs, for airfields, camps, and storage depots *etc.* for the Armed Forces - who numbered 3.5m. by mid-1941 even before the arrival of any US servicemen - brought about a large increase in freight as well as passenger traffic over routes lightly loaded in peacetime. As it supplied three airfields, the freight traffic on the Easingwold Light Railway from Alne mushroomed in 1943 to 37,000 tons - nearly five times its pre-war level. Likewise, the Derwent Valley Light Railway had its carryings multiplied three-fold at that time, and the North Sunderland Railway from Chathill carried 3½ times the peacetime traffic.

All this wartime freight traffic gave rise to much of new interest in the locomotive workings, for the pleasure of such railway enthusiasts as were around. With those on the troop specials as well, this compensated a great deal for the loss of the glamorous express trains and special holiday trains of peacetime. However, in considering the locomotive workings in wartime, one must bear in mind that for the *staff*, who had to *run* the railway, an 'interesting' locomotive from an 'unusual' Shed normally meant *Trouble*: some shed-master or running foreman was short of his normal stud of motive power, on account of 'failures' or extra traffic. Under wartime circumstances the return of such 'foreigners' to their home depots was not ensured by the District Motive Power Controller with the same diligence as was normal in peacetime. After the war this was done much more conscientiously, but the train-spotter was still given his surprises.

For the footplate-men and guards, wartime freight working might mean a lot more overtime but also long frustrating hours out on the road, perhaps crawling along from block to block, or queuing interminably on Permissive Block stretches waiting for a path or for space in a yard. Even without bad weather, men might work a whole shift queuing and not moving their train an inch - and this still occurred to some extent just after the war. A serious problem in these circumstances was that engines held up for hours in sidings could run out of water and their fires would have to be dropped. To avoid this, Controllers tried to have trains backed into sidings to allow the engines to uncouple and go off light to replenish their tanks, although water-columns were installed at many of the new wartime loops. Being out in the Black-Out was eerie, and could be dangerous: it was much easier to get lost, and men anyway might have to work on lines with which they were not very familiar - and under the sheets draped from cab to tender to hide the glow of the fire from enemy aircraft, it was claustrophobic. Then again they might quite likely be handling a load of ordnance - like the brave men

who were blown up at Soham in June 1944, at Gascoigne Wood in April 1945, and elsewhere. Still, at least train crews were issued with 'tin hats'.

In terms of *timetabled* freight services, there were really remarkably few changes during the war compared with pre-war (*see* Table 6.1). Even the braked freight trains were not markedly reduced, and the paths provided for non-fitted trains were essentially the same, in routes and in numbers. Perhaps the most obvious difference was the insertion of paths for the Convoy coal trains and for certain corresponding empties trains from New England to the NE Area in the Down direction, also for some ironstone trains from Highdyke to the NE and Scottish Areas. Undoubtedly the intention remained, even in the middle of the war, to have a schedule of regular freight workings much as in peacetime. Of course it was very often not possible to adhere to the WTT, and the innumerable extra trains on Government Account had to be fitted by the District Control Officers into the WTT in the best way they could.

POST-WAR FREIGHT UNTIL THE END OF THE 1950s

Once the war was over in Europe in May 1945, there was an easing up in the volume of freight traffic - but this was *relative*. For example, in the LNER Southern Area freight tonnage originating in the 12 weeks to 20th October 1945 was only 7.2% less[33] than in the same period of the hectic previous year, coal traffic being 9.8% *higher*; moreover, fish traffic was *double* that of pre-war. In November 1945 congestion again forced the LNER to place embargoes from time to time on the dispatch of traffic for south of Peterborough. Then in the winter of 1946/47 embargoes once again had to be put - even before the Great Freeze began (*see* Appendix K), on account of shortage of serviceable locomotives.

Commencing as early as July 1945, the LNER built up, again as in 1939, an extensive service of fast fitted and semi-fitted trains between the main goods depots of the principal cities, running mostly at night. However, study of the WTTs for freight trains on the ECML in Winter 1945 shows that immediately after the end of the war, the majority of trains were still running unbraked, but much of the New England - Ferme Park coal traffic, which persisted at a high level in the first ten post-war years, had already been up-rated to Class A speed. There were significantly more scheduled unbraked trains than before the war, and both braked and unbraked trains were running between a greater variety of yards, and often for longer distances than pre-war. Moreover, a number of trains were still instructed "to run under Control orders", which had applied to so many during the war. The new destinations included Connington Sidings, to which as well as to New England Down empties trains ran from London. Of the 16 daily Down empties between New England and Doncaster, half ran *via* Sleaford or *via* Boston. Furthermore, the legacy of wartime left through workings between Doncaster and West Hartlepool or Heaton, and a number of conditional paths between Doncaster and York (some *via* Knottingley). There were several through workings over the Hertford Loop, which included at least one train each way to/from Temple Mills Yard *via* the Bounds Green link, and certain braked trains continued to come up through York from the Yard at Thirsk which had been reopened in the war. By the early 1950s these paths had been taken out of the WTTs.

In 1953-54 five daily Express Parcels trains ran from King's Cross to York, while Marylebone sent one to York which joined

B16/3 No.61453 (LNER No.2382) pulls away northwards on a Class C freight on the avoiding-lines at Darlington Bank Top, in the mid-1950s. The station and North Box can be seen behind the vans, while the large sign on the right announces the forthcoming building of a depot for DMUs. *P.Hay.*

An Up Class H coke train of typical NER and BR high-capacity wagons drifts into Durham station, behind Austerity 2-8-0 No.90482 (LNER No.3161, ex-WD No.78690), on 16 July 1951. This north end view shows the small engine shed on the left and North Box on the right. *E.R.Morten.*

V2 No.60810 (LNER No.4781) heads an Up Class D freight past Heaton shed and ex-LMS 4MT 2-6-0 No.43016, 1950s. *B.Morrison.*

The Gresley 4' 8" J38 0-6-0s were not seen on the ECML until you got near Edinburgh: here at Niddrie North on 21st April 1956 No.65919 (LNER No.1422) heads a goods towards Niddrie West from the Portobello direction, while a V2 approaches with another on the Lothian Line having probably come off the ECML at Monktonhall Junction. The lines bearing left in front of the J38 are those to Niddrie South and the main Waverley Route, and the line above converging to the overbridge is a loop from Niddrie South onto the Lothian Lines that lead to South Leith Junction and South Leith. Niddrie South Box is visible on the horizon towards the right. *J. Robertson.*

TABLE 6.3: **TIMETABLED THROUGH FREIGHT TRAINS ON THE ECML, 1950**s

The following summary table was compiled from WTTs for Winter 1953 (Eastern Region), Winter 1952 (North Eastern Region) and Summer 1955 (Scottish Region). It serves for comparison with Tables 6.1 and 6.2, indicating the booked ECML freight services soon after Nationalization and before the downturn of traffic after the ASLEF Strike in June 1955, and with Table 6.4 for Winter 1959. Similar reservations to those noted under Table 6.1 apply regarding the differences in the nature of the Up traffic and of the services which are *not* listed.

London - York, and beyond:-

BRAKED, CLASSES C - E

King's Goods to: Niddrie[1]; Haymarket (*meat empties*); Dringhouses; York Yard; Leeds (2); Doncaster Decoy; Colwick (*via Hertford North*); Lincoln Holmes; New Clee (*fish empties*); Heaton.
Clarence Yard to: New England; Doncaster Decoy.
Ferme Park to: New England.
Welwyn Garden City to: Colwick *via Grantham*.
Hitchin to: Colwick *via Grantham*; Doncaster Decoy.
Peterborough Westwood to: York.
Newark to: Doncaster Decoy.
Burton-on-Trent *via Newark and Doncaster* to: York.
Colwick *via Newark and Doncaster* to: York; Hull Hessle Haven.
Woodford Halse *via Tuxford North* to: Doncaster Decoy.
Thames Wharf *via March and Doncaster* to: Niddrie.
Whitemoor *via Doncaster* to: Niddrie (2); Stockton; York.
Hexthorpe *via Doncaster* to: York.
Doncaster Decoy to: Heaton (2).
Grimsby *via Joan Croft Junction* to: York.

UNBRAKED, CLASSES E, F, H and J

King's Cross Goods to: New England (4).
Ashburton Grove to: New England (3).
Highbury Vale to: New England.
Ferme Park to: New England (17, 9 *via Hertford North*).
Hatfield to: New England.
Letchworth *via Hitchin* to: New England.
Tempsford (Little Barford Generating Station) to: New England.
New England to: York (2); Doncaster Decoy (5).
New England *via Grantham* to: Colwick (7); Worksop *via Retford*; Scrooby. (In addition, there were about 8 paths booked from **New England** *via Spalding and Boston* to Doncaster Decoy, and *via Sleaford* 2 to Mansfield Concentration Sidings and 1 to Warsop Junction).
Highdyke to: Frodingham (4, *3 via Grantham, and Lincoln - or Sleaford, 1 via Doncaster*); Colwick; Aldwarke *via Retford*.
Sleaford *via Barkston North Junction* to: Newark.
Colwick *via Newark* to: Doncaster Mineral (2); Doncaster Decoy; Hull Hessle Haven (2); York.
Coundon Road (Coventry) *via Newark* to: Hull Hessle Haven.
Northampton *via Newark* to: Doncaster Mineral.
Welham Sidings *via Newark* to: Doncaster Decoy (2).
Mansfield Concentration Sidings *via Tuxford and Doncaster* to: Hull Mineral (2).
Warsop Junction *via Tuxford and Doncaster* to: Hull Hessle Haven (2)
Whitemoor *via Lincoln and Doncaster* to: York; Hull Hessle Haven.
Doncaster Decoy to: York (3).
Hexthorpe to: Skelton Sidings.
Frodingham *via Joan Croft Junction* to: York (3).
Stainforth *via Joan Croft Junction* to: York.

York - Newcastle (in addition to any of the above running north of Doncaster):-

CLASSES C - E

Dringhouses to: Niddrie; Newcastle New Bridge St. (2); Gateshead Warehouse (1), Gateshead Park Lane (2, *via Stockton and West Hartlepool*).
York Yard to: Heaton (4); Newcastle Forth; Newport (4).
Park Royal (London) *via GC and York* to: Newcastle Argyle St.
Croft to: Heaton; Newcastle Forth (2).
Starbeck to: Croft.
Northallerton (Low Gates) to: Croft.
Stockton *via Ferryhill* to: Heaton.

CLASSES F, H and J

Woodford Halse *via GC and York* to: Newport (3).
Ashwell, Storefield, Toton, and Wellingbrough (1 each) *via LMR and York* to: Newport.
Tibshelf *via LMR and York* to: North Stockton.
Healey Mills *via Normanton and York* to: Newport.
Dewsnap *via Penistone, Wath and York* to: Newport.
York to: Newcastle Forth (3); Heaton (2); Gateshead Park Lane (3, *1 via Durham, 2 via Stockton and West Hartlepool*); Newport (3); West Hartlepool (4); North Stockton (3); Croft (4).
Neville Hill to: Croft (2).
Hull *via Sherburn and York* to: Newport (2); Croft.
Gascoigne Wood *via York* to: Croft.
Croft to: Low Fell; Heaton (3); Gateshead Norwood; Sunderland South Dock (2); Blaydon Addison; Consett; Gateshead Park Lane *via Ferryhill and Leamside* (2).
Newport *via Ferryhill* to: Low Fell (3); Heaton (3).
Port Clarence and **West Hartlepool** (1 each) *via Ferryhill* to: Heaton.
Haverton Hill *via Ferryhill* to: Low Fell (2).

Newcastle - Edinburgh, not including those already listed starting south of Newcastle:-

(Trains on Sc.R. section only are from June 1955 WTT).

CLASSES C - E

Heaton to: Aberdeen Craiginches (2); Portobello (2); Niddrie (3); Meadows (4); Townhill; Glasgow High St.; Leith Walk; Tweedmouth.

CLASSES F and H

Heaton to: Niddrie; Granton; Tweedmouth.
Morpeth to: Granton; Tweedmouth.
Tweedmouth to: Niddrie; Meadows.
North Berwick to: Glasgow High St.

Note:
1. 266 Down 'Scotch Goods' had booked stops only at Peterborough Westwood and Doncaster Decoy before Skelton Sidings, which were reached in six hours.

TABLE 6.4: TIMETABLED THROUGH FREIGHT TRAINS ON THE ECML, WINTER 1959

The following summary table was compiled from WTTs for Winter 1959 (Eastern, North Eastern and Scottish Regions). It serves for comparison with Tables 6.1, 6.2 and 6.3, indicating the booked ECML freight services to some extent modified in the early years of the Modernization Plan. Similar reservations to those noted under Table 6.1 apply regarding the differences in the nature of the Up traffic and of the services which are *not* listed.

London - York, and beyond:-

BRAKED, CLASSES C - E

King's Cross Goods to: Aberdeen (*fish empties*); New Clee (*fish empties*); Niddrie (2)[1]; York Yard; Dringhouses; Newcastle Forth; Gateshead Park Lane; Leeds; Hull; Sheffield *via Retford*; Doncaster Belmont.
Clarence Yard to: York Yard; Peterborough Westwood.
Ferme Park to: Niddrie; Heaton; New England (3, *2 via Hertford North*); Hitchin.
Welwyn Garden City to: New England.
Hitchin to: Peterborough Westwood.
Yaxley to: York Yard.
Peterborough Westwood to: Doncaster Belmont; Manchester Ducie St. *via Grantham*.
New England to: York Yard; Doncaster Decoy; Colwick *via Grantham*.
Grantham to: Dringhouses.
Sleaford to: Retford *via Barkston North Junction*.
Colwick *via Newark* to: Doncaster Belmont; Hull; York Yard (2).
Woodford *via Tuxford* to: Hull;
Annesley *via Tuxford* to:Hull.
Dagenham Dock *via March, Lincoln and Doncaster* to: Niddrie.
Whitemoor *via Lincoln and Doncaster* to: Niddrie (2); Newcastle Forth; Stockton; Croft; York Yard (2, *1 via Knottingley*); Carlisle *via Blaydon*; Doncaster Belmont.
Boston *via Lincoln and Doncaster* to: Dringhouses.
Doncaster Belmont to: York Yard (2).

UNBRAKED, CLASSES E, F, H and J

King's Cross Goods to: New England; Welwyn Garden City (2).
Ashburton Grove to: New England.
Highbury Vale to: New England.
Ferme Park to: New England (8, *4 via Hertford North*).
New Southgate to: New England.
Palace Gates to: New England.
Hertford North to: New England.
Hitchin to: New England.
Letchworth *via Hitchin* to: New England.
Little Barford CEA to: New England.
Goldington CEA *via Sandy North Junction* to: New England.
New England to: Colwick *via Grantham* (6); Doncaster Decoy (3); York Yard *via Knottingley*; Ranskill[2]; Scrooby (In addition, there was one train from New England to Doncaster Belmont *via Boston*, 2 to Worksop *via the Joint Line and Retford*, and 2 to Warsop Junction and 2 to Mansfield Concentration Sidings *via Lincoln and the LD&EC*).
Highdyke to: Frodingham (3, *2 via Lincoln, 1 via Doncaster*); Colwick; Aldwarke.
Welham Sidings *via Newark* to: Doncaster Decoy.
Northampton *via Newark* to: Doncaster Belmont.
Colwick *via Newark* to: Hull (2).
Mansfield Concentration Sidings *via Tuxford* to: Hull.
Warsop Junction *via Tuxford* to: Hull.
New Clee *via Retford* to: Rossington.

Doncaster Decoy *via Knottingley* to: York Yard (4); Stockton.
Doncaster Belmont to: York Yard. (In addition, there were a number of through trains from Whitemoor etc. passing through Doncaster to Leeds, Hull, Wath etc.)

York - Newcastle, in addition to any of the above running north of Doncaster:-

BRAKED CLASSES C - E

Grimsby *via Joan Croft Junction and York* to: Croft.
Immingham *via Joan Croft Junction and York* to: Consett.
Dringhouses to: Newcastle New Bridge St. (AA)[3]; Gateshead Park Lane (3); Stockton; Niddrie.
Hull *via Sherburn and York* to: Glasgow High St. (AA).
York *via Durham, or Leamside* to: Newcastle Forth (2); Gateshead Park Lane (2); Wearmouth; Croft (2); Heaton (4).
Via York:- Woodford *via GC* to: Newport.
Healey Mills *via Normanton* to: Gateshead Park Lane (2); Newcastle Forth; Croft.
Normanton to: Heaton.

UNBRAKED CLASSES E, F, H and J

Frodingham *via Joan Croft Junction* to: York Yard; Croft (2).
Via York:- Manchester Brewery Sidings *via Normanton* to: Newport (2);
Guide Bridge Dewsnap Sidings *via Wath* to: Newport (2);
Rotherham Road to: Croft;
Normanton to: Stockton (2); Croft (2); Newport (2);
Toton (1) and Storesfield (2) to: Newport;
Mansfield *via GC* to: Uphall *via Edinburgh*;
Woodford *via GC* to: Newport (2);
Healey Mills *via Normanton* to: Newport (4); Stockton (3); Croft (3);
Hull *via Sherburn* to: Croft.
York Yard to: Croft (2); Northallerton (2); Newport (4); West Hartlepool (2); Stockton (3); Heaton *via Leamside*.
Skelton Sidings to: West Hartlepool (2).
Thirsk to: Newport.
Newport, and **Stockton** (1 each) to: Addison Yard *via Ferryhill and Low Fell*.
Croft to: Heaton (3); Newcastle Forth; South Dock Sunderland; Addison Yard (2); Consett; Gateshead Park Lane *via Leamside*.

Newcastle - Edinburgh, not including those listed above as starting south of Newcastle:-

BRAKED CLASSES C - E

Heaton to: Aberdeen Craiginches; Leith South (3); Niddrie (4, *1 AA*); Portobello (AA); Glasgow High St. (AA); Tweedmouth.
Morpeth to: Niddrie.

UNBRAKED CLASSES E, F, H and J

Heaton to: Alnmouth (2); Tweedmouth; Pegswood; Leith South.
Morpeth to: Niddrie; Tweedmouth.
Tweedmouth to: Niddrie (2).

Note:
1. 266 Down 'Scotch Goods' now running non-stop to Skelton Sidings, and an hour faster than in 1953.
2. Crippled wagons; taken on to Doncaster after repair.
3. AA = 'Assured Arrival'.

One of the numerous J6 0-6-0s that worked in the Peterborough area, No.64206 (LNER No.3557), brings an Up Class K ballast train off the Nene Bridge, with the electricity generating station prominent beyond, 1958. *A.C.Ingram.*

The most modern BR Steam motive power: one of the 9F 2-10-0s with double chimney, No.92188, speeds up the Vale of York 'race-track' at Otterington with an oil train in the late 1950s, while a Down express recedes into the distance. *E. Sanderson.*

London Midland Region freight at Hitchin: two ex-Midland 3F 0-6-0s (43808 and 43766) bring a heavy train - with three ex-GNR fitted brick wagons at the head - into the Up platform line, 2nd November 1957. *Author.*

continued from page 119

the ECML off the former GC at Tuxford North, and one ran down the GN&GE Joint line from March joining the ECML at Doncaster. York ran two Express Parcels trains to Edinburgh and no less than five to Newcastle, while one other ran from Newcastle to Edinburgh. Up services were similar, although at least one Express Parcels ran through from Edinburgh to King's Cross. There was one Express Meat train from Aberdeen to East Goods Yard, and nine Express Fish trains to King's Cross Goods: two from Aberdeen, one from York, three from Hull, two from New Clee, and one from Grimsby. Actually, Grimsby dispatched daily eight fish trains and Hull five, all running at least briefly on the ECML. The urgency of the fish traffic after the war is exemplified by the fact that one of the Aberdeen-London trains was given priority over the Up *NORTH BRITON*. The equally urgent seasonal seed-potato traffic from Scotland continued to be very heavy, the ER handling no less than 300 trains between November 1950 and January 1951. All these Class C trains were worked largely by the Pacifics and V2s, but often also by B1s or K3s. To smooth their ordered assemblage, the refrigerated and insulated wagons needed for these Express Fish and Meat trains was arranged by the Central Freight Rolling-Stock Control Office at BR Headquarters. This office superseded the wartime ICRC, and collated nationally the information sent to Regional Freight Wagon Stock Control Offices (a combined office at York for the ER and NER) by the District Offices, to which individual depots and yards sent daily details of their stock positions. The same system was conducted with respect to mineral wagons at collieries, quarries, *etc.*

The ECML in the 1950s was still a very important freight artery, and as late as 1958 the total on the ER was still 3,300m. ton-miles, of which respectively 56% of the merchandise, 75% of the minerals and 91% of the coal originated on the (new) Great Northern Line (London - Doncaster, inclusive). The pattern of freight services on the ECML at the relatively prosperous time in the early 1950s is shown by the list given in Table 6.3. In Part II (Appendix M) will be found a complete listing of all scheduled freight trains at York in Winter 1952/53.

It will be apparent that by 1953-54 the number of braked freight trains down the ECML was now similar to that before the war, although the proportion that was fully-fitted was much larger. Their destinations were likewise similar, except for the notable omission of any to Manchester or Liverpool, and four instead of one going down north from Whitemoor plus one from Thames Wharf. With all new freight and mineral wagons from 1957 being fitted with power brakes, changes that were made between 1953-54 and 1959 comprised primarily the introduction of more Express Freight trains, including some engaged in the

new 'Assured Arrival' - usually overnight - service now offered to traders. Also many of the workings between Ferme Park and New England, New England and Doncaster - and certain others, were speeded up to Class E (limited load with or without at least four piped wagons next to the engine). Entailing in several cases the reintroduction of lodging-turns for the footplate-men, the new fast braked train workings included, for example, King's Cross to Hull[34], to Sheffield *via* Retford, and to Aberdeen, from Clarence Yard to Colwick, to Heaton and to Niddrie, from Woodford to Hull (*via* Tuxford), from Boston to York (*via* Doncaster), from Immingham to Consett, and from Hull to Glasgow High Street - the 'Humber-Clyde'; the Aberdeen - Newcastle overnight train was dubbed the 'Geordie'.

There was a deliberate policy during the 1950s of running through trains further between remarshalling. The outstanding example on the ER of this kind of rationalization in the period was the scheme undertaken at Peterborough in 1953, when three yards were closed, saving the shunting and tripping of 2,000 wagons a day and an average of six hours in the transit time of these wagons - and this was at a time when rail freight was still booming and not being lost to road to any great extent. Moreover, in this period, existing marshalling yards were being modernized and even new ones were being built. Examples of new long-distance freight workings on the ECML included, from Mansfield to Uphall (West Lothian), and from the upgraded new marshalling yard at Healey Mills near Wakefield - and from Normanton - to destinations in the North-East.

The output of iron and steel in the Scunthorpe area increased by over 50% in the 1950s, providing more traffic onto the ECML. The Highdyke - Frodingham ironstone workings flourished, and came to be re-routed *via* Sleaford, Boston and Grimsby - or by the ECML and Doncaster, to obviate reversals at Lincoln and Barnetby. Workings between Frodingham and York and thence to the North-East expanded, and in the reverse direction much larger tonnages of coking coal than formerly were passing from North-Eastern pits to Frodingham.

With the radical changes on the ECML in Winter 1957, there was a revision of the freight services as well as the passenger

In the 1950s a number of LMS-type Class 4MT 2-6-0s were allocated in the North-East: this one, No.43065, working an Up Class E freight past Northallerton power box, is however from New England and is a long way from its usual haunts of the M&GN lines. *N.E.Stead coll.*

B16/1 No.61436 (LNER 2365) passing through Selby on an Up Class H freight: a general view of the station area from the south on 5th April 1957. The lines on the left are the Down Loop off the Leeds line, also leading to the locomotive shed, and the main goods station is on the far side. *Author.*

One 'overgrown schoolboy' at least is thrilled as A4 No.60010 (LNER No.4489 DOMINION OF CANADA comes through Wood Green on an Up Class C freight, July 1952. *B.Morrison.*

timetable. The celebrated 'Scotch Goods', which a few years earlier had been diagrammed to run non-stop to Retford (Babworth), was now made non-stop to York (Skelton) - a record non-stop run for a British freight train, and conveying wagons for Scotland only. In addition, the 02.55 King's Cross to Niddrie was also made non-stop to Skelton, and the 16.30 King's Cross to Dringhouses non-stop to Selby. By this time a quarter of the ECML freight workings were Express, comprising almost all long-distance trains other than coal, minerals, and iron and steel; there was now also a fully-fitted brick train from Fletton to York[35]. Merchandise - as well as meat - was now coming to London in only four hours from Leeds, six hours from Newcastle and eight hours from Edinburgh, with 70-80% not more than 30 minutes late on schedule. Such performance depended largely on the employment of Pacifics and V2s, and latterly the powerful and fleet-footed 9F 2-10-0s.

By Winter 1959 (Table 6.4), there were 30 regular braked freight trains running down the ECML and originating at points between London and Doncaster, compared with 19 in Winter 1953; almost a half of these were Class C and many involved Top Link engines and men. There were also about 12 coming off the Joint Line at Doncaster (six in 1953), and another six joining at Newark or Tuxford (four in 1953). More noteworthy was that the number of unbraked trains (mainly empties) from the London District down to New England was only half those run in Winter 1953, although there were four more braked empties trains down to New England in 1959 - enabling more economical out-and-home rosters. North of York the pattern in 1959 was still quite similar to that in 1952, but with a tendency towards longer overall journeys and many more trains from Healey Mills Yard. Otherwise, the reduction - such as it was - in traffic up to that date must have been reflected in the loading of trains and in the number of unscheduled or irregular workings.

Undoubtedly, apart from the traffic in domestic coal[36], little change occurred in the 1950s in the nature of the freight carried on the ECML. The movement of coal to East Coast ports, for export or bunkering, never again came anywhere near to the pre-war level, and much more coal was still moved inland; indeed - by 1957 already, coal was being *imported* through these ports. The annual consumption of coal by public utilities nationally at this time was 40m. tons more than before the war, and some 3,000 wagons a day of coal still left the Doncaster, Nottingham, and Lincoln Districts for the South and East Anglia. Over half of this coal was conveyed on the ECML, while heavy lateral flows continued through Doncaster, Selby, York, Ferryhill, Newcastle and Edinburgh. The ironstone traffic from the East Midlands had rather fallen off, but on the other hand the heavy traffic in ore from Tyne Dock to Consett[37] was transported with the latest modern equipment. Indeed, under the Modernization Plan, in addition to the standard 16-ton steel wagons built to replace the old 10- or 12-ton wooden ones, 21- and 24½-ton steel hopper wagons for coal and minerals were now being used extensively, the hopper wagons being introduced without difficulty in the NE Region where they had been used traditionally. Trials were undertaken also in the late 1950s between New England and London of vacuum-fitted coal trains (hauled by 2-10-0s), but they proved premature. As well, wagons specialized for particular bulk traffics came into widespread use, and the loading methods at goods depots were mechanized, with pallets, fork-lift trucks and conveyors. All these facilities, along with the radical reduction of intermediate marshalling and trip working, were leading to substantial reductions in overall transit times. Yet the railways were by this time already under-utilized by about 30%, and the construction of motorways was soon to abolish any advantage they had - even over long distances - in speed of conveyance of merchandise.

Notes:

1. To the LNER it was always 'goods' (or 'mineral'), but 'freight' is used normally in this account as a generic term to cover all non-passenger-rated traffic or services.

2. That is not overnight Sunday - Monday, and in the Summer timetable many did not run on Saturdays.

3. Several other wayside stations dealt with similar negligible quantities. Intermediate figures (tons respectively inwards and outwards) included: Acklington 460 and 3,810; Berwick 19,000 and 5,100; Cowton 940 and 620; Darlington 228,000 and 145,000; Morpeth 10,100 and 1,100; Northallerton 10,100 and 5,100; Selby 27,500 and 76,600; York 125,000 and 118,000.

4. Goods trains from Forth southbound on the ECML *reversed* out before proceeding to Newcastle Central, whence they went over the High Level Bridge, and conversely trains arriving at Forth reversed into the Goods station. Otherwise these trains went *via* Blaydon Main and the loop to Norwood thence to the ECML at Low Fell.

5. Closed as early as January 1956, after which the spur for the banking pilot for southbound trains was moved to the King's Cross end of Farringdon station, the signalling and the system of communication between train-engine and banker drivers improved, and also the limit on train lengths raised from 30 to 50 wagons.

6. The Down Yard built at Connington during the war also had a hump, and Dringhouses acquired one in 1961.

7. Built near Blaydon for extra wartime traffic and opened October 1941.

8. One Down train stopped when required at Wiske Moor on Thursdays "to leave groceries", and one Up train stopped at Danby Wiske and Cowton on Fridays "to deliver wages bags".

9. This train was routed *via* the Hertford loop.

10. 'Not many people know' (perhaps) that Biggleswade - and also Crow Park, further down the ECML, were major souces of traffic in *flowers*.

11. While **773** 20.30 to Deansgate and **774** 21.00 to Huskisson (Liverpool) ran *via* Grantham, Colwick, then Annesley and the GC line through Sheffield and over Woodhead, **584** took the ex-GN Leen Valley line to Brinsley Junction, then over to the LMSR Erewash Valley line at Codnor Park Junction and so to Manchester *via* the Hope Valley line. Only the Huskisson train ran after the War for a while, but the LMS route continued to be used until 1952 by a train in the former timings of the Deansgate train but it ran only from Colwick.

12. Connington to Leys, near Three Counties to Stevenage, and Hatfield to Marshmoor on the Up; Wood Green to Potters Bar, near Hatfield to Digswell, and Huntingdon to Leys on the Down.

13. Sleaford and Lincoln were both in fact by-passed by their respective avoiding-lines.

14. One of these trains waited *three hours* at Grantham before proceeding.

15. Trains to and through York from Hull impinged on the ECML going westwards at Selby before turning north at Gascoigne Wood Junction and approaching York *via* Sherburn-in-Elmet and Church Fenton. An exception was the nightly Express Fish train from Hull to Edinburgh, which took the direct route through Market Weighton to York.

16. By mid-1942 there were *18* daily paths (including two *via* the Border Counties line) - and no less than *26* on Sundays, for freight trains on the Newcastle - Edinburgh route, although it is unlikely that all of them were ever used in practice.

17. This included 2-8-0 locomotives for the Middle East in February 1941 - even though they could not negotiate most of the dock lines.

18. One notable shipment was a 75-ton transformer, which although quite out-of-gauge was brought along the ECML from Stockton, with great difficulty.

19. In June 1944, while Southampton received 248 special trains of stores for shipment, Hull dealt with no less than 303, Grimsby 66, Middlesbrough 38, Newcastle 10 and Leith 8. In the same period - many having used the ECML, London Docks received 223 trains and Tilbury 152. The total to all ports was 2,187.

20. One factory in Eastern Scotland dispatched 2m. jerricans in 4,000 wagons - presumably up the ECML - in the month before D-Day.

21. On a Thursday afternoon in November 1941- before the wartime widenings were carried out, the Ministry Inspector counted 17 Down and 14 Up freights on a run he made between Northallerton and Skelton Junction (28 miles), with a freight waiting at *each* of the nine colour-light stop signals on eight miles of the Down Slow between Northallerton and Thirsk, and five freights on the Up Slow with two more waiting in Thirsk Yard.

22. Overall, the distribution of freight traffic (in terms of wagons) at Northallerton at that time was roughly: Ministry of Mines 34%, Ministry of Supply 24%, Ministry of Food 7.3% (excluding seed potatoes), War Office 2.7%, miscellaneous 18%, empties 14%.

23. Only 1% terminated at York, and southwards from York the distribution was 43% towards Doncaster, 32% to the Swinton & Knottingley line, and 24% to the LMSR *via* Normanton.

24. Originating points of these coal trains were:- Blaydon Mineral, 1; Cliff House, 1 (Sunday); Heaton Mineral, 3; Percy Main, 4; Preston Colliery, 1; Tynemouth, 1; Washington, 6; West Hartlepool, 7. (In 1941 other starting-points included Stella Gill, Whitburn Junction, and West Dunston).

25. Thus on 14th September 1940, a week after the real Blitz began in London, 12,224 wagons were on hand in LNER London yards and only 5,058 had been moved in the previous 24 hours; at Ferme Park the respective numbers were 1,791 and 1,200.

26. Perhaps not unconnected with the floods, a pilot engine was derailed at Newark and blocked the Up lines for three hours on 1st March 1940, and on the same day no less than *four succesive* derailments occurred on the Hotel Curve off the Widened Lines at King's Cross.

27. In the climax of the week ending 14th October 1941, when 215 'Convoy' coal trains were dispatched, 49 were from Northumberland collieries, 24 from the Dunston area, 6 from around Bishop Auckland, and no less than *66* from mid-Durham and *70* from East Durham.

28. Much of this concrete was indeed recovered many years later - to provide hard-core for the motorways.

29. Between mid-1942 and mid-1943 minerals traffic in East Anglia increased by 73% and that of merchandise by 22%, and severe congestion occurred at Whitemoor Yard.

30. See *The Second World War, 1939-1945. Royal Air Force: Maintenance*, Air Ministry, 1954.

31. It seems from the records that Admiralty depots, like many others, were unable to handle munitions at the rate they were supplied, and hundreds of wagon-loads accumulated up and down the country. One set of sidings devoted to them near the ECML was at Haxey on the GN&GE Joint.

32. On or near the ECML, such trains were allocated to:- Finchley Central, Meldreth & Melbourn, Godmanchester, Bawtry (2), Catterick Bridge, Marston Moor, West Auckland (2), Shildon, and Alnwick.

33. Loaded wagons forwarded by King's Cross District were down by 8.9% and by Doncaster District down 8.3%.

34. The Hull service - non-stop to Hougham - had to be worked by a B1 because the weight restriction of bridges beyond Doncaster prohibited not only Pacifics but V2s and K3s also.

35. Also a piped coal train from Mansfield to Temple Mills - not on the ECML.

36. Much was now however brought, in hopper wagons, to a new coal concentration depot at Palace Gates, opened in July 1958, which was reached off the wartime link from Bowes Park.

37. In the late 1950s running on the ECML between Gateshead and Ouston Junction.

Appendix A

BACKGROUND FACTS RELEVANT TO THE ECML, 1939-1959

The circumstances of the Railways of Britain in general just before the outbreak of the war, during it and in the first 15 post-war years have been described in Chapter III. However in order to assess - rather indirectly - the situation on the ECML it is necessary to record some facts about the LNER and the successor Regions concerned with the line. It would be interesting, but is not possible, to give statistics relating to the ECML separately, to show how this essential part was affected. At a rough estimate, perhaps some 60% of the passenger and freight traffic of the LNER as a whole was handled at some stage on the ECML; after Nationalization a similar proportion of the combined ER and NER traffic and perhaps 10 to 20% of that of the ScR would be ECML-related (south of Edinburgh).

Mainly on account of road competition, the net operating revenue (adjusted to the price index) of the LNER had fallen since Grouping in 1923 from £9.5m. to £6.1m. in 1938. When road transport was severely restricted during the war - by 1943 lorry numbers were down to only 120,000 nationwide - the figure rose dramatically to a peak of £18.8m. in 1943 although the Company was only allowed to retain the 'agreed revenue' of £9.9m. The operating ratio - traffic expenses/revenue, which before the First World War had been about 60 on the NER, was as high as 87.0 in 1938, falling to 71.6 by 1943. In the 16 years between Grouping and the end of 1938, rail passenger journeys had declined on the LNER by 27% to 288.2m. and the freight tonnage originating had fallen by 23% to 104.0m. Total freight tonnage carried by the LNER was 121.3m.; this was made up of 78.7m. tons of coal, 18.3m. tons of other minerals (merchandise classes 1 - 6)[1], and 20.3m. tons of merchandise classes 7 - 21 (plus livestock).

Expressed in ton-miles, total LNER freight traffic in 1938 was 5,642m. (3,385m. in the Southern Area, 1,483m. in the North-Eastern Area, and 774m. in the Scottish Area). The Southern Area moved 1,934m. ton-miles of coal traffic, 699m. of 'other minerals', and 752m. of merchandise (Classes 7 - 21); in the NE Area, 672m. ton-miles of coal was moved, 269m. of 'other minerals', and 542m. of merchandise; in the Scottish Area, 364m. ton-miles of coal were moved, 131m. of 'other minerals', and 279m. of merchandise. Included in the 104.0m. tons of freight originating on the LNER in 1938 were (m. tons): iron ore 4.77, iron and steel (finished and semi-finished) 4.40, bricks and tiles 1.66, grain and flour 1.22, pig-iron 0.69, fertilisers 0.66, timber 1.61, vegetables 0.99; finally, 0.83m. head of cattle and 1.40m. of sheep were conveyed. Moreover, the *revenue* (in 1938) of merchandise traffic (Classes 7 - 21), at 60.7p/ton, was much greater than for minerals (22.3p/ton) or coal (15.9p/ton), and therefore its loss to road haulage was commensurately more serious.

On the LNER in 1938 total passenger-journeys had been 288m., rising slightly to 290m. in 1939. Wartime at first brought a fall to 227m. in 1940, but then there was a progressive rise, to 240m. in 1941, 286m. in 1942, 315m. in 1943, 316m. in 1944, and a peak of 322m. in 1945. Meanwhile, coaching train-miles (loaded and empty) on the LNER fell from 74m. pre-war to a constant 52 to 53m. during 1940-44.

During the war, on the LNER as a whole, freight train mileage increased from 454,000 pre-war (1938) to 545,000 in 1940 but then rose only a little more to a peak of 551,000 in 1943. Thus by far the greater part of the increases on the LNER occurred in the first year or so of the war. (The trends were similar on the LMSR, but on the GWR and the SR on which increases in tonnage of freight traffic were even greater, the greatest expansion occurred later in the war). On the LNER - with which we are concerned here - net ton-miles of all freight climbed eventually to 8,200m. in 1944 (43% above pre-war) - and fell only to 7,400m. in 1945. All-line forwardings of loaded wagons reached their peak (929,000) in the week ending 24th September 1943; on the LNER the peak was 328,000 in the week ending 22nd October. By September 1947 the figures were respectively 772,000 and 267,000. Total loaded wagon-miles on the LNER had attained 1,395m. in 1944 (33% above pre-war), while empty wagon miles had gone up by only 5% to 551m. The shift from short- to longer-haul movement was revealed most starkly in the LNER Scottish Area, where loaded wagon-miles had increased by the peak period of mid-1944 to about 70% above pre-war, although at that time loaded mineral wagon-miles were 87% above pre-war in the Southern Area and 37% up in the NE Area. The combined loaded plus empty wagon ton-mile figure on the whole LNER was only 25% above mid-1938 (21% up in the Southern Area, 29% up in the NE Area, and 33.5% up in the Scottish Area).

Relatively, the greatest wartime expansion was in merchandise traffic. On the Railways as a whole, from 1941 the ton-mileage figure for Class 7 - 21 merchandise traffic rose at the phenomenal rate of 15 - 20% per year. The trend applied as much to the traffic on the LNER as to any other railway, although on the GWR the growth was considerably greater. It is interesting also to note that the tonnages of freight being handled at the main city goods stations were in fact *lower* than in peacetime, further emphasizing the enormous increases in traffic loaded elsewhere. Already in the last quarter of 1939 on the LNER merchandise ton-miles were no less than *29%* up on those of the same quarter in 1938. By July 1940 the four-weekly ton-mileages on the LNER of merchandise, minerals and coal were increased by 35, 42 and as much as *62%* respectively over the average 1939 figures; in the NE Area, the corresponding increases were 33, 54 and *102%*. The tonnages of merchandise class traffic originating on the LNER then increased - trends being very similar in all three Areas - during the course of the war to peaks of respectively 25m. tons (in 1944) in higher-rated merchandise and of 23m. tons (in 1943) in minerals, while its originating coal class traffic *decreased* by 15% from 74m. tons in the last pre-war year to 63m. tons in 1944. The reason for this decrease in tonnage of coal, which also applied to the other three Railway Groups, is probably largely accounted for by the profound drop in the traffic of coal for export and for the bunkering of foreign ships, nearly all this export coal being hauled only over short distances between mines and ports. The tonnage of coal shipped from East Coast ports - excluding Scotland - fell from 17.0m. in 1938 to 7.9 m. in 1943; it never recovered after the war to the pre-war level, but had risen in 1946 to 10.2m. tons.

In spite of the upheaval of the war, there were remarkably few changes in the parameters of the LNER system between 1938 and 1947. The total miles of track, the numbers of stations and depots, and of locomotives and rolling-stock, remained almost unchanged. The greatly increased traffic during the war had been hauled by very much the same number of total locomotive stock: the loss of 92 2-8-0s requisitioned early in the war was roughly compensated by new construction, while during 1943-44 - but not in 1945 - vital extra needs were met by the loan of 518 2-8-0s from the Ministry of Supply and the US Army. In fact, the LNER managed its extra traffic with a considerably larger proportion than before the war of locomotives laid up under or awaiting repairs. The LNER had quite the worst figures of the Big Four: in August 1945 20.6% of its locomotives were not available for traffic, a year later the proportion was *24.6% (32.5%* of engines of tractive effort above 25,000 lb). The rate of locomotive repair actually fell directly after the war, thanks to shorter working-hours, extended holidays, and more work being needed on each locomotive. Moreover, most of the Austerity 2-8-0s coming back in 1946 from service on the Continent, on which the LNER depended so heavily to meet its needs, required Heavy General Repairs before they could be taken into traffic. Locomotive shortage on the LNER was a prime factor in its failure to capture the market and improve receipts after the war to the extent that the demand was there.

With the markedly enhanced carryings of passengers and freight during and after the war, the efficiency of locomotive utilization, in terms of passenger-miles and freight ton-miles per engine-hour, was considerably increased and was still high in 1947. During the war, LNER rolling-stock vehicles destroyed amounted to 1,583[2] (with 9,120 damaged) but the coaching-stock losses (278) were not made good, and in spite of new building directly after the war the number of coaching vehicles (16,400) was still in 1947 16% below the 1938 total. (In January 1945, the LNER had to convert some 85 first-class (three-a-side) coaches to third-class, to ease the overcrowding). One year after the end of the war, 2.5% of the LNER fleet of passenger coaches were over 50 years old and 14% were 40-50 years old, figures much higher than on the other three Groups. The Company's wagon fleet, at 241,600 in 1947, was 6.5% less than in 1938, but there had been some new construction: this was of larger-capacity wagons, and the average wagon capacity in 1947 became 13.77 tons (10.6% up on 1938).

In staff, there had been an increase on the LNER during the war of 10% (to 195,100), and not surprisingly the number of women had almost doubled (to 15,744), their proportion of the whole having risen from 4.5% in 1938 - after a maximum of 14.6% in 1945 - to 8.1% in 1947. Efficiency in terms of labour had changed little, for the total 'conciliation' labour force in 1947 (at 108,500) was 11.6% higher than in 1938, locomotive grades being 20.5% up, and traffic grades 15.2% higher - reflecting the extra demand for operating staff.

Just after the war, with traffic still buoyant, the LNER was able to maintain its net operating revenue at least up to the 'agreed' figure, but after allowing for charges on capital the true net revenue fell back to £4.8m. in 1946 and then to a *deficit* of £0.75m. in 1947. Nonetheless, in 1947 the net revenue from its operations was still 71% above that in 1938, roughly in line with inflation. The post-war decline in the operating ratio, which had risen to 101.4 in 1947, was due to inflated costs of labour, fuel and materials compounded by unusually heavy expenditure on maintenance that had run into arrears during the war. At this time (July 1947), the LNER Board seriously considered a daring plan to introduce main-line diesel traction onto the ECML expresses, but Nationalization - which the Board strenuously opposed - intervened, nothing was done and the plan remained a pipe-dream for 10 years.

Moreover, at £26.1m., LNER passenger receipts in 1947 were 104% above those in 1938. As fares were only 33% greater (55% from October 1947), the figures represented a substantial increase in passenger carryings, in spite of the fact that travel by Servicemen and the number of special trains on Government account were coming down by 1947 to near the normal peacetime level. The proportion of first-class receipts (13.0%) in 1947 was significantly above the 9.2% of 1938, probably owing to the continuing restrictions on private motoring. Passengers on the LNER in 1947 were still travelling a good deal *further* on average than in 1938, for revenue per passenger (overall and corrected for fare increases) was double that in 1938, and that from excursion and week-end reduced fares was up 2.4-fold. After the great Holiday Rush of the summer of 1945, there was nevertheless a considerable falling off in passenger-journeys on the LNER immediately after the end of the war in August 1945; in 1946 the figure was down to 299m. journeys, then 269m. in 1947. This was due not only to the rapidly diminishing numbers of Servicemen, but also to the release of fuel oil for both buses and private cars, the bus services especially quickly expanding their share of the passenger market. Broadly indicative of the trends of ECML traffic are the figures for passenger journeys originating in the NE Area, which fell by 24% in 1946 to 48.1m.

Although rates for most of the year were only about 33% above those being charged in 1938, the LNER's freight revenue in 1947 was £40.0m. (at 1938 prices), compared to £28.9m. in 1938. Freight tonnage originating in 1947 was 80.6m., or 18% less than in 1938, the decrease being mainly in coal carryings for shipment, but total net ton-miles of freight had fallen in 1946 from its peak in 1944 by only 16% to 6,890m. and to 6,675m. in 1947, and were thus still 18.3% above the figure for 1938. Total wagon-miles on the LNER in 1947 (1,558m.) were almost the same as in 1938, as was coal traffic, but there was considerably less empty wagon mileage and minerals traffic was still half as much again as it had been before the war.

After Nationalization, in terms of net operating receipts the ER did better than BR as a whole, showing a profit every year until 1957, while the NER fared very much better, showing operating profits *every* year (ranging from £7.11 to £14.1m.); on the other hand the ScR made a loss every year except in 1948 and 1951. The best of these years was 1952, when BR as a whole made £39.6m. The ER's working expenses in the same period fell just from 17.8% of the total for BR to 16.15%, while those of the NER *rose* from 8.0% to 11.2% - no doubt as a result of boundary changes, and on the ScR they remained constant at 11.1 - 11.2%.

As a proportion of the total for BR, which rose by about 10% in the period, passenger-journeys on the ER rose suddenly - due to the incorporation of the Tilbury section, from 101.9m. in 1948 to 158.6m. in 1949 after which they rose gradually to 179.8m. in 1957. Those on the NER tended to parallel those on the ER, whereas on the ScR passenger journeys remained constant. During that ten-year period, total BR passenger train-miles rose only from 363m. to 384m. The proportion on the ER rose slightly from 16.2% to 17.5%, while that on the NER was constant at 7.5 to 8.0% until after 1955, when (in an enlarged Region) it rose to 10.5%. Train-miles on the ScR fluctuated only between 11.1% and 12.4% in the period.

A major census of passenger traffic in a week in October 1952, covering all the Regions individually, revealed some differences relevant to the ECML and its associated traffic. Thus the operating ratio (movement costs/revenue) for fast trains on the ER, NER and ScR (0.26, 0.28 and 0.28 respectively) were close to the average, but higher than on the WR and lower than on the LMR. On Edinburgh - London ordinary express trains the average load factor (passengers/seats) over different portions of the ECML was 56% for first-class and 83% for third-class (73 and 71% respectively on Pullman trains), but was only 26 and 49% respectively on Edinburgh - Leeds services, and 25 and 74% on Edinburgh - Colchester trains. For semi-fast trains the operating ratios (about 0.70) were well above the average, and the ratios (about 2.2) for stopping services - roughly 40% of train-miles run - were not only appallingly high but double those on the SR with its many electrified services. The October 1952 analysis revealed that the best load factors on branch-line services in East Anglia were 22% and the worst 6% - i.e. about two people on a three-coach train. All these figures give a pointer to the level of passenger loadings and profitability on the ECML and some of its feeder services at non-holiday times, and were probably the best that were achieved at any time after the war, as 1952 was one of BR's 'Best Years'. Subsequently, in 1955 just before the DMUs were introduced, detailed surveys were made on East Anglian branches in March (winter service) and September (summer service); they showed that the operating ratio on these services averaged 2.4, and fell to 0.73 when DMUs were brought in.

The RE's response to these telling exposures of the loss-making local steam services was slight. The inertia maintaining the *status quo* took more than another ten years to overcome, the substitution of the much more economical DMUs later in the 1950s coming too late to prevent the 'Radical Reshaping' of the network in the 1960s. By 1959 stopping passenger trains, *in spite of* the introduction of DMUs to many of them, were calculated to be producing an *operating* loss of £39.0m. a year, and more than the corresponding profit of £31.3m. being made by the fast and semi-fast trains (suburban trains were breaking even). Meanwhile, before the eventual proliferation of private cars, public bus services grew rapidly in the early years after the war. These included long-distance coach services, such as on the London - Edinburgh route on which - in spite of their being much slower than the trains, carryings doubled between 1947 and 1951, and fares were considerably lower than by rail.

As we have seen, net ton-miles of freight on BR as a whole was constant (at 20,880 - 22,900m.) between 1948 and 1957. The traffic on the ER, NER and ScR also remained remarkably constant over the period, at 20.3 - 21.9, 9.1 - 10.3 and 10.1 - 11.6% of the total respectively - except that in 1956-57 the proportion on the now larger NER rose to 13.8 - 14.0%. (The NER was second only to the LMR - by far the largest Region - in the originating tonnage of coal, and in 1957 this was 43.6m. tons - 26.2% of the BR total). At the close of the 1950s the ECML could not yet have been in decline, for in 1959 freight traffic on the GN Section (3.6m. loaded wagons forwarded) was slightly up on 1958, as were passenger receipts (at £6.68m.) with the King's Cross and Doncaster Districts showing significant *increases*.

Efficiency expressed as net ton-miles per total engine-mile rose on BR as a whole by 18% from 543 to 643 in the period. It differed however between Regions: on the ER, thanks to widespread adoption of out-and-home engine and crew diagrams and strict scheduling[3], the figure went up by 30%, whereas on the NER it rose by 22% and on the ScR by only 6.8%. Total staff numbers on BR fell from 648,300 in 1948 to 519,300 in 1959; after boundary changes in 1950 a constant 15-17% of these worked on the ER, 11-12% each on the NER and on the ScR.

The very detailed studies made in the late 1950s, culminating in the Test Week ending 23rd April 1961, formed the basis of the Beeching Reshaping Report of 1963. They underlined but greatly amplified the findings of the earlier post-war traffic surveys, and by extension provide a measure of traffic on the ECML and its branches. It seems appropriate therefore to summarize them here, for although Modernization was well under way - especially in the shape of dieselization - there would have been little change in traffic patterns in the 16 months after the end of 1959, and the findings indicate levels at the end of the period covered in this book - prior to the falling of the 'Beeching Axe'. However, the reader must bear in mind that the figures are basically *flawed in at least one vital respect*: they take no account of seasonal variations in traffic. The third week of April is an almost totally 'non-holiday' week, and on main lines passenger traffic fluctuated by a factor of two between 'high' and 'low' seasons, while on branches serving holiday resorts it varied by more than ten-fold.

From King's Cross as far as Hitchin the ECML was carrying 100,000 to 200,000 (100K - 200K) passengers per week (p/w); the number fell to rather less than 100K p/w on to Doncaster and were of the same order between York and Darlington. Between Doncaster and Selby, and from Darlington through Newcastle to Edinburgh, carryings were about 50K p/w, and rather less between Selby and York. Of the feeder and branch lines of the ECML, Wood Green - Hertford North, Hitchin - Cambridge, Retford or Doncaster - Sheffield, Doncaster - Hull, Doncaster - Leeds or Bradford, York - Malton, Darlington - Redcar, Darlington - West Hartlepool - Newcastle, Newcastle - Hexham, Newcastle - Tynemouth, and the main lines west and north of Edinburgh Waverley, were all carrying more than 10K p/w and were therefore not candidates for closure under the Beeching Plan[4]. Even the lines Peterborough - March - Ely*, Peterborough - Grimsby, Grantham - Sleaford (as far as Honington)*, Grantham - Nottingham*, Retford - Lincoln*, York - Hull, Northallerton - Harrogate, Northallerton - Eaglescliffe*, Darlington - Bishop Auckland* - Crook, Hexham - Carlisle*, Drem - North Berwick*, and Edinburgh - Hawick[5], were carrying only 5-10K p/w. The remaining ECML branches still operating passenger services all had densities of less than 5K p/w, and were undoubted candidates for closure: Hatfield - Dunstable, Hertford North - Stevenage*, Hitchin - Bedford, Sandy - Bedford (as far as Willington), Sandy - Cambridge, Peterborough - Northampton or Rugby, or Leicester* (as far as Manton), Honington - Lincoln or Sleaford and Boston*, Doncaster - Gainsborough*, Selby - Goole, Selby - Market Weighton, York - Harrogate* (as far as Knaresborough), Darlington - Richmond, Bishop Auckland - Durham - Sunderland, Tweedmouth - St. Boswells, and the Edinburgh South Suburban line.

The freight traffic data in the Beeching Report showed that London - York and Newcastle - Edinburgh on the ECML were carrying 50-100K tons per week (t/w), the higher levels being on the Sandy - Grantham and Newark - Doncaster stretches, while Newcastle - Morpeth was at the lower end of the range. Not surprisingly, the density on the York - Northallerton stretch was well over 200K t/w, while along the Northallerton - Darlington - Newcastle axis it was about 100K t/w. Of the connecting lines, Sheffield or Barnsley - Doncaster - Scunthorpe was carrying over 200k t/w, and also very healthy (with more than 100K t/w) were: Peterborough - March, Sheffield - Retford - Lincoln, Shirebrook - Lincoln, Doncaster - Lincoln[6], York - Normanton, Northallerton - Tees-side, Tees-side - Ferryhill, and the Edinburgh South Suburban line. Traffic was satisfactory (more than 50K t/w) on: Wood Green - Hertford North - Stevenage, Sandy - Bedford, Peterborough - Rugby or Leicester, Peterborough - Spalding - Boston - Grimsby, Nottingham - Grantham - Sleaford, Newark - Bottesford, Doncaster - Hull, Leeds - Selby - Hull, Eaglescliffe - Darlington - Bishop Auckland, Ferryhill - Leamside - Newcastle, Durham - Bishop Auckland or Consett, Newcastle - Carlisle, Morpeth - Bedlington, and the South Leith and Granton branches in Edinburgh. Lines carrying between 5K and 10K t/w, and therefore on the margin of being unprofitable, were: Hatfield - Dunstable, Sandy - Cambridge, Doncaster - Knottingley, Selby - Goole, York - Malton, Ferryhill - Bishop Auckland, and Newcastle - Tynemouth. All the remaining branches connected with the ECML, on which either passenger services had been discontinued already or were those listed above with very low passenger densities, carried less than 5K t/w.

Most of the lines conveying less than 10K p/w (or less than 5K t/w of freight) were closed in the 1960s. Those that were not are marked above with an asterisk; in many cases they were kept open because they were part of a through route, and in any case their wayside stations were closed, virtually all having passenger receipts of less than £5,000 per year and/or goods turnover of less than 5,000 tons per year - as were those on the ECML itself not already closed. There were very few lines where freight traffic density alone justified their being maintained. Exceptions included: Peterborough - Leicester, Peterborough - Grimsby, the lines from Shirebrook or Retford, or Doncaster - Lincoln, Northallerton - Eaglescliffe, and several lines in Co. Durham; conversely, Hitchin - Cambridge and Newcastle - Tynemouth were saved by their passenger traffic. On the other hand, Sandy - Bedford, Peterborough - Rugby, and Peterborough - Grimsby, which all seemed to have sufficient freight but were only marginal for passenger traffic, succumbed to the 'Beeching Axe' - probably largely because alternative routes were available, whereas York - Malton has remained open, no doubt on account of the heavy summer traffic and the absence of alternative routes.

It is interesting to note that the Beeching Report identified very substantial flows of freight (50-100K t/w) - *not* including coal - that was 'favourable to rail but not on rail' passing along the Great North Road artery, especially southwards. This was so even in 1961, when almost the only motorway then in use was the M1 (London - Birmingham).

Capital expenditure on the ER was relatively high in the first decade after Nationalization, with the completion of the Liverpool St. - Shenfield electrification[7] early in 1950, and its extension to Chelmsford in June 1956 and to Southend Victoria in December 1956, completion of the electrification[8] from Manchester to Sheffield and Wath in June 1954, and work in hand on the London, Tilbury & Southend electrification. However none of these relate directly to the ECML, where the only major works carried out in the period were the York[9] and Newcastle resignalling and the quadrupling between New Barnet and Potters Bar. Just after the war the advantages in financial terms of converting principal ECML expresses to diesel traction were not seen to be very great, and while the ideas were resurrected immediately after Nationalization it was to be over ten years after that before the diesels came, nearly 19 years before the GN London Suburban lines were electrified, and 40 - 42 years before the wires were carried down the main line through to Edinburgh. Earlier schemes in the 1955 Modernization Plan had had to be shelved for lack of funding - and of confidence in the financial benefits to be derived from the Plan itself. Indeed

in September 1960, Ernest Marples had *cut* planned investment on BR by 30% - in favour of more Motorways.

Changes on the ECML before the end of 1959 related principally to motive power. Many of the 218 main-line diesels already ordered (for £21.4m.) to replace 400 steam locomotives on the ECML were at work, and the prototype 'Deltic' was showing its potential, but it was two to three years into the 1960s before a radical acceleration of ECML express schedules could be brought into operation with the new diesels. Meanwhile, DMUs were taking over in wholesale fashion almost all the suburban and local passenger services by the end of the decade. In fact, the NE Region forged ahead faster than any other Region with conversion of regional passenger services to DMU operation. Commencing with the Bradford Exchange - Leeds Central - Harrogate - Knaresborough service in June 1954, by October 1958 most of the Region's stopping and semi-fast services had been converted and 24.3% of its coaching mileage was diesel - double the all-BR average. In 1955 it could be said that receipts (internal branch bookings *only*) had risen 300-400% in the West Yorkshire scheme, 50% on the Newcastle - Middlesbrough service and 30-35% on the Newcastle - Carlisle and Darlington - Saltburn services, but - strangely - hardly at all on Darlington - Richmond or Crook. Indeed, with the rapid proliferation of private cars in the 1960s, the upward trends in receipts were not sustained, and some dieselized branches (*e.g.* Hull - Hornsea/Withernsea, where initial improvements in receipts were 55-80%) were closed in the Beeching Era.

Notes:

1. Merchandise classes 1-6 comprised minerals other than coal, classes 7-10 other bulk traffic not requiring cartage by the Railway Company, and classes 11-21 merchandise requiring collection or delivery, in order of value, class 21 being the most valuable.
2. Of the Tyneside electric stock, one luggage-motor composite and an articulated twin-set of open thirds were destroyed by bombing in the war, and replaced shortly after. Of the total losses, 81 passenger stock and 442 wagons were lost during the Blitz (*i.e.* up to 17th May 1941), so the remaining majority may have been destroyed mainly by V-weapons.
3. The Annesley - Woodford 'runners' were the outstanding example.
4. Doncaster - Leeds, Darlington - Middlesbrough, and Newcastle - Sunderland were carrying rather more than 50K p/w.
5. Hawick - Carlisle had less than 5K p/w.
6. The rest of the GN&GE Joint line down to March was conveying about 150K t/w.
7. Budgeted and started before the war.
8. Budgeted and started before the war.
9. Budgeted and started before the war.

Appendix B

CAUSES OF SERIOUS DELAY TO ECML EXPRESSES, OCTOBER 1944

(Excluding those resulting from the accidents at Yaxley on 12th October, and at Essendine and Skelton on 16th October) (Extracted from the Chief General Manager's Monthly Report on the Working of the Railway - PRO RAIL390/1228)

October 1944

2nd: 10.15 Edinburgh to King's Cross: 34 min late - time lost at Newcastle in detaching a defective guards van and transferring contents.

16.00 King's Cross to Leeds: 63 min late - defective brake on engine, necessitating change of locomotives at Dukeries Junction.

4th: 10.00 Edinburgh to King's Cross: 37 min late - engine short of steam between Peterborough and King's Cross because of injector trouble.

9th: 10.15 Leeds to King's Cross: 48 min late - delayed between Wakefield and Grantham through locomotive trouble on relief train ahead.

13.10 Edinburgh to King's Cross, and 17.30 King's Cross to Newcastle: both 26 min late - diverted *via* Askern and Knottingley owing to aircraft crash on line near Selby.

13th: 10.00 King's Cross to Edinburgh: 50 min late - train lost 25 min through engine failure at Hitchin (hot driving box) involving change of locomotive, and 25 min between Peterborough and Grantham from shortage of steam caused by inferior coal.

16th: 07.50 Leeds to King's Cross: 44 min late - delayed by military special ahead.

17th: 07.50 Leeds to King's Cross: 33 min late - time lost between Huntingdon and Hitchin through reaction goods train ahead being stopped because of hot axle box on wagon.

18th: 07.50 Leeds to King's Cross: 41 min late - delayed near Hitchin through goods train ahead having become divided.

23rd: 07.00 Newcastle to King's Cross: 46 min late - delayed by military special ahead which lost time through locomotive trouble.

25th: 10.30 King's Cross to Leeds: 45 min late - delayed by derailment at Holbeck of three coaches on the 16.00 parcels train from Doncaster to Leeds.

27th: 17.30 Leeds to King's Cross: 49 min late - failure of points at Hatfield.

28th: 07.50 Leeds to King's Cross: 31 min late - reaction from delay caused to goods train ahead through defective wagon.

30th: 17.50 King's Cross to Leeds: 52 min late - delayed between Wakefield and Leeds because of defective sandpipe and priming of engine.

31st: 10.00 Edinburgh to King's Cross: 48 min late - engine short of steam, requiring an assisting engine from Retford.

Appendix C

EXCURSION TRAINS & THEIR ROUTES

1939

Study of the Special Traffic Notices (STNs) along with the WTTs relating to the ECML for some key dates in 1939 reveals the great extent and variety of special trains worked in those days. Maundy Thursday was always one of the busiest days of the year on the railways. On 6th April 1939 no less than *51* relief trains were dispatched from King's Cross down the ECML - 42 of them in the nine hours from 15.00 to midnight, mainly by dividing normal trains into many (up to 7) separate portions.

Their destinations were: Aberdeen (2 trains), Glasgow (4, one to Fort William also), Edinburgh (6, *in addition to* the above - one with coaches for Perth, another for Inverness), 13 (apart from the Scottish trains) to Newcastle (one *via* West Hartlepool); one each to Darlington, South Shields, Sunderland, and York; one to Ripon *via* Knottingley and Church Fenton, 14 to Leeds and/or Bradford (including one through to Halifax); five to Hull, one just to Doncaster, and another just to Grantham. Most of this parade of trains were balanced by corresponding Up reliefs, but not so the *six* parts of the (unadvertised) overnight train from Marylebone to Newcastle, the empty stock for most of which had to be worked up from Doncaster *via* Tuxford and the GC main line.

Further down the ECML, many other relief trains ran on 6th April 1939. One each ran from Hitchin to Doncaster, and from Letchworth to Manchester (Central) *via* Retford. Through Retford ran reliefs from Manchester (Central) to Ipswich, Liverpool (Central) to Harwich and another to Cleethorpes, and through Doncaster a relief ran from Liverpool (Central) to Hull. At York, four reliefs were run to Newcastle, and other reliefs ran from Bournemouth to Newcastle, York to Bournemouth, Newcastle to Swansea (*via* Bourton-on-the-Water), and no doubt a number on the Sheffield, Leeds and Scarborough lines (see below for Easter 1955). Finally, several services from Newcastle to Lancashire, and to Carlisle and Edinburgh were duplicated, and a number of extras were run on the other more local services.

The relief trains run down the ECML in the day or two before Christmas were comparable to those on Maundy Thursday. However, perhaps of more interest were the extra and excursion trains run over the August Bank Holiday in 1939, for not only were there a remarkable number of relief trains on Saturday 5th August 1939 in addition to the Saturdays Only (SO) ones in the timetable, but a host of excursions were put on, mainly on the Sunday and Bank Holiday Monday (6th and 7th August). A measure of the immense number of people expected to be going on their seaside holidays on the Saturday is indicated by the notes on strengthening the *SO* 07.52 Burton-on-Trent and 09.48 Basford (North) trains to Mablethorpe to each accommodate *1,000* passengers. Down the ECML from King's Cross 27 relief trains were run, principally by the division of normal trains into several portions, and many others ran on part of the ECML or passed through its major centres.

From King's Cross, there was one overnight extra to Aberdeen and another to Glasgow and Perth, one to Newcastle and one to Leeds/Bradford. During the day there were: one relief to Edinburgh, five to Newcastle, two to Saltburn, seven to

Leeds/Bradford, three to Hull, one to Doncaster, one to York, and one to Grimsby, while the 15.00 Down was also divided to give separate portions to Cromer, Boston, and Cambridge. In addition, the overnight Marylebone-Newcastle train ran in *eight* portions. Through Doncaster or through Retford ran extras from: Liverpool (Central) to Yarmouth/Lowestoft, Manchester (London Road) to Skegness, and Sheffield to Boston, while two extras were run from Peterborough to Cleethorpes. Up specials were very similar, and included an overnight troop special from Newcastle to Bude which ran *via* Canonbury and the North London onto the SR.

Further down the ECML the reliefs included: Rugby (Central) to Scarborough, Nottingham (Victoria) to Bridlington, March to York, Skegness *via* Grimsby to Newcastle, *three* overnight trains from Birmingham to York plus one from Leicester (LMS) to York, and (in daytime) one each from Birmingham, Kings Norton, and Heeley to Scarborough, and three extras from Leeds to Scarborough; one each from Castleford to Scarborough and Leeds to Whitby and *five* extras from Leeds to Bridlington, one each from Leeds to Hull, Leeds to Saltburn, and York to Newcastle. Generally speaking, corresponding reliefs were run in the opposite direction, but some extra long-distance empty stock workings were needed. If one had been observing the ECML where it crossed the LMS lines to the East Coast resorts near Little Bytham, the Nottingham - Sleaford line near Barkston, or the West Riding & Grimsby line near Shaftholme Junction, one would have seen also *numerous* extras and excursions going to the resorts from the Midlands and West Yorkshire. For example, there were *seven* reliefs just from Nottingham (Victoria) to Skegness or Mablethorpe on 5th August.

Over the long weekend 5-7th August, numerous Return Excursions were run, mainly but by no means entirely on the Sunday and Monday. For many of these trains non-corridor suburban stock was employed, and the LNER even found it necessary to borrow stock from the LMSR.

On Monday 7th August, they ran the following:- To King's Cross from Bradford/Leeds (two trains); to Skegness from King's Cross (two trains), and one each from Hitchin, Letchworth, Peterborough North, Doncaster, and Leeds (Central); to Yarmouth/Lowestoft from Luton *via* Cambridge, to Yarmouth from Peterborough North; to Hunstanton from Peterborugh North *via* King's Lynn and March; to Buxton from Peterborough East *via* Leicester; to Newcastle from Doncaster; to Cleethorpes one each from Barnsley, Castleford, Morley/Leeds (Central), and from Leeds (Central) (three trains), and to Bridlington and Scarborough *via* Selby one each from Bentley Crossing[1]/Wakefield Westgate/Bradford, Drighlington *via* Castleford, Normanton, Moorthorpe, Castleford, Bolton-on-Dearne, Chapeltown (LMS), Knaresborough *via* Wetherby, and Leeds (City); to Liverpool from Hull; to Bridlington from York; to Scarborough from York (two trains); to Scarborough *via* York one each from Heeley, Bradford (Forster Square), Leeds (City), Morley, Batley, Castleford, Halifax/Keighley, and from Sunderland and Newcastle (two trains); to Whitby one each from Sheffield (Victoria) and from York, and from Leeds (City) (two trains); to Blackpool from York (two trains); to Ripon from Hull *via* York; to Harrogate one each from Newcastle, South Shields, Seaham, and York; to Saltburn one each from Bradford (Forster Square), Leeds (City), Harrogate, and Crook; to Redcar from Liverpool; to Balloch Pier from Saltburn (overnight); to Middlesbrough from Edinburgh *via* Darlington; to West

Hartlepool from Liverpool; to Edinburgh one each from Durham and from Newcastle; from Newcastle two each to Alnmouth/Alnwick and to Carlisle, and one each to Glasgow (Queen St), Berwick-on-Tweed, Rothbury, Warkworth, Brampton Junction, Bellingham, and Hexham; from Sunderland one each to Alnwick and Carlisle. (Total of 77 excursions).

As already mentioned, several Race Courses were served by the ECML, and all the year horse-boxes (with their compartment for the groom or trainer) were conveying racehorses between racing stables and training centres such as Newmarket; also in the hunting season horses travelled by train to major meets such as in the East Midlands and Vale of York[2]. Before the War, but to a rapidly diminishing extent after it, the ECML at Doncaster had its St Leger Week each September. For the whole week the LNER Plant and other Works closed down, coal traffic was diverted as much as it could be, and the sidings at the Plant, at Decoy, at West Yard and at Bentley Colliery were cleared in order to accept the empty stock of numerous Race Specials. On St Leger Day itself these came from far and wide, as much from the LMSR as from the LNER, and in 1936 their origins were as follows. LNE:- Cambridge, March, Barnsley (2), Peterborough, Arkwright Town and Kirkby-in-Ashfield, King's Cross (2, one Pullman), Leeds (Central) (4), Bradford (Exchange) (2), Drighlington, York (2), Hull (2), Newcastle (2), Halifax/Keighley, Cleethorpes, and Harrogate; LMS:- Heeley, Gloucester (2) and Hinckley, Northampton (*via* GN&LNW Joint), Luton (*via* Sheffield), Coventry, Kidsgrove, Low Moor/Wyke, Colne, Meltham/Holmfirth, Leeds (City), Southport, Blackpool, Manchester Victoria, and Barrow.

All these 39 specials arrived between 09.15 and 13.15, and along with 29 normal trains dealt with in the same four hours made a frequency of one train every $3^1/2$ minutes. Apart from the St James' excursion platforms, two special extra platforms in the Plant locomotive sidings had to be brought into use for their discharge. Almost as many specials were run on the three other days of St Leger Week, and moreover horse-box specials were run, mostly each on several days, to and from Waltham (on the GN&LNW Joint), Witham (Essex), Newmarket, Newbury, Thame and Lambourn, Cheltenham, Battersea, and Holyhead.

Finally, an indication of the trains run for horse races even well off the ECML, those for the Grand National Handicap at Aintree provide another sample. The ECML itself carried as far as Retford two first-class only trains (one consisting entirely of Pullmans) from King's Cross to Aintree, also a special from Newcastle *via* Sunderland, York, Sheffield and Manchester, and another by the same route from Darlington. That morning Doncaster dispatched its own special to Aintree and passed through another from Hull, and through Retford passed one from Cleethorpes and Skegness and one from Colchester *via* March and Lincoln.

1955

The STNs show that the numbers and destinations of relief and excursion trains were virtually the same on Maundy Thursday in 1955 as in 1939. Thus on 7th April 1955, King's Cross dispatched *46* reliefs (25 of them third-class only), a high proportion running overnight, and rather more to Scotland than in 1939; the similarity applied also to those further down the ECML away from London.

Major football fixtures still needed countless specials across the country, and even justified the opening of new (primitive)

After Nationalization former LMS locomotives regularly worked to Scarborough: here Fowler 'Crab' 2-6-0 No.42890, of Burton shed, brings an excursion returning from Scarborough into York station, 8th September 1951. The train will only traverse the ECML as far as the junction at Chaloners Whin whence it will proceed to the Midlands via the S&K line. *E.R.Morten*

stations, one built in 1950 for the Hibernians at Easter Road Park on the Leith (Central) branch served *arriving* fans only. For the F.A. Cup Final on 26th April 1951 (Newcastle United *v.* Blackpool), 18 specials ran up to London from Tyneside, and when Newcastle United played Manchester City on 7th May 1955 no less than 14 Excursions were sent up overnight to King's Cross from Newcastle (Central) alone (returning between 19.00 and 02.15), two to Marylebone and three to Wembley Hill. In addition there was one each from Newbiggin, Monkseaton, and Bradford and Leeds, to King's Cross, and from Edinburgh, Blyth, Hebburn, and West Hartlepool to Marylebone; Marylebone also handled some from the Manchester and Sheffield areas. The Illuminations at Blackpool and Morecambe drew numerous Evening Excursions (Evex) not only from the North-West but also from the North-East, 170 in August to October 1952. (The NE Region also ran no less than 85 specials for *Ladies Only*, with restaurant cars, in 1953, many to the Hockey at Wembley. A further example of their enterprise in the post-war era was the running of an Evex from Morpeth to Rothbury, a line already closed to passengers, in September 1953 for a *cocktail-party*, with stops between stations to pick up guests!)

The STN for the GN Section for the August Bank Holiday week in 1955 ran to 157 pages. The programme for Saturday 6th August 1955 included Pigeon Specials from King's Cross to Newark and to Pinchbeck, and from York to Retford and to Grantham. *In addition* to advertised SO trains, there were 11 Down reliefs (9 third-class only) from King's Cross, and a programme of extra holiday trains to and from East Coast resorts quite as prolific as in 1939, as were also the Excursions to the seaside and elsewhere on the Sunday and Monday.

On Sunday 7th August 1955 - when considerably more were run than on Bank Holiday Monday (1st August), there were 74 scheduled excursions on the GN lines, of which the following went through ECML centres:- One each from Hull, Bradford, and Leeds to King's Cross and one from King's Cross to Hull, one to Southend from Hertford North (*via* the Palace Gates link), one to Clacton from Hitchin (*via* Canonbury), one to Yarmouth Beach from Peterborough North *via* the M&GN, and

one from Sheffield to Newcastle. There were 18 ER Excursions to Skegness, 10 to Mablethorpe, two to Woodhall Junction, *21* to Cleethorpes, four to Bridlington, six to Scarborough[3] and one from Scunthorpe to Buxton. Most of these latter passed through Retford or Doncaster, or crossed the ECML at Barkston or near Shaftholme Junction. (A 'train-spotter' at these crossing points would therefore have found them as busy and interesting on a Summer Sunday as on any other day). In fact the pattern was remarkably similar to that of Excursions in Summer 1939 (see above), and nationalization of the railways seems to have had only a slight effect on through running of trains from former LMSR stations to the East Coast. One can conclude that in regard to special passenger traffic, as to regular passenger and freight flow, the railways were still being operated very much as if Nationalization had not occurred, and the ER and LMR, for example, were still isolated entities.

Although the total number of relief and Excursion trains was beginning to decline by the end of the 1950s, examination of STNs for 1958 and 1959 show few differences in routings from those of 1955. The NE Region STN for the 1958 August Bank Holiday Sunday (3rd August) was typical: it showed four overnight Starlight Specials from Marylebone to Edinburgh plus one to *Cardenden*, overnight trains (probably military) from Whitby to Carlisle and from Ollerton to Edinburgh, and there were the following Day Excursions:- three to Newcastle (from Bradford Forster Square, Leeds, and Hull), one to Glasgow (from Seaburn), one to York (from Altrincham), one to Edinburgh (from Newcastle), one to Dumfries (from Morpeth), two to Saltburn (from Bradford and from Leeds), one to Leyburn (from Spalding), one to Monkseaton (from Nottingham), five to Bridlington, 24 to Scarborough (some *via* Selby and Bridlington, and including four from Leeds plus one from Kippax and one from Penda's Way, also - the furthest - from Burton-on-Trent), and lastly one from Sheffield to Whitby.

Notes:
1. *Not* a passenger station.
2. Hence perhaps the naming of D49 locomotives after Hunts.
3. *Not* including NE Region Excursions.

Appendix D

DOCUMENTED JOURNEYS[1] ON THE ECML OF THE ROYAL TRAINS, 'GROVE' AND 'DEEPDENE', 1940-1959

(Journeys of TM The King and Queen together before 1952, then of HM The Queen and Prince Philip together thereafter, unless stated otherwise)
(Not including sectors over which the Royal Train was not conveying the Royal Party)

1940:
25th - 28th Feb: KX to Forth and Clyde Districts.
31st Jul - 1st Aug: KX (23.00) to Hull; Scunthorpe to KX (22.00)
22nd - 23rd Aug: KX to Norwich; Thetford to KX.
27th - 29th Aug: KX (23.00) to Crimple (arr. 03.30 28th Aug). Departed 08.35 for Catterick Bridge (arr. 10.00) *via* Eryholme (reverse). Richmond (dep. 17.00) to Garstang Town (arr. 21.50, *via* Leeds City South, Blackburn and Preston). (Return 29th Aug - *via* Rock Ferry - to Euston by LMSR).

1941:
6th Jan: Peterborough to Sheffield.
17th - 19th Jun: KX to Newcastle, Blyth, Birtley, and back to KX.
11th Sept: KX to Brandon.
28th - 30th Oct: KX to Thorp Arch *etc.*
12th - 14th Nov: KX to Grantham *etc.*
24th - 26th Mar: KX (19.00) to Crimple (or Ripley Valley), to Beningbrough (arr. 10.00 25th Mar). Northallerton (17.00) to Crimple (or Ripley Valley) (17.55 - 09.00 26th Mar) to Bradford Forster Square (arr. 10.00). (Return by LMSR to St Pancras).

1942:
11th - 12th Jun: KX to Hertford North (night halt), then to East Anglia.
6th - 7th Aug: KX (22.00) to Hertford North, departing 06.55 7th Aug to Melton (arr. 09.55 *via* Ipswich). Back to Ipswich, then calling at Claydon, Bury St Edmunds, Ingham, Bury, and to KX (arr. 19.17).
11th - 13th Nov (HM The King only): KX (19.35) to Leadenham (22.20 - 09.45 12th Nov). Then calling at Waddington, Lincoln, and Bingham (dep. 17.00), and returning *via* Spalding to Peakirk (night halt 18.45 - 09.28 13th Nov) to Huntingdon North.

1943:
6th - 9th Apr: KX (19.30) to Ripley Valley (00.25 - 08.10 7th Apr). Then to Newcastle, and Hebburn, departing there 17.10 to the Alston branch (night halt 18.55 - 08.50 8th Apr). Back to Sunderland, then Durham (lunch on train), Aycliffe, then to night halt at Hertford North, arriving KX 09.02 9th Apr.
25th - 27th May: KX (19.15) to Hertford North (20.00 - 09.08 26th May), then Royston, and Royal Party rejoined the train at Downham, left at 16.30 and spent the night at Leadenham (20.02 - 07.50 27th May). Then North Thoresby and Digby were visited, and return to KX was at 21.00.
29th - 30th Jul: After travelling by LMSR from Euston to Renfrew, TM slept overnight at Aberlady and returned from Inveresk to KX.
7th - 9th Dec: KX (19.20) to Leadenham (22.12 - 08.10 8th Dec). Then to Wakefield Westgate (arr. 10.00); train rejoined at Doncaster and taken to Leadenham (17.30 - 08.30 9th Dec), then Huntingdon, and Tempsford (dep. 17.00) to KX.

1944:
8th - 10th Feb: KX to a tour of Yorkshire.
22nd - 24th Feb (HM The King only): KX (19.15) to night halt (probably Warren Hill). Then Sudbury (arriving 09.00 23rd Feb), departing 13.00 for Halesworth (arr. 14.30), departing 16.30 for night halt probably at Warren Hill, and arriving Brandon 10.00 24th February.
21st - 23rd Mar (with Princess Elizabeth also): KX (18.50) to Leadenham (21.47 - 06.45 22nd Mar). Then to Bridlington (arr. 09.45); TM rejoined train at Helmsley, departing at 17.30 for Ripley Valley (19.20 - 08.55 23rd Mar), then to Otley (arr. 09.45), and rejoined train at York, thence 15.50 to KX (arr. 20.00).
26th - 27th Apr (HM The King only): KX to night halt at Warren Hill. Then visited Bury St Edmunds, Tivetshall, and Beccles, rejoined train at Yarmouth Vauxhall and travelled on to Thetford:
4th - 6th Jul (Princess Elizabeth also): KX (18.45) to Warren Hill (20.45 - 09.45 5th Jul). Then to Ely, where Party left train and rejoined it at Cambridge, departing at 17.20 for Warren Hill (17.50 - 08.45 6th Jul). Train then rejoined at Huntingdon North at 17.30 for journey to Hatfield (arr. 18.25).
10th - 12th Aug (Princesses Elizabeth and Margaret also): KX (19.20) to Leadenham (22.12 - 07.48 11th Aug). Then to York (arr. 10.00), where the Party alighted, and rejoined the train at Darlington and departed at 18.00 for Ballater (arr. 08.30 12th Aug).
20th - 23rd Sept (Princess Elizabeth also): Ballater (15.00) to Aberlady (arr 20.00). The Royal Party then used the train for most meals and for sleeping two nights. On 22nd Sept 'Mr and Mrs Grove' were then conveyed from Inveresk (19.30) overnight to KX (arr. 10.00 23rd Sept). Meanwhile a second, smaller Royal Train was sent up by LMSR to Edinburgh Princes Street and on to Aberlady, and with two coaches transferred from the 'Grove' train carried 'Miss E. Grove' on 23rd September back at 12.00 to Ballater.
12th - 13th Dec (Princess Elizabeth also): KX (19.15) *via* Kings Lynn to Wells-on-Sea (arr. 22.50). Party slept on train, and returned at 16.05 to KX.

1945:
1st - 2nd Feb (HM The King only): Wolferton (19.00) to Hertford North (21.30 - 08.30 2nd Feb), then to KX (arr. 09.45).
9th - 10th Mar: Originating point not known, but joined NE Area at Mexborough West Junction at 19.10 8th Mar and passed Edinburgh at 02.15 9th Mar on the way to an unknown destination. Then Rosyth Dockyard to KX (no details at hand).
15th - 17th May (the two Princesses also): KX (19.30) to Aberlady (arr. 05.30 16th May), then on to Edinburgh Princes Street (*via* South Suburban line). Party returned from Waverley (19.00) direct to KX (arr. 10.00 17th May).
15th - 16th Jun: KX (22.00) to Warren Hill overnight, then to Brandon (arr. 11.00). Returned (13.00) to KX (arr. 16.45).

1946:
11th - 12th Apr (Princess Elizabeth also): KX - Newmarket and back (probably sleeping on train at Warren Hill).
29th - 30th Apr (Princess Elizabeth only): KX (22.30) to Baldersby (03.47 - 09.50 30 Apr). Party alighted, and rejoined train at Sunderland, departing 11.30 for Peterborough North (arr. 20.15).

1947:
25th - 26th Jun: KX (23.00) to Warren Hill (01.05 26th Jun), departing 09.05 for Norwich Thorpe (arr. 10.45). TM alighted, and the Royal Staff returned on train *via* Kings Lynn to Wolferton.

1948:

17th - 18th Mar (HM The Queen only): in two Royal coaches attached to the 22.00 service KX to Newcastle, then worked on to Ponteland (04.25 - 09.23 for 'lie-in'), then back to Newcastle Central (arr. 10.00). HM returned to KX in coaches attached to the 16.20 service.

5th - 7th Jul (after extensive tour of Scotland starting from Euston on 23rd Jun; Princess Margaret also): Edinburgh Waverley (18.00) to Leadenham (01.13 - 14.30 6th Jul), then back to Sledmere (arr. 17.55 *via* Selby) for night halt - but no dinner. Departed 08.50 7th Jul for York (arr. 10.20), then returned at 17.00 to KX (arr. 21.10).

10th - 11th Sept: Ballater (19.00) (*by LMSR Aberdeen to Carlisle*, then Newcastle and ECML) to Bawtry (Misson branch arr. 08.44 - no night halt). TM then alighted at Bawtry at 10.15[2] and rejoined the train to return at 17.00 to KX (arr. 21.00, but with a halt at Stapleford on the Hertford Loop).

1949:

28th Feb - 4th Mar (Princess Elizabeth and Prince Philip): KX (22.00) to Edinburgh Waverley (arr. 09.30 1st Mar). Returned 22.35 3rd Mar to KX overnight (arr. 10.02 4th Mar).

12th - 13th Jul (Prince Philip only): KX (22.50) to Louth (02.01 - 07.32 13th Jul), then Grimsby Town (arr. 08.00).

26th - 29th Jul (Princess Elizabeth and Prince Philip): Marylebone (21.55) *via* Penistone to Clayton West Jct (02.08 - 09.15 27th Jul), then on to Halifax (arr. 10.15). Party alighted, and rejoined train next day at York, leaving at 18.00 for KX (arr. 09.35 29th Jul, after night halt somewhere).

King George VI[3] died and HRH Princess Elizabeth became Queen from 6th Feb 1952 and Prince Philip, Duke of Edinburgh. Journeys listed below were by Their Majesties only, unless stated otherwise.

1952:

11th Feb (HM The Queen and Duke of Edinburgh, accompanying the *body of His Late Majesty King George VI*): Wolferton (12.05) to King's Lynn (12.16-12.20), and on to KX (arr. 14.45).

12th - 13th Sept (HM The Queen only): Ballater (19.00) overnight to Bawtry (arr. 11.45). HM alighted, then rejoined the train at 17.30 for return overnight to Ballater (arr. 05.45 14th Sept).

26th - 27th Nov (Princess Margaret only): three coaches attached to the 23.00 from KX to Newcastle.

1953:

9th - 11th Jan (Princess Margaret also): Wolferton (22.00) *via* Ely North Curve and Peterborough to Leadenham, departing there 07.03 10th Jan for Edinburgh Waverley (arr. 13.45). Return was at 16.30 direct to Wolferton (arr. 01.22 11th Jan); Party alighted 10.00.

17th - 18th May (HM The Queen only): Aberdeen (19.10) as 4-coach 'Deepdene' train to Edinburgh Waverley, then on to KX attached to 22.45 service.

11th - 12th Sept (HM The Queen only): Ballater (19.00) to Bawtry (Misson branch), then Bawtry (arr. 11.40). Party alighted, then returned and left at 17.30 for overnight return to Ballater (arr. 05.45, detraining 09.45 12th Sept).

1954:

26th - 31st Oct: KX (23.10) to Leadenham (arr. 01.50 27th Oct). Depart 07.55 for Barnsley Exchange *via* Retford, Darnall Curve and Chapeltown, arriving 10.00. Royal Party rejoined train at Sheffield Midland, and left at 17.40 for Tinsley Park Sidings arriving 18.00, and returning at 20.40 to Sheffield just until 22.50

to stay at Tinsley Park overnight (23.10 - 08.15 28th Oct). Royal Train then conveyed TM to Dewsbury Central *via* Upwell Street Junction, Oakenshaw Junction and Wakefield Kirkgate and Westgate. Royal Party then left train, which made a complicated perambulation *via* Batley, Normanton and Leeds to pick up Royal Party again at Manningham, whence they travelled *via* Leeds, York and Newcastle to a night halt on the Monkseation - Hartley line (20.55 - 09.55 29th Oct). Royal Party left train again at Monkseaton, and rejoined it at Sunderland, to travel to a night halt on the Denny branch from Larbert (arr. 21.40), before proceeding next day to Perth. (The Royal Party eventually travelled back to Euston, and naturally all these complex maneouvres involved more elaborate planning than ever).

1955:

6th - 8th Sept (HM The Queen only): Ballater (20.00) to Bawtry (arr. on Down line, 09.00 7th Sept). Return at 19.30 to Ballater (arr. 07.05 8th Sept).

31st Oct - 1st Nov (Duke of Edinburgh only): KX (00.00) to Leadenham (night halt, 02.50 - 08.10), then York (10.00). Left York (16.45), stabled at Bolton Percy (17.00 - 21.45), and then on to Malpas, *via* Leeds and Crewe. (The Duke left the 'Deepdene' train at Malpas and joined the Queen in the 'Grove' train, which had come from Euston).

15th Nov (Duke of Edinburgh only): KX (01.15)[4] to a night halt at Castle Hills (on the Hawes branch near Northallerton, arr. 06.03). Departed 09.37 for Darlington (arr. 10.15). (Royal Train returned empty from Newcastle, *via* York, Rotherham and Market Harborough).

1956:

4th - 5th Apr (Duke of Edinburgh only): Windsor (22.45), *via* Oxford, Banbury, Sheffield (Darnall curve), Mexborough and Doncaster, Goole, Hessle Road and Beverley to Cherry Burton (night halt, 05.23 - 09.10, 5th Apr), then back to Hull Paragon. (Train was not needed for the return journey, so was sent empty *via* Selby, Rotherham, Market Harborough and Northampton, to Wolverton).

3rd Jun (HM The Queen and the Duke of Edinburgh): KX (20.00) to Redmarshall East (night halt, 03.15 - 09.30 4th June)[5], then Stockton (09.45 - 10.00), and Redcar (special platform, 10.25). Meanwhile, 'Special coaches' (carrying other members of the Royal Party) were conveyed at the rear of the 23.45 from KX to Darlington and then sent on to Redcar, arriving 06.00. (The 'Grove' train was worked empty from Redcar back to Wolverton, *via* York, Rotherham, Market Harborough and Northampton).

7th Jul (HM The Queen and the Duke of Edinburgh; part of Royal Tour of Scotland, 2nd - 9th Jul): Edinburgh Waverley (09.35) - Dunbar (10.10 - 10.35) - Berwick-on-Tweed (arr. 11.15). (Empty stock worked to Tweedmouth and then *via* Waverley to St Rollox Paint Shop in Glasgow - apparently only for cleaning, as the train was returned the next day to Edinburgh to convey the Royal Party back to Paddington *via* the WCML, Bletchley and Oxford).

11th - 13th Sept (HM The Queen): Ballater (20.00) - Bawtry (arr. 08.52, reverse, dep. 09.10) - Doncaster (09.25), returning 17.45 to Bawtry (18.00), leaving 19.30 for Ballater (arr. 07.05 13th Sept).

1957:

17th - 18th May (HM The Queen and the Duke of Edinburgh): KX (23.00) *via* Goole and Hessle Road to Cherry Burton (night halt, 03.35 - 09.38 18th May), then Hull Paragon (10.00) (Empty stock returned to Wolverton as on 5th Apr 1956).

9th - 11th Jul (HM The Queen and the Duke of Edinburgh): KX (21.45) to Catterick Bridge (night halt, 02.42 - 09.40), then to Catterick Camp (10.00). Departed Catterick Camp 12.30 to Harrogate (14.00 - 16.55), then Hessay (17.23 - 17.46), and York (18.00). Empty train turned *via* York Yard South and Waterworks before stabling at Clifton. Then, York (dep. 21.15, 22.00, 22.45 *or* 23.30, *as required* - with pause at Ulleskelf to fill in time if necessary) *via* Leeds and Todmorden to night halt at Lowton, before continuing next day on visits to Chester, Wallasey *etc.* and returning to Euston.

8th - 9th Sept (Princess Margaret): 'Deepdene' coaches attached to rear of 19.00 from Aberdeen for KX (arr. 07.00).

8th - 9th Oct (Princess Margaret): 'Deepdene' coaches attached to rear of 20.35 Aberdeen for KX (arr. 07.44).

16th - 17th Oct (Princess Margaret): 'Deepdene' coaches attached 22.15 KX for Aberdeen (arr. 09.30).

5th Dec (Princess Margaret): 'Deepdene' coaches attached to rear of 22.15 KX to Edinburgh (arr. 05.20), where detached and run as a Special - with a BG and restaurant car added, departing 05.45 for Dundee West *via* Perth (with halt 06.35 - 08.40 on the Denny branch). The Princess returned on 9th Dec from Dundee Tay Bridge (22.27), in coaches attached to the 20.35 Aberdeen - KX (arr. 07.44 10th Dec).

19th Dec (Duke of Edinburgh only): 'Deepdene' coaches attached to rear of 23.45 (relief) KX to Newcastle (05.36 - 05.52) and South Gosforth (West Cutting) (06.04 - 09.12) and return to Newcastle (arr. 09.25).

1958:

19th - 21st Feb (Duke of Edinburgh only): Four coaches attached to 23.35 from KX and run under 'Deepdene' instructions to Edinburgh Waverley (arr. 07.10 20th Feb). Departed Waverley 07.25 (behind a V3) for Longniddry (arr. 07.55) returning to Waverley 09.35, arr. 10.00. (Empty stock to Craigentinny, then round *via* Morningside Road for turning and back to Waverley). Waverley dep. 22.50 for KX (arr. 06.34 21st Febraury).

23rd - 28th May (Princess Margaret): 'Deepdene' coaches attached to 01.00 from KX and detached at Perth at 11.35. Returned 27th May attached to 20.35 from Aberdeen, arr. KX 07.50 28th May.

26th - 27th Jun (HM The Queen and Duke of Edinburgh): KX (21.55) to night halt at Sleaford on Bourne branch (00.13-09.15 27th June), then on to Lincoln (10.00 - 13.00) and *via* Gainsborough and Doncaster to Scunthorpe (14.25-14.40) and Immingham Dock (15.25). (Empty stock returned to Wolverton, *via* Swinton and Market Harborough).

21st - 22nd Sept (Prince Charles): two coaches attached to 20.30 Aberdeen to KX (arr. 07.53 22nd Sept).

28th - 29th Sept (Princess Margaret): two coaches attached to 20.30 Aberdeen to KX (arr. 07.53 29th Sept).

15th - 16th Oct (Princess Anne): coach attached to 19.05 Aberdeen to KX (arr. 07.15 16th Oct).

18th - 19th Nov (Duke of Edinburgh): five coaches attached to 23.45 KX - Newcastle, detached at Peterborough North (01.11-01.23 19th Nov) to continue to night halt on the Spilsby branch (02.40 - 08.10), then on to North Thoresby (arr. 08.55). (Empty stock continued to Cleethorpes and returned to *Cricklewood, via* Nottingham).

11th - 12th Dec (Princess Margaret): four coaches attached to 23.20 from KX to Edinburgh (arr. 07.10 12th Dec), then run as a Special to Perth (arr. 09.16).

1959:

29th - 30th Apr (Princess Margaret only[6]): four coaches attached

to 23.20 KX to Newcastle; detached and run to night halt at South Gosforth (West Cutting), returning to Newcastle at 10.00. (Empty stock returned as Special to Wolverton *via* Wath Road Junction, Chesterfield and Market Harborough).

12th - 13th Aug (Princess Margaret only): two coaches attached to 22.15 KX to Aberdeen.

20th - 21st Sept (Prince of Wales only): two coaches attached to 20.30 Aberdeen to KX.

25th - 26th Sept (Princess Margaret only): three coaches attached to 20.30 from Aberdeen and detached at Newcastle, then worked as a Special *via* Durham and Bishop Auckland to Barnard Castle (arr. 10.15)[7].

10th - 11th Oct (Princess Anne only, with nurse and other children): Ballater (17.43), then coaches attached to 19.05 from Aberdeen to KX. (Picnic baskets provided by Balmoral Castle for supper).

14th - 15th Oct (Princess Margaret only): coach attached to 20.30 Aberdeen to KX.

1. Details of certain journeys have not become available.

2. On these visits to Bawtry, Her Majesty was met by Lord Scarborough, and after being entertained by him at Sandbeck Hall they would then all go to the St. Leger.

3. The King however made many journeys on the Royal Train in 1950 and 1951 (including a brief emergency journey to and from London from Balmoral in September 1951 for medical examination), but none was made on the ECML.

4. Probably the Duke joined the train sometime earlier.

5. The train was hauled by A4 No. 60007, and was restricted to 15 m.p.h. through Barnet, Hadley South and North, and Stoke Tunnels.

6. HRH always had just fresh fruit and China tea for breakfast.

7. This route was changed by HRH at the last minute from one arranged *via* Carlisle and Kirkby Stephen - apparently to save money.

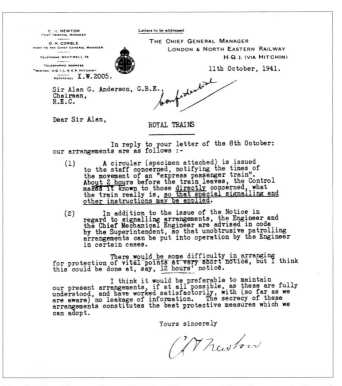

Facsimile of letter from Charles Newton with reference to Royal Train security in 1941.

Appendix E

MILITARY AND OTHER GOVERNMENT INSTALLATIONS SERVED BY THE ECML IN THE SECOND WORLD WAR
(mid-1942 to mid-1945)

The following is a list of depots established just before and during the war for military and other Government purposes which would have contributed substantial traffic (either passenger or freight) to the ECML more or less directly. Many had rail access with sidings and dealt with at least 10 to 100 wagons a day, for example the Cold Stores for the Ministry of Food listed below had 6.8 miles of sidings between them. Depots *known* to be rail-connected are printed in *italics*, but there were many others. Those that still existed in 1956 are marked '#', with where applicable the Department or firm to which they were handed over after the end of hostilities.

The list is collated from - secret - lists compiled during the war for the REC, with additions from other sources including - at mid 1944 - for the RAF the secret Locations of Units documents[1]. *Table I* lists depots served by main-line ECML stations, *Table II* those by stations on its connecting lines. The distinction as to which were or were not important to the ECML is naturally subjective. The criterion for inclusion in *Table II* broadly was that traffic to the rest of the country would have to pass along the ECML or through one of its major junctions, such as York or Doncaster. Depots in all of Lincolnshire, East and North Yorkshire (excluding the Hull & Barnsley line), Co.Durham, most of Northumberland, and some in the Border Counties are included. *Not* included are depots beyond Seaton on the LMSR lines going west from Peterborough, in East Anglia (other than those served by the M&GN west of Kings Lynn), broadly east of Cambridge, St Ives or March, those in much of the East and North Midlands, the West Riding of Yorkshire, on the western part of the Newcastle-Carlisle line, and nearer the Waverley route in the Borders, and - most importantly - those in Scotland beyond Edinburgh. The list[2] cannot be vouchsafed to be entirely complete[3]. At the very least it constitutes a representative sample of all the numerous depots established for war purposes all across the country, and it is interesting to note how many of the HM Government sidings were extant in 1956.

TABLE I
Depots on the ECML

STATION: DEPOT.

King's Cross: RAF No.232 MU[4] Equipment Depot, White City, West London.
New Barnet: POW Camp, Trent Park, Cockfosters; Militia Training Camp, Whetstone; WD Records and Pay Office, Barnet.
Hatfield: *Ministry of Food Buffer Depot, Marshmoor Siding*; RAF (MAP, De Haviland's) Airfield, Hatfield; No. 64 MU (Ammunition Park and Oxygen Depot).
Welwyn Garden City: RAF Airfield & Training Depot, Holwell Hyde (Panshanger). RAF Airfield Construction Depot.
Knebworth: WD Signals Development Branch.
Stevenage: Dept. of Education Stores Depot.

Three Counties: *RASC Duplicate Supply Depot, RASC Siding, Arlesey.*
Biggleswade: RAOC No.27 Sub-Depot, Shefford (also served from Sandy).
Tempsford: RAF Airfield, Tempsford.
St Neots: RAF (later USAAF) Airfield, Little Staughton; Ministry of Food Slaughterhouse, Eynesbury; Eaton Socon Militia Training Camp.
Offord & Buckden: RAF Airfield, Graveley; War Hospital, Diddington Hall, Buckden.
Huntingdon North: RAF Airfield, Wyton; HQ 2 Group (later HQ 8FF Group), Castle Hill House; Ministry of Works Depot; RE Stores Depot (Mail); US Army Engineers' Depot; HQ USAAF 1Bombardment Division; *RAF Petroleum Depot.*
Abbots Ripton: *USAAF 2nd Strategic Air Depot, Abbots Ripton; RAF (later USAAF) Airfield, Alconbury.*
Holme: USAAF (later RAF) Airfield, Glatton.
Fletton Sidings: *RAF Petroleum Depot, Fletton; Ministry of Food Cold Store*[5]*, Botolph Bridge Siding.*
Yaxley & Farcet: Royal Engineers' Camp, Yaxley.
Peterborough: *RAF Station, Peterborough Westwood*[6] *(M&GN)*; AA Training School, Peterborough; #*RAOC Depot, Sage's (WD) Siding, Walton.*
Essendine: RAF Ammunition Park, Park Farm.
Little Bytham: RAF Airfield, Woolfox Lodge; Army Tank Corps Training Centre, Grimsthorpe Park.
Corby (Lincs.): RAF (later USAAF) Airfield, North Witham; RAF Airfield (later USAAF Airfield and Maintenance Base), Folkingham; RAF Landing Ground, Swinstead (Swayfield).
Great Ponton: RAF (later USAAF) Airfield, Saltby (later Waltham-on-the-Wolds); RAOC Dump, Waltham-on-the-Wolds.
Grantham: RAF Airfield, Grantham - Spitalgate from 1944 (HQ 5 Group - later HQ USAAF IX Troop Carrier Command - was adjoining, at St Vincent); RAF Airfield, Harlaxton; RAF Regiment Depot, Belton Park.
Claypole: RAF Emergency Landing Ground[7], Claypole.
Newark: RAF (later USAAF) Airfield, Balderton; Bowbridge Militia Camp; RAF Depot, Coddington Hall; *RAF Maintenance Depot, Lincoln Road*; RAF Airfield, Winthorpe; RASC Depot, Winthorpe Hall; MoS Home Grown Timber Depot, Stapleford Wood; RAF No.203 Maintenance Unit.
Carlton-on-Trent: RAF Airfield, Ossington.
Tuxford North: Militia Training Camp, Tuxford.
Retford: RAF Airfield, Gamston.
Ranskill: #*ROF (Explosives), Torworth, later MoS Siding;* 2nd Armoured Division, Barnby Moor.
Bawtry: RAF Airfield, Bircotes; #*RAOC Dump (later, Ministry of Works).*
Rossington: Royal Engineers' Barracks, Rossington Hall.
Doncaster Carr: Brigg's Sidings-*MAP Depot, Brigg's Motor Bodies Ltd.*; Crompton-Parkinsons's Siding; SPC Wagon Repairs Ltd Siding; *MoS Depots.*
Heck: RAF Station, Snaith.
Henwick Hall Sidings, Selby: #*RAF Airfield, Burn, later WD Siding.*
Selby: Militia Camp, Brayton; *Royal Ordnance Depot, Selby.*
Riccall: RAF No.80 MU Holly Carrs Wood Ordnance Depot, Escrick; RAF Airfield, Riccall; Skipwith Common Ordnance Dump.
York: #*Ministry of Food Cold Store, Eason View, Dringhouses*; #*RAF Airfield (RAF No.60 MU, Salvage & Repair), Shipton, later WD Siding; No.87 MU Equipment Park*; Northern Command HQ Depot.
Beningbrough: RAF Maintenance Unit No. 60, Beningbrough (Shipton).
Tollerton: RAF Station, Linton-on-Ouse; RAF Airfield, East Moor.
Raskelf: RAF Airfield, Tholthorpe.
Sessay: RAF Airfield, Dalton Moor.
Thirsk, or Topcliffe (Thirsk-Melmerby): RAF Station, Topcliffe; RAF Station, Skipton-on-Swale.
Northallerton: #*Ministry of Food Cold/Food Stores, Boroughbridge Road*; RAF Hospital.
Darlington: #*RE Depot, Black Banks WD Siding*; *RAF Repair Depot, Geneva Works*; RE Stores, Nestfield.
Birtley: #*ROF, Birtley Ministry of Supply Siding.*
Gateshead, Team Valley Estate: Ministry of Works Store.
Killingworth: 7th AA Division Ordnance Depot; Mobilisation Stores, Killingworth.
Morpeth: RAF Airfield, Saltwick (Morpeth).
Chevington: RAF Airfield, Northstead.
Acklington: RAF Station, Acklington; RAF Airfield, Eshott.
Longhoughton: RAF Airfield, Boulmer.

Chathill: RAF Airfield, Brunton.
East Fortune: RAF Airfield, East Fortune.
Drem: RAF Airfield, Fenton Barns (Drem).
Longniddry: RAF Airfield, Macmerry.
Edinburgh: *RAF No.205 MU Universal Equipment Yard.*

TABLE II
Depots fairly directly served by the ECML, with approximate locations.

SOUTHERN AREA, and LMSR connections:

Aby (Firsby - Louth): RAF Landing Ground (later, Airfield), Strubby.
Alford Town (Firsby - Louth): Military Camp, Well.
Ancaster (Grantham - Sleaford): RAF Airfield, Barkston Heath.
Ashwell & Morden (Hitchin - Cambridge): RAF (later USAAF) Airfield, Steeple Morden.
Aslockton (Grantham - Nottingham): Militia Training Camp, Watton-in-the-Vale.
Bardney (Lincoln - Boston): RAF Airfield, Bardney.
Barnetby: RAF Airfield, Elsham Woods; RAF Airfield, Kirmington, Ulceby.
Barnstone (GN&LNW, Saxondale - Harby & Stathern): RAF Airfield (later USAAF), Langar.
Bingham (Grantham - Nottingham): RAF Airfield, Newton; RAF Airfield, Syerston.
Blankney & Metheringham (Lincoln - Sleaford): RAF Airfield, Metheringham.
Blyton (Gainsborough - Barnetby): RAF Airfield, Blyton.
Bottesford (Grantham - Nottingham): RAF (later temporarily USAAF) Airfield Depot, Bottesford/Normanton; *#No.17 RASC Petrol Depot, WD Siding.*
Boughton (Lincoln - Shirebrook: *#US Army Stores Depot, Boughton WD Siding.*
Brigg (Retford - Barnetby): RAF Nos.207 and 209 MU, Broughton Equipment Park.
Carcroft & Adwick-le-Street (Doncaster - Wakefield): *Ministry of Food Store, Carcroft.*
Cardington (Hitchin - Bedford): *#Air Ministry Siding*; RAF No.26 MU Repair Depot.
Cole Green (Hatfield - Hertford): RAF Training Depot, Hatfield Hyde.
Collingham, LMS (Newark - Lincoln): *Air Ministry Sidings, Swinderby.*
Coningsby (Lincoln - Firsby): RAF Airfield, Coningsby.
Digby (Lincoln - Sleaford): RAF Airfield, Digby.
Doddington & Harby (Lincoln - Shirebrook): RAF Airfield, Wigsley.
Doncaster, Edlington (LMSR): Wadworth Woods Ordnance Depot.
Doncaster, Hexthorpe Sidgs: MoS Depot, Sprotborough.
Doncaster, Marshgate or **York Rd.**: RAF Airport, Doncaster.
Doncaster, Wheatley Park Sidings: *MoS Depot (Crompton Parkinson Ltd)*; *#Ministry of Food Cold Store, Churchill Road.*
Donnington-on-Bain (Bardney - Louth): RAF No.23 MU Forward Ammunition Depot, Market Stainton.
Dunstable LNER: *#Ministry of Food Cold Store, Luton.*
Enfield Chase (Wood Green - Hertford): Home Office Regional Store, Great Cambridge Road, Enfield; Military Training Camp, Great Cambridge Road, Enfield; Military Training Camp, Slades Hill, Enfield.
Eye Green (Peterborough - Sutton Bridge, M&GN): *Ministry of Food Grain Silo, Dogsthorpe.*
Finchley Central (Highgate - High Barnet): AA Unit Station, Territorial Army.
Finningley (Doncaster - Lincoln): RAF Airfield, Finningley; RAF Airfield, Lindholme.
Firsby: RAF Airfield, Spilsby; *RAOC Ammunition Sub-Depot.*
Gainsborough (Central): Ministry of Food Buffer Depot.
Gamlingay, LMSR (Sandy - Cambridge): RAF Airfield, Great Gransden.
Great Dalby, later Melton Mowbray (GN&LNW): RAF Airfield, Melton Mowbray.
Grimoldby (Louth - Mablethorpe): RAF Airfield, Manby.
Grimsby Docks: *#Admiralty Siding.*
Haxey & Epworth (Doncaster - Lincoln): *RN Mines Depot.*
Henlow Camp, LMSR (Hitchin - Bedford): *#RAF Airfield and Army Camp,*

Henlow WD Siding; *RAF No.13 MU Repair Depot.*
Hertford North: RAOC Dump, Hertford.
Hill End, or Smallford (Hatfield - St Albans): *#Ministry of Food Cold Store, Butterwick.*
Histon (Cambridge - St Ives): WD Technical Stores Depot; *USAAF Equipment Depot.*
Holbeach (M&GN): RAF Bombing Range, Gedney Drove End; RAF Bombing Range, Long Sutton.
Honington (Grantham - Sleaford): RAF Works Repair Depot, Honington.
Horncastle (branch from Woodhall Jct.): *RAF Petroleum railhead;* RAF No.233 MU Chemical Weapon Depot, Hemingby.
Immingham Dock: *RN Depot.*
Killingholme, Admiralty Halt (New Holland - Immingham): *#Admiralty Oil Fuel Depot, East Halton; Admiralty Siding;* RAF Petroleum Depot.
Kimbolton, also Long Stowe Siding (Huntingdon - Kettering, LMSR): RAF Airfield, Longstowe.
Kingscliffe (Peterborough - Market Harborough, LMSR): RAF Station, Collyweston; RAF Camp, Kingscliffe; MAP Depot, RAF Airfield, Wakerley (later USAAF, Spanhoe).
Kirton Lindsey (Gainsborough - Barnetby): RAF Airfield, Hemswell (Harpswell); RAF Airfield, Kirton Lindsey.
Langworth (Lincoln - Barnetby): RAF Airfield, Dunholme Lodge.
Langworth, or Reepham (Lincoln - Barnetby): RAF Airfield, Fiskerton.
Lea (Doncaster - Lincoln): RAF Airfield, Sturgate.
Leadenham (Grantham - Lincoln): RAF Airfield (later USAAF), Fulbeck.
Letchworth (Hitchin - Cambridge): WD AFV Depot, Letchworth.
Lincoln (LNER): RAF Airfield, Scampton; RAF Airfield, Ingham; Boultham Gate Siding *Ministry of Food Cold Store*; Ruston & Hornsby Siding *RN Armament Depot, Sheaf Ironworks.*
Lords Bridge, LMSR (Sandy - Cambridge): *RAF Sidings, and No.95 MU Ammunition Park and Oxygen Supply.*
Louth, or Ludborough (Louth - Grimsby): RAF Airfield, Kelstern.
Lowesby (GN&LNW Leicester branch): WD Ammunition Distribution Centre, Lowesby.
Luffenham (Peterborough - Manton, LMSR): *RAF Depot, Luffenham;* Militia Camp, North Luffenham.
Luton (Hatfield - Dunstable): *Admiralty Victualling Depot & Salvage Stores, Balmforth's Siding.*
Maltby (Kirk Sandal - Dinnington): *#ROF Maltby, later Ministry of Supply.*
Market Rasen (Lincoln - Barnetby): RAF Airfield, Binbrook; RAF Airfield, Ludford Magna.
Melton Mowbray (GN&LNW): Militia Training Camp; US Forces Ammunition Dump.
Mill Hill East (branch from Finchley): *Mill Hill Barracks Depot and Ammunition Dump.*
Misterton: *Air Ministry Petroleum Depot.*
Moortown (Lincoln - Barnetby): RAF Landing Ground, Caistor.
Navenby (Grantham - Lincoln): RAF Airfield, Colbey Grange; RAF Airfield, Wellingore.
Netherfield & Colwick: *MoS, Colwick Depot WD Salvage Unit Siding.*
Newark, LMSR: *RAF No.58 MU (Salvage & Repair) and No.203 MU (Supply);* Hawton Road Militia Camp; *RAF Petroleum Depot, Langford.*
New Holland: RAF Airfield, Goxhill, Barton-on-Humber; WD Site 'F'.
North Thoresby (Louth - Grimsby): RAF Airfield, North Coates.
Old North Road (Sandy - Cambridge, LMSR): RAF Airfield, Bourn; RAF Station, Caxton Gibbet; Royal Ordnance Depot, Caxton.
Ollerton (Tuxford - Mansfield): Militia Camp, Ollerton; Militia Camp, Rufford Abbey.
Oundle, LMS (Peterborough - Northampton): RAF (later USAAF) Airfield, Polebrook.
Peterborough (LMSR), Crescent Wharf Sidings: *RAOC Sub-Depot.*
Potton, LMS (Sandy - Cambridge): WD Stores Depot, Belle Vue.
Ramsey, North or **East**: RAF Airfield, Upwood; Militia Training & Cemetery Camps.
Rauceby (Grantham - Sleaford): RAF Hospital.
Redmile (Bottesford - Harby & Stathern, GN&LNW Joint): *RAF Petroleum Depot.*
Royston (Hitchin - Cambridge): Militia Camp, Royston; *#Ministry of Food (WD 1943) Depot, The Drift;* RAF (later USAAF) Airfield, Bassingbourn; *WD Petroleum Depot.*

Sandtoft (Axholme Joint): RAF Airfield, Sandtoft.
Sandy (LMSR): *Air Ministry Petroleum Depot, Sandy Heath.*
Saxondale Sidings, Bingham (GN&LNW Joint): *RE Stores Depot, Bingham Road.*
Scawby & H. (Gainsborough - Barnetby): RAF Airfield, Hibaldstow.
Shefford (Hitchin - Bedford): RAF Depot, Creaklands Priory Hutted Site.
Shepreth (Hitchin - Cambridge): RAF (later USAAF) Airfield, Fowlmere.
Skegness: RN Training Establishment, HMS 'Royal Arthur'.
Skellingthorpe (Lincoln - Shirebrook): RAF Airfield, Skellingthorpe.
Sleaford, Cranwell Sidings: *RAF Training Establishment, Cranwell.*
Snelland or **Wickenby** (Lincoln - Barnetby): RAF Airfield, Faldingworth; RAF Airfield, Wickenby.
Spalding: RE Searchlight Corps, Fulney Park.
Stamford (branch from Essendine, or LMS Peterborough - Manton): RAF Airfield, Wittering.
Stickney (Lincoln - Firsby): RAF Airfield, East Kirkby.
Stow Park (Doncaster - Lincoln): *Air Ministry Petroleum Depot, Brampton.*
Sutton Bridge (M&GN): RAF No.3 Armament Training School, Sutton Bridge (Holbeach).
Swinderby, LMSR (Newark - Lincoln): *RAF Depot, Swinderby;* #*RAF No.93 MU, Norton Disney (Oxygen Supply and Chemical Weapons Dump).*
Theddlethorpe, or **Saltfleetby** (Louth - Mablethorpe): RAF Airfield, Donna Nook.
Thorne South (Doncaster - Scunthorpe): Militia Camp, Hatfield, near Doncaster.
Thorp Culvert (Firsby - Skegness): RAF No.233 MU Satellite Ammunition Depot.
Thrapston, or **Kimbolton** (LMS, Kettering - Huntingdon): RAF (later USAAF) Airfield, Molesworth.
Thurlby (Essendine - Bourne): AA Searchlight Co HQ, Obthorpe, near Bourne.
Tumby Woodside (Woodhall Jct - Firsby): RAF No.93 MU Equipment Park.
Ulceby (Barnetby/Immingham - New Holland): RAF Airfield, North Killingholm.
Waddington (Grantham - Lincoln): RAF Airfield, Waddington.
Waltham (Louth - Grimsby): RAF Airfield, Waltham.
Waltham-on-the-Wold (mineral branch from Scalford, GN&LNW): RAF (later USAAF) Airfield, Saltby; Military Hut Storage.
Wansford, LMSR (Peterborough - Northampton/Market Harborough): RAF Airfield, Sibson.
Warsop (Lincoln - Shirebrook): RAF No. 66 MU General Equipment Park, Cuckney.
Whittlesea (Peterborough - March): *WD 38th VR Depot, Saxon Sidings, Pingle.*
Woodhall Junction, or **Woodhall Spa** (Horncastle branch): RAF Airfield Woodhall Spa (Tattershall Thorpe).
Worksop (Harriecroft Sidings), or **Ollerton** or **Checker House** (Retford - Sheffield): Royal Ordnance Depot, Clumber Park.
Worksop, or **Checker House** (Retford - Sheffield): RAF Airfield, Worksop; RAF Training Station, Firbeck.

NORTH EASTERN AREA

Akeld (Alnwick - Coldstream): RAF Airfield, Millfield, Wooler.
Alnwick (Alnmouth - Coldstream): RAF Petroleum Depot.
Amble (branch from Chevingon): RAF Marine Base, Warkworth Harbour.
Arram (Hull - Driffield): RAF Airfield, Leconfield.
Barlow (Selby - Goole): #*WD Mobilisation Depot.*
Barnard Castle (West of Darlington): Barnard Castle Training Camps.
Bedale (Wensleydale branch): RAOC No.23 Sub-Depot.
Benton (Newcastle - Backworth): RAF Balloon Centre, Benton.
Boroughbridge (Pilmoor - Knaresborough): RAF Airfield, Dishforth.
Bowes (Barnard Castle - Kirkby Stephen): RAF Chemical Weapons Store, Bowes Moor.
Brafferton (Pilmoor - Knaresborough): *RAF No.92 MU Air Ammunition Park, Brafferton;* Cundall Oxygen Depot.
Brancepeth (Durham - Bishop Auckland): Durham Light Infantry Training Camp.
Brandon Colliery (Durham - Bishop Auckland): #*Ministry of Fuel & Power*

Sidings, Broom Park.
Brough (Doncaster/Selby - Hull): RAF (also Blackburn Aircraft Co.) Airfield, Brough.
Bubwith (Selby - Market Weighton): RAF Station, Gunby (Breighton).
Burton Agnes (Driffield - Scarborough): RAF Airfield, Lissett.
Callerton, or **Woolsington** (Gosforth - Ponteland): *RAF No.83 MU Salvage & Repair Depot Woolsington.*
Carnaby (Bridlington - Driffield): RAF Emergency Airfield, Carnaby.
Castle Eden (Ferryhill - Hartlepool): Air Ministry Experimental Station, Old Shotton.
Catterick Bridge (Richmond branch), also **Richmond**: #*Catterick Camp, Military Units and Depots, NAAFI canteens etc., including traffic over Catterick Camp Military Rly;* RAF Station, Catterick.
Cawood (branch from Selby): RAF Bomb Dump.
Church Fenton (York - Leeds/Sheffield): RAF Station, Church Fenton.
Copmanthorpe (York - Church Fenton): RAF Airfield, Acaster Malbis.
Cottingwith (DVLR): MoS Mustard Gas Factory.
Croft Depot (Croft branch): RAF Airfield, Croft.
Danby (Picton-Battersby-Whitby): RAF Wireless Station, Danby Beacon, Lealholm.
Darlington, Fighting Cocks: RAF Station, Middleton St. George.
Driffield: RAF Bomb Dump, Cottam; RAF Airfield, Eastburn, Driffield; *RAF No.91 Maintenance Depot, Southburn;* Watton Siding; *WD Site, Watton Crossing.*
Eaglescliffe: *MAP Factory and Metal Products Recovery Depot, Urlay Nook;* #*Admiralty Siding;* HQ 59 Division.
East Boldon (Newcastle - Sunderland): 7th AA Division, Advanced Ordnance Depot.
Elvington (DVLR): RAF Airfield, Elvington; WD Ordnance Depot (from 1952).
Everingham (Selby - Market Weighton): RAF Airfield, Melbourne.
Fangfoss (York - Market Weighton): RAF Airfiel, Full Sutton.
Fencehouses (Ferryhill - Pelaw): #*Ammunition Depot, Finchale WD Sidings.*
Filey: RAF Airfield, Hunmanby Moor; French Air Force Depot.
Garforth (York - Leeds): RAF Bomb Dump, Parlington.
Gilling (Pilmoor - Malton): RAOC Ammunition Sub-Depot.
Goldsborough (York - Knaresborough): #*MoS Cold Store.*
Goole: *RAF Petroleum Depot, Hook.*
Greatham (Stockton - West Hartlepool): RAF Landing Ground, Greatham.
Guisborough (Middlesbrough - Whitby): Militia Camp, Hulton Lowcross.
Harrogate: Militia Camp, Harrogate.
Haxby (York - Malton): RAF Mines Depot, Haxby.
Heighington (Darlington - Bishop Auckland): *ROF (Filling Factory), Aycliffe;* #*Ministry of Works Siding.*
Hedon (Hull - Withernsea): New Mobilisation Store, Paull, Hedon, Hull.
Hessay (York - Harrogate): #*Ordnance Stores Depot, Hessay WD Siding;* RAF Airfield, Tockwith (Marston Moor); RAF Airfield, Rufforth.
Hetton (Ferryhill - Murton - Sunderland): Lambton, Hetton & Joicey Works; *MAP No.1 Store.*
Hexham: #*Ministry of Food Cold/Food Stores, Tyne Mills.*
Holme Moor (Selby - Market Weighton): RAF Station, Holme-on-Spalding-Moor.
Hornsea: RAF Airfield, Catfoss.
Hull, Wilmington: Balloon Barage Depot, Sutton, Hull.
Hutton Cranswick (Hull - Driffield): Mobilisation Store; RAF Airfield, Hutton Cranswick; *RAF Petroleum Depot, Watton.*
Kenton Bank (Ponteland branch): RAF No.13 Group Depot, Kenton Bank.
Knaresborough: Farnham Small Arms Factory.
Leeming Bar (Wensleydale branch): RAF Station, Leeming.
Market Weighton: *RAF Reserve Supply Depot, Market Weighton.*
Marske (Middlesbrough - Saltburn): #*25th Medium Heavy Regt., RA, Training Camp, Marske Airfield.*
Masham (branch from Melmerby): RAOC No.23 Sub-Depot.
Melmerby, MOS Sidings: #*Ministry of Supply Ordnance Storage & Inspection Depot.*
Middlesbrough: #*Post Office Telegraph Pole Yard.*
Murton Lane (DVLR): *WD Northern Command Petroleum Depot.*
Nawton (Gilling - Pickering): #*Ministry of Food Cold Store; RAF Airfield, Wombleton.*
Norham (Tweedmouth - Kelso): RAF Airfield, Winfield.

60022 (LNER No.4468) - the famed MALLARD, comes away from York past Dringhouses Up Yard (on the right) with the Up *TEES-TYNE PULLMAN*, early 1950s. On the left is the former Ministry of Food cold store at Eason View. Many of these purpose-built wartime facilities got an extended lease of life during the 'Cold War' period of the 1950s and 60s. *Treacy/ Appleby coll.*

Norton (Shaftholme Jct. - Knottingley, LMS): Askern Brick & Tile Co. Siding; *MoS MT Depot.*
Norton-on-Tees, Bells' Siding: *Mobilisation Depot, Stockton.*
Pocklington (York - Market Weighton): RAF Airfield, Pocklington.
Ripon: Militia Camp, Ripon.
Ryhope (Ferryhill - Sunderland): 7th AA Division Advanced Ordnance Depot, Ryhope.
Scorton (Richmond branch): RAF Airfield, Scorton; RASC Depot and Kiplin Air Ammunition Park, Scorton.
Scruton (Wensleydale branch): Engineers' Store Depot, Scruton.
Sedgefield (Ferryhill - Stockton): Hardwick Militia Camp, Sedgefield.
Slingsby (Malton - Gilling): *WD Ordnance Dump.*
South Bank (Middlesbrough - Redcar): *#Admiralty Depot.*
Southburn (Selby - Driffield): *RAF No.91 MU Air Ammunition Park.*
Spennymoor (Ferryhill - Bishop Auckland): *ROF Spennymoor.*
Staddlethorpe (Doncaster/Selby - Hull): RAF Relief Landing Ground, Bellasize.
Starbeck (York/Leeds - Northallerton): *Air Ministry Fuel Depot, Starbeck.*
Stocksfield (Newcastle - Hexham): RAF Station, Ouston, Stamfordham.
Stockton, South: RAF Station, Thornaby.
Stokesley (Picton - Battersby): Mobilisation Depot, Stokesley.
Strensall (York - Malton): Mobilisation Store, Huntington, York; RAF Airfield, East Moor.
Tadcaster (Church Fenton - Harrogate): Air Ministry Contracts Depot.
Thirsk Town (goods branch): *#Ministry of Food Cold Store.*
Thorp Arch (Church Fenton - Harrogate): *#ROF (Filling Factory No.8), Thorp Arch (Boston Spa).*
Topcliffe (Thirsk - Knaresborough): Mobilisation Store, Topcliffe.
Usworth (Ferryhill - Pelaw): RAF Station, Castleton (Usworth), Sunderland.
Waskerley (Crook - Consett): *#MoS Ordnance Storage Depot, Burnhill.*
West Auckland: *#Ministries of Food, Works and Home Security Stores, Bishop Auckland;* RASC and NAAFI Stores.
Wetherby (Church Fenton - Harrogate): RAF Repair Depot, Wetherby.
Wheldrake (DVLR): RAF Airfield, Melbourne, also *Petroleum Dump for FIDO (fog dispersion); #Ministry of Food Cold Store*
Whitby: Mobilisation Depot.
Whitedale (Hull - Hornsea): WD Site, Rise Park, Skirlaugh.

Willington (Durham - Bishop Auckland): *#Min.of Food Cold/Food Stores, Sunnybrow; #MoS, Bowden Close Siding.*
Willington Quay (Riverside line): Militia Camp, Willington Quay.
York, Layerthorpe (DVLR): WD Ordnance & Supply Depot, York; *Petroleum Depot for RAF Linton-on-Ouse and RAF Full Sutton;* Rowntree's Siding: *Ministry of Supply Depot No.14, Haxey Road.*

SCOTTISH AREA

Duddingston (South Suburban line): *#RE Dump, Duddingston & Craigmillar*
Haddington (branch from Longniddry): RAF Landing Ground, Lennoxlowe.
Granton, East: *#Northern Lighthouse Commissioners' Siding*
Leith: *RN Base.*
Marchmont (Reston - Duns): RAF Station and No.54 OTU, Charterhall.
Edinburgh, Leith Walk or **Waverley Goods**: Ministry of Works Store, McCleod St.

Notes:
1. In PRO file AIR 10/3960.
2. It is based mainly on an REC list of September 1942 and many amendments to the end of the war, in PRO file AN2/1045, with additions and corrections kindly made by John McCrickard, Bill Corser and Mike Christensen (World War Two Railway Study Group). Amendments or additions offered by readers would be very welcome.
3. They are probably more complete for the RAF than for any other service.
4. MU - Maintenance Unit; other abbreviations: MAP - Ministry of Aircraft Production; MoS - Ministry of Supply; PFF - Pathfinder Force; RE - Royal Engineers.
5. After the war most Cold Stores were taken over by National Cold Stores Ltd.
6. Rail-connected with LMSR at Wisbech Sidings.
7. Most Landing Grounds became Airfields later in the War, when they were provided with concrete runways and hard standings.

Appendix F

SIDINGS AND WORKS ON THE ECML, 1938 - 1962

(for HM Government Depots and Sidings, see *Appendix E*)

The following list is compiled largely from the *Railway Clearing House Handbooks of Stations* for 1938 and 1956, and from the *Appendices* published between those dates as well as that for 1962. (As no *Appendix* was published between 1956 and 1962, the precise situation at 31st December 1959 - the cut-off date for the rest of this book - could not be used).

In general, Sidings and Works belonging to the Railway are not listed here, but are cited in Chapter VI or incorporated in the text of Chapter VII in Part 2. The entries are headed by the name of the Railway Station having charge of the Siding. All facilities (other than Railway installations) listed in the RCH *Handbooks* under the heading of an ECML station are given below. Those added by the RCH after 1938 are marked '*' and those not in the 1956 *Handbook* (and/or closed before 1962) are marked '#'. In a number of instances the establishment operating the installation changed during this period, and this is indicated in most cases. The designation 'Siding' is left to be inferred in many cases.

At the larger towns, many of the works and sidings listed were not directly adjacent to the ECML; only those coming under the auspices of an ECML station are cited. Where the location was on a branch this is indicated.

King's Cross Goods:
Camley St. coal bays
*Rowntree & Co Ltd, Blundell St. Siding
Holloway:
Islington Electric Light Works (later Central Electricity Authority, CEA)
*Turner, Burns & John Inns Ltd (Holloway Mill)
Ashburton Grove Sidings - Islington Borough Council
Finsbury Park:
#Clarence Yard Siding (public)
LNER Engineer's Siding
*MacFisheries Depot
*Stoneyard Siding
Hornsey:
Hornsey Gas Works (later North Thames Gas Board)
Wood Green:
Metropolitan Water Board
Alexandra Park Siding
New Southgate:
LCC Colney Hatch (later Friern) Hospital
Standard Telephone & Cables Ltd
Southgate & District Gas Co (later Eastern Gas Board)
New Barnet:
Barnet Gas Works (later Eastern Gas Board)
Hatfield:
Marshmoor Siding:
    Calder & McDougall's Ltd
    *Holland, Hannen & Cubitt's Ltd
    *Massil & Sons (Wood Turners) Ltd
    *Measures Bros. Ltd
    *John Mowlem & Co Ltd
Sherrif & Sons Ltd
Smart's Siding
Blackbridge Siding (Dunstable branch)
Fiddle Bridge Public Siding (St Albans branch)
Mount Pleasant (Hertford branch)
Welwyn Garden City:
*Associated British Picture Corporation (Welwyn Studios)
*Crown Macaroni Co
Hertfordshire Gravel & Brick Co
*Lincoln Electric Co Ltd
Mouldrite Ltd
*Nabisco Foods Ltd
*Roche Products
Shredded Wheat Co
Twentieth Mile Siding
Unity Heating Co
Dunstable branch:
    #Horn's Sdg., Welwyn Garden City Co
Hertford branch:

Attimore Hall Public Siding
Dawnay's Ltd
New Town Trust Ltd
*Norton Grinding Wheel Co
Knebworth:
#Rowe's Lime Siding
Stevenage:
#Ellis & Everard Ltd
#Inn's Coal & Grain Sdg., W. Pearman Ltd
Langley Public Siding
Wymondley Public Siding
Hitchin:
Cadwell Public Siding
Hitchin Gas Works (later Eastern Gas Board)
Ransome's North Siding: P.H.Barker & Sons Ltd
Ransome's South Siding:
  *Concrete Proofing Co
Wallace & Bros. Lime Works
*Wilmott & Sons
Three Counties:
Arlesey Brick Co (later London Brick Co)
#Associated Portland Cement Manufacturers
Three Counties Mental Hospital
Arlesey:
#Gault Brick Co
#London & Arlesey Brick Co
Biggleswade:
#Gas Light & Coke Co. (later Eastern Gas Board)
Tidman's Ltd (Wisbech)
Sandy:
#Love's Brick Yard (H. Cope)
#Pym's Sand Sidings
Tempsford:
*Little Barford Power Station, Beds. Cambs. & Hunts. Elec. Co. later Edmondson Electricity Corp (later CEA)
Huntingdon North:
Huntingdon County Council Siding:
*Chivers & Sons Ltd, Fuel Oil Installation Siding
#Thackray & Co
Holme:
Highney Estates Co
*Lark Ltd (formerly H.M. Knighton & Co)
Fletton [1]
*AEI Hotpoint Electric Appliance Co Ltd
Beeby's Brick Co
Botolph Bridge Siding (Botolph branch):
British Sugar Corporation
    *British Thomson-Houston Ltd
Eastwood's Ltd, Yaxley Brickworks
Farrow & Co Siding
Hicks & Co (Fletton) Ltd Nos. 1, 2 & 3 Sidings
#Kemil Ltd, Celta Works
London Brick Co Ltd:
    Farcet Brick Works
    Fletton Crown Siding
    New Peterborough Nos. 1, 2 & 3
    *Noble & Mushroom's Ltd
    Norman Cross Siding
Peterborough District (later Midland) Tar Distillers Ltd
Plowmans' Brickfields Ltd
Yaxley Brickworks Siding
Peterborough North - Werrington Junction:
Peterborough Corporation Electricity Works, (later CEA)
Southeast England Electricity Sdg. (LMS, Mid)
Spital Cattle Docks
Air Ministry Siding (M&GN):
    Baker, Perkins Ltd, Arktos Siding
    *Baxter Guion Ltd
    W.P. Hartley Ltd
    *Post Office Siding
Crescent Cattle Docks (LMS, Mid)
Crescent Wharf Public Siding (LMS, Mid)
    S. Thomson & Sons
LMSR C&W Siding
Brotherhood's
Gilstrap, Earp & Co, Paston Siding
New England:
    Burnett & Co
    *Cambrian Wagon Works
    Peterborough Cooperative Equity Co (later Co-op Wholesale Soc Ltd)

Cripple Sidings
    *New England Angle Siding (public)
Sage & Co' Siding, Walton
Shell Mex & BP Co Ltd
Tallington:
*Dow-Mac Products Ltd
Etton Siding:
    Peterborough Corporation Water Works
Essendine:
#Wilsthorp Siding (Bourne branch)
Little Bytham:
Lawnwood Siding:
    Adamantine Clinker Works
#T.E. Gray & Co, Bulk Storage
Stainby:
Highdyke - and other - Ironstone Sidings
Grantham:
Ambergate Yard (Grantham Canal station, Public Siding, on branch from Nottingham line):
    H. Bell's Siding
    #Grantham Gas Works (later East Midlands Gas Board)
    Bristowes, Tavia Siding
Barnstone Cement Co, Little Ponton Siding
#Gonerby Public Siding:
    W.F. Swallow & Son (Wheeldon's Siding)
Grantham Water Works, Saltersford Siding
Lee & Grinley's Siding
*Lion Emulsions Ltd
Ruston & Hornsby Siding
    *Aveling Barford Ltd
    *Ransome's, Simms & Jeffries Ltd
*Shell Mex & BP Ltd ?
Newark:
Abbott & Co's Siding
Hugh Baird & Sons Ltd, Cliff Nook Kilns
Barnston's Maltings
British Glues & Chemicals Ltd Siding:
    *Calfoss Ltd
    *Croid Ltd
    Kerol Ltd
Cafferata & Co Siding
Pure Bone Phosphate Co Ltd
Cotham branch:
    Bowbridge Siding
Cross St. Siding
Jericho Siding
Lowfield Siding:
    T.W. Ward Ltd
    Worthington, Simpson Ltd
Newark Gas Co (later East Midlands Gas Board)
Newark Gravel & Concrete Co, Balderton
Gilstrap, Earp & Co's Maltings
Joint Curve:
    H. Baird & Co, Spital Kiln No.1
    Branstone's Riverside Malt Kilns and
    Farrar's Boil Works
    Fish Meal Plant
    Gilstrap, Earp & Co's Cow Lane and Massey Maltings
    *W. Peach & Co, Cow Lane and Spital Maltings
    Ruston & Hornsby Ltd Ironworks
    Trent Concrete Co
    Warwick & Richardson Ltd
*S.B. Moore Ltd
Muskham Siding
*Newark Egg Packers Siding
Ransome & Co's Siding
    Ransome & Marles Bearing Co Ltd
Tuxford North:
East Markham Public Siding
Retford, Babworth Sidings:
A.J. Fisher
*J. Bibby & Sons
Ranskill:
*Eric Fawcett Ltd
*Ministry of Supply (later WD) Sidings:
    *Courtaulds Ltd
    *Kingsbury Concrete Co
Bawtry:
Associated Quartzites Ltd
#Bawtry Coke Ovens & By-Products Ltd

*General Refractories Ltd
    *Brick Marketing Co Ltd
Oates Siding
South Yorkshire & Derbyshire Gas Co (later East Midlands Gas Board)
Yorkshire Amalgamated Products Ltd
Harworth Colliery branch:
    Harworth Main Colliery
    *Glass Bulbs Ltd
Misson Siding:
    *Ministry of Works
Doncaster - GN lines [2]
Branch from Rossington: Amalgamated Denaby Collieries Ltd, Rossington Colliery
Belmont Sidings:
    Arnold & Son Ltd
    *Briggs Motor Bodies Ltd
    British Ropes Ltd
    Darlington Fencing Co Ltd
    *SPC Wagon Repairs Ltd
*Ford Motor Co Ltd Siding
Carcroft line:
    Doncaster Corp. Highways Dept. Siding
Doncaster - GC, and Joint, lines:
Allen & Orr's Siding
#Anglo-American Oil Co
*W.S. Arnold & Sons (Executors, of) Siding
Balby Public Siding
Bentley Colliery (GC & H&B Jt. line)
British Bemberg Ltd Siding
Burnett's Wagon Works
Cherry Tree Lane Goods
    Doncaster Amalgamated Collieries Ltd,
    Bullcroft Colliery (GC & H&B branch)
Doncaster Canister Co
Doncaster Cooperative Society Coal Siding
Doncaster Ice & Cold Storage Co's Siding
Doncaster Wagon Co Ltd Siding
Farmer's Co. Siding
Marsh Gate Goods and branch:
    *East Midland Gas Board Siding
    *International Harvester Co.
    S. Parkinson & Sons Ltd Siding
    *Wheatley Park Goods:
        *Bowser, Monks & Whitehouse
Stevens' Wagon Works
York Road Goods, and GC & H&B Jt. line:
    C.F. Booth Ltd
    Doncaster Cooperative Society Siding
    *J. Fowler & Co (Leeds) Ltd
Arksey:
Bentley Colliery
#Bentley Colliery Goods Siding
Heck:
Yorkshire Amalgamated Products
Selby:
Bell, Berry & Co
Brayton Siding (public)
*British Oil & Cake Mills Ltd
Britsh Sugar Corporation Ltd
Dents' Siding
E.M. Fawcett's Siding
Fletcher's Siding
#Henwick Hall Siding (public)
*Kirby's (Selby) Ltd Flour Mills
#Olympia (formerly Selby) Oil & Cake Mills
Selby Flour Mill
Selby Gas Works (later NE Gas Board)
Selby Urban District Council
Thorp Gates Public Siding (Leeds line)
Yorkshire Dyeware Co
York, including Foss Islands Goods and branch:
Anglo-American Oil Co.'s Depot & Siding
*W. Bridge Ltd
Burton Lane Coal Siding
*Carlton St. Siding
Corporation Siding
*Derwent Rubber Co, Layerthorpe
*Esso Petroleum Co. Ltd. Depot Siding
Holgate Dock
Leatham Flour Mills

Logan & Hemingway's, Skelton Bridge
Rowntree's Sidings
St Cuthbert's Siding
Shell-Mex & BP Ltd, Layerthorpe
Station Hotel Laundry Siding
Waterworks Siding, Clifton
*Waterworks Siding, Layerthrorpe
Workhouses & City General Hospital
York Gas Co's (later NE Gas Board)
British Sugar Corporation (Poppleton branch)
Raskelf:
Hodgson's Coal Depot
Pilmoor:
#Moor Siding (public)
Thirsk:
Jackson's, later Calvert Scrap Metals
#Manor House Siding (public)
Thirsk Town Goods:
Anglo-American Oil Co's Siding
    Shell-Mex & BP Ltd Siding
    Stirke & Sons Siding
    J. Toser's Siding
Northallerton:
#Logan & Hemingway's (Construction) Siding
Eryholme:
Rolling Stock Co Ltd
Croft Depot:
Croft Gas Works (later Northern Gas Board)
Darlington, Bank Top [3]:
Alliance Boiler Works
Black Banks Chemical Works (Thos. Ness Ltd)
Boyd's Siding
Cleveland Bridge & Engineering Co Ltd
*Darlington Cooperative & Industrial Society
Haughton Bridge Depots & (public) Siding:
    *R. Blackett & Son
    Dawson, Forcett Ltd Works
    Grieveson & Whitwell Ltd
    Haughton Road Brickworks
    *L. Wynn-Williams' Works
North of England Maltings Siding, Burnip's Brickyard
W. Richardson & Co's Siding
J. Tinsley Engineering Works
Victoria Works
Wagon Repairs Ltd
Weardale Steel, Coal & Coke Co
J. Weeks & Co Horticultural Engineering Works
Darlingon, Hope Town:
Albert Hill and Skerne Works & Sidings:
    Albert Hill Foundry
    British Still Tube Works
    Darlington Gas Works (later Northern Gas Board) Albert
Hill Works and Skerne Works
    Darlington Wire Mills Ltd Works
    Goldsborough Patents Ltd
    *A.R. Jolly
    T. Oldham's Scrap Yard
    Premium Radiator Co
    Railway Appliances Works
    J. Shewell & Co Ltd
    Skerne Iron Works Ltd
    J. Tinsley Engineering Works, Skerne
Brown's Saw Mills, Pearson's Siding
Chemical & Insulating Co
Darlington Corporation, Hunden's Lane Siding
Darlington Electricity Works (later CEA):
    Bunker, Manure & Cement Siding
Darlington Forge Co's Works
Darlington Railway Plant & Foundry Co's Siding
Darlington & Simpson Rolling Mills Ltd, Rise Carr and West Works
Dunwell Bros' Whessoe Brick Works
*Esso Petroleum Co Ltd
Grieveson & Whitwell Ltd, Cockerton and Rise Carr Depots
Jubilee Siding
*Morley Bros
*NAAFI Sidings, Whessoe Lane
Nestfield Engine Works and Wagon Works
Northern Gas Board, Albert Hill Works
Northgate Coal Depots
#North of England School Furnishing Co, Scholastic Sidings

Patons & Baldwin's Siding (Fighting Cocks branch)
Pease & Partners' Granary and Warehouse
Redline Glico Ltd
Rolling Stock Co Ltd, Nestfield Wagon Works
R.P. Simpson & Co (Alnwick) Ltd, North of England Maltings
R. Stephenson & Hawthorns Ltd (Springfield) Locomotive Works
T. Summerson & Co's Foundries
T.W. Ward Ltd
Whessoe Lane Siding, *Russell & Wringham
Whessoe Ltd Foundry and Siding
H. Williams Ltd Railway Appliance Works
Aycliffe:
Aycliffe Lime & Limestone Co (later Gjers, Mills & Co)
Ord & Maddison's Lime Works
Ferryhill:
Barker & Co's Slag Works, Coxhoe Junction
Coundon Depot (Leasingthorne branch)
F.W. Dobson & Co:
    Chilton Limeworks & Quarry
    Cornforth Basic Works
Earl of Eldon's Sand Tip Siding
Ferryhill North Slag Works
Ferryhill South Slag Works
Fishburn Colliery (branch from Sedgefield)
LNER Gas Works (later BR, NER)
Mainsforth Colliery
*Mainsforth Lime Works
North of England Electric Co (later CEA)
Pease & Partners Ltd, Bishop Middleham Quarry
Steetley Dolomite Quarry Ltd
#Thrislington Colliery, Coke-Ovens & By-Products Works
Tursdale Colliery & Coke Ovens (later NCB Central Stores, Leamside line)
West Cornforth Chemical Works (Leamside line)
Plawsworth:
Kimblesworth Colliery
Chester-le-Street:
Chester South Moor Colliery
Horner's Confectionery Works
Birtley:
*AEI Ltd
#Bewick Main Colliery
Birtley Brick Co, Union Brick Works
Birtley Cartridge Case Factory (later ROF, Birtley)
#Birtley Co's Siding
#Birtley Gas Works (later Northern Gas Board)
#Birtley Grange Brick Works
#Birtley Iron Works & Gas Works
#Black Fell Siding
#Black House Siding
Blue Barns Manure Siding
#Blythe's Brick Works
*Caterpillar Tractor Co Ltd
*Durham Chemicals Group
#Eighton Banks Siding
*Goodall's (Disinfectants) Ltd
*W.T. Henley (Telegraph Works) Co Ltd
#Newcastle-on-Tyne Elec Supply Co, Change of Frequency Stores (later CEA)
#Newcastle-on-Tyne Zinc Oxide Co
#Ouston Colliery 'A' Pit and Gas Works
Ouston Colliery 'E' Pit (Birtley Colliery)
#Ouston Grain Warehouse & Saw Mill
#Ouston Manure Depot
#Pelaw Grange Saw Mill
#Pelaw Grange Siding and Depots
*Ravensworth Ann Colliery
*Ravensworth Betty Colliery
Ravensworth Brick & Tile Works
*Ravensworth Shops (NCB)
*J.O. Scott, Pelaw Grange Brick Works
#Urpeth Colliery ('B' and 'C' Pits) & Coke Ovens
#White Hill Bank Head Siding
#Whitehouse Siding
Gateshead [4]:
Armstrong, Whitworth & Co's Close Works
*S. Bowran, Shipcote Works (Felling line)
*Bramwell's Siding
#Carrick & Wardle, Redheugh Engine Works
Clark, Chapman & Co.:
    Victoria Works
    *Coronation Works (Allhusens branch)

#Eagle Depot (E.S. Holdsworth & Co)
Gateshead Cooperative Society Depot
Gateshead Corporation Depots
Goodall, Bates & Co
#Hope & Co's Raby Depot
ICI (General Chemicals) Ltd Works
*Jenning's Siding
Kirkpatrick & Barr's
Marple & Gillott, St James's Siding
Oakwellgate public Siding
Park Lane Glass Works (Ferry & Son)
#Redheugh Colliery
Rivet, Bolt & Nut Co's Tyneside Works
Sowerby Ellison Glass Works
Team Valley Trading Estate [5]:

    *British Road Services (Parcels) Ltd
    *Cadbury-Fry Ltd
    *De La Rue Developments Ltd
    *Durham Steel Co
    *Fusarc Welding Co Ltd
    *Huwood Mining Engineering Co
    *NE Trading Estate Ltd
    *Reed, Millican & Co Ltd
    *Team Valley Cold Storage Ltd
    *H. Wood & Co Ltd
    Wright, Anderson & Co's Coulthards Lane Siding

Newcastle-on-Tyne (*excluding* Elswick, Blaydon, Jesmond loop, and Riverside line):
Forth (Goods):

    English Steel Corp, Elswick Works
    #Hawthorn, Leslie & Co
    Newcastle Gas Works (later Northern Gas Board), Elswick Works
    #R.H. Patterson & Co
    Railway St. Coal & Lime Depots
    Robert Stephenson & Hawthorns Ltd
    Vickers-Armstrong Ltd, Elswick Ord. & Eng. Works, and Wharf

Newcastle Central:

    #Benwell Colliery
    Forth Cattle Dock
    Forth Hydraulic Engine House
    Forth Provender Store
    Walker, Parker & Co (later Associated Lead Manuf. Ltd)

New Bridge St. Goods & Coal Depot:

    #Backworth Coal Depot & Siding
    Carruthers' Granary
    *Guinness & Co Warehouse
    *J. Heinz' Warehouse
    Newcastle Corporation Electricity Generating Sidings, and

Newcastle Electricity Supply Co, Pandon Dean Power Station (later CEA)

    Red Barns Manure Wharf
    Schweppes Ltd Warehouse

Quayside Branch:

    *Cooperative Wholesale Society Grain & General Warehouse
    Newcastle Corporation Sheds 1, 2 & 3
    Newcastle Corporation Wharves Nos. 3 - 26
    *Spillers Ltd, Tyne Mills

Heaton Junction:

    *J. Arnott & Co's Siding
    #H. Down & Co
    Heaton Foundry Co Ltd
    #Heaton Manure Loading Wharf
    Heaton Junction Public Siding
    *Hunter's Coal Depot
    *Imperial Tobacco Co Ltd
    *Metal Box Co Ltd
    *Needlers Ltd
    Newcastle Cooperative Society Coal Depot
    Newcastle Corporation Sidings
    Nicholson's Chemical Works; Dope & Varnish Works
    A. Parsons & Co Ltd, Heaton Works
    F. Turnbull & Co

Killingworth:
Burradon Colliery & Sidings
#Burradon Lizzie and Weetslade Pit
#Dinnington Colliery,. Depot & Brickworks
*Havanneh Colliery
Hazelrigg Colliery
#Hope Cottage Siding
Killingworth Colliery
Killingworth Saw Mill

Scorer's Manure Siding
Seaton Burn Colliery & Depot
*Weetslade Colliery & Washer
Annitsford:
#Annits Village Siding
#Ann Pit
Cramlington Lamb Pit & Brick Works
Dam Dykes Siding
Dudley Colliery & Depot
#Hartford Colliery (Scott Pit)
Shankhouse Colliery (Amelia Pit)
#Wrightson Colliery
Cramlington:
Cramlington Coal Co Siding
Stannington:
#W. Slater
#W. Younger
Morpeth:
J.R. Temple's Siding
*Shell-Mex & BP Ltd Siding
Pegswood:
Bothal Park (or Ashington Junction) Siding
*Longhirst Public Siding [6]
Pegswood Colliery & Siding
Widdrington:
Burn Fireclay Co
Stobswood Colliery & Siding
#Widdrington Old Colliery
Chevington:
Amble Junction Siding
Warkworth:
South Shilbottle Colliery
Shortridge Farm Siding
#Southside Colliery
Alnmouth:
Shilbottle Colliery
Little Mill:
*Howick Whinstone Quarry & Pipe Works (later Trollop & Colls Ltd)
*Littlehoughton Concrete Pipe Works
Little Mill Lime Kilns
#Little Mill Whinstone Quarry
Christon Bank:
#Christon Bank Tramway Station Siding
#Fallodon Siding & Depot
Belford:
Appleby's Siding
Craigmill Siding
*Grain Drier Siding
Scremerston:
#Billingdean Colliery
#Scremerston Colliery
Tweedmouth:
Allan Bros.
*J.T. Dove Ltd
Johnson & Darling's
McCreaths'
Tweed Dock:

    Esso Petroleum Co
    *Fisons'
    *Northern Gas Board
    *Roofing & Building Supply Co
    H.O.Short & Sons
    J.P. Simpson's Maltings

Berwick-on-Tweed:
Berwick Auction Mart Co
Reston (Chirnside branch):
Auchencrow Public Siding
Billiemains Public Siding
Dunbar:
Thomas Allandale & Sons Ltd.
#Battlebent Siding
Beltenford public Siding
British Malt Products Ltd., Westbank Mills
Oxwellmains Limestone Siding:

    Associated British Portland Cement Co

Oxwellmains Public Siding
West Barns Siding
Drem:
Ballencrieff public Siding
Longniddry:

#Longniddry West Siding
Prestonpans:
Meadowmill Mine (branch)
#Morrison's Haven Siding
Northfield Siding
Ormiston Road Coal Depot
Prestongrange Colliery
Prestongrange Brick & Fireclay Works
Preston Links Colliery
Seton Siding
Summerlee Iron Co. Ltd.
Tranent and Tranent Colliery Branches:
#Bankton Colliery
Kingslaw Siding
Myles' Siding
Tranent Public Siding
Tranent Mains Siding
#Wester Windygoul Siding
Windygoul Siding
Inveresk:
Inveresk Paper Co., Musselburgh
*NCB Siding, Wallyford Colliery
Niddrie:
*Edinburgh Corp. Water Dept., Pipe Works
Newcraighall Colliery
Niddrie Sanitary Fireclay Works
Woolmet Colliery
Portobello:
Buchanan & Co Wagon Repairs, Joppa Saw Mills
J. & P. Cameron Corn Store
#Craigentinny Gas Works (later Scottish Gas Board)
#Edinburgh Corporation Refuse Bank
LNER (later BR, ScR) Materials Store
Meadowbank Siding
Palace Brewery, Rose Lane
Portobello Bottle Works
Westbank Power Station (later South of Scotland Electricity Board)
Woods Park Repair Depot
Edinburgh Waverley:
*Bruce & Sons, Abbeyhill
Central Fruit Co
Lindsay & Sons & Scarlett
Lochend (Moray Park) Siding (W. Younger & Co)
#London Road Foundry (Miller & Co) (Piershill loop)
Rankins' Siding
Scotsman Siding:
        A.S. Clarke & Co
        #HM Stationery Office
        Ormerod, Wood & Co
        M. Ritchie & Co
        Veital, Moore & Erskine

N.B.: *Not* listed above are a large number of Sidings in the Greater Edinburgh/Leith area, amounting to over 100 entries in the *RCH Handbook*. These came under the jurisdiction of various stations on the branches from Portobello or on the South Suburban line (including the St Leonards branch), some being worked jointly from LMSR stations.

1. Extensive changes of ownership and organisation here between 1938 and 1956.
2. The LNER workshops are not included here.
3. LNER Works and Sidings *not* included. Almost all other Works and Sidings came under either Bank Top or Hope Town and are listed here.
4. Not included are the many Works and Sidings coming under stations in the Gateshead and Newcastle areas, close to but not on the ECML, such as Dunston-on-Tyne, down the river towards Wallsend, North Shields, Jarrow and South Shields.
5. In 1938, rail-connected factories in the Team Valley Trading Estate came under Dunston-on-Tyne (not ECML)
6. After closure of station.

Appendix G

SPECIFIC WARTIME LOCOMOTIVE WORKINGS

The train-watcher observing during the War at major centres like Doncaster, York and Newcastle was rewarded - as indeed he was at most other places in the country - by the spectacle of 'organized chaos' resulting directly or indirectly from military operations, and at times from bomb-damage after enemy air-raids, which rendered memorable both the sight of special workings of one kind or another and the fascinating appearance of unexpected locomotives outside their normal sphere of operations. Unfortunately it seems that hardly any STNs or Movement Orders giving details of the scheduling of wartime special trains have survived, let alone records of the locomotives used. The following is a tantalizingly short example of details that the author for one would treasure.

The Convoy coal trains caused a lot of trouble, partly due to frequent breakdowns of grease-lubricated private-owner wagons on the long journeys, and a sample report on Convoy coal trains running during the Blitz winter of 1940-41 is intriguing. It cites the progress of a sample of five actual block coal trains from Co.Durham on Friday and Saturday 14th and 15th March 1941.

No.1 - left West Hartlepool at 11.55 on 14th March for Westbury, arriving 02.35 16th March; it had O4 No.**6574** to Normanton (*via* York), LMS 4F No.**4337** on to Branston, LMS 4F No.**4171** on to Stoke Gifford, then GW 'Saint' No.**2951**, with assisting engine from Bathampton.

No. 2 - left West Hartlepool at 17.02 on 15th March for Ferme Park, arriving 21.10 on 16th March; it had O4 No.**6193** to York, where it was delayed two hours waiting for an engine, that turned out to be A1 No.**2579** which took the train on to New England, where O1 No.**3468** took over.

No. 3 - left Stella Gill at 09.05 on 14th March for Brimsdown, arriving at 10.50 on 15th March; it had Q7 No.**907** to Doncaster, O4 No.**5400** on to Whitemoor, then J20 No.**8274**.

No. 4 - left Whitburn Junction at 14.25 on 14th March for Hartford Exchange Sidings, arriving 18.00 15th March; it had V2 No.**4825** to York, then O4 No.**6235** right through to Northwich, assisted by J6 No.**4173** from Wath to Dunford Bridge, plus O4s Nos.**6500** and **6224** from Wath to West Silkstone Junction (Worsborough Incline).

No. 5 - left West Dunston at 20.35 on 15th March for Heywood, arriving 16.40 on 17th March (having been held over the Sunday at Rochdale); it had Q6 No.**1131** to Normanton (*via* York), then LMS 7F No.**9519** to Rochdale.

Appendix H

THE IMPACT OF THE AIR WAR ON THE ECML

Damage And Disruption Due To Enemy Action On The ECML And Some Connecting Lines

No account of the railway scene during the war can suffice without an attempt to recount the various episodes of damage and disruption caused by enemy action. In fact, on the LNER the ECML came off relatively lightly. Considering that it was virtually impossible at that time for a bomber to hit a specific railway target at night, the list of damage and disruption given below is actually an impressive indication of the intensity of the air-raids. Nonetheless, in any account of air-raids in Britain in the Second World War, it is salutary to remember how minor was the damage done by the Luftwaffe in this country compared with the devastation meted out later in the war by the Allied Air Forces, both as a result of area bombing and when the railways of Germany and of Occupied France, Belgium, Holland and Luxembourg were subjected to a campaign of targeted interdiction in 1944-45. For example, on the night of 14th October 1944 alone Duisburg in the Rühr received as many tons of bombs as did *all* British targets during the worst *month* (September 1940) of our Blitz.

What follows here relates primarily to the ECML, and the reader should bear in mind that other railways - and many other places in Britain - suffered much more severely from air-raid damage, and at one time or another incidents of some kind due to enemy action occurred in almost every part of the country. The indirect effects of for example raids on London, Hull, Leeds, Glasgow and other places connected with the ECML were often as great as the direct damage on ECML centres. The first significant damage inflicted by the enemy on the LNER was a bomb on the Down Goods line between Barnetby and Brocklesby in the early hours of 13th June 1940. Other bombs fell in Humberside that night, and as is well known Hull and Grimsby suffered severely during the Blitz and later. The LNER's property in the area was heavily damaged, as it was in Norwich, Yarmouth, Lowestoft, Nottingham, Leeds, Sheffield, Middlesbrough, West Hartlepool, Clydebank and elsewhere. There is not space here to describe the damage done at all these places, and reference is made to only a few of the numerous incidents that happened on the lines branching off the ECML. Moreover, it was far from just direct damage by blast or fire that was suffered: traffic could be interrupted for hours or days by the mortal danger from delayed-action (DAB) or unexploded bombs (UXB). When a high-explosive (HE) bomb - or worse, one of the hefty land-mines that were dropped by parachute - failed to explode, accidentally or deliberately, it could often cause more disruption than if it had, for until it did explode or was defused its mere presence on or near a line necessitated the closure of that line and diversion of all trains. Often UXBs were found hours or days after a major raid, and lines had to be closed for longer than it took to repair actual damage. Anti-aircraft (AA) shells were inclined to shower shrapnel on people on the ground, and if the shells failed to explode they were also a menace. For example, in 1940 unexploded AA shells at New Barnet on 20th September and at Ferme Park on 29th December each caused interruption of traffic for over three hours.

In the initial, violent and almost continuous phase of the London Blitz, in September - November 1940, a number of incidents of serious damage on or near the ECML occurred, and these are listed below. However, compared to the damage done on many other lines in London this was not so very disruptive. The main effects of the Blitz on the ECML were indirect. Thus, from the first heavy daylight raids early in September 1940 to the end of the Blitz in May 1941, the passage of the heavy mineral and freight traffic onto the SR from Ferme Park Yard *via* the Widened Lines and over Blackfriars Bridge was interrupted directly by destruction of adjacent buildings, including Farringdon Goods station, but also especially of bridges *etc.* on the SR lines. During September and October 1940, not only were the routes over Blackfriars Bridge and *via* either Herne Hill or London Bridge cut for prolonged periods, but there were also serious interruptions of the routes to the SR by the North London, West London and East London lines.

When bombs actually exploded on plain track, by dint of hard work it did not take many hours to restore traffic - if at first with hand-signalling, but when bridges and other major structures were hit it was a different story. Right from the beginning of the Blitz in September 1940 the SR suffered many serious incidents of this kind, and as a result when the direct route to the SR *via* the Widened Lines was out of action on several occasions there was a great build-up of traffic in the ECML yards. For example, on 14th September no fewer than 1,791 wagons were held up at Ferme Park and another 2,300 at East Goods, Clarence and King's Cross yards, and the LNER expected to be able to clear only about 1,350 in the next 24 hours. It was therefore diverting coal traffic to South London *all the way round* through Bletchley, Oxford, Basingstoke, Eastleigh and Chichester.

Bridges and locomotive sheds were prime targets, but hard to find and hit. The enemy could hardly fail to hit the vast Stratford complex, but the damage they did to King's Cross, South Blyth and York engine sheds (see below) was probably incidental, as was that to Norwich shed - where on 9th July 1940 the first LNER railwayman was killed. However, raids on Louth shed on 19th February 1941 and on Tweedmouth shed on 10th February 1942 were well directed, the first virtually destroying the little depot, killing one man and injuring two others.

Air-raids themselves obviously could have dire consequences, but it must be remembered that the most serious delays and disruption were caused in the early stages of the war by trains being stopped or slowed to a crawl simply because there was an air-raid *warning* in force, and also by the difficulties of operating in the Black-Out. Until November 1940 it was ruled that after the sounding of the 'Alert', all passenger trains must be stopped and warned by a signalman - and the passengers given the opportunity to detrain at the next station. The trains then had to crawl at *15 m.p.h.* (10 m.p.h. for freight trains) until the 'All Clear' had sounded. After October 1940 the speed-limit in Alerts was raised to 25 m.p.h. in daylight but remained at 15 m.p.h. in darkness, but the delays naturally caused absolute havoc with timetables and with the rostering of men, locomotives and stock, and trains - more especially freight trains - often had to be controlled on an *ad hoc* basis. Fortunately these restrictions were soon recognized to be impractical and unnecessary: even if drivers went very slowly they still might run into an obstruction or fall into a crater in the dark - as did happen several times. Therefore from February 1941 all trains were allowed to run at normal speeds during Alerts in daylight or at 30 m.p.h. during Black-Out hours, and the order to stop to inform passengers of an Alert was rescinded because few people took any notice. At night trains still had to be stopped for the driver to be warned of an Alert - also the guard, who had to turn off the train lighting - until December 1944; who told the train-crew when the All Clear had sounded is not clear. During the Flying Bomb emergency in London and the South-East in 1944, in daytime signalmen put out white boards with a black upward-pointing arrow to warn drivers of Alerts. The heavy air-raids on London led to the practice of having expresses call at a major suburban station to help passengers keep away from main termini; on the ECML Up expresses stopped at Finsbury Park if an Alert was on, to let passengers transfer to the Tube there if they wished.

For some reason best known to the Germans, virtually the only city on the ECML to be bombed heavily was London. Newcastle-upon-Tyne, in spite of its prime importance as an industrial target, had only two major raids throughout the war, on the nights of 9th and 25th April 1941, and these were widely dispersed over the Tyneside area, bombs falling mainly well downstream from Newcastle. Peterborough and Darlington each had several incidents, none doing grievous harm to the railways. Grantham town was struck no less than twelve times in the last three months of 1940 and in one raid 39 people were killed, but the railway was little affected. Doncaster, on the other hand, was fortunate to escape, for on 21st December 1940 a major - but accidental - fire at the Carriage Works (which began in the Paint Shop and burnt out the Carriage Body and Joiners' Shops) attracted a number of enemy bombers whose sticks entirely failed to explode. It could have been that the failure of the enemy to bomb major railway centres on the ECML (and elsewhere) was to a certain extent thanks to the installation of decoy lighting (QL sites) and fires (QF sites), which in addition to smoke-screens were employed to mislead the German bomber crews. In November 1940 QL sites were set up at Loversall near Doncaster, to represent the lights of Decoy (!) Yards, and at Eye to represent New England Yard; in November 1941 one was brought into use at Upper Poppleton, south-west of York, but it confused RAF crews approaching nearby Rufforth Airfield and was abandoned two years later. There were of course several decoy sites in other parts of the country.

As described later, the railway installations at York were the most unfortunate on the ECML, receiving a pasting in one of the relatively small-scale Baedeker raids in 1942. Edinburgh, Britain's second capital, never had a major raid; the only recorded railway damage in the Edinburgh area occurred in minor incidents at Leith LMS on 18th July, at South Leith on 22nd July and at Portobello on 4th August 1940, and at North Leith and Junction Road stations on 7th April 1941. In London, by far the greatest damage in the Blitz was done in the City and East End, and therefore on the LNER it was the Great Eastern section that was most affected. London also was the prime target of the Flying Bombs and Rockets in 1944-45, and again the LNER suffered principally in the East End. Indeed one in seven of all V2s (German rocket weapons) that fell in Britain damaged LNER property.

The earliest reported incidents on the ECML itself were at Darlington, where on 27th June 1940 minor damage was done to signal and telephone wires - cutting communications with Tees-side for a few hours, then at Newcastle on the night of 2nd July 1940 one bomb fell near the station, one near the High Level Bridge and another at Gateshead West, causing minor damage and interruption of block working.

LONDON AREA

The London Blitz had begun with a vengeance on 7th September 1940. Havoc in the East End was so widespread that the LNER stopped *all* traffic in the Stratford District that night - a Saturday, and for the first time of many to come the SR stopped all inter-Company exchange traffic. From then on London was bombed almost every night until the end of November. The first incident on the ECML itself occurred in the early hours of 9th September, when the Potato Market at King's Cross was severely damaged, and several bombs fell in the Top Shed area. One in particular landed next to the main-line shed, destroying one wall and the roof over two stabling roads. Stores buildings were damaged, the glass of the Suburban shed blown out and the dividing wall with the LMSR brought down; a water main was burst, the coaling-plant put out of action and telephones cut. Several locomotives were damaged (notably O1s Nos.3462, 3473 and N1 No.4571), but in all this only five men were injured - none seriously, and engines still came and went. A bomb struck the Shed area again on 23rd October and an AA shell hit it on 21st December.

King's Cross was again affected on the night of 17th September, with debris and damage on the Down main and slow lines to Belle Isle, delaying but not interrupting traffic for several hours. And it was not only bombs: on the evening of 20th September an AA shell exploded in the station forecourt, killing two and injuring 27. On 9th October York Road station was hit, although traffic was not affected. At King's Cross Goods, UXBs disrupted work on 2nd, 11th and 21st October (when Outwards traffic had to be diverted to the Inwards shed), and then on the morning of 9th November major damage was suffered there, with 28 people being killed (10 bodies not being found in the wreckage until several days later) and 102 injured. Further extensive damage was sustained by the Outwards shed and No.1 Office in raids on 13th and 15th November, and on 30th January 1941 - nine people being injured on that occasion.

On the night of 17th April 1941 - in London's worst raid of the war, Farringdon Goods station was destroyed in the fires, but apart from relatively minor damage suffered on 15-16th November 1940, 12th January and 17th April 1941, King's Cross passenger station was spared (although bombs fell in the Milk Yard) - until the night of 10-11th May. At 03.15 on that night, HE smashed about 75 feet of the west side of the main station roof between the booking-hall and the footbridge, killing five staff and eight soldiers in the RTO's office. On No.10 platform, the booking-office and its entire stock of tickets - but not the cash, secure in a safe - buffets, stores and many Headquarters offices were all destroyed. One engine (N2 No.4761) and fifteen vehicles on No.10 and the adjoining track were damaged. Roof girders fell across platform lines 6, 7, 8 and 10, and more of the west wall was in danger of collapsing, but the station was partially reopened in 24 hours; it took two weeks to effect repairs sufficient to allow Platforms 7 and 8 to be used. A temporary booking-office was established in the Georgian tea-room, and the latter substituted by a buffet car at the buffers of Platform 10. The great hole in the roof was not repaired until over a year after the end of the war, and while this was being done the roof was again extensively damaged - by a *fire*.

(left) **King's Cross Goods: bomb damage to the Outwards side, 9th November 1940. The sign says: "Beware of Moving Wagons".** *GNR Soc.*

(opposite, left) **A composite view of platform 10 at King's Cross, showing the still smouldering debris surrounding N2 No.4761 (which survived to become BR 69540), after the night of 10-11 May 1941.** *GNR Soc.*

(opposite, right) **King's Cross: the gap on the west side made by the bombing of 11th May 1941, as seen from the west on 7th July 1941. The middle wall is shored-up awaiting more permanent repair which until it was carried out kept two valuable platform roads out of use. Other signs of the times include the RAF airman, the NER milk van (probably for the traffic from Leyburn) and the pigeon baskets.** *Herbert/Duffell.*

(left) **King's Cross Goods: further bomb damage to the Outwards side, 9th November 1940.** *GNR Soc.*

(opposite, bottom) **King's Cross, platform 10 later in the day of the 11th May after an HE bomb fell through the Western Offices and exploded in the main booking hall at 03.15 on the awful night of 10-11 May 1941, killing 13 (staff and soldiers). Some clearing of the debris had begun from the time that the photograph above left had been taken but still the effect of a 500 lb HE bomb exploding on the ground floor, bringing down the great roof and the Western Offices, can be appreciated. Notice, in the background, that the roof of St Pancras station is also severely damaged.** *GNR Soc.*

(left) **King's Cross, York Road: view looking across from the locomotive yard to where a bomb demolished the station buildings (but not the air-raid shelter) adjoining York Road itself during the night 9-10th October 1940.** *GNR Soc.*

Men hard at work filling the large crater left after a German rocket (V-2) exploded at Palmers Green station at 18.45 hr. during the evening rush-hour of 26th October 1944. There was *very nearly* terrible carnage, for the 18.20 Finsbury Park - Hertford North was just departing full of 'commuters' and was only 150 feet from the explosion -near where N2 No.2679 (BR 69585) is with a train in this picture, which was taken the next day when a shuttle service was being run from Wood Green (see locomotive at the other end). However, Norman Crump, in his 1947 book about the LNER in the war, *By Rail to Victory*, has left an element of mystery about what really happened. He wrote "Like Dr. Watson I must maintain a certain discretion. For example, many years must elapse before it becomes possible to tell the story of the Palmers Green Rocket, the Foreign Railway Delegation, and the Volga Boat Song. That must remain locked up in the vaults of the bank, together with Dr. Watson's notes on the politician, the lighthouse and the trained cormorant." Sherlock Holmes devotees may be able to solve that riddle, but the author for one remains mystified. Surely a Down train leaving the station would have been quite severely damaged, but according to the official records (supported by photographs) the locomotive was "undamaged" and the coaches suffered no more than broken windows and a hole in the roof caused by the falling back of a large lump of clay. Casualties are recorded as "11 injured" no more explicit than that. The Ministry of Home Security Incident Report shows in photographs a number of houses very badly damaged in the adjoining roads. The report adds that an Up train was approaching, "but was able to stop 100 yards from the explosion." It all makes one realize that train drivers - even more than the rest of us - carried on, not knowing when they might run into a crater or when something awesome would drop on them out of the blue and wipe them out. *C.C.Herbert/NRM.*

(*opposite, top*) **Finsbury Park: bomb damage during the night of 8-9th October 1940 by the north end of the station at the corner of Stroud Green Road and Wells Terrace; the bridge in the middle distance carried the branch to Finsbury Park Goods Depot.**

(*opposite, centre*) **Finsbury Park: a view north-west from the railway bridge, showing complete blockage of Stroud Green Road, 9th October 1940.**

(*opposite, bottom*) **Finsbury Park: evidence of a near miss to the main ECML bridge over Stroud Green Road at the north end of the station.** *All GNR Soc.*

New Southgate: bomb damage in the Up coal yard during the night 15-16th November 1940; the view is southward, the station being beyond the bridge faintly visible in the murk. *GNR Soc.*

continued from page 149-

Traffic on the Widened Lines and/or to Moorgate was suspended for many hours or days - even weeks - on many occasions during the Blitz, by bombs, debris, fires, also flooding and derailments. Indeed, Moorgate and Aldersgate stations were so completely destroyed that the suburban service from Moorgate was suspended from October 1940 for the duration of the war. King's Cross Metropolitan station was struck on 9th March 1941, and on the night of 10th May bombs penetrated through St Pancras main station down to the Midland connecting line to the Metropolitan, and others also severely damaged the Circle line just west of King's Cross. As a result it was $2^1/2$ months before any LMSR trains could run through onto the Widened Lines, and almost *five* months before the Circle line was reopened through from Euston Square.

Broad Street station was closed when the viaduct between Shoreditch and Dalston Junction was severed in a raid on 13th October 1940, followed on the next night by further damage at Canonbury. Broad Street station was out of action until 11th November, but all lines were not restored until February 1942. All services, except those to Poplar, had been restored progressively by mid-January 1941, but the LMS steam suburban trains to the GN suburbs were never reinstated. The terminus was again isolated for a few days after bomb damage to the viaduct at Haggerston on the night of 16th April 1941.

At Holloway, on the evening of 12th October 1940 much damage was caused to buildings, coaches and wagons in Clarence Yard; two men were killed, and the Down Goods and Carriage lines were blocked for 21 hours. Then on the evening of 14th October first the cattle pens were hit at 19.35, the bombs penetrating down to the Piccadilly Line tunnel, and an hour or so later much damage was caused by HE that fell on an Up coal train, when also two passenger trains were damaged; two people were injured in the 19.30 from Hertford North as it passed, and the debris blocked all Up lines. Most lines were cleared within 21 hours, but it took over a week to restore normal working. The Caledonian Road coal depot was struck on 8th November, and on the night of 11th January 1941 a DAB fell at Holloway South and all traffic - including that on the Piccadilly Tube line - was interrupted for 13 hours until the bomb had exploded; full normal working was not restored until nearly six days later.

Just down the line in the area of Finsbury Park there were a number of incidents. Firstly, at midnight on 26th September 1940 a land-mine fell near the station without exploding and all traffic was suspended until the next evening. Next, on the evening of 29th September a bridge was damaged near the station and all lines were blocked for an hour, normal traffic not being restored for 11 hours. Then in the evening of 8th October the station itself was struck at the north end of the Down side, damaging the 20.20 Down local from King's Cross standing at No.8 platform. Five railwaymen and two others were killed and eight injured, and debris blocked Down Slow lines Nos.1 and 2 for 36 hours. The station was further damaged early on 15th October. In the evening of 10th October a goods train was hit on the Down Canonbury line next to No.1 Box, damaging the engine and blocking the line for 12 hours, and Ashburton Grove and East Goods Yards were closed on account of UXBs. On the night of 13th October, 25 wagons of meat which would normally have been unloaded at Farringdon were hit in Clarence Yard. The Up Canonbury loop was blocked by debris for seven hours on 8th November, and on the nights of 19th March and 10th May 1941 both Canonbury lines were blocked for 14 hours by overbridge damage. In the Fire Raid of 29th December 1940, apart from the Widened Lines once again being blocked by burning buildings all around, the Down Goods lines between Finsbury Park and Harringay were blocked for 16 hours by debris.

The Ferme Park/Hornsey area was struck several times. On the night of 1st October 1940, virtually all traffic was stopped for 12 hours after a DAB was found, while another bomb cracked the flyover viaduct. In the early afternoon of 3rd November a bomb wrecked the footbridge at the north end of Hornsey station, forming a crater across all the Up lines, which were severed for 24 - 48 hours. Then at midnight on the following night a bomb fell in the Down yard, injuring three men, damaging an engine, and seriously impeding yard work for several days, while on 29th December the Down Slow line was damaged by an AA shell.

Further down the line, at Wood Green on 5th October a bomb fell at the 'Khyber Pass' a little before 11 p.m., causing the Down Slow, Goods and Enfield lines to be blocked for 20 hours. The station-master at New Southgate was bombed out shortly before noon on 27th October, and then tragically he was killed (and four men were injured) when working in the goods yard there on the morning of 16th November and a DAB exploded; much damage was caused to signalling and for five days trains had to be hand-signalled. A UXB fell by the line at New Barnet in the early hours of 20th September, suspending all traffic for three hours, and early the next morning more were suspected between Potters Bar and Brookmans Park - and an empty train was sent along to investigate (!). The signalbox at New Barnet was hit just after midnight on 18-19th March 1941, two men were injured and traffic was interrupted for 13 hours. On 9th October in the early hours, bombs nearby affected Hadley Wood North Tunnel - but trains were allowed to pass through after being diverted for three hours. Potters Bar station was damaged in the evening of 26th February 1941.

Strangely, traffic was interrupted - often for at least 12 hours - by enemy action more frequently on the Hertford Loop than on the corresponding stretch of the main line, there being no less than nine occasions during the nine months of the Blitz, and isolated ones later, Enfield Chase station sustaining extensive damage on 15th November 1940. The High Barnet, Edgware and Alexandra Palace branches were blocked for many hours on at least six occasions; on 25th September 1940 a bomb by the signalbox at Finchley Central caused interruption of LPTB trains for four hours, and Cranley Gardens station was badly damaged on 15th November. On the evening of 19th April 1941 a bomb cracked the north end of the new Northern Line Tube tunnel at Highgate, and then an hour later another bomb demolished the tunnel mouth. The branch was blocked again after HE landed at Park Junction in the late evening of 7th October 1943. Each of the other branches off the ECML in the King's Cross District was affected by bombing incidents at some time, the Hitchin - Cambridge line being hit and blocked on two occasions in September - November 1940.

Down the ECML in Hertfordshire, bombs fell on or near the railway at Hatfield on 14th September 1940, but damage (if any) was not recorded. Welwyn Garden City had several incidents: traffic was interrupted by a UXB for eight hours on the morning of 3rd October, and immediately after that a DAB exploded, damaging the signalling. Three days later all lines there were blocked by debris for 14 hours. Then on 30th October an exploding AA shell made a large crater in the Down Slow line, which took 12 hours to repair. Lastly, on 2nd November three UXBs fell near the Up side, and Up and Hertford line traffic between Hatfield and Welwyn Garden City was diverted for some hours.

Early in 1944 the Germans attacked London again, albeit on a smaller scale, giving it what was called the Little Blitz. The most important incident affecting the ECML occurred at Canonbury on the North London line in the early hours of 19th February, when HE caused a blockage that took no less than 58 hours to clear. There were four occasions when traffic on the Hertford loop was interrupted for several hours, and damage on the SR halted freight exchange on several occasions, whereas on the ECML itself there were few incidents. On 22nd January, incendiaries on the line at Hadley Wood interrupted traffic for an hour and then a UXB caused interruption of passenger trains (freight went on running at 5 m.p.h.) for 36 hours. Two UXBs fell in the area of King's Cross Shed and Goods yard on 19th February but did not cause much disruption, and there was a certain amount of damage at New Southgate on 20th February and at Wood Green Tunnel on 25th February. Our defences were now very powerful, and from the AA barrage one shell blocked the exit from Hornsey engine shed on the night of 22nd February, and another on 1st March destroyed the offices at the King's Cross Potato Market.

German Flying Bomb (V1) and Rocket (V2) offensives (June 1944 - March 1945)

The GN section of the LNER bore its share also during this later time. Although the damage caused was considerable, disruption of traffic was a good deal less than in the Blitz, when there had been so many UXBs to contend with and also the exigencies of yard work at night when the lights were turned off in 'Alerts'. With South London receiving so many of the V1s, as in the Blitz the SR lines were cut several times, causing problems with interchange freight traffic. Individual incidents on the ECML and its branches were as follows.

On 26th June 1944 at lunchtime, buildings at Kings Cross Goods were damaged. On 4th July in the evening - a V1 blast near Finsbury Park station caused interruption of signalling on the Down line to Harringay, but this was restored by midnight. On 14th August at 07.00 a V1 fell in St Pancras Junction coal bays, causing extensive blast damage at Kings Cross Goods, six men and a horse being injured. On 10th October in the early morning, a V1 near Hatfield station damaged No.3 Box and interrupted signalling to Welwyn Garden City; trains had to be hand-signalled for over three hours. On 26th October the Hertford line was blocked by a V2 that exploded at the end of the Up platform at Palmers Green - just as the 18.20 Finsbury Park - Hertford North was about to leave. Eleven passengers were injured and the line was blocked for 24 hours, local passenger trains being cut back with shuttles between Hertford and Winchmore Hill, and Wood Green and Palmers Green, the gap being covered by buses. On the morning of 10th November, a V1 at Hornsey goods yard severely damaged buildings, but there was no interruption of traffic. On 1st December in the early evening, a V2 rocket exploded close to Muswell Hill station, doing extensive damage and blocking the Alexandra Palace branch, which was not reopened until 48 hours later.

On 13th January 1945 in the early hours, a V2 rocket exploded right on the main lines 200 yards south of Wood Green. All lines except No.2 Down Slow (the 'Khyber Pass') were blocked. The station, four signal-boxes and 55 carriages in the sidings were seriously damaged. Before mid-morning No.1 Down Slow was repaired and used for Up traffic, which was sent over to the Up by the flyover at Ferme Park, Up night expresses suffering massive delays as a result. Down suburban services were cancelled and Up local services reversed at New Southgate or Bowes Park. Six of the eight running lines were back in use before the evening rush, and suburban services were reinstated from Kings Cross starting with the 17.35 - a good example of the efficiency and hard work that was normally shown by the Engineering Department staff in the war to restore normal working as quickly as possible. On 17th January about midday, a rocket in the vicinity of Moleswood Tunnel followed soon after by a second explosion, although doing no damage to track cut No.2 Control circuits and severed all telephone communication between Hertford North and Watton-at-Stone. On 25th January at first light, a rocket explosion damaged Gordon Hill station. Finally in Central London, the rocket that landed on the crowded Farringdon Market in mid-morning on 8th March, causing great carnage, seriously damaged the goods station and retaining walls, and the depot was closed for two weeks.

YORK

On the night of 28th April 1942, as one of their retaliatory Baedeker raids, which were not on the scale of the Blitz and involved less than 100 raiders, the Luftwaffe went to York. They not only caused great damage in the city, but also this time turmoil on the railway. At about 02.30, the station was struck by HE smashing through the roof of Platforms 2 and 3, and showers of incendiaries fell, starting major fires that destroyed the booking, telegraph, parcels and stationmaster's offices. Unfortunately, the 22.15 Kings Cross - Edinburgh *NIGHT SCOTSMAN* was in the station, and the middle six of its 20 carriages - an unremarkable length in those days - were burnt out, together with stock at adjoining platforms. The *NIGHT SCOTSMAN* had been in the station for some seven minutes before it was hit, and there had been time for passengers to take shelter - although many did not. Courageous and prompt action by the station staff enabled the other 14 coaches to be drawn clear, and for much valuable property to be saved from the fires.

Clifton carriage sidings were severely damaged, Leeman Road coal depot was wrecked and the Civil Engineer's shops were set on fire, as were also the stables - but the horses were saved. Last but not least, at the main locomotive depot, No.4 shed received a direct hit that ravaged A4 No.4469 and B16/1 No.925 quite beyond repair. (O4 No.6283 was also badly damaged, and J39 No.3095 less severely). The damage extended to Nos.1 and 3 sheds, and 20 locomotives were damaged in some way and 50 imprisoned. Fifteen coaches at York were destroyed and 220 damaged. Human casualties on the railway (passengers and railwaymen) were 4 killed and 81 injured. On top of all this, the main line to the North and the Harrogate branch were blocked at Skelton Junction.

No traffic was able to pass through the station until the morning of 30th April, when Platform 8 was available for Down trains[1]. Freight was stopped entirely and passenger traffic was diverted *via* Church Fenton and Harrogate to/from Thirsk, until 18.00 on 29th April. After that just one Down and Up line were made available on the Goods lines, by which time most of the passenger trains and half the normal freight trains were passing York - by the Goods lines. In spite of the great damage - and six UXBs remaining on Railway property, immense hard work and improvisation enabled traffic to move again fairly freely in a remarkably short time, normality being restored by 3rd May. Later in 1942, on 17th December, damage was done by bombs to the power supply at Foss Islands Goods depot - but this may have been accidental, from 'one of Ours'.

Restoration of the buildings destroyed in the April raid naturally took time: it was a year before temporary (flat) canopies were put up over Platforms 8 and 9. Initially, refreshments were served in the former left-luggage and parcels offices, then a combined dining/tea room was restored and the former tea room converted to a staff canteen. As soon as possible a temporary parcels office (with new electric hoist from the subway) and a left-luggage office were built, and the telegraph office was re-housed in the HQ Building[2]. After the war, in 1948 the roof spans were repaired, rather than being demolished, and so remain today.

This raid naturally gave rise to a number of reports and correspondence, and the annexed letter opposite is illuminating.

NEWCASTLE AREA

The first serious damage to the LNER in the north-east during the war had been at Sunderland, where the station was largely destroyed in a sharp raid on 6th September 1940. In 1941, on the night of 9th April considerable damage was done at North Shields, Monkseaton, Jarrow, South Shields and Tyne Dock between 22.00 and midnight, electric stock being severely damaged, lines blocked and services interrupted. On the night of 25th April, Sunderland and the Tyneside towns below Newcastle were heavily attacked, but serious damage was done to the railways only at South Blyth, where the station and shed were largely destroyed; a bomb fell in the yards at Heaton, the Blyth & Tyne was blocked between Seghill and Seaton Delaval, and damage was done at Tynemouth then - and on several other occasions. Then again, on the night of 30th September, the passenger and goods stations at North Shields were severely damaged - albeit fortunately with no casualties, and on the night of 2nd October South Shields had a sharp raid and damage was done to the railway there, at other places on the coast, at Wallsend and between Benton and Backworth. Relatively minor damage, including at St Peters on the Riverside line, was done in small raids on the nights of 29th December 1941, of 30th April 1942, and again on the night of 12th March 1943. Sunderland station was hit again in small raids on 14th March and 16th May 1943. Also off the ECML itself, the Coast line was blocked at West Hartlepool on both 4th and 8th May 1941, while Middlesbrough station (and V1 class No.416 on an empty train) were badly damaged in a brief daylight raid on 3rd August 1942, with two people being killed and 13 seriously injured.

The railways in Newcastle itself suffered most on the night of 1st September 1941 (from 22.15 until 23.00), when a sharp raid by a mere 28 German bombers caused disproportionate damage. The large New Bridge Street Goods warehouse was hit, and it was completely destroyed by an enormous fire that burned fiercely for three days; 5,200 tons of goods, including 2,000 tons of flour were consumed by fire, and four people were killed and three injured. However, they managed to save 33 wagon loads, containing "bicarbonate, potatoes, Horlick's product, biscuits, oil *etc.*, 300 packages of hams, Andrews' salts, syrup and glass, and two trailer loads of tobacco and apples." At least one of several courageous and resourceful men received official Commendations for their actions that night. Temporary repairs were undertaken in 1943, to enable the goods station to be of use again for 'smalls' traffic in case Forth Goods was bombed - which fortunately it was not. The New Bridge St. depot was not fully restored after the war, its pre-war traffic having been principally from Newcastle Quayside and the amount of trade through there remained restricted after the war.

Meanwhile on 1st September a bomb at Argyle Street badly damaged the signalbox, and other bombs damaged the signalbox

Caption to the letter opposite - **This communication from the NE Area Divisional General Manager to the Chief General Manager reveals quite a lot about the contrasts between heroism and pettiness that characterize the behaviour of people in wartime - or other - emergencies. The letters Mr. Jenkin Jones was rebuffing had complained about how badly some passengers had been treated by Railway staff when the Down *NIGHT SCOTSMAN* encountered that raid on York.**

THE DIVISIONAL GENERAL MANAGER   (N.E. Area)
LONDON & NORTH EASTERN RAILWAY
YORK

13th May 1942

THE CHIEF GENERAL MANAGER.

DAMAGE BY ENEMY ACTION AT YORK, 29TH APRIL 1942.

I am obliged to Mr.Corble for letting me see Mr.Cole Deacon's letter to Mr.Bell and also a copy of his letter to Sir Alan Mount.

I have also received Miss Gifford's letter to Mr.Mather, which I return, and the copy of Lt.Commander G.I.Clark Hutchison's letter to Mr.Noel Baker, which we have received by telephone.

I think that most of the points in both these letters are covered by my report of the 8th May dealing with the letters of Mr.Boothby and Mr.Henderson Stewart. It may, however, be convenient if I recapitulate the facts briefly in relation to each letter.

Taking first of all Lt. Commander Hutchison's letter:-
(1) The siren did not sound after the train had drawn into the station, but about 13 minutes before its arrival.
(2) The first bomb fell in the neighbourhood of the station not 20 minutes after the arrival of the train, but 7 minutes after, and the direct hit was obtained on the station 32 minutes after the train's arrival.
(3) The Assistant Station Master and a Station Inspector ran the whole length of the train (20 vehicles) immediately on its arrival and advised passengers to alight and take cover. Two policemen were on the platform to guide passengers to shelters. Later, the guard is stated to have advised passengers who did not leave the train to lie down on the floor.
(4) The majority of the passengers left the train immediately they were advised to do so and certainly none of them lay down between the lines and the platform.
(5) The shelters in York Station provide accommodation for 1,048 people; accommodation for over 500 being either immediately adjacent or comparatively close to the train in question.
(6) Loud Speakers. The Assistant Station Master who was in charge of the station, tells me that on the arrival of the train he considered whether he should make announcement by the loud speakers but came to the conclusion - I think rightly - that it would give more confidence to the passengers if he and the Inspector actually went on to the platform so that they could advise them in person.
(7) It is the general policy of all the Railway Companies to keep passenger trains moving after air raid alerts. In this case the train would in the normal course have proceeded from York Station, but this was rendered impossible by damage to the line immediately to the North. In actual fact, the passengers were probably far safer in the station than they would have been outside, and the injuries to only three of them are stated to have been serious.
(8) It is not our practice to lock any of the carriage doors.

With regard to Miss Gifford's letter:-
(1) Passengers were advised what they should do to the best of the station staff's ability.
(2) The shelters were not inadequate and there is no evidence that any of them became uncomfortably hot. If they did so, there would have been nothing to prevent passengers leaving them, especially as no bombs fell on the station after the attack which caused the fires.
(3) Some passengers (certainly not the majority) found their way to the Hotel where the staff did every-thing possible for them, especially having regard to the fact that their supply of gas and water had been cut off. The statement that only one member of the First-aid detachment worked long and well is absurd. Many members of the staff performed very meritorious service in dressing passengers' injuries, and one man lost his life while fetching additional equipment for this purpose. About 75 people altogether were given First-aid treatment, and according to my information none of them have succumbed to their injuries.
(4) The staff did very well to get a train away from York Station by 8 o'clock in the morning, and Leeds was clearly the most advantageous point to send passengers for further distribution in any direction. It is very unfortunate that passengers should have undergone the long journey to Edinburgh without food, but if they did so I think they, rather than the Railway Company, must bear the greater portion of the blame. It must be borne in mind that telephonic communication with York Station was entirely cut off, and that the normal arrangements which might have been made for the comfort of passengers were quite impossible. It is surely not too much, in all the circumstances, to suggest that passengers themselves could have made enquiry at Leeds or during some subsequent stage of their journey whether any arrangements were being made to provide food, in which case something would, no doubt, have been done. Alternatively, they could easily have left the train either at Leeds, Darlington or Newcastle and obtained any food they needed and pro-ceeded on their journey by a later service. It must be borne in mind that all the staff in York Station were devoting the whole of their energies to matters of extreme urgency and that the provision made in the City for air raid victims was fully extended in dealing with inhabitants of York who had suffered far more severely than the passengers in York Station. I think that the general reply to the burden of Miss Gifford's letter is that in wartime, and particularly during active operations, passengers cannot expect the usual attention from railway staffs and must be prepared to a considerable extent to use their own initiative.

(Sgd.) C.M.JENKIN JONES.

The 'classic' official view of the 'shambles' at York on the morning after the air-raid of 28th-29th April 1942. The view is southwards from the footbridge. The remains of the burnt-out coaches from the middle of the Down *NIGHT SCOTSMAN* stand at platform 9. *LNER/Armstrong coll.*

and the platforms at Manors North. A UXB at Manors North put all lines north and east from Central out of commission until the evening of 2nd September, when two of the four lines towards Heaton were reopened. Some ECML traffic was then able to go north to Morpeth *via* Tynemouth. In addition Jesmond station was badly damaged and the line blocked, as was the Riverside line at Carville for four to five days. Manors North reopened at 18.00 on 3rd September, and traffic was running normally by the evening of 5th September. On 2nd September, 16 passenger and 27 freight trains on the ECML to or from Edinburgh were diverted *via* Carlisle - and also *via* North Wylam for 10½ hours until debris had been cleared at Blaydon. Between 2nd and 4th September four Up passenger trains and five Up and seven Down freight trains were diverted *via* Carlisle and the LMSR (Settle & Carlisle line to the Leeds area, and/or Caledonian routes). The LNER was singularly unlucky in such an otherwise small raid, and the congestion was cleared only by the evening of 8th September.

MISCELLANEOUS ENEMY ATTACKS on or near the ECML

From the outset, coastal towns were particularly susceptible to 'tip-and-run' raids, as was the ECML. These began once the 'Phoney War' was over in the summer of 1940. The initial incidents at Darlington and Newcastle have been mentioned,

and these were followed by similar ones at Ferryhill on 6th and 7th July 1940, between West Monkseaton and Backworth where bombs slightly damaged the track on 8th July, and at Portobello on 4th August. Thereafter, there were many relatively minor incidents throughout the war on or near the ECML, as follows.

1940: On the night of 24th August, bombs fell close to the ECML at Highdyke, causing slight damage. During the night of 29-30th August, UXBs were reported near the ECML at Stannington and traffic was diverted *via* Backworth and Newsham. On the night of 13th October, HE landed on the Up side at Everton Box (near Sandy), and the Up lines were blocked for six hours. On the afternoon of 23rd October, an overbridge was damaged and a water-main burst at Spitalgate (Grantham), blocking all lines but only for 20 minutes after which the Up Goods line was usable, normal working being restored in four hours. In the evening of 27th October, all lines at Alne were blocked after a bomb landed on a York - Newport special goods train; all traffic was diverted *via* Ripon and Church Fenton for over six hours. On 4th December in the afternoon, a DAB exploded at Grantham, causing damage to sidings and killing a platelayer.

1941: On the evening of 5th January, several bombs at Darlington caused extensive damage to Stooperdale Boiler Shop, Faverdale Wagon Works, and to the Paint and other Shops; there was also a problem at the Works with UXBs. On 15th January at

Further devastation at York station on the morning of 29th April 1942: bay platforms 3 and 2, which received a direct hit from a high-explosive bomb, and the parcels office area gutted by fire. *Appleby coll.*

22.45, in a minor raid on Peterborough, bombs fell on the main line between New England North and Werrington Junction, causing interruption of traffic on the Down Main, Goods, and Engine lines for over three hours. The south end of New England locomotive yard was also hit, two large cranes and a locomotive were derailed and three locomotives damaged, and the Mineral Office was badly damaged. In the yards 112 wagons were damaged, and the Locomotive and Empties Yards were blocked for 42 hours; Wisbech Sidings Box was also heavily damaged by a bomb. In all that night one railwayman was killed and 14 injured. ECML trains were diverted *via* the Joint line for about four hours, and access to New England locomotive depot was restored by the evening of 16th January. The Peterborough area also received attention on 30th January, when the M&GN line was completely blocked by HE at Eye Green, and only restored after four days.

Late on 15th January, the Up Main and Goods lines between Grantham and Great Ponton were cut by HE, for nine hours. In the afternoon of 19th February, HE hit a stationary goods train (of *chocolate* from Rowntree's to Faslane Military Port) at Sessay Wood, causing blockage of the Down lines for six hours. As there was then only one Up line at that point, much traffic had to be diverted - and this was also the time of the Great Blizzard. On 7th March in the early afternoon, the South Junction Box and the station at Newark suffered some damage, but traffic was not interrupted. On 8th March, following a 'sneak' raid at lunchtime, traffic on the main line was interrupted by a UXB at Longhoughton; for five hours traffic was diverted to other lines, but at least one main line express was diverted at Alnmouth onto the Alnwick and Wooler branch and so to Tweedmouth *via* Coldstream. On 15th March, Langford Box (near Biggleswade) was damaged and communication cut. On 1st April, Christon Bank Box was damaged by blast, but was repaired in 44 hours and traffic was not interrupted. On 8th April in the very early hours, the Up and Down Main and Up Independent lines were blocked at Annitsford for three hours and trains diverted onto the B&T. On 10th April in the early hours, during the fairly major raid mainly affecting the North and South Shields areas, the station at Low Fell was set on fire, delaying traffic.

On 16th April, the 07.20 York - Pickering local was derailed when its engine fell into a bomb crater at Coxwold; three staff were injured, and the line was blocked for 14 hours. On 25th April in the late evening, debris blocked the main and electric lines at Heaton for two hours, and electric stock was damaged;

an electricity sub-station was destroyed by a bomb on the same night at Benton. On 4th May just after midnight, seven wagons were damaged at Gateshead; soon afterwards a bomb fell near the High Level Bridge and traffic had to be diverted for five hours. Towards midnight on 2nd May, HE fell close to the line at Barnby (near Newark), cutting communications and forcing diversions for a few hours. On 9th May in the very early hours, Retford station suffered slight damage; on the 10th May a UXB was found at Burnmouth in the morning and traffic had to be diverted for 8 hours *via* Kelso or *via* Carlisle. On 3rd June, slight damage was caused at Tweedmouth shed in the early hours. On 14th June in the early morning, traffic was interrupted at Northallerton and at Pilmoor for several hours by damage to the signalling. Early on 9th July, the lines were blown out at Honington, and Colwick - Whitemoor traffic had to be diverted onto the ECML. Two days later HE landing between Werrington Junction and Essendine caused damage to signalling and some interruption of traffic, while on 15th July Grantham also received some attention but damage then was slight. On 13th August, the Down Main at Alnmouth was severed by HE during the morning, and a UXB was suspected for a while and traffic disrupted. In the afternoon of 17th August machine-gunning at Innerwick damaged a bridge, the main line was blocked for six hours and traffic diverted *via* Carlisle; one workman was killed and seven injured. In the very early hours of 13th September, a goods train ran into a bomb crater near Knitsley on the Durham - Consett line; the line was blocked for nine hours. In the late evening of 7th November, a bomb landed near the line between East Linton and Dunbar, severing the telegraph. Lastly, on the morning of 21st November, bombs exploded on the line at Goswick, severely damaging the signalbox. In addition, the locomotive (C7 No.2207) and first coach of the 06.45 Newcastle - Berwick were damaged; three passengers were injured, and on account of suspected UXBs traffic was diverted *via* Coldstream or *via* Carlisle for a time.

1942: On 4th January, Tweedmouth station and signalbox were severely damaged by HE; three men were killed and four injured, but the main line was not blocked and normal working

continued on page 162.

AIR RAID PRECAUTIONS
IF THE EMERGENCY COMES
ALWAYS KEEP RESPIRATORS HANDY

WHEN AN AIR RAID ALARM is sounded:

1. As both Passenger and Freight trains will continue to run during Air Raids, it is essential that such staff as is necessary to deal with them en route, at Stations, in Yards, at Motive Power Depots and at other points concerned with train movement shall remain on duty.
All other staff—TAKE COVER.

2. Ensure that no lights are visible to aircraft, and avoid use of matches or unscreened electric torches in the open.

3. PRECAUTIONS AGAINST POISON GAS.
Remember that any cover which will keep out ordinary rain will also protect you from the rain of LIQUID POISON GAS.
IF CAUGHT IN THE OPEN, put on RESPIRATOR.
Remember that Liquid Gas falling in your eyes will blind you, so do not look up unless protected by a respirator, until half an hour has passed since the " RAIDERS PASSED " signal.

   If any unusual odour is noticed, such as mustard, geranium, garlic, etc., characteristic of POISON GAS, put on RESPIRATOR whether under cover or not.

   IF YOU SUSPECT LIQUID GAS has fallen on your clothes, REMOVE YOUR OUTER CLOTHING as soon as practicable, if possible at a CLEANSING CENTRE.

4. REMEMBER that if you are contaminated, you are a DANGER to OTHERS until your clothing has been removed and you yourself cleansed AND FOR YOUR OWN SAKE IMMEDIATE ACTION is necessary to avoid serious results.

5. AFTER THE RAID—AVOID TOUCHING ANYTHING in a contaminated area, unless protected by protective clothing or bleach ointment.

6. KEEP CALM—If the instructions are adhered to, these precautions will guard you from injury from Poison Gas.

FURTHER PRECAUTIONS OF A LESS URGENT NATURE.

THE DANGERS FROM AIR RAIDS MAY BE DIVIDED INTO TWO CATEGORIES

The chilling notice prepared in May 1939, well in advance of hostilities, and issued soon after the outbreak of the war.

SECRECY OF MILITARY MOVEMENTS.   9/2/40

     The War Office state that instances have been reported of military troop trains bearing destination labels and of goods wagons being chalked with overseas addresses of the consignments they contain.   In some cases these marks have been made by the military forwarding depots, all of which have been warned by the War Office against this practice.

     The attention of Railway staff dealing with military traffic is drawn to the fact that any destination markings which are not strictly necessary must be avoided, and if such markings are found, they should be erased.

     It is also imperative that there should be absolute secrecy in regard to overseas movements.
                                                                T/7.

AIR RAID PRECAUTIONS : LIGHTING RESTRICTIONS :
     CALLING OUT OF STATION NAMES.

     An improvement is necessary in the manner in which the announcement of station names is made, and the following instructions must be observed:-
                                                                6/3/40

     Train Attendants must walk along the whole of the train immediately before arrival at a station and announce that the next station at which the train will stop is.........

     Station staff must call out the name of the station loudly and clearly.

     Sleeping Car trains - station staff must go up to the compartment vehicles and announce quietly name of station.
                                                                T4/91882.W.

Internal LNER documents issued in early 1940. The confusion caused by the state of hostilities in the early days of the war must have been incredible for passengers and railway staff alike, but the railways managed to keep going no matter what disruption was caused.

An A.R.P. poster issued in September 1940 by the LNER indicating where air raid shelter accomodation was available on certain station premises in the London area.

LONDON AND NORTH EASTERN RAILWAY.

District Superintendent's Office,
BLANKNEY.

CONFIDENTIAL

15th November, 1939.

G. Emg.Pad.
15.11.39.

AIR RAID DAMAGE - INFORMATION TO THE
PRESS AND PUBLIC.

The question has been raised as to the procedure to be followed in the event of Railways sustaining damage through air raids, in informing the Press and public of necessary service adjustments.

It has been decided that no statement should be made to the Press as to the nature or location of any damage, but notices may be exhibited at stations, and information communicated to the Press regarding service adjustments which may be necessary for the convenience of the travelling public.

The usual notices exhibited at stations in the event of a breakdown will meet requirements, and it should be noted that information shown on such notices when brought into use consequent on air raid damage must be limited to what appears at present, and must not refer in any way to air raid action.

Please note, arrange accordingly and acknowledge receipt.

for DISTRICT SUPERINTENDENT.

A.

LONDON AND NORTH EASTERN RAILWAY.
District Superintendent's Office,
BLANKNEY.   28th April 1944.

G.Emerg.Pad.2/35.

LANDING OF ENEMY AGENTS.

At the present stage of the war it is considered there is reason to suppose that an intensification of effort on the part of the enemy to land agents illegally in this country is likely to occur.

Such agents if successfully landed, whether by parachute or on the coast by small boat, or by other methods, are likely, if not immediately apprehended, to make their way by rail or road to London or some populous centre where they may have contacts and facilities for maintaining themselves undetected.

A notice on these lines will be inserted in the next issue of the Permanent Way Programmes. In the meantime please draw the attention of all concerned to Clause (36) of the Booklet "Emergency Arrangements" sent you on 4th August 1942 and remind them at the present juncture the necessity for vigilance.

Where serious suspicion is aroused concerning an individual travelling or about to travel by train or by railway operated bus, the proper authority to which to report is either Special Branch New Scotland Yard, or the local civil police authority best placed to detain such a person for investigation.

for FRANK PROBERT,
DISTRICT SUPERINTENDENT.

(left and above) **Further internal LNER correspondence from the early and latter days of the conflict. Railway enthusiasts of the period had to be careful not to draw attention to themselves when taking numbers. Even observing trains could alert a member of the public to contact the authorities and many enthusiasts 'had their collars felt' by the law. As for taking photographs!**

continued from p.159: resumed within 24 hours. Again, on 10th February in the evening, bombs partially demolished Tweedmouth engine shed, damaging five locomotives and other buildings, and blocked the main line by hitting an overbridge; seven locomen were injured and one shunting locomotive standing near Billindon bridge was damaged. In the early hours of 30th June, incendiaries landed on railway property at Peterborough, setting fire to the Great Northern Hotel and Engineers' Stores, and on 24th July a bomb landed at midnight at Peterborough East but only damaged cables. On the morning of 2nd September, UXBs were discovered at Doncaster station and Decoy Yard; traffic was disrupted until they were made safe.

1943: At Warthill (on the York - Hull line) on the night of 23rd September, several canisters of anti-personnel bombs were dropped by the Enemy close to the station. Most of the bombs failed to explode, but the line had to be closed for nine days before all bombs had been found and disposed of.

1944: On 22nd January in the early morning, as the 21.40 Leeds - Kings Cross express emerged from Potters Bar Tunnel the crew saw incendiaries falling on the line. They stopped and picked them up! However, UXBs were also reported, so trains had to be diverted *via* Hertford North for 26 hours.

Attacks on Moving Trains

Almost throughout the length and breadth of the country but mainly on the eastern side, there were occasions when lone German aircraft attempted to bomb or machine-gun moving trains, especially during the first half of the war. Indeed there were also instances when British or Allied aircraft shot up trains, or even dropped bombs - presumably accidentally. Incidents on the ECML included the following.

In the afternoon of 31st October 1940, the locomotive (O4 No.6364) of the 06.44 Worksop - New England freight was shot up at Werrington Junction; damage was confined to puncture of the tender tank, but the driver had to be taken to hospital. On 23rd December 1940 between Essendine and Little Bytham, the 08.00 Newcastle - Kings Cross and the *FLYING SCOTSMAN* (hauled by A4 No.2510 - which suffered a punctured smoke-box) were almost simultaneously gunned; one passenger (a soldier) was killed. On 20th January 1941, the 16.08 Hitchin - King's Cross was gunned (without harm being done) between Hitchin and Stevenage, while near St Neots V2 No.4801 was shot up and its tender holed. On 1st April 1941, B16 No.1384 sustained minor 'gunshot wounds' on a freight at Christon Bank. In the early hours of 7th May 1941, a freight train was gunned at Tuxford North and slightly damaged. In the afternoon of 3rd June 1941, a freight was shot up at Alnmouth and the guard injured. Very early on 14th July 1941, the 18.55 Newcastle - King's Cross was gunned at Langley (near Knebworth); damage was slight, but three Servicemen were injured, also damage was done to two ambulance trains (Casualty Evacuation) stabled in the sidings[3]. In the evening of 10th November 1941, between Marshall Meadows and Burnmouth, V2 No.4886 and D49/2 No.247 on the 09.50 King's Cross - Edinburgh suffered fairly minor damage from aerial gunning, although one of the drivers was injured. Next day the Up *FLYING SCOTSMAN* was machine-gunned at the same place but suffered little damage and no serious casualties.

Finally, on the night of 3rd March 1945 the Luftwaffe had their 'last fling' - OPERATION GISELA, sending 70 fighter-bomber intruders ranging widely over airfields in the East and Midlands. In the course of the operation, the 22.25 Newcastle - Kings Cross was gunned near Temple Hirst soon after midnight, receiving little damage and no injuries. Shortly afterwards, the 00.25 empty stock train from Helmsley to York was gunned between Husthwaite Gate and Sunbeck Junction, killing a relief signalman travelling on it, and at Northallerton 45 minutes later, a freight for Newport Yard was gunned - twice in 15 minutes while taking water - and damaged, as were wagons and buildings in the goods yard.

AIRCRAFT CRASHES and RELATED INCIDENTS on or near the ECML

During the war huge numbers of aircraft crashed in Britain, the great majority of which were 'Ours' - especially bombers taking off or landing in the eastern half of the country, and it is not surprising that some of these crashes affected Railway Company property. While crashes right on the tracks were not infrequent, more often either the line had to be closed while UXBs from a crashed aircraft were dealt with or the aircraft cut the telecommunication equipment. Sometimes bombs jettisoned by Allied aircraft fell on the lines, and Allied planes even occasionally shot up trains. Such pranks were normally forbidden, but at one site on the ECML - Goswick, on the Northumberland coast, superannuated locomotives[4] and coaches in a special siding were *officially* used for practice in the art of 'train-busting', which proved very profitable before and during the Liberation of Europe in 1944.

Barrage balloons proved very susceptible to storms, and when they broke loose they sometimes landed on the railway or more often trailed their cables across the telegraph wires. At Finsbury Park on 11th May 1940 a balloon fell on the roof of the station and in February 1944 one floated down on the great roof of King's Cross.

The following is a compilation of all known incidents on or directly affecting the ECML and of the more serious incidents on its branches, the majority of crashes being at points close to a military airfield. The few cases where the aircraft have been identified here from other sources[5] provide a small sample of the circumstances involved:

1940: In the afternoon of 30th July, a crashing RAF plane cut the telegraph at Baldock. During the night of 16-17th August all lines were blocked between Baldock and Ashwell by a crashed RAF bomber. In the night of 16th September, balloon cables brought down telegraph wires between Doncaster and Arksey, and on 15th October a balloon came down between Escrick and Naburn and blocked the ECML for four hours.

1941: Very early on 8th April, all lines at Little Bytham were blocked for 3½ hours after a Hampden bomber on a training flight was shot down onto the railway by a German night-fighter intruder.

1942: On 25th April, an engine ran into a parachute (believed to be carrying explosives) at Tempsford and remained entangled for 95 minutes. In the afternoon of 12th November, a plane crashed into the embankment at Stukeley, causing interruption of the telegraph. Early on 18th November, the Richmond branch was completely blocked by an RAF plane between Scorton and Moulton. On 20th December, a Spitfire crashed on the Clifton fish stage at York, setting it and three coaches on fire. The pilot was courageously rescued by Driver Imeson; traffic was not affected.

1943: On 8th January at 12.40, between Eaglescliffe and

Dinsdale, the 11.30 Saltburn - Darlington local (hauled by A8 No.1519) ran at over 45 m.p.h. into the burning wreckage of an RCAF 427 Sqn Wellington on transit which had overshot the runway at Middleton St. George Airfield and crashed on the line. To save the passengers, Driver Barber although badly burned drove on and then with Fireman Blunt - who was killed - jumped, and the engine overturned. Yet the line was cleared in 45 minutes. On 26th January at 23.00 hrs. a 466 Sqn Wellington bomber, bound from Leconfield to Lorient, suffered engine failure and crashed at Barnby Moor & Sutton station, but no railway damage was reported. On 29th January shortly before midday, a 51 Sqn. Halifax on test and coming in to land at Burn Airfield[6] crashed on the ECML between Heck and Temple Hirst, killing in their hut one platelayer and injuring three. In the early hours of 5th April, between Alne and Raskelf, the locomotive of the 20.20 Edinburgh - Kings Cross picked up in its water-scoop a *container of incendiaries* believed to be from an RAF bomber; the bombs burned out under the engine and the train was able to continue. On the morning of 10th April, at Temple Hirst - *again*, a plane crash on the ECML cut the telegraph for five hours. Soon after midnight on 14th April, a plane crash on the ECML at Saltersford (Grantham) blocked all lines for several hours. At noon on 17th May a plane crash near Beningbrough station cut the telegraph for three hours. On the morning of 22nd June, a loaded RAF bomber crashed close to the line from Grantham at Bracebridge Brick Siding near Lincoln; the signalbox was evacuated and the line closed for three hours until it was safe. On 29th June in the early hours, an RAF plane crashed in flames on the Up line 30 yards from the signalbox at East Fortune. In the afternoon of 2nd October, two planes collided and fell on the track near Market Weighton station, blocking all lines. In the late evening of 22nd October, the Church Fenton - Harrogate line was blocked for 11 hours between Tadcaster and Newton Kyme after a 427 Sqn. Halifax from Leeming aborted a raid on Kassel and crashed on the Up line and then the other line was blocked by a fire-tender that attended the incident but broke down. Very early on 20th November, a plane crash on the Selby - Market Weighton line at Bubwith blocked the line for 14 hours.

1944. In the afternoon of 20th January, a plane crashed on the ECML between Westwood (Peterborough) and Werrington Junction, blocking both main lines for 10 hours, but traffic was able to pass over the goods lines. In the morning of 23rd February at Haxby (on the York - Scarborough line), a plane crashing into pylons brought them down onto the railway. On the night of 15th April, a Halifax on taking off (probably from Topcliffe airfield) on a night traing flight hit the bridge over the ECML at Sowerby (a mile south of Thirsk) then struck and severly damaged lineside cottages recently rebuilt in connection with the ECML widening, and buried one of its engines in the Up Goods line; apart from the crew of five, three people on the ground were killed. On 7th June, UXB from an RAF bomber held up traffic at Goswick for some hours. From soon after midnight on 17th June the Selby - Goole branch was closed for 2-3 days while a number of UXBs from a crashed Allied aircraft were blown up near Airmyn & Rawcliffe. On 12th August in the morning at Alne, a bomber crashed on fire by the ECML; no bombs exploded, but the telegraph was cut, and all traffic was interrupted and diverted *via* Starbeck until safety from explosions was assured. Early in the evening of 27th August, a fully-laden bomber crashed near the Northallerton - Eaglescliffe line at Welbury; traffic had to be diverted *onto* the ECML for 19

hours until the area was deemed safe. Early in the evening of 9th October at Heck - *once again*, a fully-laden bomber crashed into wagons in a siding; traffic was diverted *via* Knottingley for five hours. In the morning of 18th December, a plane crash blocked one line on the Grantham - Lincoln branch between Caythorpe and Honington. On 24th December in the morning, a USAAF B17 bomber, fully laden with fuel and bombs, crashed on the ECML between Connington and Holme[7]; a signalbox was damaged and the line blocked totally for two hours until UXBs were removed, signalling not being restored for *16 days*.

1945. On 9th February late in the afternoon, a crashing plane cut the telegraph for 8 hours between Connington and Holme *again*. On 24th February early in the afternoon *once again* at Heck, the telegraph was cut by a low-flying plane. In the late afternoon of 5th March, two planes crashed near the ECML at Dringhouses (York); UXBs were suspected on the Down side, so for four hours trains were run only on the Doncaster lines. Shortly before midnight on 14th March, Heck *yet again* witnessed a crash near the ECML; trains were diverted until the line could be declared safe. Finally, in the afternoon of 25th October - after the war was over - a plane crash blocked both lines for several hours between Dunbar and Innerwick.

An incident that caused immense disruption on the railway but no actual casualties was the **explosion in a bomb store at RAF Snaith** at 13.35 on 19th June 1943. The explosion was caused by "airmen disregarding regulations on the handling of explosives in the open", when they were setting fuses. It must have caused pandemonium and there were a number of Service casualties. The windows of Heck signalbox were blown out, and the ceilings came down in the stationmaster's house. Because much ordnance was left in a 'pre-activated state' and the dump was only 500 yards from the ECML Shaftholme Junction - Selby section, the LNER had to divert all passenger traffic *via* Knottingley or Hull for 10 days (albeit goods traffic for only 36 hours), with consequent congestion and delay. From 16.00 on 28th June until 05.30 on the 29th June all traffic had again to be diverted while the RAF deliberately exploded further bombs every 45 minutes. The result of this incident was an extended fuss about the location of bomb dumps near enough to railways to cause damage to trains if the ordnance blew up, and afterwards much more severe restrictions on the siting of bomb dumps were imposed. Nevertheless, subsequently there were several instances across the country of exploding ordnance affecting the railways. Associated with the ECML were the following.

At 17.10 on 8th September 1943, **Hexham station** had to be evacuated after the **accidental explosion of small arms ammunition** - which killed three soldiers engaged in loading it. Much heroism was shown by railway staff who coupled up and removed wagons to comparative safety in case they blew up. The goods station and engine shed were extensively damaged, and trains were not allowed through until midnight.

Then again, just after 16.00 on 4th February 1944, **Catterick Bridge station** was wrecked by an **accidental explosion of bombs**. Eight people were killed (including the stationmaster and two women clerks), and 88 injured (10 staff).

Great heroism was displayed at **Moulton** on the same branch at 05.40 on Sunday 25th March 1945. **Fire** broke out on the 05.00 Darlington - Catterick Camp goods, **loaded with bombs**. Driver T. McLoughlin set the train back to the platform, and he and Fireman J.C. Northcott, Guard M. Campbell, and (Lady) Porter D. Rowe tried to put out the fire with buckets then took the wagons to a safe place. There was *no* explosion.

Darlington North Box, on 23rd May 1939 - a little over three months before it became the interfacial box between the newly electrified signalling south to York (to the left) and the old mechanical signalling. The windows of the relay room have been bricked up for air-raid protection even some five months before war was declared. Compare this former North Eastern signal box with the wartime (ARP) design below which offered far more protection from either shrapnel or strafing. *Appleby coll.*

A very nasty incident occurred at **Gascoigne Wood Yard** at 19.35 on 18th April 1945 - very near the end of the war. Driver T.H. Stainton and Fireman J. Talbot, on J21 No.1513, were working a goods from Selby which included - next to the engine - **12 wagons of 50 lb bombs** for RAF Wheldrake (on the Derwent Valley Light Railway). On passing Hag Lane Box they noticed that the eighth wagon was on fire, and pulled up. Helped by Inspector T.H. Popplewell - and all aware of the bombs, they uncoupled the front seven wagons and drew them forward into the reception sidings. But the **burning wagon and two others exploded**, 98 bombs (13 tons of TNT) going up. There was first a small explosion - which allowed the men to take cover, followed by a massive blast that unfortunately killed the fireman on another locomotive (J6 No.3522) standing nearby, and produced a crater 50 feet deep and much damage to surrounding wagons

and buildings. Driver Stainton was awarded a George Medal, and Taylor and Popplewell received Commendations.

The gallantry shown by those men - and many others - stands in stark contrast to the man who fabricated several letters to the authorities about his *own* gallantry at Newport Yard, Middlesbrough!

Finally, a mishap on the ECML, which might be considered 'transitional' between the war and present-day circumstances, occurred on the morning of 5th August 1957 (August Bank Holiday), when a hoax 'bomb' planted on the line at Tempsford was so realistic that trains were diverted for 100 minutes while the Police and Army blew it up.

Notes:

1. Although that was stated in reports, the late W.B.Yeadon travelled through the station (platform 8) at 19.00 on the 16.18 Newcastle - Leeds (with two 'Hunts'), which was able to "crunch its way through the broken glass".

2. York District Works Superintendent, H. Love, received the BEM for his great efforts in organizing the restoration of York station, also the widening works down the line to the north.

3. During the first three years or so of the war, two Casualty Evacuation trains were stabled at Langley and two at New Barnet - out of 36 nationwide.

4. Locomotives known to have been exposed to this strafing included an ex-NER D21 4-4-0 and a GWR 'Aberdare' 2-6-0.

5. Mainly from *Royal Air Force Bomber Command Losses of the Second World War*, by W.R.Chorley, Midland Counties Publications, 1992-1996.

6. Snaith (east of the ECML and south of the ex-L&Y line) had runways running roughly W-E and NW-SE close to Heck station, so aircraft approaching to land upwind of the prevailing westerlies if they over-shot might well end up on the ECML, whereas at Burn the airfield was west of the ECML (between Temple Hirst and Henwick Hall), albeit with NW-SE and SW-NE runways that ended just a few yards from the railway.

7. Very probably this plane was trying to take off from Glatton Airfield, which had a W-E runway ending only 400 yards from the railway.

The signalbox built at Sessay at the time of widening of the ECML during the war to replace the existing ground-frame and enable signalling of the infrequent stopping passenger trains by 'Block Conversion'. The official title for this type of wartime box was an Air Raid Precautions (ARP) box. Its design afforded a semblence of protection for those inside. *K.Appleby coll.*

Appendix J

ACCIDENTS ON THE ECML, SEPTEMBER 1939 TO DECEMBER 1959

SERIOUS ACCIDENTS, UNTIL THE END OF 1959

Although ultimately someone is almost always to blame, accidents can be separated broadly into three classes: (A) those due to human operational error, (B) those caused by mechanical failure, and (C) those caused by 'Acts of God'. On the railway, (A) can be divided between errors of signalmen and others 'on the ground' - here designated 'Aa', those of train drivers ('Ab'), and those due to wrong-doing by other staff or members of the public ('Ac'). Mechanical failures can be divided broadly again, into defects on locomotives or rolling-stock ('Ba'), and defects of track or signalling equipment ('Bb'). Logically category 'C' would include accidents due to HM's Enemies, to terrorists or to vandals; the first are listed in *Appendix H* in the account of war damage, while - unlike in more recent times - there were only two instances of vandalism causing trouble on the ECML during the period covered, and one of those caused no *accident* as such.

Below are lists setting out the accidents of which the author is aware, occurring on the ECML alone between September 1939 and December 1959, in summary form and in chronological order, with classifications as above in so far as they can be discerned. (Significant accidents *not quite* on the ECML are in parentheses).

The list is of accidents that were relatively serious in terms of casualties and/or damage. Full description of them all would fill another volume, and the list cannot be vouchsafed to be complete, especially as records of incidents not resulting in fatalities may not have survived. Moreover, during the war official reports to the Minister of War Transport were limited by decree to generalities, except in the case of accidents involving death or serious injury or extensive damage to rolling-stock. (The most comprehensive summary accounts appear to be in the Daily Situation Reports of the REC to the Ministry of Transport. Other accounts are in the Ministry's own Reports, and for the LNER in Monthly Reports of the Working of the Railway by the Chief General Manager).

Considering the amount of traffic it carried, serious accidents to trains on the ECML during this twenty-year period seem to have been relatively rare, and few were very disastrous in terms of the number of people killed. The last is, however, usually a poor index of an accident's severity, although there was a rather justifiable public outcry in the immediate post-war years when accumulated arrears of maintenance to track and rolling-stock led to a spate of derailments at speed. It should be borne in mind that the ECML had an excessive number of level crossings for a trunk route, and they were the scene of several accidents. Their replacement by the now almost universal automatic lifting-barriers began soon after the first such barrier was installed in November 1952 at Warthill on the York - Hull line.

LESS SERIOUS ACCIDENTS, UNTIL THE END OF 1947

Far outnumbering the relatively serious accidents there were numerous mishaps that did not involve injury, loss of life, or major damage to rolling stock or track - a criterion that is admittedly rather subjective. It would be tedious to enumerate these mishaps individually, for between September 1939 and the end of 1947 - that is during the period of the REC - there were over 200 recorded on the ECML in addition to the 'Serious' ones listed above. Regretably, the author has not discovered records of 'less serious' accidents which occured after Nationalisation - for example, as depicted in the photograph of K1 No.62049 derailed on 18th August 1958.

In this modern age of motorways and an endless choice of alternative road routes it seems trivial that it was a serious matter if a mishap involved a few hours of interruption of traffic, its diversion to other routes or just the imposition of Single Line Working (SLW). But in the Railway Age - and in the war in particular - such occurrences were indeed serious, because of their knock-on effect on the normal, never-ending flow of traffic on a trunk route such as the ECML.

An unfortunate N2/4 No.2679 (BR 69528) being lifted free from the buffer-stops of the Up bay at Potters Bar after the multiple collision on the evening of Sunday 10th February 1946. It began when a local, hauled by this engine, derailed on account of a signalling error, then a Down express collided with the coaches, followed by an Up express running into the engine of the Down express. It was remarkable that only two people were killed and 11 injured. *J.Aylard coll.*

A2/1 No.60508 (LNER No.3697) DUKE OF ROTHESAY in an undignified position at New Southgate on 17th July 1948, after bad track - still blamed three years after on the back-log of maintenance caused by the war - had derailed it working the overnight 19.50 from Edinburgh. (Driver W. Hoole was injured and his fireman was killed. The staff at King's Cross shed collected a large sum for the fireman's wife and three children). *Author.*

A general scene looking north of the recovery work on the derailed 19.50 Edinburgh - King's Cross near New Southgate, 17th July 1948. There were no serious injuries to passengers. *Author.*

During those eight years or so there were at least 60 occurrences when all traffic was interrupted on some section of the ECML between London and Edinburgh for at least an hour, and trains had to be diverted to other routes to keep traffic flowing. (Local passenger traffic was usually dealt with in these cases by the hiring of buses). A similar number of mishaps blocked one line on a two-track section, but the traffic was continued by resort to SLW on the other line and perhaps some diversions. In about 20 instances on multi-track sections the extra tracks could be used, but as these were at the same time the busier sections anyway the disruption of traffic flows could be just as bad. For example, on at least seven occasions mishaps at the north end of York station necessitated the re-routing of passenger trains on the freight lines past York Yard and reversal in and out of the station at the south end. Again, at King's Cross on 15 to 20 occasions - including as well as derailments the flooding of Gas Works tunnel or a fire in the temporary roof over the main train-shed - when part of the station was blocked, local trains were cut back at Finsbury Park and goods trains on the Widened Lines were held up.

On the ECML generally there was usually an alternative and roughly parallel route that could be used, although in the war when all routes were so fully occupied these diversions caused considerable inconvenience. The principal alternatives were: the Hertford Loop; *via* March and Cambridge - perhaps also up to Liverpool Street; the Joint line *via* Sleaford or Boston and Lincoln; the Knottingley or Gascoigne Wood - Church Fenton route - combined with Starbeck - Ripon if York was blocked; *via* Bishop Auckland; the Leamside line; the Jesmond - Benton NW curve route; all the way round *via* Carlisle and the Waverley route; and the Kelso - St Boswells line. There were also some occasions when accidents blocked other routes and traffic had to be diverted *onto* the ECML, *e.g.* the GN&GE Joint line[1], Northallerton - Eaglescliffe, *etc*. During the night of 11th-12th February 1942 there were extensive diversions off the GC main line onto the ECML following the tragic accident near Beighton Junction, when a displaced girder on a freight train in Holbrook Colliery Sidings ripped into a passing troop train, killing 11 soldiers and injuring 36. There were also occasions when the ECML was used for WCML traffic when the latter was blocked for some reason. This occurred more frequently after Nationalization, such as after the Harrow disaster of 8th October 1952, but during the war some LMSR traffic was occasionally passed to the LNER, for example when an express collided with a barrow at Wembley on 13th October 1940 and the main lines into Euston were totally blocked.

Derailments of a few defective wagons were the commonest mishap, but there were numerous collisions involving two freight trains. When no injuries were recorded presumably these were slow-speed occurrences, but they must have been due to lapses on the part of drivers or of signalmen. Collisions involving *one* freight train only were common, resulting from a 'snatch' causing the division of the loose-coupled train followed by the rear portion catching up with the front portion. Occasionally coaching stock also became divided, and apart from those already listed as 'serious', there were a further 15 - 20 derailments or minor collisions on the ECML involving coaching-stock trains. Frequently - and especially towards the end of the war and shortly after it - there were many major locomotive failures, when big ends, coupling-rods or other main components broke and the engine was totally immobilized and/or damaged the track, and because it could not be moved without the breakdown gang it

completely blocked the line. There were also several occasions when single-line working had to be instituted for some hours while a broken rail was replaced. Sometimes a passenger train was derailed at catch-points when after being stopped on a bank (*e.g.* several times at Egmanton, south of Retford), the train was allowed to run back while restarting was being attempted.

Lastly and most poignantly, there were at least two instances of traffic interruption due to a trespasser being knocked down and killed, and one when the communication cord was pulled because it was thought that someone had fallen from the train ahead. (In that instance, the locomotive was detached and went forward in the dark to search the line).

Not included of course in the above are the traffic interruptions caused by enemy action, nor are aircraft crashes on the line. These are all recounted in *Appendix H*, while those due to severe weather are discussed in *Appendix K*. During the war, there were also often problems caused by barrage balloons and their cables, and not a few by road vehicles - most often Military - driving or falling onto the railway; these are not itemized here.

SERIOUS ACCIDENTS

27/11/39 16.48 - **Hitchin.** The engine off the 15.05 local from King's Cross collided with the 16.45 to King's Cross. Two coaches were derailed, and both crew of the light engine were injured. The Up lines were blocked until 04.30 28/11. (Ab?).

16/12/39 c.19.30 - **Barlby, Selby.** A succession of derailments: three vehicles of the 18.30 Doncaster-York, then the leading and rear vehicles of the 16.00 King's Cross-York (hauled by A4 No.4485), later causing damage to the locomotive of the 19.55 Leeds-Hull, one vehicle of which was also derailed. No further details. (Bb?).

2/2/40 02.17 - **Holloway.** The engine of an empty stock train ran into Holloway North Down Box, injuring the signalman; the Down Slow line was blocked for nearly seven hours.

13/6/40 c.10.30 - **Hett Mill, between Ferryhill and Durham.** Three platelayers were knocked down and killed by the 08.45 York-Newcastle express, the body of one man being carried on the buffer-beam of the engine for a quarter-mile before the driver was able to stop. (Ac).

(2/1/41 19.08 - **Haywoods Crossing, Askern.** A troop train collided with an Army lorry, killing two of its occupants and injuring another. Rail traffic delayed only 1½ hours. (Ac)).

28/4/41 15.40 - **Westborough Box, near Claypole.** Fire broke out in the second-to-last coach of the second portion of the 12.45 King's Cross-Newcastle express, hauled by V2 No.4779. The coach was occupied by boys of Ampleforth College (near Gilling) who were returning to school for the Summer Term, and the fire was started by boys flicking lighted matches. On account of the draught caused by the speed of the train, the fire was fanned so rapidly that in the 90 seconds it took for the train to stop after the communication cord had been pulled the coach was engulfed in flames. Moreover, it then spread to the third-to-last coach so quickly that the front of the train could only be uncoupled ahead of that coach, and the last three vehicles were burnt out. In the awful mêlée of fire and smoke, six boys died and seven were seriously injured. All trains were diverted off the ECML *via* Bottesford, Lincoln, and Retford or the Joint line until 19.00 (Ac).

17/9/41 21.53 - **Hitchin.** The 18.30 Highbury Vale-New England empties collided with the 20.44 King's Cross-York parcels,

An accident in the early hours of 19th February 1949: clearing up after A3 No.60107 (LNER No.4476) ROYAL LANCER on the 05.25 parcels King's Cross to York ran into a Down empties that had divided, New Southgate. Unfortunately during the clearing operations, one of the two breakdown cranes attending the incident fell over on its side, no doubt causing a lot of embarrassment to one and all. In this view the crane has just been righted but its jib is prone on the ground. *D.A.Dant.*

derailing the engine of the latter and also several wagons. Most lines were blocked until 18.00 18/9; Cambridge trains were diverted to Liverpool Street.

18/12/41 22.35 - **Tweedmouth Junction.** On being diverted onto the Kelso branch on account of a mishap at Dunbar, the first four coaches of a Pacific-hauled express were derailed when a rail shattered to pieces. (The rail was laid in 1890 and had been thoroughly worn by locomotives slipping).

14/2/42 03.18 - **Sessay.** The 22.15 King's Cross-Edinburgh express collided with a freight train, and the locomotive was derailed. No details seem to be available, but there were no casualties. All lines - including the new Down Slow that had only been opened two weeks before - were blocked until 13.30, and trains were diverted *via* Starbeck and Sinderby. (Ab?).

28/3/42 03.50 - **East Linton.** The 19.05 King's Cross-Edinburgh express was derailed completely, due to fracture of a connecting-rod, but the locomotive and all the coaches remained upright and there were no injuries. Both lines were blocked however until 21.15, with diversions *via* Kelso and Carlisle and some freight over the Border Counties line.

31/8/42 early hours - Between **Hougham and Claypole.** The 23.15 King's Cross-Edinburgh express, loaded to 20 coaches, became divided, and the last two coaches of the front portion of 15 and all the last five coaches were derailed. Both lines were blocked until 18.00 and the Down line until 20.00.

18/9/42 22.58 - **Selby.** The first coach of the 19.00 King's Cross-Edinburgh derailed. Main lines blocked until 07.00 19/9.

4/11/42 - Between **St Neots and Tempsford.** One Up coal train ran into another, blocking all lines for an hour, and all Up lines for much longer.

28/11/42 evening - **Peterborough North.** An Up train, hauled by V2 No.4879, ran into the back of a Grimsby train, telescoping the last van.

19/12/42 16.25 - **Newcastle, High Level Bridge.** The 15.57 local EMU from South Shields collided with a light engine (a D17/2) at the north end of the bridge. There were several injuries, and the bridge was blocked until 20.00.

2/1/43 18.40 - **Egmanton Box, near Retford.** On restarting from a signal stop, the fourth coach of the 15.30 King's Cross-Newcastle express became derailed on catch-points. The driver continued for 1,000 yards before he realized, and the track was much damaged. The ECML was blocked until 04.35 3/1/43. (A scenario repeated several times).

10/1/43 17.00 - **Newcastle Central.** An electric parcels car collided with empty stock in No.4 platform, telescoping two vehicles; the motorman was injured.

25/1/43 09.57 - **Newcastle, High Level Bridge.** The 08.20 Middlesbrough-Newcastle collided with an electric parcels car. The locomotive and two coaches of its train were derailed, and all lines were blocked until 16.30, Up lines until 17.30.

29/1/43 13.09 - **Christon Bank.** The 10.40 Edinburgh-King's Cross, held at a signal, was run into by the runaway rear portion of a freight train that had divided. The locomotive was derailed, and all lines blocked until 18.55 (22.30 for Down lines). (Ba?).

30/1/43 12.25 - **Newcastle Central.** The 10.05 passenger train from York collided with a station pilot, and a wagon was derailed blocking Platforms Nos.7-10.

20/3/43 20.44 - **Werrington Junction.** The locomotive of a Down freight derailed and overturned. All lines blocked until 03.00 21/3.

10/6/43 13.19 - **King's Cross.** The 08.40 express from Cleethorpes (hauled by A4 No.2509) collided with the buffer-stops of Platform 8. Minor injuries to 27 people. (Ab).

13/6/43 18.22 - **Manors Junction** (gantry) **signalbox** burned down, due to an electrical fault. Lines blocked by debris until 20.00 (to electric trains until 02.40 14/6). Normal working from 17/6, but trains had to be hand-signalled until a temporary Box was installed.

8/7/43 17.27 - Between **Peterborough North and Spital Junction.** A coach caught fire on a King's Cross-Newcastle express, but it was removed and no-one was hurt.

(**8/8/43** 14.12 - **Church Fenton.** The 10.15 (Sun.) Liverpool-York LMS train was derailed and divided. Several passengers were severely shocked and bruised. All lines except the Down Leeds were blocked until 18.55 10/8, and trains were diverted *via* Gascoigne Wood and Selby).

13/8/43 16.40 - **Lincoln Road Box, between Tuxford and Retford.** The 13.25 King's Cross-Hull express was in collision with a lorry that crashed the gates. Three were killed and four injured in the lorry. All lines were blocked, but only until 17.25. (Ac).

20-21/8/43 Midnight - **Tuxford North.** The locomotive of the 22.05 Doncaster-King's Cross parcels train was derailed after a glancing collision with the 23.30 Ranskill-Mansfield munition workers' train. There were no casualties, but all lines were blocked until 02.25 and trains were diverted *via* Lincoln.

21/8/43 14.15 - **Carlton-on-Trent.** A van on the 07.23 King's Cross-Doncaster train came off the rails - but the train was not stopped for another two miles. All lines were blocked and trains diverted *via* Lincoln until 15.55.

(**11/10/43** 07.13 - **Middle Road Crossing, near March.** The 22.20 Edinburgh-Colchester express collided with a car in dense fog, killing three and injuring two. (Ac)).

28/10/43 06.15 - **Hitchin.** A light engine collided with an empty stock train, causing derailment of both and blockage of both Down lines until 14.10.

1/11/43 15.53 - **Connington.** Collision of a special stock train with a lorry on a crossing - no casualties.

2/11/43 01.25 - **Tweedmouth.** An Edinburgh-King's Cross parcels train, hauled by A3 No.2795, collided with the rear portion of a divided freight train. The locomotive overturned and five vehicles were derailed; the fireman was injured. All lines were blocked until 03.05 3/11.

15/11/43 09.27 - **York.** A special Forces Leave train from Thirsk collided with the buffers in Platform 12. Several men were slightly injured. (Ab?).

30/11/43 19.30 - **Selby South.** The 18.30 Leeds-Hull collided with a pilot engine. One person was injured. All lines were blocked for 12 hours, and ECML traffic was diverted *via* Knottingley and Church Fenton. (Ab?).

4/12/43 05.50 - **Newcastle Central.** An EMU from Benton collided with a light engine, injuring the driver. All lines were blocked until 08.00 (This occurred just seven hours after the 22.45 Newcastle-South Shields EMU ran into a light engine at Gateshead East, two coaches being telescoped but causing only minor injuries).

17/12/43 22.00 - **Finsbury Park No. 6 Box.** The driver of the empty stock for the 22.25 Down Sleeper ran into a light engine, pushing it onto coaches for the 22.05 in front. Much delay.

1/1/44 17.40 - **Biggleswade.** The leading coach of a King's Cross-Doncaster relief train caught fire, but it was detached, and there were no injuries.

16/1/44 16.03 - **Hatfield.** A local train from King's Cross collided in fog with a light engine on the wrong line. Twelve people were slightly injured. (Ab?).

13/3/44 09.50 - **Newark.** The 08.45 Doncaster-King's Cross express, hauled by V2 No.4844, was derailed by a piece of cast iron on the track and then by distortion of a check-rail on Newark Dyke Bridge. The ECML was blocked until 21.30, with buses and/or diversions and SLW until 16.15 on 14/3.

2/5/44 07.22 - **Essendine.** Two freight trains collided. All lines except the Down main blocked until 11.45.

29/5/44 16.40 - Between **Skelton and Beningbrough.** The rear coaches and five fish vans of the 14.30 Newcastle-Leeds were derailed. One person was injured and several shocked. All lines were blocked until 18.10-21.45, and trains diverted *via* Ripon.

31/7/44 00.46 - **Christon Bank.** Both lines were blocked for five hours after the collision of a Down special fish train with the 02.11 Little Benton-Meadows empties whose driver had overrun signals. *Then*, after restoration of the Up line, the engine and front coach of the first train through - the late-running 22.00 King's Cross-Edinburgh express running wrong-line - became derailed because staff had failed to clamp the facing-points. All lines were blocked until 10.25; all cleared at 16.40. (Ab, Ac).

5/8/44 Midnight - **King's Cross.** The locomotive leaving on an express for Edinburgh became derailed. The recovery breakdown-train was then *also* derailed, and Platforms 8-10 and the Suburban lines were blocked until 11.00.

21/8/44 16.29 - **Wood Green.** The engine (A4 No.2512) and 10 coaches of the 16.00 King's Cross-Leeds derailed at the junction of the Down Main and Down Slow No 1, the engine coming to rest in the station. Three people were injured. The Down lines were blocked and Up traffic was affected by cranes working from the Up Main; all not fully clear until 21.05 22/8. (Ab?)

29/8/44 17.30 - **Wood Green.** The 17.22 Finsbury Park to Gordon Hill (with N2 No.2675) derailed on the flyover, because the driver was going too fast; the first coach ended up on top of the engine. Six people injured. Normal working restored 12.15 30/8. (Ab).

13/9/44 16.36 - **Doncaster, Marshgate Junction.** The 10.15 Edinburgh-King's Cross express collided - at slow speed - with the Newcastle-Hornsey stock train, derailing its last vehicle. Two passengers were slightly injured. SLW was imposed from Arksey on the Down line.

12/10/44 11.53 - **Yaxley.** The 22.20 King's Cross-Leeds freight train derailed because a bale of cloth fell off. Considerable damage was done to track, bridge and gantry. Most lines were blocked until 21.30.

8/11/44 20.51 - **Grantham.** The 17.30 Leeds-King's Cross express overran signals and collided with a Colwick-New England freight crossing from the Down to the Up side. Damage was minor, but all lines were blocked until 03.25 9/11. (Ab).

3/12/44 - **Tweedmouth.** A Down freight while being propelled to the Up line to allow another to pass was run into by an Up freight that overran a signal. No injuries, but some diversions. (Ab).

24/12/44 - **Pilmoor.** The 01.00 express parcels York-Newcastle became divided and partly derailed. All lines blocked, but Up Slow available within the hour.

V2 No.60968 (LNER No.3680) has come to grief at the east end of Newcastle Central station, after being hit by ex-LMS 2-6-4T, No.42073, on a train arriving from Middlesbrough, 19th April 1955. *I.S.Carr.*

31/12/44 - Edinburgh Waverley. The 22.30 to Colchester on leaving collided with an empty stock train whose driver disobeyed signals. Several coaches of both trains derailed, but no casualties. Disruption was caused for 10 hours.

4/2/45 - King's Cross. Due to partial failure of the locomotive's steam sanders, the 18.00 express to Leeds/Bradford, consisting of 17 coaches hauled by A4 No.2512, stalled in Gas Works tunnel, and - *without either the enginemen or the guard being aware of it* on account of the smoke and noise - ran back 200 yards. The signalman was unable to switch the points in time and the last coach was derailed, killing two and injuring 26. It was common for these heavy trains to stall in Gas Works tunnel, and inadvertent reversal had happened before - but this was serious.... The derailment also brought down part of the signal-gantry and bridge next to the signalbox, and the resulting chaos lasted three weeks because the breakdown gang cut the otherwise intact cables and the area was devoid of power signalling. Hand-signalling, and the use of Finsbury Park as the terminal for local trains went on until 23/2. Following the Accident Inquiry, lights marked with the distance into the tunnel were placed at 50-yard intervals, and stricter rules about the use of banking engines instituted. (Ab).

9/3/45 04.50 - **Barlby North Junction, Selby.** On colliding with an Engineers' train, the locomotive of the 23.15 King's Cross-Newcastle was derailed. All lines were blocked and trains diverted *via* Church Fenton.

15/9/45 20.00 - **Newcastle Central.** Due to a signalman's error, the 19.17 EMU from Monkseaton *via* Riverside running into Platform No.2 was struck by a light engine. Only one injured,

despite considerable damage to train. Up and Down Main and Platforms 1-3 blocked; all cleared by 16.20 16/9. (Aa).

6/10/45 16.23 - **Newcastle Central.** The 16.00 from North Wylam running into Platform No.13 collided with a light engine just derailed. Engine and train derailed. Slight injuries to 20 people.

22/10/45 - York. Due to a signalling fault, as the 18.40 to Sheffield was leaving Platform No.3, a shunting engine proceeding from No.2 struck the fifth coach, causing derailment. No injuries.

31/10/45 - Carcroft & Adwick-le-Street. A 12-coach express (hauled by K2 No.4633 and B4 No.6098) was derailed shortly after leaving the ECML, due to failure of a connecting-rod big-end on the K2. (Ba).

5/1/46* 05.40 - **Browney Box, just south of Durham.** The 03.40 Low Fell-Doncaster freight, hauled by B16/1 No.842, divided on account of a coupling snatch after surmounting the 'hump' at Relly Mill. The signalman at Browney stopped the front half of the train, which was then run into at speed by the rear half. He also set all his Down line signals to danger, but one of the derailed wagons caught the wires and pulled them 'off' again. The approaching 23.15 King's Cross-Newcastle express (hauled by V2 No.4895) therefore ploughed into the resulting wreckage at 50 m.p.h. Ten people were killed and 29 injured in the consequent pile-up. Trains were diverted *via* Bishop Auckland and Leamside until 22.35 6/1, and again on 7-10/1 to allow clearing of wreckage. (Ba, + C?).

29/1/46 - Grantham South. A King's Cross-York parcels train ran into the rear of the 22.10 King's Cross-Edinburgh. Two passengers and the guard were slightly injured. (The Southern

Area Passenger Manager, C.G.G. Danbridge, was on board).

10/2/46 - Potters Bar. Due to a signalling error, the 21.32 Hatfield-King's Cross local, hauled by N2 No.2679, was derailed and the engine ran into the buffer-stops. The 21.45 King's Cross-Edinburgh (hauled by V2 No.4876) then collided at speed with the coaches of the local. After that the 17.00 Bradford/Leeds-King's Cross (hauled by V2 No.4833), which was nearly but not quite able to stop in time, ran at 5-10 m.p.h. into the first V2. Two people were killed and 11 injured. All trains were diverted *via* Hertford North for the next 48 hours, and a push-and-pull with F2 No.7106 operated between Wood Green and Potters Bar. (Aa).

24/2/46 20.48 - Thirsk. The driver of the 18.50 Newcastle-Bristol express, hauled by V2 No.4878, failed to observe a speed restriction over newly relayed track and derailed his train. Almost all trains were diverted via Ripon and Starbeck, but the Up Slow was used by some freights. Normal working resumed 17.30 on 25/2. (Ab).

15/7/46 19.30 - Red Hall, south of Hatfield. Faulty track was thought to have been the cause of the total derailment at 60 m.p.h. of the 19.05 King's Cross-Aberdeen (hauled by V2 No.3645). The engine broke loose and was derailed 50 yards ahead of the train. Eleven people were injured. Trains were diverted *via* Hertford for 24 hours. (Bb).

10/11/46 22.35 - Marshmoor Box, south of Hatfield. Yet another V2, No.905 (ex-4876) - in its second accident in nine months, on the 16.45 Newcastle-King's Cross was totally derailed on faulty track. There were only seven injured, none seriously. All lines were blocked and trains suspended or diverted *via* Hertford, until 11.30 on 11/11 for the Down and 18.00 for the Up. This was the last straw for H.M. Inspector, and after that part of the blame for these successive derailments of 2-6-2s was attributed to the design of their pony-truck suspension. This was urgently altered on some of the class, but track maintenance improved anyway, and there were no more of these derailments.

30/12/46 11.20 - Doncaster Central. The 09.05 Ripon-King's Cross express, running 'permissively', collided with the rear of the 09.40 Hull-King's Cross express in Platform 1. The driver of the Ripon train had been given a green hand-signal by the signalman, but "failed to control his engine adequately". Several coaches were derailed and damaged, and the Up lines were blocked until 17.30 - partly because further coaches were derailed when moved. There were 40 injured, four seriously. (Ab).

8/7/47 15.14 - King's Cross. The 09.05 express from Ripon - *again* - collided with the buffers. Three coaches were damaged and 26 people were injured (two badly). (Ab?)

31/7/47 01.05 - Between Balderton and Barnby Boxes (south of Newark). A tyre came off the wheel of the fourth coach of the 22.15 King's Cross-Edinburgh; it passed through the floor and roof without hurting anyone. The coach was re-railed several hours later. (Ba).

9/8/47* 16.41 - Doncaster, Bridge Junction. A terrible mistake by a signalman during the confusion of the changeover from semaphore to colour-light signalling, on a very busy Summer Saturday, resulted in the 13.25 King's Cross-Leeds express (hauled by V2 No.936) colliding at 40 m.p.h. opposite Sand Bank Box with the 13.10 King's Cross-Newcastle (hauled by A3 No.50), which was held at Bridge Junction awaiting entry to the station. Four coaches of the front train were smashed, 18 people were killed and 120 injured (76 of them seriously). (Aa). Traffic had to be run over the goods lines for the ensuing 25 hours, -

but on the Summer Saturday two weeks later a locomotive derailment at Retford Crossing blocked the ECML completely for two hours.

26/10/47* (Sunday) 12.47 - Goswick. Another occasion when a driver ignored a temporary speed-restriction, in this case at a crossover connection to the Down line, by taking it at 65 mph. The train was the 11.15 Edinburgh-King's Cross, hauled by A3 No.66. The train derailed, and 28 people lost their lives, 65 were injured (many of them seriously). All lines were blocked for 15 hours and trains were diverted, principally *via* Carlisle. (Ab)[2].

1/3/48 01.00 - Connington North Box. A light engine collided (in fog) with a lorry at a level crossing. The lorry was carrying ten German ex-prisoners-of-war, one of whom was the driver; five were killed and the others seriously injured. Subsequently, at 17.26 on 16/10/48, at the *same* crossing a man was killed in his car by an Up empty stock train hauled by a Pacific. (Ac, ?+Aa). As a result of these accidents, Connington North Box was moved in 8/54 - bodily - to beside the crossing, so that the gates could be controlled directly from the Box.

9/7/48 - Little Bytham - Essendine. The right-hand injector blew out on V2 No.943, working an Up fish train. Although badly scalded, the driver stayed on the footplate to stop the train.

17/7/48* c.06.00 - New Southgate. Bad track was the cause of the derailment at 70 m.p.h. of the 19.50 Edinburgh-King's Cross express (hauled by A2/1 No.60508). The engine parted from its train, slipped along the track for 100 yards and ended up on its side. The fireman was killed, but as only one coach overturned only one passenger lost his life. (Bb).

29/1/49 - Holloway. In dense fog, the Up *ABERDONIAN* (18.45 Aberdeen-King's Cross, hauled by V2 No.E924) collided with an empty stock train. The locomotive was extensively damaged, but there were no casualties. (Ab?).

16/2/49 - York. LMS Class 5 No.4781 on its way to the shed collided at the main crossover at the north of the station with J25 No.5656 working a freight from Foss Islands. Both engines were derailed, but the lines out of the station were only partially blocked.

19/2/49 - North of Wood Green tunnel. The 05.25 King's Cross-York parcels, hauled by A3 No.60107, ran into the rear portion of a Down freight that had divided. The A3 was derailed and the lines blocked for several hours, with diversions *via* Hertford, partly because the King's Cross crane fell over while clearing wreckage. (Ba, ?+Aa).

23/6/49 20.40 - Penmanshiel tunnel, between Cockburnspath and Grantshouse. Fire, probably due to a lighted match in a corridor igniting inflammable cellulose lacquer paint, in one minute engulfed the last two coaches of the 10-coach 19.30 Edinburgh-King's Cross express (hauled by A3 No.60035). It was a fine evening and many windows were open. The train, travelling at speed, was brought to a stand by the action of the guard in a little over a minute after the fire started, with the burning coaches *only just* outside the tunnel. However, the unbelievable fierceness and rapidity of the fire forced some of the passengers to have to escape by smashing windows, and seven were hurt, two of them seriously. The first eight coaches were soon taken on to Grantshouse, and after the other surviving passengers had walked there or had ridden by car, the train proceeded at 22.30, only 105 minutes late. No sign of the fire had been seen by the Cockburnspath signalman or by a railwayman passenger who passed through the coach a few moments before the fire broke out. In addition, an asphyxiating gas was produced, and the consequences would have been even

On 1st September 1955, the W1 4-6-4 No.60700 suffered a broken front bogie frame as it was leaving Peterborough North on the 15.50 King's Cross to Leeds and Bradford. The scene shows the resulting mayhem, and men trying to decide - or waiting to be told, what to do. It is also an informative view from Westwood Bridge down the line. On the left is Wisbech Junction (ex-MR) Box with the M&GN lines leading left off the MR Leicester line; in the centre, immediately behind No.60700, is Westwood Junction Box and the connections going from the ECML into the New England Yard complex, the tracks to the right including the Down and Up Goods/Coal lines, shunting spurs for the Old Coal and North Yards and the Engine lines from New England shed, the water tower and coaling plant of which are visible in the distance.

The view of 60700 from Westwood Junction signal box shortly after the incident of 1st September 1955. This dramatic close-up reveals how lucky the signalman was and who must have got the fright of his life. *Facing and this view P.Waszak coll.*

worse if the whole train had stopped a second later - entirely in the tunnel. (Ac).

5/6/50* 14.32 - **Tollerton.** In a heat-wave the track became distorted. The previous train merely suffered a shaking and minor damage, but the rail broke as the 12.15 Newcastle-York (hauled by A1 No.60153) derailed at 45 m.p.h. and nine people were injured. Traffic on the ECML north of York had to be diverted *via* Starbeck and Sinderby. (Bb).

8/9/50 - Selby. The 18.30 York-Swindon, hauled by B1 No.61250, was derailed on entering the station. Trains had to be diverted *via* Church Fenton and Knottingley.

c. 21/10/50 - Peterborough. Within a few days, there were two runaways and a collision, all of light engines. In the first, J52 No.68789, un-manned, pushed J52 No.68866 (also without a crew) off New England shed and up the main line to near the North station, where they collided with J3 No.4128 on a ballast train. Secondly, J3 No.4123 took the wrong line out of Eastfield Yard and collided with and derailed an Austerity 2-8-0. Lastly, J6 No.4191 set off without a crew from New England Shed and ran to Werrington Junction before it was derailed. (Ab or Ac).

16/3/51 10.09 - **Doncaster, Bridge Junction** - *again*. Owing to track defects, the 10.06 Doncaster (08.45 Hull/09.15 York)-King's Cross, hauled by A2/2 No.60501, was derailed as it was leaving Doncaster. Four people were killed and 29 injured. Main line trains had to be diverted *via* Darnall and Retford. (Bb).

14/7/51 17.00 - **North of Huntingdon.** Fire, believed to be caused by an ember from the engine, destroyed the second coach of the Down *WEST RIDING* (15.45 King's Cross-Leeds/Bradford, hauled by A3 No.60058). Unfortunately, the coaches involved were a crowded articulated twin from the pre-war *WEST RIDING LIMITED* and egress was possible only at each end of the set. Therefore passengers had difficulty in escaping and there were 23 injured. The guard, believing smoke reported earlier was merely coming from a hot axle-box, had tried to have the train stopped by *throwing a message attached to a potato* to a signalman, - but without success, and the train was brought to a stand by a passenger pulling the communication-cord. (As this was a Summer Saturday, there must have resulted much chaos on the line, trains presumably being diverted from Peterborough *via* Cambridge). (C).

17/8/51 10.36 - **Newcastle Central.** The motorman of the 10.35 EMU to Tynemouth *via* Wallsend departed on the guard's authority without checking the signal - a common mistake - and collided with the incoming EMU from Tynemouth *via* Benton. Three people were killed and 41 injured. (Ab).

21/12/51 17.05 - **Piershill Junction, Edinburgh.** Due to a signalman's error, an Outer Circle local from Leith Central (hauled by V1 No.67630) collided with a light engine (A4 No.60018). (Aa).

22/1/52 - King's Cross 'Hotel Curve'. N2 No.69569, running

173

light, collided with and derailed the rear of the 09.54 King's Cross-Hertford North (hauled by N2 No.69492), blocking the local line from Moorgate for several hours. (Ab?).

16/7/52 19.59 - **Riccall.** Due to the gatekeeper reversing the signals and allowing a car to cross at Riccall Gates Crossing (on the Selby-York main road), two people were killed in the car by the Down *TEES-TYNE PULLMAN* (16.45 King's Cross-Newcastle), hauled by an A4. The train was relatively unscathed, but the gatekeeper was sentenced for manslaughter. (Aa).

14/11/52 08.55 - **Three Counties.** The 07.35 Clarence Yard-Doncaster semi-fitted freight, hauled by V2 No.60880, became divided and the rear portion ran into the front portion at speed. All four tracks were blocked and trains were diverted *via* Cambridge and Ely until 16.00 (Ba ?+Aa).

28/10/53 - **Goswick** - *again*. The collapse of a big end on A2/1 No.60509, hauling the 21.15 Glasgow-Colchester caused it to be derailed at points at 55 m.p.h. Remarkably, little damage was done to the train and there were no serious injuries. (Ab).

17/12/53 - **Longniddry Junction.** An obstruction that had just fallen off a Down freight derailed at 60 m.p.h. the 00.41 Edinburgh-King's Cross special parcels (hauled by A2 No.60530). The engine crashed through the station, became detached from its tender and fell down an embankment. The fireman was killed and the driver seriously injured. Trains diverted *via* Kelso. (Ac).

20/1/54 18.15 - **Thirsk.** Electrical points failure caused the sudden change of 'clear' colour-light signals to 'danger' as the Down *HEART OF MIDLOTHIAN* (14.00 King's Cross-Edinburgh, hauled by A1 No.60126) was approaching at 75 m.p.h. Although it was brought down to 20 m.p.h., it still left the tracks, but stayed upright and damage was slight, and there were no casualties. Trains were diverted *via* Starbeck and Ripon. (Bb).

10/4/54 early hours - **Oakleigh Park.** The driver of the 22.35 Ardsley-King's Cross fitted freight, on V2 No.60861, was unaware that he was on the Up Goods line that ended there and ran at some speed through the sand-drag. (Ab).

3/9/54 - **Sessay.** J27 No.65827, on a Burdale-Thirsk goods, derailed when it ran at speed into the brake-van of the 07.00 York-Thirsk goods. The van had been left unprotected on a 'permissive block' line, but the driver of the York train averted a more serious accident by speeding his engine out of trouble. (Aa ?+Ab).

19/4/55* - **Newcastle Central.** Due to misreading of signals by one of the drivers, two light engines (V2 No.60968 and LMS 4MT 2-6-4T No.42073) collided heavily at the diamond crossing at the east end of the station and were both derailed. (Ab).

21/6/55 03.34 - Between **Huntingdon and Offord.** A Hull-King's Cross fitted freight (hauled by a V2) suffered division and

derailment after travelling at 40 m.p.h. for two miles following derailment of one wagon due to a suspension defect. Both parts of the train were stopped and there were no injuries. (Ba).

1/9/55* 17.23 - **Peterborough, Westwood Junction.** The 15.50 King's Cross-Leeds/Bradford, hauled by W1 No.60700, was derailed as it was leaving Peterborough North, due to failure of an engine bogie frame. The bogie design was subsequently modified. (Ba).

7/1/57* 07.12 - **Welwyn Garden City.** In this serious accident, the 19.10 (Sunday) Aberdeen-King's Cross, hauled by A2/3 No.60520, ran through adverse signals and collided at a closing speed of 30-35 m.p.h. with the 06.18 Baldock-King's Cross local (hauled by L1 No.67741). One person was killed and 43 injured, mainly in the local although it was on the move, casualties in the express being minimized by the stronger steel bodies of its coaches. Although AWS was in operation, No.60520 was not yet fitted for it. Soon after, on 8/3/57, the *same train*, hauled by A2/3 No.60514 (also not fitted with AWS) overran the self-same signals; the 06.30 King's Cross-Welwyn Garden City narrowly escaped a converging collision. Drivers had already been complaining vehemently about the siting of the signals in question, and after this they were substituted by colour-lights. (Ab).

27/2/57 - **Hadley Wood.** The 00.35 Ferme Park-New England Class H broke in two and the rear part ran back through Potters Bar tunnel and collided with the 02.15 King's Cross-Grantham newspapers; there were no injuries. (Ba ?+Aa).

3/8/58* 09.26 - **York.** A3 No.60036, on the 07.32 from Sunderland, overran the buffers, demolished a kiosk and slightly injured 11 people. (Ab, or Ba?).

19/11/58* 04.30 - **Hitchin.** In thick fog, the 03.25 Ferme Park-New England freight (hauled by 2-10-0 No.92187) passed an automatic signal at 'danger' and ran at 15 m.p.h. into the 02.28 Ferme Park-New England freight (hauled by another 2-10-0, No.92145). Wagons were thrown across the Up lines and were struck firstly by the 22.35 Ardsley-Ferme Park freight (hauled by V2 No.60885), which was derailed and tore up the track. Some of its vans were then smashed into by L1 No.67785 running on the Up slow and this engine turned over, covered with wreckage. Casualties were confined to four train-crew slightly injured. All lines were blocked until 11.00, when just a single line became available. Many Down expresses were cancelled, and there had to be major diversions of traffic, up the GE section from Peterborough (in one case, Sandy) and Cambridge to Liverpool St. A complete embargo was put on all Up ECML freight south of Peterborough, and the most urgent Down traffic from London was diverted to the LMR. All lines were not cleared until 08.05 20/11, and certain overnight expresses were diverted once more to Liverpool Street (Ab).

18/1/59 - **Newcastle Central.** The 06.42 Long Benton-Newcastle EMU collided with an empty EMU outside the station. The driver was killed, and three passengers injured. Only the electric services were disrupted.

27/7/59 - **Benton Bank, near Heaton.** A train of empties, hauled by Q6 No.63399, collided with derailed wagons. The driver was killed and the fireman injured; all traffic had to be diverted *via* Jesmond and Benton NW Curve.

20/8/59 12.51 - Between **Relly Mill and Bridge House Boxes, south of Durham.** Fire destroyed the kitchen-car of the Up *ELIZABETHAN* (09.45 Edinburgh-King's Cross, hauled by A4 No.60031). No one was hurt. The rear seven coaches of the train were reversed to Durham and continued on *via* Bishop Auckland.

(opposite) **An aerial view of the terrible accident between Balby Junction and Bridge Junction Boxes on the approaches to Doncaster at 16.41 hr. on 9th August 1947. The picture shows the locomotive (V2 No.936 (LNER No.3663)) of the 13.25 King's Cross - Leeds on its side after ploughing under clear signals into the rear of the preceding 13.10 King's Cross - Leeds, ripping the bodies off and totally wrecking the rear three Gresley teak coaches of the latter. The front train was just on the move, but the collision speed was still 40 mph and the V2 came to rest 90 yards beyond the point of impact. Both trains were crowded, and from appearances it would seem unlikely anyone in those three coaches survived; in fact 18 people were killed and 76 seriously injured.** *NRM*

15/9/59 - Stobswood Crossing, near Widdrington. The 10.35 Alnwick-Newcastle, comprising a two-car Metro-Cammell DMU, collided at 50-55 m.p.h. with a lorry on a crossing that had been kept open (against the rules) by the crossing-keeper following the passage immediately beforehand of a Down mineral train. The DMU, which was running under clear signals, was derailed and eventually came to rest after smashing into a brake-van in a siding. The driver was killed, and five passengers and the lorry-driver were injured. All traffic was run on the Down line from 12.15 until 20.50 (Ac).

9/11/59* - Finsbury Park. A goods empties, hauled by an N2, ran out of control down the branch from the Highgate direction and collided violently with empty stock in the station. The crew of the N2 were able to jump clear and no one was hurt, but there was much wreckage to be cleared from over the Seven Sisters Road. (Ab, or Ba?).

1. The first such incident in the period covered here was on 3rd February 1940, when the 13.50 Colchester to York collided with the crossing gates at Stow Park.

* These accidents have been well illustrated in the series, *Trains in Trouble*, published by Atlantic.

2. The driver allowed a sailor - who wanted to become a engineman, to travel on the footplate, but there was no evidence provided that this man distracted the crew. All three men were injured, the driver and fireman severely.

(above) **A3 No.60036 (LNER No.2501) COLOMBO, having 'run out of track' at York's No.12 bay platform on a train from Sunderland, 3rd August 1958.** *J.Hooper coll.*

(below) **Railwaymen and onlookers watch, as A2/3 No.60520 (LNER No.520) OWEN TUDOR is lifted, after its collision south of Welwyn Garden City with a stopping train from Royston while working the Up** *ABERDONIAN*, **7th January 1957.** *Author.*

(above) **Uumm! K1 No.62049 derailed near the Ouse Bridge at Skelton on 18th August 1958, as seen from the Up *FAIR MAID*, which was halted at the site. This is also a study in human poses, perhaps.** *I.S.Carr.*

(below) **As it is showing express head-code, J38 No.65929 (LNER No.1442) and the St Margarets breakdown train at Niddrie North, is going to attend an incident, 10th March 1956.** *J.Robertson.*

Appendix K

SNOW AND FLOODS ON THE ECML IN THE 1940s AND 1950s

SNOW ON THE LINE

The severe weather, with snowstorms and great frosts in several of the winters of the 1940s and 1950s caused widespread chaos due to failures of the block signalling system, and freezing of points, water-troughs, water-columns, locomotive injectors, and carriage-heating pipes - even brake-blocks. During the blizzards, ploughs had to be run over hundreds of miles of track and often failed to prevent snowdrifts blocking lines, derailments were common and of course ice and snow interfered with the running of third-rail electric trains - as on Tyneside. The problems caused by severe weather were especially serious under the conditions of intensive traffic during the war. In Britain as a whole, the worst problems of this kind occurred in the first winter of the war, even before enemy action was causing difficulties.

For about six weeks from the third week of January 1940 there was a period of the 'worst winter weather for a century', with prolonged frost and severe blizzards at times. It affected most of the country and many lines were blocked by snowdrifts - 390 miles on the LNER alone. Work in many marshalling yards - already hampered by the Black-Out and fog, was brought to a standstill by ice and heavy snow. The snow-ploughs were first out on the Newcastle - Berwick stretch of the ECML on 16th January, the Ouse froze at York on 23rd January, and the Tyne froze as far down as Dunston with the temperature in Newcastle falling to -4⁰ F. Yet the ECML was in fact just kept open, although traffic was impeded by snow at Biggleswade and at Corby (Lincs.). Naturally punctuality suffered severely, the *average* lateness of ECML expresses declining to 40 - 100 minutes in the four weeks ending 3rd February.

With most of the main lines over the Pennines impassable, including the Settle - Carlisle line, and also the WCML blocked by snowdrifts on 31st January not only in Scotland but also in the most unlikely places such as between Preston and Lancaster and at Golborne, the weather brought freight traffic to a virtual standstill in the northern half of Britain for days at a time. The result was a severe shortage of coal, and households were restricted to two hundred-weights a week. For a few days the Waverley Route was also blocked and all traffic in and out of Scotland had to pass over the ECML. In the last week of February 1940 widespread floods came with the thaw, and interrupted traffic at various places; for example, there was three feet of water in Gainsborough and flooding seems to have been the cause of a derailment at Newark.

In 1941 it was nearly as bad - and for the ECML worse. In the North-East there had been continuous frost for five weeks up to the beginning of February, and the water froze in Wiske Moor troughs - severely damaging them, with fog for 12 of the days. Moreover, up to a quarter of the staff were off sick. There were heavy falls of snow on 19th January and the ECML was blocked for two hours between Selby and Riccall. In the next three days many branch lines were blocked in Yorkshire and Lincolnshire and yards made inoperative. Constant use of snow-ploughs was needed, and the Military were called in to assist, but there was still much congestion. More snow caused 'working

difficulties' in East Yorkshire and Lincolnshire on 5th - 6th February, and possibly related to it there was a serious derailment at Bawtry when five coaches of an empty stock train came off the rails in the early hours of 6th February and blocked both lines for over two hours (after which single-line working was operated), with trains being diverted *via* the Joint line.

However, as far as the ECML was concerned the worst blizzards came on 19th - 21st February, with *56 hours* of almost continuous snowfall - 'the worst in living memory'. First, there was disruption in the Darlington area, and ECML trains had to be diverted *via* Stockton, Ferryhill and Leamside. Freight traffic north of Darlington was already suspended on 20th February, and then *two feet* of snow settled on the City of Newcastle, and even Newcastle Central became snow- and ice-bound. The ECML was blocked by snow-drifts between Darlington and Ferryhill and at Forest Hall, as were the lines to Sunderland and to Carlisle; the Tyneside electric services had to be worked with steam engines or suspended entirely. Anglo-Scottish trains were diverted to the LMSR - although the Waverley Route was also blocked by a derailment, and freight was virtually halted. The snow brought down miles of telegraph lines and they were strewn across the tracks. Block telegraph communication and telephones failed over the whole area, with District Controls completely out of touch, and the few trains that ran had to do so under a 'time-interval' system. There were numerous derailments to add to the chaos, one at Bishop Auckland blocking another alternative route to Newcastle, another between Darlington and Eaglescliffe; only the Coast line remained open - to Sunderland. Three expresses from London were 'lost' south of Durham, becoming snowbound, the passengers and crew having to be nourished with food brought partly by road and partly by foot through the snow. The passengers of the 23.30 from King's Cross of 19th February were finally detrained at Darlington at *03.00 on 21st February*, after many adventures. Passengers for Scotland on trains that eventually got through to Newcastle - in over 24 hours - were put up for the night on the floors of the public rooms of the Royal Station Hotel.

To clear up the mess and restore all the communications took several weeks, and at times 300 extra men were so employed. Signalling repairs needed 10,000 new insulators, 4,000 miles of copper wire, and much help from men from the LMSR and the Royal Corps of Signals. Then, after the snow came the almost inevitable floods - and at Beamish a major embankment slip resulted in a J39 finding itself in a field. Block working was restored on the ECML by 23rd February, but passenger services - which for Scottish traffic had been diverted to the LMSR Midland Division - were still restricted a week later, when only 160 miles of lines out of 600 in the North-East were back to normal block working. Normal traffic operations were not achieved until 10th March, and on the branches by 17th March. As the freight and coal traffic that was held up had first to be cleared, there was a total ban on acceptances in the NE Area north of Darlington for several days, being relieved gradually until 3rd March. Only 50 Convoy coal trains moved during the week of the storm - compared to the normal of about 175, and the shortfall had to be made up from collieries further south.

The Divisional General Manager NE Area (C.M. Jenkin Jones) ended his report of the episode: "We have experienced what is without question the greatest dislocation of railway facilities which has ever occurred in this country.... Men voluntarily remained on duty as long as they could be of service - in many cases for thirty hours - in some cases for over fifty hours.... the staff of the Area by the determination and endurance with which they faced a great devastation have quickly brought it within manageable limits, and by their spirit of service to the public and to the country they have shown an example of the highest conception of the duty of Railway-men." Nevertheless, in those days equal devotion and heroism was being displayed in other parts of the country under the Blitz, from the worst of which Tyneside was lucky to be spared.

In view of the even greater burden of traffic the railways were having to bear in the final three winters of the war, it was fortunate that there were no great blizzards comparable to those earlier in the war. Still, in late January and early February 1942, a blizzard in the North-East and Scotland again brought freight traffic almost to a standstill. On 3rd February the ECML was blocked by drifts between Dunbar and East Linton, also all four lines to Scarborough were blocked and so were all lines north of Aberdeen, but all were clear in two days on this occasion. Then, in the first week of March, severe weather caused some difficulties further south. In 1944, snow on 26th - 27th February did cause damage to signalling and consequent severe delays on lines in Lincolnshire and Nottinghamshire, the North-East and Scotland, and problems continued for a week or so in certain places. The ECML was spared, but had to carry traffic unable to pass on the Joint line. In January 1945, there was heavy snow again especially in Scotland, and blockage of various branches; on the ECML there were block failures but no actual interruption. On all these occasions the weather hold-ups forced very extensive embargoes.

Before the days of lines electrified with overhead wiring, gales were not such a hazard, but there was a widespread severe gale on 7th April 1943, indirectly affecting the ECML. A tree fell on the 10.15 York-Scarborough between Weaverthorpe and Ganton, injuring the guard and slightly hurting four passengers. On the same day a tree blocked the Border Counties line near Hexham, and near Darlington a signal gantry was swaying so badly that trains were suspended on the Bishop Auckland line.

The Great Freeze-Up of 1947, for seven weeks from late January to the middle of March, was probably the worst. This, and the ensuing floods when the snow suddenly melted, brought chaos to the country and privations - in terms of power shortages - unknown even in the war, with industry reduced for a period to a three-day week, mainly on account of the inability of the Railways to move the coal from the pits to the power stations, gas works and docks. Colliery and other branches were so snowed up that many thousands of loaded wagons were stranded at the pits, and when they could be moved the cold was so intense that the coal was frozen solid in the wagons, while the Arctic weather hindered the movement of empty wagons to the pits and of loaded ones away from them. On 12th February, the Cabinet decided that absolute priority must be afforded and emergency measures taken for the movement of coal - for 30,000 loaded wagons were now held up. To save fuel, numerous passenger trains were cancelled, and severe limitations were put on the consumption of fuel for industrial and also domestic purposes. Given the priority for coal there had to be extensive embargoes on merchandise traffic, although the effect of them was lessened by the fuel shortage causing a sharp drop in manufacturing output. Loaded wagons forwarded on the LNER fell in the first three months of 1947 by 15% compared with the same period in 1946. The LNER cut loaded passenger train-miles by 27,000 from 22nd February, then by 124,000 (the countrywide figure being 420,000) from 17th March, cuts which were not restored until the Summer 1947 service began - belatedly, on 16th June.

Beginning in East Anglia, intense frosts came on 23rd January and remained almost unbroken until mid-March, causing severe delays due to freezing of locomotives and their watering facilities. This was especially so in London on 29th January, when three ECML expresses were delayed an average of 4½ hours due to frozen locomotives. Having already overcome trains down in Devonshire, snow came to the East on 28th January. Main lines and branches were blocked by snow-drifts on many occasions and for lengthy periods in the north and east of England, with several instances of even passenger trains having to be abandoned, the engine fires dropped and passengers marooned either in the unheated trains - or if they were lucky, in cottages or station-masters' houses. The Darlington - Penrith/Tebay line was blocked for no less than *eight weeks*, with a train abandoned near Stainmore for much of the time.

Helped by violent blowing-off of the locomotive of the 17.55 King's Cross - Hull, on 22nd January the glass fell from the roof at Peterborough North onto the train. On 4th February, the roof of Grantham station partially collapsed under the weight of snow, blocking the ECML for some hours. The ECML was first completely blocked by snow-drifts on 21st-22nd February, between Newcastle and Berwick. Also the GN&GE Joint line was blocked at that time at Cowbit, forcing diversions onto the ECML. A worse snowstorm struck the north on 26th February, blocking many branch lines and the ECML itself once more between Newcastle and Berwick for 36 hours. Operations at York and Newcastle were brought almost to a standstill, and traffic was also interrupted by drifting snow near Retford and between Berwick and Edinburgh. Freight traffic in the NE Area had got back to 70% of normal by 1st March, but further snowstorms on 27th February in Scotland and on 1st March in Co. Durham and in the Midland and Eastern Counties on 4th-5th March brought traffic again almost to a halt. Finally, the worst storms of all in the North on 12th-13th March blocked both of the LMS routes south of Carlisle and the ECML had to take the LMS traffic from Scotland. But then on 13th - 14th March both the ECML and the Waverley LNE routes became blocked in several places by drifts on 13th-14th March. However on this occasion, after a block on the Newcastle - Carlisle line had been cleared, most ECML traffic could be diverted to the Settle - Carlisle route which by then had been reopened by the LMSR. On two successive nights 2,000 passengers were stranded at Newcastle, many off diverted expresses from St Pancras, and - as in 1941 - they were bedded down in the Royal Station Hotel and in the refreshment rooms. Nevertheless, by running light engines and snow-ploughs and somehow keeping the traffic moving in spite of frozen signals and point-work, the ECML itself was otherwise kept clear in the blizzards of 1947 - albeit with delays to ECML expresses of six to eight hours. Thanks to the herculean efforts of the staff, coal *was* kept moving and accumulations at the collieries did not exceed two days' output. Still, when a thaw came the LNER had to convey 170 extra coal trains a week up to London early in March. Locomotive shortages - and shortcomings, already serious owing to the number needing repair, were accentuated by so many being frozen up or needed to clear snow; the percentage availability on the LNER fell to 73% in the period. Wagon stocks - another critical factor - were kept up by Military and other Government depots assisting in their repair.

After the Great Freeze came the Great Thaw, and lines became flooded in many parts of the country. The first were in the Lea Valley and Cambridge district, necessitating the diversion of GE line trains *via* Hitchin and the new connection from Bowes Park to Palace Gates. After that there were floods in the Lincoln and Doncaster Districts, and a hurricane-force gale in the South caused widespread disruption of telecommunications by fallen posts and trees. On 24th March the ECML was flooded between Selby and York, with part of the main-line embankment at Barlby north of Selby being washed away. Selby engine shed was put out of use - and 42 engines isolated, by the floods, fully until 28th March and partially until 13th April. Trains between Doncaster and York had to be diverted *via* Askern and Ferrybridge and those from Leeds *via* York. Various other lines were flooded, including that from York to Scarborough, on which the station and yards at Malton were inundated for several days.

All this caused the average delay to principal ECML expresses to rise from 50 minutes in January 1947 (also in January 1946) to 75 minutes in February and 87 minutes in March; these were figures typical of trains as a whole - and without taking account of complete curtailments of services. In the eight weeks ending 22nd March, 75% of King's Cross - Leeds trains were over 45 minutes late and the *average* lateness was 65 minutes. For trains through York and beyond, delays due to the floods varied between two and three hours. Moreover, a general speed limit of 60 m.p.h. was imposed from 15th March until 19th May and even after that at certain points on the ECML, because of the effects of a general waterlogging of track that was already suffering from wartime arrears of maintenance. Indeed, the upshot of all this severe weather in the first part of 1947 was that the public timetable was no longer worth the paper it was printed on.

The ECML did again succumb to the snow on some later occasions. In 1955, on 20th December at the height of the pre-Christmas rush, a blizzard in the North completely interrupted traffic at York - of all places. For some hours nothing could move at this great centre[1] and diversions round the city had to be made *via* Knottingley, Starbeck and Melmerby. Similar disruptions of services by snow occurred in 1958: on 8th-10th February at Newcastle (*see* appended memorandum opposite) and down the ECML to Berwick trains were held up for hours by snowdrifts, and although the main lines were never *completely* blocked, a freight train was abandoned in the snow right behind Newcastle Central station. Then on 25th February it was the turn of the south: the ECML was *just* kept open, but trains were cancelled or heavily delayed, and a Cambridge line train - hauled unusually by BR Standard Class 5 No.73157 - was marooned in a snowdrift between Ashwell and Royston.

THE DELUGE IN THE BORDERS IN AUGUST 1948, AND ITS AFTERMATH.

A natural calamity that radically affected the ECML was the disastrous flooding in south-east Scotland on 12th August 1948. The disaster was vividly described by George Dow[2], and the following is based largely on his account.

After six days of very wet weather in the districts on both sides of the Border, "on August 12 the rain became a deluge, unabated for 24 hours, during which period it is estimated that over 200 million tons of water fell on the Berwickshire hills alone.... Rivers rose between 15 and 20 feet, bursting their banks and sweeping all before them... On the railway between Dunbar and Berwick [*i.e.* the ECML] 11 bridges and culverts were washed away, three others were damaged and there were major landslides, washouts and slips at 14 different places." However, the Berwick - Dunbar stretch was by no means the only,

or the first, one to be severed. The ECML was first blocked a little to the south at Scremerston and at Goswick in mid-afternoon. Then "from 3.40 p.m. on August 12th until 5.25 a.m. next morning Edinburgh District Control Office received more than 80 reports of mishaps." The line was blocked by extensive flooding between Cockburnspath and Grantshouse, Burnmouth station was under 3 feet of water, water poured in torrents through Penmanshiel tunnel. There were landslides to the east of the tunnel, and later no less than *seven* bridges between Grantshouse and Reston were washed away - with in some places the tracks left hanging in the air. It soon proved useless planning diversions, for "At 9.00 p.m. the driver of the first northbound express to be diverted by the Waverley Route, the 9.50 a.m. from Kings Cross, reported a landslide on the down line between Borthwick Bank and Gorebridge and almost simultaneously another landslide blocked both up and down lines at Tynehead. Thus the Waverley Route became unusable for through traffic, and by the early hours of August 13th even its tributaries, the St Boswells - Reston and the St Boswells - Kelso - Tweedmouth lines, were partially out of action. There was no alternative left but to divert trains to the West Coast route *via* Carlisle, Carstairs and Haymarket West." In fact, apart from the main lines - the ECML and the Waverley Route, eleven branch lines of the former NBR in the Borders were affected by floods, landslides and bridge washouts, some so devastatingly that they were never reopened.

That night there must have been chaos, for two main-line trains, the 19.00 Carlisle-Edinburgh and the 10.05 Kings Cross-Edinburgh (diverted onto the Waverley Route), and a St Boswells - Reston branch train, were isolated and their stranded passengers had to be rescued by buses - convoyed along the flooded roads by the police. In addition, a number of freight trains and light engines were cut off. The *FLYING SCOTSMAN* reached Edinburgh Waverley *10 hours late*, having retreated from Alnmouth back to Newcastle, then over to Carlisle and up the Waverley Route as far as Hawick, and finally retreating to Carlisle *again* to come up to Edinburgh *via* Carstairs.

It was found that certain branches could be reopened without much delay, but not so the ECML between Berwick and Dunbar. The blockages in Northumberland were cleared quickly, but not even one line of the Waverley Route could be restored until 20.00 hr. on 15th August. Meanwhile, all essential passenger and freight traffic between Edinburgh and England had to be diverted *via* Carstairs and Carlisle, thence mainly up the WCML or the MR line *via* Leeds, the *FLYING SCOTSMAN* for example running *via* Carstairs, Carlisle, Leeds and Selby. This diversion was very awkward because to reach the ex-CR line to Carstairs each train from Waverley had to be reversed both at Haymarket West and at Dalry Road junctions, using a pilot engine between them. Moreover, Carlisle could hardly cope with all this extra traffic for any length of time. At first all freight but perishables was cancelled, and this led to a great backlog. In the meantime, while would-be passengers at Borders stations on the blocked main and branch lines could be collected by buses, lack of lorries in those days meant that freight at these stations had to wait many days before it could be collected.

The complete destruction of so many bridges on the ECML between Berwick and Cockburnspath meant that the line would be out of use for months. The diversion of traffic through Carlisle *via* the reopened Waverley Route could only be a very temporary expedient for the reasons given. Therefore the somewhat revolutionary decision was made to send (from 16th August) all the ECML traffic over the (reopened) St Boswells - Kelso - Tweedmouth branch, in spite of its having an uninterrupted stretch of over 11 miles of single line. But the Gresley Pacifics

The following memo from the Newcastle District in 1958 records a sample
of the problems even a short-lived snow-storm could cause[1].

OFFICE MEMORANDUM

10th February 1958.

MEMO TO:- <u>PASSENGER TRAINS SECTION, WORKS SECTION</u>
MEMO FROM:- ASST. TO D.O.S.

SNOW STORM AT NEWCASTLE: SATURDAY MORNING
8TH FEBRUARY 1958.

The position when I arrived about 8.0am (having been called out at 4.15am) was as follows:-

<u>NEWCASTLE CENTRAL</u>
  Working had almost stopped due to points failure at Newcastle No.1 and No.3 and also at Gateshead
High Street and Greensfield. The 05.43 from Sunderland was still standing at Gateshead High Street at
7.30am and the engine for the 05.05 Newcastle - Middlesbrough was also at High Street.
  WTT.114 (23.20 King's Cross - Edinburgh, due 04.20) arrived Newcastle 07.26 and left 08.19 after
waiting engine from Gateshead.
  WTT.116 (23.35 King's Cross - Edinburgh, due 04.44) arrived Newcastle shortly afterwards and did
not leave until 10.28 after waiting engine from Gateshead.
  WTT.110 (23.30 King's Cross - Edinburgh, due 04.01) was standing on the King Edward Bridge.
  WTT.237 (00.12 Manchester Exchange - Edinburgh *News*, due 03.49) left Bensham for King Edward
Bridge at 08.30.
  WTT.140 (23.45 King's Cross - Newcastle, due 05.36) arrived Bensham at 08.55.
  WTT.324 (19.20 Bristol - Newcastle, due 04.55) was standing at Low Fell.
  WTT.8 (01.00 King's Cross - Edinburgh, due 06.27) was standing at Lamesley.
  WTT.1194 (01.42 York - *via* Bishop Auckland - Newcastle *Parcels*, due 05.09) had been put to the
Slow lines at Ouston.
  WTT.270 (20.40 Whitemoor - Niddrie, due 04.55) was behind WTT.1194.
  The Central Area Section Controller was unable to ring out on any circuit. There was a block
failure between Heaton South and Benton Bank.
  The situation eased from 10.00 onwards and WTT.116 left for the North at 10.28 followed by 110 at
10.35.
  WTT.237 arrived at 10.19, WTT.140 at 10.30 and WTT.324 at 10.36.

<u>NORTH MAIN LINE</u>
  There was no reliable telephone communication beyond Benton Bank, although it was sometimes possi-
ble to speak to Dudley or Dam Dykes. The trunk line to Tweedmouth Yard was, however, working. A total
block failure had been reported between Plessey and Stannington. A telegraph pole was down on the
Royal Border Bridge blocking the Up Main Line. The following information was available about trains:-
  WTT.1003 (07.28 Berwick - Newcastle, due 09.28) was standing in Berwick Station ready to leave.
  WTT.108 (20.20 King's Cross - Edinburgh, due dep. Newcastle 02.34) had left Newcastle at 05.30 and
passed Morpeth at 05.56.
  WTT.104 had passed Alnmouth at 05.24.
  WTT.262(c) (13.30 Clarence Yard - Niddrie, due dep. Newcastle 23.50) had passed Tweedmouth at
08.15 and had been put into Berwick Yard.
  WTT.2 (00.30 York - Edinburgh *parcels*) had passed Benton Bank at 06.50.
  WTT.100 (22.15 King's Cross - Aberdeen, due dep. 03.07) had left Newcastle at 06.42.
  Information was received from Alnmouth Station at 10.30 that there was a complete block failure on
the Down Main Line between Warkworth and Wooden Gates and a partial block failure on both Up and
Down lines North and South of Alnmouth. The following Main Line trains were then reported by
Alnmouth:-
  WTT.108 (due 03.21-03.24) arrived 06.22, left 06.26.
  WTT.2 (due pass 03.05) arrived 08.50, left 09.11 after taking water.
  WTT.100 (due pass 03.45) arrived 09.23, left 09.44 after taking water.
  WTT.114 (see above) arrived 10.30 and was standing in the station.
  WTT.251 (00.30 Niddrie - Whitemoor, due pass 03.09) arrived 07.43, left at 07.44.
  WTT.273 (00.30 Inverkeithing - East Goods Yard, due pass 04.09) arrived 08.18, left 08.19.
  WTT.1001 (07.27 Alnwick - Newcastle) arrived 08.39, left 08.40.
  WTT.385 (00.42 Inverkeithing - Heaton, due pass 04.49) arrived 08.38, left 09.00, after taking
water.

continued over-

WTT.1005, the 10.20 from Alnwick to Newcastle, was expected to run and would make a special stop at Shilbottle to pick up 43 passengers for Newcastle who had been stranded all night in a 'bus.

Information was received from D.O.S. Edinburgh by G.P.O. line at 11.00 that WTT.49, the 10.00 Edinburgh - King's Cross, had left Waverley 27 minutes late and passed Prestonpans at 11.02. WTT.137, the 10.15 Edinburgh - Leeds, would be following.

Scottish Region snow ploughs were working between Edinburgh and Reston and the Tweedmouth snow plough would precede WTT.100 from Berwick to Reston.

Telephone lines were down between Grantshouse and Berwick.

WEST LINE

WTT.4853 (02.35 Carlisle - Newcastle, due 04.02), which had been standing outside Newcastle, eventually arrived at 07.37. WTT.4857, the 05.45 diesel from Hexham, was standing at Scotswood. There had been no trains out of Newcastle for the West. The 05.05 empty diesel (WTT.4882) from Scotswood to Hexham left Blaydon at 08.25 for Hexham as a stopping passenger train. The telephone circuits were working, except that it was impossible to ring out.

Blaydon Yard was stopped but there were 2 freight trains, 1 for Blaydon and the other for Addison, running up from Carlisle in front of WTT.4871 diesel which had left Carlisle at 07.54 (59 minutes late).

NORTH TYNESIDE ELECTRIFIED AREA

Four electric sets had left Gosforth Car Sheds to go into Newcastle via Tynemouth and Wallsend owing to the derailment at South Gosforth, but all 4 sets were stopped on the Up line between Wallsend and Manors waiting acceptance into Newcastle Central.

One Diesel set had also left Gosforth Car Sheds for Monkseaton where it was to turn round and return to Newcastle via Jesmond.

As soon as the crossover road had been cleared at Benton and the electric sets on the Up line had been accepted into Newcastle, the first service was arranged between Newcastle and Benton via Wallsend in each direction. A steam set was also provided to run from Monkseaton to Newcastle via Benton.

The Gateshead tool vans had been ordered to South Gosforth but were still at Gateshead Shed unable to get out owing to the points being fast.

Telephone circuit No.10 was the only one working and it was impossible to ring out.

There was considerable delay in getting the boat train empty stock away from Heaton Carriage Sidings to the Tyne Commission Quay and in any event it never reached the Quay as information was received that the passengers off the boat had been brought into Newcastle by 'bus and the empty set was sent to Newcastle Central.

BLYTH AND TYNE AREA

There was no passenger service due to the derailment at Newsham North which blocked the Up and Down lines. No telephone circuits were working and it was understood that conditions were particularly difficult due to snow between Newsham and Newbiggin.

The Blyth tool vans had been ordered to Newsham, but it was not known whether they could deal with the derailed engine.

SOUTH MAIN LINE

Information was received from Central Control that owing to congestion on the Down line WTT.14 (06.40 York - Newcastle) would probably turn round at Darlington but WTT.1088 (06.42 Bradford - Newcastle) would run through to Newcastle if possible. Information was later received that WTT.138 (10.10 York - Edinburgh) had been cancelled and WTT.16 (09.15 Leeds - Glasgow) would cover its stops between York and Newcastle. WTT.138 eventually left Newcastle at 13.40 and an earlier special, X.204, left at 11.44, with the Edinburgh Sleeping Car off WTT.8.

We were instructed to cancel the empty set (WTT.53) from H.C.S. for the 07.53 Sunderland - King's Cross, as alternative arrangements had been made for the Sunderland passengers.

The 08.15 Newcastle - Cardiff was also cancelled and a corresponding train started from York.

The 08.55 Newcastle - Liverpool was also cancelled between Newcastle and Darlington.

We were asked to run WTT.143 (08.00 Newcastle - King's Cross) as early as possible in order to take all passengers from Newcastle for York and the South, but this train did not leave Newcastle Central until 10.28, running as WTT.33 (09.55 Newcastle - King's Cross).

WTT.1169 (10.05 Newcastle - Liverpool) was also cancelled and the set run as an 11.15 Newcastle - Leeds, probably going through to Liverpool.

COAST LINE

It was reported that two Diesel sets were coming through from Middlesbrough, but it was not known when they would reach Newcastle.

Note:

    1 Amended from a copy kindly provided by its author, Walter Dendy.

Restoration of the ECML after the great Border Floods of 12th August 1948: D49/1 No.62706 (LNER No.266) FORFARSHIRE and A4 No.60012 (LNER No.4491) COMMONWEALTH OF AUSTRALIA test one of the temporary bridges over the Eye Water between Ayton and Grantshouse, 24th October 1948. It all looks perhaps a bit rickety, and redolent of 19th Century American railroads. *BR.*

were game - if often with a banker - for the 10 miles of 1-in-70 facing Up trains on the Waverley Route from Hardengreen Junction to Falahill Box - the climb up to Falahill for Down trains being more gradual, and the bridges on the branch could take them. Nevertheless this diversion added 93 minutes to the London - Edinburgh express journey, and to prevent Newcastle passengers having to wait, extra expresses to London were added for them to the timetable. The 'Non-Stop' (the *FLYING SCOTSMAN*) now had a run of 409 miles, which it did indeed manage on 17 occasions without stopping at all in spite of the extra 16 waterless miles between Lucker troughs and Edinburgh. However, by dint of hard restoration work on the Kelso line, the scheduled delay in the overall time was cut early in September to 70 minutes, and train times adjusted to allow the withdrawal of some of the extra trains from Newcastle.

"The emergency schedules for diverted freight trains were prepared on the 'pre-deluge' basis of a thousand wagons each day in each direction between Edinburgh and Berwick, and with the knowledge that the Kelso route could take only ten express freight trains a day, so taxed was it already with passenger trains,....after taking full advantage of the remaining capacity of the Waverley Route to Carlisle and the St Boswells - Kelso - Tweedmouth line, the balance of the freight traffic that would normally have been operated by way of Berwick and Dunbar was sent *via* Kilmarnock and *via* Carstairs and, after passing through Carlisle, was distributed *via* Newcastle and *via* the Midland and Western Divisions of the London Midland Region to Eastern Region exchange points at Wakefield, Ashton Moss (near Manchester) and Peterborough...Intensive working was adopted at weekends, and, by running numerous freight trains on Sundays, congestion was avoided at any point." Dow omits to mention, however, that considerable use was also made of the Riccarton Junction - Hexham line for freight diversions.

Thanks to a massive effort by the Civil Engineers using, for temporary bridge replacement, military type bridging on

steel trestles with foundations protected by steel sheet-piling, and a labour force of up to 500, the diversion of ECML freight from the Berwick - Dunbar section was ended on 25th October. Passenger trains were restored on 1st November, although speed restrictions still made all trains between the Capitals slower by about 25 minutes. The permanent rebuilding of the bridges would take many months more, and the branch from Burnmouth to Eyemouth was not reopened until June 1949. The Reston - St Boswells branch was permanently severed between Duns and Greenlaw, and worked as separate branches from Reston and from St Boswells for a few more years - as long as the traffic justified keeping them open.

Apart from the several instances noted under Accidents above, the Kelso line was used for diverted ECML trains briefly again in December 1953 after the crash at Longniddry, and indeed the ECML was breached once more by floods on 28th August 1956, but this time only the Pease Burn between Grantshouse and Cockburnspath was washed away at a culvert; trains were diverted to the Waverley Route (the Up *FLYING SCOTSMAN via* Beattock) for a few days until a temporary bridge was built. In October 1954 a reverse situation occurred, when for two days both the former LMSR main lines between Glasgow and Carlisle were blocked by flood damage, and trains diverted through Edinburgh Waverley - mainly down the Waverley Route but also some by the ECML, bringing for the first time 'Duchesses', 'Royal Scots' and 'Jubilees' down to Newcastle.

Notes:
1. Although a novel use was found there - dispersing snow - for the high-pressure air supply for the signalling.
2. Dow, G. (1968). *Deluge over the Border.* In: *Railway World* 29, 402-405, 452-454, 493-495. London: Ian Allan.

In the great Flood Disaster of 12th August 1948, Grantshouse station was inundated, and the depth of water was recorded for posterity by this plaque on the wall of the station house on the Up side. *C.J.B.Sanderson.*

CONTENTS OF PART II

Chapter VII - The East Coast Main Line and its Centres.
Chapter VIII- Alterations to the Way and Structures, 1939-1959
Chapter IX   - Locomotives on the ECML, 1939-1959.
Chapter X   - Locomotive Depots on the ECML, their Allocations and Workings.
Chapter XI   - Passenger Rolling-Stock on the ECML in 1939, and its Changes in the Ensuing Twenty Years.
Chapter XII - Management and Staff of the ECML in 1939 and Changes in the Ensuing Twenty Years.

APPENDICES:
L - Notes on ECML Wayside Stations.
M - Tables of Trains Departing, Arriving and Passing some Major ECML Centres, Summers 1939, 1942 & 1955.
N - Directors of the LNER; Railway Executive Committee; British Transport Commission & Railway Executive; Some of the Chief Officers (1939-1959).
O - Representative Staff Returns, October 1939.

TABLES:
1. List of Stations and Signal Boxes - King's Cross to Edinburgh Waverley.
2. List of Tunnels and Principal Underbridges - King's Cross to Edinburgh Waverley.

INDEX

BIBLIOGRAPHY